Cecil Brown

CECIL BROWN

*The Murrow Boy
Who Became Broadcasting's
Crusader for Truth*

REED W. SMITH

McFarland & Company, Inc., Publishers
Jefferson, North Carolina

ISBN (print) 978-1-4766-7202-1
ISBN (ebook) 978-1-4766-3088-5

LIBRARY OF CONGRESS CATALOGUING DATA ARE AVAILABLE

BRITISH LIBRARY CATALOGUING DATA ARE AVAILABLE

© 2017 Reed W. Smith. All rights reserved

No part of this book may be reproduced or transmitted in any form or by any means, electronic or mechanical, including photocopying or recording, or by any information storage and retrieval system, without permission in writing from the publisher.

Front cover: Cecil Brown holding audio recorder, 1951 (Wisconsin Historical Society WHS-82982; cropped)

Printed in the United States of America

*McFarland & Company, Inc., Publishers
Box 611, Jefferson, North Carolina 28640
www.mcfarlandpub.com*

For those who esteem truth

Table of Contents

Acknowledgments — viii
Preface — 1

1. Growing up Jewish in America — 5
2. A Cub Reporter Becomes a Pioneering Broadcaster — 19
3. A Correspondent's Rewards: Evicted, Strafed and Censored — 34
4. Sounding the Alarm for Singapore — 50
5. Reporting History Up Close and Personal — 67
6. Out of the Sea but into Hot Water — 82
7. Welcome Home to Accolades and Controversy — 100
8. A Cause Worth Quitting For — 119
9. Exercising a Liberal Voice — 137
10. Fighting for Unpopular Causes — 162
11. Back to the Far East for a New Medium — 191
12. Return to the U.S. to Open More Eyes — 215

Epilogue — 240
Chapter Notes — 249
Bibliography — 270
Index — 281

Acknowledgments

This project is the culmination of a four-year research and writing journey that owes a debt of gratitude to several institutions and numerous individuals. Cecil Brown's life story could not have been written without their kind and gracious assistance.

The journey began with a semester sabbatical Georgia Southern University granted me in spring 2013. With sixteen weeks available to select a topic and conduct research, I landed upon the George Foster Peabody Awards website at the University of Georgia Grady College of Journalism and Mass Communication. Nineteen forty-one was only the second year the awards were granted, and upon scanning the winners, I came across the name Cecil Brown, CBS Radio, for "Outstanding Reporting of the News." I have done a great deal of broadcast history research during my academic career, but Cecil Brown is a name that I had not previously encountered. Thus began an investigation into who he was, and why the Peabody Committee esteemed him. Upon pulling together bits and pieces of his career from a variety of online and print sources, I discovered that he had been a member of Ed Murrow's renowned World War II CBS news team, but little had been written about him.

But I soon discovered that the archive at the Wisconsin Historical Society in Madison served as a repository for his papers. Upon downloading the index for the Cecil Brown Papers, I found that the collection was voluminous and included a treasure trove of radio and television news scripts, diaries, newspaper and magazines articles, correspondence, photographs and recordings. It soon became clear that Brown's career deserved book-length treatment. This led to multiple trips to Madison to read and take notes on the collection. Thankfully, Brown was a packrat, saving practically every scrap of paper related to his career, right down to thank you notes and dinner receipts. We have renowned stage and screen actor Frederic March to thank for the existence of the collection. He and Brown became close friends in New York just after World War II. Brown had no connection to Wisconsin, but March graduated from the University of Wisconsin, and he talked Brown into donating his papers to the Historical Society's Mass Communications History Collection. There, Brown's documents resides alongside those of such notable journalists as David Brinkley, H.V. Kaltenborn, Howard K. Smith, and Joseph Harsch.

A memo in the archives led me to John Moore, Emeritus Professor of History at California State Polytechnic University, Pomona. Upon contacting him, I discovered that he and Brown had been colleagues in the 1970s when both taught at Pomona, and that Brown had tutored him in hosting several television productions. From Moore, I learned that Brown's widow, Martha, who was 100 years of age at that time, was still living in Los Angeles. Moore was kind enough to contact her and ask several questions on my behalf regarding her late husband's journalism career. Upon learning that I was proposing to write a book about Cecil, Martha agreed to participate in multiple phone interviews during the next couple of years. Despite her age, she demonstrated that she possessed a remarkable memory for incidents that had occurred decades previous. While devoted to her husband's memory, expressing on several occasions that he was "a kind, generous and wonderful person," she was candid in discussing his career and their relationship. She also provided contact information for her nephew, Jonathan Brown (Cecil's brother Eugene's son), and he readily agreed to be interviewed as well. Both Browns were open to sharing personal anecdotes about Cecil as well as filling in details that were missing in the Wisconsin files.

Subsequent trips to the Library of Congress in Washington, D.C., and to the American Broadcasting and Public Broadcasting Archives at the University of Maryland at College Park yielded additional primary sources and audio recordings. Supplementary documents, transcripts and recordings were secured from the CBS and NBC Network Archives and WNYC Radio Archives in New York City, the Edmund Muskie Collection at Bates College, and the Edward R. and Janet Murrow Collections at Mount Holyoke College and Tufts University. The online historical newspaper sources, Newspapers.com and Newspaperarchive.com, also were extremely helpful in yielding dozens of articles that contained details of Brown's activities. Numerous other websites, containing information ranging from radio, war and journalism, to television and presidential history, helped construct a fuller context of the times, people and events with which Brown participated or on which he commented. The staff at Georgia Southern University's Henderson Library was supremely helpful in processing many inter-library loan transactions, and the public libraries of Youngstown and Mahoning and Warren-Trumbull counties in Ohio were also accommodating in securing historic documents and photographs that added to the study's depth. It never ceases to amaze how eager librarians and archivists are to become personally involved in a project such as this. When they do, they go the extra mile to find materials that provide illumination. The staff at the Wisconsin Historical Society, who were willing to answer any question and make my visits efficient undertakings, also were exceedingly supportive and patient with me as I navigated the archives. They rescued me during one weeklong visit when my laptop computer quit working. Because I was unable to get it repaired in a timely manner, one of the staff members who was also a university student volunteered to check out and renew a laptop in his name from the University of Wisconsin Library for the week. My visit to Madison would have been a disaster without his assistance.

I am most grateful to the Brown family members who were so willing to comply with my requests for interviews and documentation, and to devote significant amounts of time to sharing with me—at first, a total stranger—their lives with Cecil Brown. During the process, we became friends. My research also led me to a much greater appreciation for the contributions Jewish-Americans have made to the field of journalism and to our nation's history. I also owe a debt of gratitude to my department chair, Pamela Bourland-Davis, for recommending me for a sabbatical, the only one granted in my department in recent memory, and to the Georgia Southern administration for approving it. Most of all, I thank my wife, Bev. She is a research savant, who time and time again displayed the ability to locate a missing date, name, or other important piece of information when I had all but given up on securing it. Beyond that, she helped me think through details, tolerated the many hours I spent pounding on the keyboard in the study, and tolerated the reading of multiple drafts of the manuscript, providing honest feedback and asking insightful questions. Most importantly, she was an encourager during times when I questioned the feasibility of completing this project, and without whom completion would not have been possible or as rewarding.

Preface

During World War II, CBS radio, under the direction of Paul White and Edward R. Murrow, created an eleven-person news team to cover events in war-torn Europe. The group of correspondents became renowned as they brought the sounds and developments of the war into Americans' homes via the airwaves. The coverage established radio as a medium that was superior to newspapers in speedily bringing the news alive for listeners, while simultaneously setting the standard for how best to utilize broadcasting to present it in a principled, personal manner. Seventy-five years later, many of those practices remain the standard of excellence for radio and television news reporting.

The members of the CBS news team distinguished themselves with their on-the-spot reporting, insightful analysis, brushes with death, and unrelenting tenacity. Of the eleven members of the lineup, which later became identified collectively as the Murrow Boys, some of them—such as Eric Sevareid and Howard K. Smith—became well-known in their own right as they enjoyed high-profile broadcast careers for decades thereafter. Others, including the team's only female, Mary Breckinridge, and Murrow's first colleague, William L. Shirer, embarked upon other pursuits. Yet another member of the latter group, Cecil Brown, left CBS even before the end of the war, but continued in broadcasting, primarily as a commentator, for the remainder of his career. Although he was recognized with all of broadcasting's most prestigious awards during his years on the air, historians have failed to recognize Brown's substantial contribution to broadcast news. Likewise, the heyday of radio commentary and the role it played in defining the parameters of broadcast press freedom have remained under-documented. Those are omissions this book seeks to correct.

Most biographical work focuses on Great Men. That is an outgrowth of the Great Man Theory that Scottish writer Thomas Carlyle promoted in the 1840s book *The Hero as Divinity*. He argued that great men (heroes) are largely responsible for mankind's developments throughout history because of their wisdom, intelligence, position or charisma. But though the theory was long ago disproven, historians continue to embrace it with the individuals about which they write. In the field of newspaper journalism, Joseph Pulitzer is the man most credited with progressing the profession in the nineteenth century. Murrow is credited with being the founding father of quality broadcast journalism practices. But the story of journalism's, and broadcasting's, development is not that simple. Pulitzer and Murrow earned their accolades, but many others who also contributed to its development have been undervalued. Numerous individuals helped build broadcast journalism into what it is today, and what it is today does not necessarily resemble the heights of achievement it previously attained. In the twenty-first century, journalism's credibility has fallen precipitously because of its devotion to the bottom line and its capricious commitment to truth. Today's broadcast journalists could gain knowledge from the experiences of radio pioneers such as Cecil Brown— awareness that, unfortunately, has also been lost to history. As a member of the first wave of broadcast journalists, he envisioned and helped illuminate the extraordinary capabilities of the medium. That is why individuals like him are worthy of study.

From the 1930s to the 1950s, dozens of radio commentators populated the airwaves. Because of the special manner in which the human voice emanating from a box of tubes and wires could connect with listeners, commentators enjoyed an intimate and powerful connection with the audience. They were clarifiers, opinion-shapers, and teachers, and audiences looked to commentators to make sense of the increasingly complicated events of those decades. At the far ends of the spectrum, and among the most well-known, were the gossipy Walter Winchell and the conservative Fulton Lewis, Jr. They are the forefathers of contemporary talk-radio hosts, and they were similar to today's talkers in that they preached from a conservative pulpit. Others, however, defined their role more circumspectly. While all the commentators embraced a partisan perspective to some degree, instead of employing sensationalism and controversy to attract an audience, some relied on intellectualism, research and rhetorical logic to build a case for their points of view. Brown was one of those. He provided a progressive, liberal perspective, in the tradition of predecessors H.V. Kaltenborn and Elmer Davis. His methods made him controversial, as he swam against mainstream opinion regarding issues, and managerial judgment regarding appropriateness. He appreciated that he was not only offering analysis—he was "testing the waters" and "exploring the boundaries" of First Amendment freedom in a medium where owners and regulators failed to grasp the role commentary could play in fostering a marketplace of ideas that could help lubricate the machinery of American democracy.

Researching broadcast history can be difficult, especially radio studies, because of the ephemeral nature of decades-old on-air work. Most electronic recordings have either disintegrated or been discarded, and few broadcasters or networks retained their scripts. But on the advice of good friend, actor and Wisconsin alumnus Fredric March, Brown donated all of his personal papers to the Wisconsin Historical Society in Madison. It seems that he was a conscientious packrat, making the collection uniquely comprehensive for a broadcaster of that era. The robust archive includes all of his scripts, personal correspondence, photographs, newspaper and magazine clippings, and recordings of his lifetime of work. Especially insightful is the extensive correspondence he carried on with his listeners. The letters document how listeners reacted to his commentaries and the copious manner in which he took additional time to clarify his positions. The archive provides not only a professional, but a personal look into Brown's thinking, motivations and strategies. In addition, interviews with his one-hundred-year-old widow (as of 2015), Martha, who displayed an astounding ability to recall events, names and places from previous decades, provided extraordinary insights into her husband's character and worldview. She was especially able to do so because, as a journalist herself, she closely participated in much of his life's work. Additionally, interviews with other family members and former colleagues provided a broader understanding of his multifaceted personality and journalistic passion.

Together, these sources were instrumental in painting a comprehensive picture of a pioneer commentator who respected Americans enough to devote his life to helping them make sense of their world. Through four decades Brown practiced a style of journalism that has largely disappeared from newsrooms today. Like Murrow, Brown thought it was his duty, his calling, to openly and rationally scrutinize the activities of elites who possessed the ability to determine the course of national and world events. That is how he earned the moniker "Crusader for Truth." As a first-generation Jewish-American, he understood what it was like to be a member of a minority that many in society ostracized and attempted to marginalize. His family heritage informed a compassion for society's disenfranchised and underdogs. Brown's career coincides with the formative years of both radio and television journalism. Fought out largely behind the scenes, they were tumultuous years in which broadcasters with integrity sought to create a stronghold for uncompromising public-service journalism. As with all innovators, their vision for what could be collided with the brutal pragmatism of a free-market industry's financial mission. Nevertheless, men and women like Cecil Brown created a model for how broadcast journalism can be practiced at an uncommonly distinguished level.

◆◆ 1 ◆◆

Growing up Jewish in America

In the late nineteenth century, 94 percent of Russian Jews occupied twenty-nine provinces in southwestern Russia. Alexander II had established the Pale of Settlement in an effort to segregate them from the rest of the population. The Jews lived in *shtetls*, wooden hovels they had constructed in circles around central markets. The Russian aristocracy forbade the Jews from practicing their religion, nor could they own land or educate their children. Most Jews made their living as tailors, cobblers or cigar makers, but there was not enough business for everyone, and thousands of Jews starved during the difficult Russian winters.[1] When anarchists assassinated Alexander II, Alexander III succeeded him. He treated the Jews even more brutally, setting about to remake Russia into a nation he could claim as having one nationality, speaking only one language and practicing a single religion. In 1882, he instituted the May Laws, which disenfranchised the Jews. Government mobs destroyed many of the *shtetls* and massacred thousands during the "pogroms" (Jewish persecutions). To escape the campaign, the Jews fled, with nearly three million emigrating between 1880 and 1914. It was the largest exclusion of Jews since the Spanish banished them in 1492. Of the total, more Jews immigrated to the United States than to any other nation.[2]

In emigrating to America, the Jews embarked on an arduous two- to three-month journey across the Atlantic in cargo ships. Many of the small vessels were old sailing or steam ships, and crewmembers treated the passengers as little more than freight, crammed into steerage where many died.[3] Upon delivery, they were processed at Ellis Island or Castle Garden in New York. If they were deemed acceptable—free of disease and a criminal record—they sought to begin a new life. The preponderance of Jews settled into shabby tenements in New York City's Lower East Side garment district, but some made their way to other eastern cities, including Philadelphia, Boston, and Baltimore. They all were determined to continue the faith-based communities that had sustained them in Russia. Unfortunately, many of them could only find low-wage employment in sweatshops, barely making enough to house and feed their families.[4]

A smaller number of families took the adventurous step of leaving the comfort of their brethren and moved further west. One of those was the Browm family. Maurice Irving Browm's parents (originally Braun) arrived from Russia with him and his two siblings in 1894 when he was ten years old. They initially put down roots in a borough of 6,000 residents in western Pennsylvania, New Brighton. Located on the Beaver River, it is thirty miles northwest of Pittsburgh. They were experienced tailors; consequently, they opened a clothing store, which became successful. The area's Jews pooled their earnings and contributed labor to construct the region's first worship house. In 1904, the Agudath Achim Synagogue opened for services in nearby Beaver Falls. Maurice became a naturalized citizen that same year, and the Browms forged a lifestyle that exceeded that of many of their fellow expatriates in New York. For families such as the Browms, they were among the fortunate Jews who achieved at least a partial version of *The Golden Medina* (land of milk and honey) in America.

In 1905, Maurice married one of the most beautiful young Jewish women in the area, Jenni Broida. Shortly thereafter, they moved to Beaver Falls, where new steel mills were attracting workers. Maurice found employment as a tailor, and within their first year there, Jenni gave birth to a son, Eugene. A second son, Cecil, was born in 1907, and three years later, a daughter, Selma, arrived. The Browms remained in Beaver Falls until 1921, when Maurice moved his family across the state line into Ohio. He did so to achieve the desire of every Jewish immigrant, which was to become *balabos far sich* (one's own boss). He opened a wholesale restaurant supply company in Warren.[5] "Father B," as his children called him, was strong-willed, practical, and firmly in charge of his household. He kept two pairs of boxing gloves in the house for when his sons disagreed. Maurice encouraged them to box to settle squabbles, but for the most part, Cecil and Eugene got along.[6]

Because of their oppression in Russia, which continued for many Jews in America, they tended to be politically liberal, and many of them became prominent labor or community leaders in the U.S. As a business proprietor, Maurice was secretary of the Mahoning Valley chapter of the Jewish Federation. Its national goals were to enhance the well-being of Jews by mobilizing financial and social resources to develop international agencies that would aid Jews worldwide. The federation promoted the concepts of *Tzedakah* (social justice), *Chesed* (caring and compassion), and *Tikkun Olam* (repair of the world).[7] Maurice passed this worldview along to his sons, both of whom would demonstrate throughout their lives that those ideals motivated their actions.

Paradoxically, although Maurice assumed a leadership position at Beth Abraham Synagogue, neither Cecil nor Eugene inherited a devotion to Judaism. The boys' ambivalence toward religion was common for the sons of immigrant Jews, as many of them distanced themselves from orthodox traditions. "They thought the impact of religion was negative, and they wanted to get as far away from it as possible.... Religion was just not part of their lives," Eugene's son Jonathan confirmed. They assumed the position of secular Judaism—not really practicing the religion—yet remaining in touch with, and committed to, fellow Jews and their causes. Instead, the Browm boys sought to integrate themselves into mainstream America. What Maurice and Jennie did pass down to both Eugene and Cecil, though, was an "incredible gratefulness to be Americans. That had a greater impact than religion," Jonathan said.[8] While they worked hard, and faced great challenges in America, Jewish immigrants never forgot how much better their life in America was than it had been in Russia.

Because many immigrant Jews were illiterate and it limited their opportunities, they made a quality education for their children a priority. The parents believed education was the surest way for their offspring to climb the economic and social ladders in the U.S. Perhaps because of his lack of formal education, Maurice was always reading a book. He passed that love of learning along to his children. The fact that all three Browms graduated college was a remarkable achievement for the majority of U.S. families in the early twentieth century, let alone first generation Jews.

Jewish Americans needed every advantage they could summon because they faced anti–Semitism. White Anglo-Saxon Protestants disliked Jews because they worshipped on a different day, ate strange food, spoke Yiddish and dressed differently. On the heels of the first Red Scare, and because of the Jews' Russian ancestry, many Americans suspected them of subversive loyalties.[9] The 1920s and '30s were especially difficult years for U.S. Jews. Many of them started businesses because Protestant-owned companies refused to hire them. They could not buy houses in certain neighborhoods, and many colleges either limited the number of Jews they admitted, or rejected them altogether. The years between the world wars was a hostile period for Jews as Detroit Priest Charles Coughlin and Henry Ford led the way in devising conspiracy theories about them. Ford charged the Jews with starting World War I for profit and that they controlled the Federal Reserve System. He believed they intended to economically dominate the U.S. Coughlin hosted an influential nationwide radio program that drew as many as twelve-million listeners and consequently Congress enacted legislation in 1921 and 1924 that limited Eastern European immigration. Coughlin later alleged that Jews had infiltrated the Roosevelt Administration (calling the president's social initiatives the Jew Deal), with the intention of overthrowing the U.S.,[10] and for causing the Depression. Public opinion polls in the 1930s and '40s found that approximately 60 percent of Americans held a low opinion of Jews, labeling them "greedy," "dishonest," and "pushy." Although Couglin's popularity waned after Pearl Harbor—when his isolationist views became suspect—distrust and abuse of Jewish-Americans lingered for years thereafter.[11]

Cecil grew up in this hostile atmosphere, but his future wife, Martha, also Jewish, said their families were never discriminated against or ridiculed.[12] Yet it would be folly to believe the Browns were unaware of the danger anti–Semitism posed to their lives, and they took steps to demonstrate they were trustworthy. One of those measures the Browns took was for the brothers to join the Boy Scouts. By joining the scouts, the brothers developed a love for adventure and the out-of-doors, including swimming, biking and camping, and Cecil rose to the rank of Eagle. He later credited his scoutmaster for teaching him how to swim, a skill that would save his life during World War II.[13]

He also began developing his journalistic skills at an early age. Selma remembered that "he was a born reporter. Even when he was a boy, he was interested in it. He wrote stories and little plays."[14] As a teenager at Warren High School, he became managing editor of the school newspaper and president of the Hi-Press journalism club. Cecil's foray into journalism prompted him to write fiction articles that reflected his admiration of O'Henry's work, but he said he had trouble devising feasible plots. However, an event that encouraged him to an even greater degree, was a review he wrote in the paper of one of the *Charlie Chan* novels that Warren High School alumnus and local resident Earl Derr Biggers had written. Cecil sent Biggers the review, and Biggers liked it enough to respond. The exchange began a correspondence that lasted several months, and in one of the letters Biggers told Cecil that if he was serious about becoming a paid writer he needed to "see life" (travel).

During his senior year, Cecil's debate team, of which he was captain, went undefeated.[15] The school had never experienced such a successful season of forensic competition, and a newspaper story called Cecil "one of the best debaters ever graduating from Warren."[16] In the final match of the year, against Grand River Academy, a cute brunette by the name of Ruth Sindlinger argued against the U.S. and Canada constructing the Saint Lawrence Seaway because of the cost. Cecil thought the view was shortsighted and he rebutted: "What difference does it make where we spend our money? Didn't we build the Panama Canal? We don't care ... as long as the expenditure will benefit the United States." Cecil said he thought the debate was a turning point in defining his worldview: He believed the U.S. was destined for an increasingly influential role in the world and from then on, he claimed he was "an internationalist." The statement foretold how he would conduct his journalistic career.[17]

In the fall of 1925, Cecil followed Eugene to Western Reserve University, in Cleveland, to begin college. He also began serving as the first editor of the Youngstown-Warren edition of the *Jewish Journal* as well as contributing anecdotes to Western Reserve's *Red Cat* magazine. Unfortunately, he found both the opportunities "obnoxious" because he had to compose advertising copy. He yearned to write original stories "well and salably."[18] About the same time, because Western Reserve professors accused the brothers of misspelling their surname, the brothers legally changed the spelling from Browm to Brown. The modification may also have been prompted by the boys believing it would make them appear less Jewish. But the name modification represented a minor alteration to their identities in comparison to how they would spend their summer vacations.

Biggers' recommendation fascinated both boys, and they sought to fulfill it. They wanted more from life than selling restaurant equipment, and they believed traveling and writing could make that happen. In the summer of 1926, they bought a canoe for $17.50, painted it tan and christened it the *Selma B*, after their sister. They shipped it to Wheeling, West Virginia, launched it into the Ohio River and paddled it nearly four-hundred miles to Cincinnati in seventeen days. The brothers camped alongside the river in a pup tent, cooked meals on a gasoline stove, and navigated the river's currents, locks, and sandbars. The canoe was overloaded with supplies to the point that the gunwales barely cleared the water. The paddling was hard work, and their muscles became sore, but they pushed on. They encountered a variety of challenges as they made their way toward Cincinnati. One night, they became caught in a rainstorm and lost their tent while navigating high waves. Fortunately, a farmer allowed them to dry out and sleep in his barn that night. Large pieces of driftwood in the water were a constant threat to their craft, yet, as they worked their way downriver, they daydreamed of Indians, frontiersmen and settlers who had paddled the same river and viewed the same terrain before them. The excursion served as a seminal event for the brothers in developing a broader understanding of the world and types of people beyond their Jewish associations. Despite the challenges, "we are, by no means, discouraged," Cecil wrote halfway through the trip. "We are merely beginning to feel the palliations of an arduous enterprise."[19] Reflecting upon the experience later, Cecil surmised, "There never were two more uncouth, carefree or unrestrained animals on the Ohio Valley than Eugene and myself."[20]

The friendliness of the people they encountered amazed the Browns when they went ashore for supplies or camped. One evening. near Rome, Ohio, an elderly man named Jim cooked catfish for their supper, and his wife stuffed their packs with ginger cookies. Few of the people would accept money. At another stop, the brothers encountered moonshiners who educated them in how to avoid the law while making a profitable, if illegal living. The Browns also learned a great deal by talking with men who worked on the river. The men told the boys stories about navigating the Muskingum, Ohio and Mississippi Rivers, or sailing farther, to the sea. The stories created visions of high adventure in the brothers' heads. One tug crew towed the Browns' canoe through a lock; a paddle-wheeler pushing a barge took the boys and their canoe aboard, where they spent the night talking late before sleeping in the wheelhouse. The worst injuries they sustained were sunburns and aching muscles.[21]

In addition to Biggers' urging, the motivation for the river trip arose from the brothers' love for Robert Louis Stevenson's *Inland Voyage*, a book in which he described his canoe trip through France and Belgium in 1876.[22] Cecil also decided to model himself after Stevenson as a writer by generating the first newspaper bylines of his career, and writing them in first person, just as Stevenson had. As they neared the Queen City, Cecil reflected: "Who will dare tell me that there is anything happier than being around boats."[23] He wrote twelve stories about their adventure on a borrowed typewriter that the *Warren Tribune-Chronicle* published. Despite his first success as a bylined reporter, Cecil was less certain about college. Back at Western Reserve in the fall, he took an assortment of courses and joined a fraternity, but ended up uninspired. He took as many English classes as he could, trying to avoid the required science courses, which he disliked. The faculty kept insisting that he take the science classes, but he resisted. His river experience motivated him to apply to the Naval Academy, but his lack of mathematical ability made that an impossibility. The next year, hoping to receive a jolt of motivation in a larger academic institution, Cecil transferred to Ohio State for his junior year.

Outside the classroom, though, is where Cecil felt most alive and where he believed he could really learn. After the river trip, he had written, "One never learns anything until he discovers it for himself."[24] Accordingly, in the summer of 1928, he and Eugene were off again—this time for a voyage on a larger body of water. For two years, Eugene wrote letter to shipping companies on the East Coast in an effort to land seafaring jobs. Cecil said they wanted to become "A.B. (Able-Bodied Seamen) instead of B.A. (Bachelor of Arts) recipients." Their goal was to sail to Europe, but a stream of rejection letters rebuffed their ambitions. Thinking they might have better luck in person, they boarded a train for New York City with ten dollars between them, and sought employment aboard cargo ships in the harbor. They did not make much of an impression because, in Cecil's words, "[worldly] seamen do not take kindly to college kids in knickers." Finally, after saying they were the requisite twenty-two years of age (Eugene was, but Cecil was only twenty-one), the chief mate on the Munson Line's *Western World* told them they could sign on as cadets for a voyage to South America. The mate put the boys to work scrubbing decks on the *Western*, a 535-foot cargo ship with a crew of twenty-eight. But before the vessel could leave port, chief officer King, a tall, broad-shouldered man, with a weatherworn face and gruff manner, informed the Browns that the mate had exceeded his authority. King said they could not remain on board because they did not have proper certification; he ordered them to go ashore.[25]

Fortunately, during their few days on the *Western*, the ship's quartermaster, Jack Lett, had taken a liking to the boys. Before they could leave he told them not to allow a "small thing like being unqualified" prevent them from sailing. He then hid them in a lifeboat and snuck them some food. They spent twelve hours there, during which time cockroaches bit them and they became dehydrated. But they had to remain hidden until the harbor pilot left the ship, which occurred when the *Western* sailed past Ambrose Light (in New York Bay). At that point, Lett told them to make their presence known. Not surprisingly, when King encountered them he was greatly displeased that they had disobeyed him, saying they "had put him in a tough spot." Regardless, it was impossible for King to turn the ship around and put them off at that point. He demanded to know why they had stowed away. Not wanting to implicate Lett, Eugene answered: "We're awfully sorry chief officer but we just had to make this trip." The response caused a smile to form on King's lips, as he realized his only option was to make the best of their presence. Accordingly, a crewmember put the brothers through the Able Bodied Seaman test. They passed part of it because they had learned how to box a compass during their scout days, but they failed miserably when it came to lifeboat procedures. Regardless, the examiner said, "You both need more learning but we are anxious to have young American workers on this ship, rather than foreigners." Thus, the Browns became shipmates, but in Cecil's words, "two more ignorant seamen could not be found on the high or low seas." Nonetheless, Eugene and Cecil were on their way to a forty-six-day cruise of 14,000 miles that took them to ports throughout South America and Trinidad, before returning to New York.[26]

King put the brothers to work, scraping and painting railings, sweeping and scrubbing decks. He paid them the standard stowaway wage, which was one cent per month along with a bunk and chow. Assigned to a ten-by-ten berth below deck, the brothers suffered from seasickness during the first two days, but their nausea and the humble work could not diminish their excitement. The crewmembers, with names like "Chips" and "Swede," found the "college kids," as they called them, entertaining, and had good-natured fun at their expense. After a week at sea, Cecil wrote that it had been seven days "of virgin experiences ... fearfully lonesome [because of] no land in sight ... [but] happy every day, talking to men from strange parts of the world."[27]

Despite the paltry wage and lack of comfort, for the two landlubbers, the trip was nirvana.

When the ship docked in Rio for a couple of weeks, the *Western's* Master of the Ship refused the crew shore leave, but in his job as quartermaster Lett had to go ashore, and he snuck the Browns off and back on without being noticed. The penalty for being ashore without leave was two days' pay, but on their salary Eugene and Cecil figured the fine was worth it if they were caught, which they were not. However, at another South American stop, their luck ran out. The ship docked in Buenos Aires for a week, and the brothers succeeded in getting themselves into trouble. While roaming the city they encountered a British reporter. He wondered what two young Americans were doing so far away from home, and the brothers responded with a tall tale. They said they were on assignment for a U.S. newspaper, and their job was to compare the beauty of the Argentine girls with those in the States. The reporter wrote a feature based on the ruse, which a local newspaper published the following day. Unfortunately, King read the story, and he threw the boys in the ship's brig for a week, but they were unharmed, and the experience became another chapter in the Browns' adventure book.[28]

Afterwards, Lett remembered that Cecil had an unrealistic idea about things in general, "and he thought a sailor's life was full of romance" but he still impressed him: "Even in those days, Cecil Brown had 'the stuff.'"[29] He meant Cecil was unafraid of the unknown, was a hard worker, and could ingratiate himself to men from different walks of life who did not usually tolerate inexperienced shipmates. Upon returning to Ohio, the *Youngstown Vindicator* published six stories and photographs from the brothers' adventure.[30] In one of the articles, Cecil credited Stevenson's *Treasure Island* for putting the idea of seafaring in their heads. Unlike many parents, the Browns did not object to their sons' nautical exploits. It is not entirely clear why not. Perhaps Maurice's memories of his own trip across the Atlantic as a ten-year old persuaded him that his sons were capable of surviving substantially less-perilous trips. Whatever the rationale, the boys' exploits and newspaper stories made the brothers celebrities in Ohio.

Eugene and Cecil returned to college in the fall of 1928. Although Ohio State had a journalism school, Cecil pursued a curriculum in business administration, and took more English courses. He found that even though he was at a new learning institution, the methods of instructions were the same, and he disliked them. He wrote that "gazing absently into a textbook or listening idly to a prattling professor" did little to arouse his interest, and, "once the smell of salt is in your nostrils, there is no turning back."[31] During this last year at OSU, Cecil wrote a play that classmates performed at University Hall, in which he cast himself as the lead. Titled "The Lonely One of God," the drama won first place for playwriting, and was accompanied by a $50 prize.

According to an article in the *Ohio Jewish Chronicle*, "The reviewers in the city papers were most enthusiastic in their praise of the production. This play was smoothly acted and gave an effective treatment of the call of the Jewish people to their own." The plot, somewhat autobiographical, concerned a young man who was unaware of his ethnicity until a seminal event in his life. He falls in love with a Jewish girl, and wonders if the relationship has a future, until, at the end of the play, his parents inform him that he, to his surprise, is also Jewish.[32] The plot that Cecil fashioned seemed to indicate that at twenty-two he was struggling with his identity. How public or how secretive should he be about being Jewish? Perhaps it would have been helpful if he had talked with playwright Robert Riskin, who years later became one of Cecil's friends. Riskin, also Jewish, once told his wife, Fay Wray: "To be Jewish was to belong to a club from which you never could, nor ever would, resign."[33]

At the end of his senior year, Cecil was finished with Ohio State, but he had not earned a degree, which did not bother him because a degree "doesn't mean anything" in his estimation.[34] He summed up his experience in Columbus by telling a colleague that he "concentrated on English, short-story writing and history, wrote reams of poetry (all of which he admitted were terrible), fell in and out of love a dozen times and met the girl who was to become my wife" because she was "as nice as his sister, Selma."[35] He said that all through his college years his "great determination was to have a novel by the time I was 21. The great fault was that I had the desire long before the ability."[36] Eugene, on the other hand, graduated from Youngstown State in 1929, and with college behind them, the brothers traveled again in pursuit of more seafaring. This time, in Cecil's words, off to "the University of the Sea to take vagabond post-graduate work in the Academy of the Heart's Desire."[37]

The Browns set out for New York again in August 1929 with the intent of securing employment on a merchant ship bound for Europe. Unfortunately, once they arrived they discovered that though they had learned much during their South American trip, they needed three years' experience before they could receive Able Bodied Seamen certification. A regulation also forbade relatives from working on the same ship. Fortuitously, they encountered their friend from the *Western* again, Jack Lett. He assured them not to worry, that the regulations were "not a big deal," and that he could help. Two nights later, Lett took them to meet a mysterious friend in Times Square. The stranger presented them with official-looking papers that certified the Browns as Able Bodied Seamen that had last served on a San Diego-based ship. He charged them nothing; the Browns never knew if Lett had paid the man on their behalf. Back at the harbor the next day, when the Browns were questioned about their relationship, they claimed they were "just good friends." After exercising, what Cecil referred to as "our elastic morals," Lett and the brothers prepared to ship out as members of a thirty-nine-man crew on the American export freighter *Exford*. The voyage would begin in mid-September, last four months, and take them to Russia and North Africa, before returning to New York. In a final surprising twist to the episode, Lett informed the Browns at the last minute that he would not be going with them because the company had transferred him. They were shocked that their supporter was abandoning them, but they were determined to sail to Europe nevertheless.

The Browns were not, of course, Able Bodied Seamen. This became apparent to their *Exford* crewmates quickly, especially after both brothers were seasick the first six days of the voyage. "Eugene and I became quite expert at heaving in unison," Cecil wrote, but once again it was too late to return to port, so the crew accepted the Browns and showed them the ropes, so to speak. Eugene and Cecil had trouble on the first part of the journey fulfilling their duties. They alternated between trying to bluff their way through jobs by modeling shipmates' actions, or admitting they needed tutoring. Fortunately, they learned quickly, and worked to pull their weight, and as the voyage progressed their abilities and confidence grew, so much so that Captain Ackerman eventually had both of them steer the huge ship for four-hour shifts. Besides that duty, he assigned them jobs on alternating shifts, which meant they did not see each other for extended periods. When Cecil finally caught a glimpse of Eugene, he was shocked: "His lips were swollen, his face emaciated, his eyes deep and haggard; a sorry sight." But seeing Eugene caused Cecil to start laughing, which made Eugene do the same. They both took their first bath since being at sea, and both felt and looked better.[38]

When they returned from the adventure nearly four months later, Cecil again wrote a series of articles that appeared in the *Youngstown Vindicator*. In them, he helped Ohioans relive what the brothers experienced. For instance, after the ship navigated the Atlantic and wound its way through the Bosporus and Dardanelles, Cecil said, "It is one of nature's rarest spots. I found it almost overwhelming to attempt to absorb so much beauty, so great and potent is the quantity." As the vessel sailed past Constantinople, he and Eugene were busy using air hammers to chip rust off the *Exford*'s railings. Yet Cecil still had the chance to marvel at the "breathtaking slopes." By this point in the voyage, his shipmates had begun calling him "Slim." At six-foot-four-inches tall and weighing nearly 190 pounds, he had always been lean, but a loss of weight from being unable to eat during the voyage's early days, and hard work, had made him even thinner. Two experiences soon thereafter taught him that crewing on such a huge ship was not child's play. Cecil was on watch up the mainmast in the mid-Atlantic one day and almost fell to his death when a violent storm swept over the ship. On watch in the early morning a few days thereafter, he could barely see thirty feet in front of the ship because of fog. The pilot slowed the ship's speed and no problems occurred until suddenly Cecil noticed a sailboat perilously close to the port bow. He clanged the *Exford's* warning bell, which alerted the pilot to steer clear of the tiny craft.[39]

The *Exford* made history when it became the first American ship to dock at a Russian Black Sea port. Its visit was noteworthy for another reason: It secretly carried equipment from the U.S. that would help build a tractor factory in Russia. The U.S. did not officially recognize the Soviet Union until four years later. Cecil said, "Huge crates dominated the deck, three score of them and more, chained or fastened.... This is the precious cargo, the unique cargo, the political dynamite cargo. The contents of the boxes and crates are about to serve to link two nations that were not linked before." As soon as the ship docked, workers uncrated the equipment and shipped it overland to Stalingrad. The Soviets hoped the tractors would help boost the Russian economy with better agricultural technology. Years later, Cecil learned that dictator Joseph Stalin later turned the tractor factory into one that manufactured tanks to help the Soviets defend Stalingrad against the Germans in World War II. Cecil modified a reference from Isaiah 2:4, when he wrote of the irony of "turning plowshares into guns."[40]

Upon arriving in Novorossiysk, the secret police boarded and searched the *Exford*. Crewmembers had warned Cecil that he could not take his camera ashore. So he hid it beneath a winch with a pile of rags thrown over it. Later, he carried the camera when he and Eugene went ashore and snapped several rolls of film. Afterwards, Cecil said, "I shudder to think what would have been the result [if he had been caught].... One forgets those things at the moment."[41] He sized up the atmosphere of the country when he wrote that "'going into Russia' is an extremely apt phrase. For once in, there is a feeling of internment. One can almost hear gates clank behind." He and Eugene felt there were invisible walls around them.[42] Cecil made no mention of their Russian heritage in the articles.

He and Eugene tried to suppress their capitalistic prejudices whenever they visited a new country. This was especially important in Russia where they attempted to absorb every element of the culture. The authorities assigned a man in his twenties to act as the boys' guide and translator. His name was Albert, and he had immigrated to Russia a few years earlier from England because of the allure of Socialism. After their first few days there, Cecil wrote that the Russian people, "as often has been said, have a genius for suffering." He also observed that Russia was a country where there are "more flies per square inch than in all the rest of the world together."[43] In discussions with Russian adults, it astounded him how complete Russian authorities controlled children's views: "They are taught that Russia and the world in general began in 1917."[44] And although the Russians were willing to engage in casual conversation, they did not trust the Browns. One of the men they met confronted them: "Who are you to come to Russia?... We need your products but not your individuals."[45] Cecil and Eugene were intrigued to learn that the title Worker was the highest distinction a Russian could attain. "Everyone had to work; if they didn't they were put on half-rations."[46] They completed their two-week visit by swimming in the Black Sea and decided that communist life was "strange, harsh and exciting."[47] Cecil concluded that if the first Five Year Industrialization Plan (conceived by Vladimir Lenin) worked, then Russians would be better off, "but it won't. The plan is failing." The analysis Cecil included in the articles provided an indication that even at this early stage of his journalism career he felt compelled to speculate on the situation. As the *Exford* left Russia, Cecil penned, "Honestly, we felt that we had escaped; we said we are 'going out.'"[48]

The *Exford* plowed back through the Dardanelles to the Mediterranean, down the west coast of Africa to Casablanca. Unfortunately, an incident on this leg of the journey left Cecil with a malady that would plague him the rest of his life. While heaving rope on the poop deck as the ship neared Casablanca, excruciating abdominal pain doubled him over. When the *Exford* docked, the company doctor came aboard and startled Cecil by saying, "You have two hours to live." Cecil laughed, thinking he was being overly dramatic, "You're kidding, Doc?" But the doctor replied that he was not exaggerating, that he had suffered a double hernia. He told Cecil he needed an operation, but he replied, "Nothing doing. I'm going back to New York on this ship. I'll take a chance on kicking off." But Captain Ackerman, upon hearing the diagnosis, interjected that Cecil would cooperate or he was going to "shove him over the side, because he was responsible" for the crew's wellbeing. Eugene volunteered that he would pay for the operation, after admitting that as Cecil's brother he was a responsible next-of-kin (a fact the *Exford's* crew had already guessed).[49] After the operation, Cecil spent nine days in the clinic before he was able to escape a "prattling French nurse" with the aid of a cane.[50] He was determined to see Morocco. As soon as he could hobble out of the building, he and Eugene boarded a bus that took them on a 135-mile trip to Marrakesh. Considering the crudeness of medical treatment in Casablanca in 1929, going on such a journey less than two weeks after surgery had to qualify as both a major risk and an accomplishment. Cecil had to have been in pain, but he was tough-minded enough to fight through it. While in Marrakesh, the brothers sampled alien but scrumptious cuisine and marveled at the beautiful, dark-skinned women.[51] They then returned to Casablanca, re-boarded the *Exford* and disembarked in New York in January 1930.

Cecil completed his last story about the journey in the *Vindicator* with advice to readers that the Brown brothers' adventures had made their lives more complete. He urged Ohioans to do something similar. "If life seems dull and stagnant give your hourglass another shake," he advised. "The world has not been discovered unless you discover it for yourself." He concluded the series with the recommendation that "life is rich and full, hardly narrow and provincial. Life is never stagnant. If we cease to move we no longer live."[52] While Eugene and Cecil had enjoyed their seafaring experiences, they realized that life as seamen was not where their futures lay. They had seen places and met people that few others their age had. And while he declared that his life as a sailor was probably over, Cecil envisioned himself combining his loves of travel and writing as a foreign correspondent.

Back in Warren, both of them had to face the reality that the year was 1930, the first full year of the Great Depression. As a result, they would have to put their plans on hold, and he and Eugene did what many families did during the 1930s: they hunkered down and supported one another. The two brothers were good tennis players, with Eugene the better of the two. They won multiple doubles tournaments around Ohio, and Eugene topped Cecil in winning a number of singles' tournaments. Competing helped keep their minds off the hard times their family was enduring. But with limited prospects for launching their careers, the brothers pitched in to help their father for two years. The Brown Company's profits were slim as restaurants bought only the items they needed, what with few members of the public having disposable income to eat out. Because Eugene displayed the mathematical skills that Cecil lacked, and he was the eldest son, Maurice employed him as company manager. The post put Eugene in a position of placing advertising in local newspapers, which allowed him to form contacts with publishers in Warren and Youngstown. He found that he liked advertising, and the experience laid the groundwork for Eugene's future in the business side of journalism.

In 1931, Youngstown librarian Margaret (Margo) Cleveland contacted Eugene about joining the board of directors of a community theater company that she and two other women were forming. The women needed a man with financial abilities to add credibility to the venture and attract investors, and Eugene's business skills and local contacts made him a partner that could benefit the venture. He agreed, and after working together for a few months, he and Margo fell in love. Eugene asked her to marry him, but she refused because she was caring for her mother, who was disabled with polio. As a result, Eugene and Margo put their relationship on hold, when in another year he left Warren to become a newspaper-advertising salesperson. After her mother died, Margo joined Eugene as he worked his way up to larger circulation newspapers, in positions that took them out of Ohio, first to Nevada, then to Long Island. In subsequent years, he became a successful newspaper and radio station manager in New York and Connecticut with the Ottaway Group.

Simultaneously, Cecil, who lacked both Eugene's interest in and ability as a businessperson, was attempting to launch his reporting career. His first few steps in this regard were halting ones. During the Depression, full-time reporting jobs were scarce, so he earned minimal wages in a number of short-term jobs as a dish washer, and chauffeur, and unsuccessfully tried to sell a variety of products. Frustrated with dead-end positions, and lacking the sales' ability of his brother, in early 1932 he decided he had to leave Ohio to make a living as a reporter. With only a few dollars in his pocket, Cecil came up with the idea of traveling to Mexico, where he planned to launch out on horseback across that nation in search of news. The Depression also had hit Mexico hard, and, in addition, a story that U.S. newspapers were largely ignoring was playing out there. Given the lack of employment opportunities in the U.S., authorities were repatriating Mexican-Americans across the border. Altogether, they deported more than 1,000,000 Mexican-Americans during the 1930s. Cecil wanted to tell their story.[53] He figured he could gather information in Mexico about the plight of the deportees and sell enough stories to U.S. magazines to make a living. Thus, he boarded a train in Cleveland that took him as far west as Phoenix. It was mid–January 1932. He wanted to get to Nogales, but at this point, he was nearly penniless. He needed to find a job to finance his trip the additional miles. He would have to call upon the resourcefulness he and Eugene had developed to finance his venture into foreign correspondence across the Mexican border.

✦✦ 2 ✦✦

A Cub Reporter Becomes a Pioneering Broadcaster

Brown walked into the temporary Phoenix office of George Beale, Los Angeles Bureau Chief for the United Press (UP), asked for a job, and showed him his portfolio of stories. There were not a lot of young men in Phoenix in 1932 with journalism credentials, and Beale needed help, so he gave Brown a chance. He assigned him the job of covering an infamous murder trial. Medical secretary Winnie Ruth Judd was accused of killing and dismembering the bodies of two female friends. The police said she had shipped body parts to Los Angeles in the trunk of a car, which resulted in her being dubbed the Trunk Murderess. For the next month, Brown sat in a nearly one-hundred-degree courtroom "about four feet away from an attractive, vacant-eyed girl [Judd] who did nothing but twist ... her handkerchief around her fingers." When the jury reached a verdict, it was that Judd was insane; Brown said the experience almost made him crazy as well.[1] Nevertheless, Beale was impressed enough with Brown's work that he offered him a job in Los Angeles. He had not paid Brown much for his work in Phoenix, and Brown figured Mexico would still be there when the Los Angeles job ended, so he accepted the offer. As events unfolded in the coming months, Brown never returned to the Mexican deportation issue.

After submitting a couple of stories to his editors, they told him he was not a very good writer, but his job as a general assignment reporter provided him with an opportunity to polish his skills. He attempted to make up for his deficiency by being aggressive: "I had long legs, unquenchable curiosity, unbounded energy and the faculty of asking penetrating and frequently insulting questions." Brown kept no notes on what he covered, other than calling his assignment "a happy hunting ground for a cub, with all kinds of fantastic stories breaking." But one memorable story occurred the following

March when he became a participant in a life-threatening disaster. He was in the UP office when an earthquake, the epicenter of which focused in Long Beach, began. The tremors made his typewriter jump across the table, but "I realized this was a big story, and I kept typing, although other reporters ran out of the room, saying the building was going to collapse."[2] Fortunately, it did not collapse and Brown contributed to the coverage of a six-point-four magnitude quake that cost 120 lives and $50,000,000 in damage.

Journalism in the 1930s was not well-paying, or easy. The UP was notorious for being stingy, which meant it had to rely on young, inexperienced reporters such as Brown to staff its bureaus. But for men like Brown, who were building a resume, it was a great place to learn the ropes. A number of the Murrow Boys began their careers with UP, including Richard Hottelet, who recalled: "UP got good kids, squeezed them like oranges, taught them the trade.... For those who could get by on bread and promises, it was a useful training ground." Another broadcaster who began his career with UP was David Brinkley. He remarked: "You can't run those big news businesses without money, but you've got to give it to the UP—they tried."[3]

Hoping to earn a little more than bread and promises, in late 1933 Brown figured he had gained enough experience in L.A. and that it was time to make a better living in the newspaper business. Thus, he returned to Arizona and took the position as editor of the *Prescott Journal-Miner*. His duties included supervising a staff of one fulltime reporter, eighteen part-time correspondents and doing most of the paper's layout and other work himself. He wrote stories and editorials, rewrote the correspondents' stories and wire copy, selected art, chose which syndicated features to run, and laid out the dummy. The publisher also expected him to participate in civic activities, and to grow the paper's circulation. Prescott had a little more than 5,000 residents, made up largely of copper miners and cowhands.

Without editorial limitations, Brown grasped the opportunity to become a crusading journalist. For his first effort, he observed that there were a great many slot machines in town, so he mounted a campaign to eradicate them. One night soon after he had published several stories about the illegality of the one-armed bandits, one of their owners sat down across a café table from Brown while he was eating supper. He told Brown that if he did not stop editorializing against the slots, "he was going to stick a knife in my innards and twist it." Brown reported the threat to the sheriff, whereupon the slot owner spent time in jail. But the machines disappeared for only two months, and returned without law enforcement interference thereafter.[4] On another occasion, he reported the lack of a fire escape from the local school's second floor, but the school board president responded, "We don't need them. If there's a fire the kids can jump."[5]

Brown also published a story about a wealthy female rancher who had

2. A Cub Reporter Becomes a Pioneering Broadcaster   21

charged a neighboring rancher with cattle rustling. He said the reason she was suing him was that the defendant had rejected her romantic overtures. She sued the *Journal-Miner* for $50,000, alleging defamation. Brown said he had reliable sources for the accusation, so he refused to retract the story, but the publisher ordered him to rescind it and print an apology. Brown declined and resigned in February 1934, recognizing that his efforts to clean up Prescott were not achieving change, and that the publisher was not supporting him. Opportunely, a reporter job was available at the *Pittsburgh Press*, and Brown was hired. The new position was particularly appealing because the Scripps-Howard chain of papers—including the *Press*—were known for dedication to orienting news to working class readers."[6]

Under the tutelage of veteran editor Edward Leech, Brown found the job the most enjoyable and instructive he had held as a newspaperman. "Leech ... conducted a vigorous paper, pulled few punches, fought fairly, called a spade a spade, and ... developed the best interests of the city," commented Brown. He broadened and improved his skills by covering practically every kind of story imaginable, including crime, politics, law and features as well as writing movie, theater and book reviews. In January 1935, the *Press* sent him to New Jersey to cover the Bruno Hauptmann trial in the twentieth-century's first "crime of the century." He was charged with kidnapping and killing aviator Charles Lindbergh's infant son. Because all the major newspapers were there, Brown looked for a different angle. He located it in a story he titled "The Brooklyn Bulldog." In it, Brown described the less-than-ethical abilities of defense attorney Edward Reilly: "[He] keeps out of jail those who kill people, always fetches out from nowhere the best in legal legerdemain to stun a jury, confounds a judge and enrages the prosecution at the proper time." Brown said Reilly understood that "publicity is money in the till."[7] Back in Pennsylvania weeks later, Leech assigned Brown to do a series about the Civilian Conservation Corps at work in rural Somerset County. The assignment gave him an opportunity to unlimber his feature writing skills: "Six thousand young men who might have 'gone to the dogs' have gone to the woods instead. They are the Depression-stricken youth who have joined [President] Roosevelt's Tree Army."[8] In another feature, Brown displayed an ability to merge tongue-in-cheek humor with straight reporting. He wrote that America's hoboes had arrived in Pittsburgh "grimy and unwashed, with high resolves and tomato-can tastes, by road and rod, by airplane and afoot." It was their twenty-seventh annual national convention, which they called a "jungle." He found that not all of the expected 100 delegates had escaped "the garbage dump to meet in Moose Temple ... because they are in jail between California and the Carolinas."[9]

But, after two years in Pittsburgh, Brown took his upgraded skills with him in January 1936 to a new position with the *Newark (N.J.) Ledger*. Part of the allure was an increase in salary, but it also provided him the opportunity to break into the nation's preeminent media market: New York City. As he left the *Press*, one of his colleagues commented, "Brownie had a terminal case of itchy feet."[10] His new editor put him to work covering sensational stories, such as the Hindenburg dirigible crash and Hauptmann's execution. Brown wrote, "I must have had a crusading gleam in my eye, because the *Ledger* set me to crusading." While digging for dirt in Newark, he helped oust a corrupt police commissioner, but such work could prove to be hazardous. Once, a gangster threatened him if he did a story about mob activities, but Brown was not intimidated. "Newark harbored many a character who was not quite a gentleman and the municipal scandals were something worth writing about." But after only a little over a year at the *Ledger*, he was off again. This time he moved across the Hudson River to Manhattan where he was in the heart of the Manhattan beat. The *New York American* hired him as a rewrite man. Unfortunately, after only a month, the *American* merged with the *New York Journal*, and Brown was unemployed.

Out of work but committed to earning a living in New York, Brown got his first taste of radio. UP acquaintance Charlie Pooler, who had moved to CBS, helped Brown get a temporary position in the network's publicity department. One of his responsibilities was to rewrite news for Andre Baruch's morning show. Brown was fascinated with the new medium, which was still in its infancy. Radio news writing was significantly different from the newspaper style to which Brown had become accustomed. He liked his introduction to broadcasting, but it was not his goal to work in radio at this point. Rather, Brown was ready to fulfill his original dream: that of becoming a foreign correspondent. He set out to achieve that by going to Europe. The European continent was in the initial stages of becoming embroiled in another war. Brown wrote former *Press* colleague Harry August what he foresaw as his opportunity. He thought a journalist in pre-war Europe had "to be ready and prepared for the next move before it happens…. The alliances were being formed secretly and spiritually."[11] He did not know how soon war was coming, but he was certain it would, and he wanted to help isolationist Americans understand the reasons why: "It was obvious that a frightful bust was coming to Europe…. When this bust-up did come, I wanted to know the reasons."[12]

Setting off with all his savings, about $1,000, in his pocket, he booked passage on the *American Farmer*, in the lowest-priced berth. It was September 1937. His plan was to tour Europe, gather information, and write articles to sell to an American magazine. He arrived in England on October 2, and because he had formed a relationship with CBS, made his way to the network's London headquarters. There, he met a man whom he had never heard of before: Ed Murrow. He had only been there for a few months himself. CBS had appointed him European Network Director, but the position had little to do with news. Murrow's job was to arrange for broadcasts that ranged from "talks by authors, and special events such as golf tournaments, children's choruses and dog shows."[13] Brown's recollection of that meeting was that Murrow was "impressive, a very handsome guy, a very nice person, and very gracious." Because Murrow had only just hired William Shirer as CBS's first European news correspondent, and formation of a European news organization still lay two years in the future, Murrow did not offer Brown a job.[14]

After departing London, Brown toured as many countries as he could. His purpose was to ascertain what motivated European dictators to govern their nations as they did, and why their people supported them. He spent five months crisscrossing England, France, Belgium, Czechoslovakia, Austria, Germany, Italy, Sicily and North Africa. By the time Brown concluded his journey in Paris, he had only $76.50 left. He faced the challenge of writing articles that would interest an American magazine enough to publish the work of an unknown freelancer. He had no connections with stateside magazine editors. As a result, on a particularly cold 1938 February morning, "in the cheapest room of the cheapest hotel in the cheapest section of Paris," he sat before his portable typewriter. He was wearing a heavy overcoat with a scarf up around his neck and ears. The unheated room was dreary.[15] His circulation was an issue, and finally his fingers stopped cooperating. He marched downstairs to the manager, a rotund man who claimed he was quite comfortable: "If Monsieur wished steam heat perhaps he should try the Ritz." The manager's response was not going to placate Brown. He argued with the man to provide some form of warmth, and after extended haggling, returned to his room with two hot water bottles from the kitchen. He placed one on his feet and the other in his lap, which allowed him to continue typing.[16]

Upon finishing the articles, he took them to the post office and put them in an envelope along with a letter to Eugene, asking him to try to sell them to a New York publisher. By this time, Eugene was the advertising manager at the *Long Island Star*. When Cecil learned that the postage would cost him three dollars, he hesitated, but he knew Eugene liked to collect stamps, so he figured that even if his brother could not sell the articles, at least he would have some new stamps for his collection. The postal clerk wanted to affix just a few large value stamps to the envelope, but Cecil insisted that he sell him a bunch of small-denomination stamps, with no two alike. By the time he had stuck them all on, they covered nearly half the envelope. He mailed what he hoped would be his future to his brother.[17]

Three weeks later, anxiety had replaced hope; Cecil was down to his last few cents. But while he had been waiting for word from Eugene, he had been pestering Ken Downs, Paris correspondent for the International News Service (INS) for a job. Opportunely, with him almost at the end of his subsistence, a welcome cable arrived from New York. Eugene had struck a deal with *Ken* (a liberal magazine that had published articles by Ernest Hemingway and George Seldes). Editor *Arnold Gingrich* had agreed to buy four of Cecil's five articles at $200 apiece Then, with the arrival of the cable, Cecil's good fortune snowballed. The same day he received it, Downs offered him a job. With the *Ken* checks on the way, and the promise of a steady salary in hand, Cecil was able to find a warmer hotel in which to sleep.[18]

Ken published the first of the articles, "A Nut between Crackers," about Czechoslovakia, in May 1938. In it, Brown was critical of Czech Party leader Sudeten Deutsch: "The Czechoslovak walks as gingerly as a tightrope artist high above the sawdust ring of war. The net of Russia, France and England may save him. He can't rely on the good will or good intensions of anyone."[19] The next two articles concerned Germany. In "The Dust Bowl of Freedom," Brown wrote of German paranoia, "Spontaneous enthusiasm simply does not grow in the land where your neighbor applauds for fear you will inform on him." Then, in "Tomorrow the World is Ours," he described Hitler Youth indoctrination: "[They] will carry into leadership an ignorance of the church, no loyalty to parents, no sense of mercy."[20] In the final article, "Mussolini's Always Right," Brown observed, "The Italian's thoughts, eyes, ears, destiny, morals, spaghetti, pocketbook, and trigger finger are controlled completely by the whim of one man.... The Italian reveres Duce."[21]

Tumultuous events during 1938 that transformed the lives of Europeans also had a major impact on Brown. On March 12, 1938, Adolf Hitler's German forces invaded Austria, which caused INS to evacuate its correspondent to Paris. INS put him in the position that Brown had occupied for only a few weeks. The following day, Germany's annexation of Austria precipitated the first CBS *World News Roundup*. Network technicians prepared a coordinated transmission from a number of European capitals, an arrangement that no radio network had attempted before. Shirer reported from London, Murrow from Vienna, INS's Pierre Huss from Berlin, Senator Lewis Schwellenbach from Washington, Edgar Mowrer of the *Chicago Daily News* from Paris, and INS's Frank Gervasi from Rome. Downs told Brown he was sorry but he was out of a job in Paris, but if he was willing to relocate to Rome, he could become the assistant to bureau chief Gervasi. Brown wanted to remain in Paris, but at the end of March he set off for the Eternal City. Upon arriving in Rome, Brown spent nine months learning about Fascist Italy from Gervasi. Then, at the beginning of 1939, INS reassigned Gervasi to the U.S. and INS named Brown bureau chief. He had made a positive impression.

He wrote a colleague that reporting in Italy was "a matter of digging, digging, digging, making innumerable contacts, spending half your salary on entertainment, knowing diplomats, ambassadors, ministers and as many as possible of the fascist government officials." The work was often frustrating

2. A Cub Reporter Becomes a Pioneering Broadcaster 25

because he had to overcome news restrictions. Nonetheless, when he did he felt gratified that he had outwitted the fascists. "The Italian system," he wrote, ensures that "the best story is the story that is not printed."[22] When Hitler reviewed Italy's military with Mussolini and King Victor Emmanuel, Brown's story about the fascist leaders read: "Never since the days of the conquering Caesars did a visitor from abroad receive a welcome surpassing in lavish splendor that which greeted the Nazi Reichsfuehrer when he arrived for a six-day sojourn." A crowd estimated at 125,000,000 cheered Hitler as he and Mussolini smiled and held clasped hands high, signifying the two country's Pact of Steel.[23]

Brown's new role also put him in a position of serving as a CBS stringer. Throughout the day and night of February 9, 1939, Pope Pius XI lay near death following a stroke, and Brown kept INS updated on the Pope's deteriorating health. Brown considered the opportunity to cover the Pope's pending death the "biggest story of the decade about one of the decade's warmest, bravest men."[24] Pius had criticized the fascists, so he was widely respected around the world. Brown slept on a cot in his office, while awaiting a call from a Vatican attaché who had promised to alert him when the Pope's condition changed. He was just dozing off at 4:45 the next morning when one of his telephones rang. Upon answering, he recognized the voice of his Vatican informant, "The Pope suffered another stroke a few minutes ago. He's slipping away very fast." Brown telephoned INS in London. For the next hour, he kept the Vatican contact on one phone and his INS colleague on another to convey updates. At 5:31 a.m., the Pope died, and Brown informed INS immediately. His world scoop of the Pope's death beat bulletins from UP and the Associated Press (AP) by a matter of minutes. Seconds were important in getting this story on the wire because 5:31 a.m. in Rome was 11:31 p.m. in New York, which was the deadline for getting the story in the next morning's newspaper.[25] Brown also informed CBS in London, where an announcer voiced the bulletin.

In the following months, Brown periodically contacted Murrow with stories about fascist developments in Italy. His hope was that the quality of his work would impress Murrow to the degree that he would hire him. In fact, CBS needed Brown almost as much as he needed it. He particularly wanted to join CBS because he recognized the valuable service radio could provide in keeping America updated on developments in Europe. He believed the future of this new mode of rapid news delivery was bright. He also thought a career in radio held more promise than the one he was experiencing as a wire service reporter. He felt INS underappreciated and underpaid him. Of course, he had little broadcasting experience. But this did not make him unusual as a prospective CBS correspondent. Neither had any of the other correspondents the network had hired, including Murrow. On the other hand,

Brown took this picture in May 1950 of President and Madam Chiang Kai-Shek as they greeted him at their home in Taipei, six months after they fled Mainland China. This was the first of many interviews Brown conducted with the deposed leader, and he and Martha became close friends with him and Madam Chiang. She was an accomplished artist, and Brown arranged for several of her paintings to be published in *Life* magazine (courtesy Wisconsin Historical Society).

Brown was impressing Murrow with the qualities he esteemed most in a colleague: "tough-minded, energetic, and aggressive."[26]

From his perspective, indications that Mussolini was going to align Italy with Germany made it clearer to Murrow every day that there was indeed a dire need for a regular correspondent in Italy. If CBS did not hire someone there soon, the network faced the proposition of missing important stories in one of Europe's leading Axis nations. Brown arranged for a number of cultural broadcasts from Rome and facilitated the broadcasts of various newspaper correspondents' reports to CBS. But one by one the newspapers stopped

2. A Cub Reporter Becomes a Pioneering Broadcaster

their correspondents from sending stories to the network. Their editors were irritated that the CBS reports were scooping their own newspaper stories. Brown's INS contract did not bar him from providing stories to radio, but just as it was threatening other correspondents' relationship with their papers, his moonlighting was putting him in a tenuous position with INS. Reporting for the new kid on the block, radio, which threatened to diminish newspaper readership, became a treasonable act, as far as publishers were concerned.

Undeniably, as the Nazis overran Europe, the American audience increasingly tuned to radio for updates because of its advantages over newsprint in speed and sound. They no longer had to wait for the following morning's newspaper to arrive at the front door to learn of the latest alarming European events. The immediacy that radio provided resulted in the growth of the audience to number in the millions. Advertisers followed with an "avalanche of advertising" profits shifting to radio from 1941 on. The newspaper business would never be the same.[27] The potential influence of radio was so evident that in Germany General Hermann Goering, Hitler's second in command, called the medium the war's Third Front, after the military and economic fronts.[28]

From New York, CBS News Director Paul White had given Murrow the go-ahead to recruit more correspondents. In addition to himself and Shirer, Murrow hired Thomas Grandin, then Eric Sevareid, to report from Paris. In September 1939, when Germany invaded Poland, war officially commenced in Europe. By then, CBS had hired thirty-nine war correspondents, and that number grew to sixty-five the following year. While all the radio networks increased their staffs to cover the war, CBS's became the largest, and Brown's persistence and CBS's need finally converged on November 24, 1939, when Murrow cabled him to prepare an audition newscast. Brown was one year older than Murrow, and a more experienced journalist by several years. Murrow, on the other hand, was more knowledgeable about broadcasting. The audition was fortuitous, because on December 7, INS abruptly fired Brown, without advance notice. The INS cable simply read, "NOTIFY BROWN DISPENSING WITH HIS SERVICES EFFECTIVE IMMEDIATELY IN VIEW HIS RECORD." The wording left Brown unsure why he had been dismissed. He had thought his reporting had been acceptable, but it is more than likely the termination had to do with his growing CBS relationship. Regardless, the suddenness of the firing did not shock him, nor did he dispute it. He called his work with INS, "A devastating experience ... a nightmare," because he never knew from one day to the next what they wanted from him, or where they wanted him. "It has taken a great deal out of us [he and his new bride]."[29] Brown had scored a world beat in his report on the Pope, and although INS sent a congratulatory telegram, he received neither a bonus nor a raise, a common practice among news outlets of the day. In his diary he recorded,

"With the money we [he and his wife] have we ought to be able to hold out for about three months."[30]

Brown had married his Columbus, Ohio, sweetheart, Martha Leaine Kohn, on July 20, 1938, in a civil ceremony in Rome. He had invited her to vacation with him for three weeks, but soon after her arrival they were married, and she remained with him for most of the next three years. Martha had cashed in her return ticket home to pay for her wedding ring.[31] She was the daughter of Adele and Jerome Kohn. Her father and uncle owned the Corrugated Container Company in Columbis. The Kohns were socially active and entertained often, inviting political and civic leaders to their comfortable home. Adele was a mentor to Jewish students at Ohio State, and one night she invited Brown to join her family for dinner. Martha was only sixteen at the time; Brown was twenty-three and had just finished his studies at OSU. He was immediately infatuated by Martha; she was a striking five-foot-nine-inch brunette with green eyes, and he later returned to the house to ask her mother if he could take her to a movie. Adele agreed, and the romance began. Martha loved horseback riding, and Brown learned to ride so he could court her. Despite the fact that Brown would soon start moving from place to place to answer his journalistic calling, they maintained a distance relationship over the next seven years. When they met, Brown himself was a striking figure. Along with his impressive height, he possessed blond hair, and his face featured a prominent, but distinguished nose. His travels had helped him develop a worldly demeanor that included social graces and a knack for engaging in stimulating conversation. Martha was especially attracted to him from the beginning because "he was simply a very good, humble man," and was always "kind to others." Initially, Jerome disapproved of Brown because he was a journalist. Before leaving for Europe, Brown had asked Martha's father for her hand in marriage. Among the questions he asked Brown before granting his approval, however, was how much money he made. He replied that his salary was fifty dollars per week. Kohn was stunned, and said that "wouldn't even keep Martha supplied with silk stockings."[32] Consequently, she had to finance her trip to Italy by selling the Steinway piano her grandparents had given her so she could take lessons. She and Cecil rented an apartment in Rome, and during this period Brown grew a mustache, which he believed made him appear more dignified. Martha approved, and he retained it for the remainder of his life.

In January 1940, while waiting to hear from CBS, Cecil and Martha embarked upon a month-long trip that took them to Malta, Tunisia, Syria, Libya, Egypt and throughout Italy. It was part-honeymoon-part-journalism tour, and hardly a luxurious journey. The Browns traveled on troop trains because it was all they could afford. He wrote that he wanted to see the desert "in preparation for coming events."[33] It was a valid premonition; in a few

2. A Cub Reporter Becomes a Pioneering Broadcaster

As part of their July 1938 honeymoon trip in fascist Italy, beautiful Martha and husband Cecil Brown enjoyed a gondola ride in Venice. She had sold the Steinway piano her grandparents had given her to finance her trip to Italy, which she had told her family was only a three-week vacation, but soon after her arrival, Martha and Cecil were married. Three years later, he sent her back to the U.S. for her safety, and he went to Yugoslavia to cover the Axis invasion (courtesy Wisconsin Historical Society).

months, he would indeed be reporting the war from there. The trip also crystalized the fact for Martha that Cecil was a working journalist twenty-four hours a day, seven days a week, regardless of his marital status. News was always on his mind. Back in Rome, on February 10, Murrow notified Brown that CBS was hiring him at a salary of $100 per week.

His new profession had to be thrilling on three counts. Not only did he have a job again, but the position allowed him to break into radio, and he had received a raise. Brown had impressed Murrow with his reportorial abilities, but employing him was also a matter of expediency: The network needed a reliable correspondent in Italy, he was already there, and they had no one else to send who knew the political landscape and who possessed the contacts Brown had developed. He was now a member of a lineup that eventually grew to thirteen correspondents that Murrow recommended and White approved to cover the war in Europe. There had never been a lineup like it before, nor has there been anything like it since. Murrow later said, "If I am remembered for anything, I want it to be for the people I have been able to persuade to work with me here at CBS. Without them I'd be nothing."[34] David Hosley says all the members of Murrow's team "had grown up distant from the [U.S.] East Coast. For the most part, they were young, in their twenties, and strong. All of them were college educated, but had not studied at Harvard or Yale."[35] They would come to be known as "Murrow's Boys."

They would spend the war reporting from a wide expanse of venues. In addition to Murrow, Shirer, Grandin, Brown and Sevareid, the team included Robert Trout, LeSueur, Howard K. Smith, Collingwood, Hottelet, Winston Burdette, Bill Downs, and one woman, Mary Breckinridge. Within a few months, millions of Americans began to recognize the names and the voices of these reporters as they alerted them to listen with one of the introductory phrases "This is London," "Paris Speaking," or "Rome Calling." The unique lead-ins made it sound "as if the announcer embodied the city itself."[36] Some historians have failed to include Brown as one of the Murrow team because he did not remain part of the unit for the entire war. Nonetheless, his tenure with the group would become noteworthy for the stories he would cover and the controversy his methods would precipitate.

As Murrow and White formed the group, there were no established models for how a radio correspondent should report, write or announce the news. Thus, CBS invented a completely new style of journalism. The geographically disparate members brought faraway scenes into American living rooms in a manner that all the networks would subsequently emulate as *the standard* for presenting broadcast news. That standard continues in practice today. They wrote for the ear, with word pictures, instead of for the eye, so the audience could cognitively visualize the scenes the correspondents were describing. The reports—often originating from a location with the sound of breaking news in the background—conveyed an on-the-spot reality and urgency that eclipsed anything newspapers could provide. Murrow urged his colleagues to "report the human side of the news, not only the facts but also how the average person reacted," and to convey the "meaning" of events.[37] The correspondents wrote to "communicate a sense of the drama unfolding before them ... to speak naturally, to be honest."[38] He told them "to be anything but intellectual. I want them [the stories] to be down-to-earth, in the vernacular of the man on the street."[39] The writing and announcing stressed creating "concrete mental images—of what shopping for food was like, or sleeping, or crossing the street—of how the war was affecting everyday people." Cloud and Olson described the reports as "part fact, part essay, part color and part editorial, all wrapped up in a crisply written two-or-three-minute account."[40] Fred Friendly, who produced documentaries with Murrow after the war, characterized the writing style as focusing on "the little picture."[41] "They used the first and second person to address their listeners directly and involve them in what the war felt like," added Douglas.[42] Latterday CBS correspondent Charles Kuralt observed of his predecessors' work: "They brought a tone of scholarship. They knew their subjects and they were able to refer easily to the past and draw conclusions for the present.... There's no one like that in broadcasting today."[43] After the war, media analysts judged the team's work "the best ever done in broadcasting."[44] Barnouw concurred: "The CBS team became a genuine all-star line-up. Any one of them could, at the moment of challenge, perform brilliantly."[45]

In selecting members of the team, Murrow valued the news instincts of the person more than the quality of their voice. Some at CBS thought Brown's voice so bad that they did not want him hired. But Murrow argued that "the power of their observations ... and their ability to write and to ad-lib vividly and well would override anything in terms of voice temper."[46] Commenting on Brown's qualifications for inclusion on the team, Cloud and Olson observed that he had gained "a reputation as tough-minded, energetic, and aggressive.... He had a terrible speaking voice—rough and raspy, with a noticeable lisp—but his fine reporting made up for it."[47] Brown definitely possessed a substandard announcing voice. For his part, Murrow's public speaking instruction in college and his baritone pitch helped him sound like he had been born to be an announcer. Brown was nowhere close to exhibiting a similarly polished speech persona, but Murrow's announcing style served as a model that the other members of the team strove to emulate. One factor that favored Brown's announcing was that his Ohio upbringing had endowed him with a Midwestern (General American) accent, which was deemed the standard for American radio announcers.[48] Like most of the members of the team, Brown sounded as if he were reading from a script, which he usually was, but often he even sounded that way though he was adlibbing. Frank Colby evaluated announcer's elocutionary skills in his nationwide column "Take My Word" during the 1940s. In analyzing Brown's voice, he described it as a "medium baritone of a grating unmusical quality that approaches stridency. Brown's voice is much too loud for good radio technique. The combination of harshness and loudness does not make for easy listening." Similar to the speech pattern of Walter Cronkite, Brown often dropped the pitch of his voice at the end of sentences. Colby assessed that, like Barbara Walters' often-ridiculed enunciation, Brown was "noted for the difficulty he has in pronouncing the letter 'l.' His 'l' usually, but not invariably, is pronounced like 'w,' as in 'wike' for 'like,' or 'Po-wand' for Poland."[49]

Nevertheless, reflecting on the CBS correspondents' announcing skills after the war, White wrote, "There aren't many so-called 'good' voices that have reached the forefront of radio news." Examples, he noted, included Walter Winchell, Hans Kaltenborn, Elmer Davis and Brown. "Any of these men," said White, "would be quick to admit that his voice is not an elocutionist's delight." But White agreed with Murrow that it was more important to evaluate what a reporter had to say than the way he said it. "You are apt to find," White added, that "in high audience appeal there are factors other than excellent diction. One of these is intensity. Another is a sincere desire to inform. A third is a community of interest with the listener, and that's something almost impossible to define."[50] Despite his vocal deficiencies, there is no record that listeners complained about Brown's announcing. Ironically, he became the victim of an announcing gaffe when a CBS broadcaster called on him for his first report on the first *News Roundup* after his hiring. Thinking Brown's forename sounded English, he introduced him as if Cecil rhymed with "vessel," the English pronunciation, instead of "diesel," as Brown had pronounced it. But he did not bother to correct the pronunciation, and he liked it so well that he retained it throughout the remainder of his life.

Murrow's initial expectation was that Brown would originate only two broadcasts each week. But fast-breaking developments in Rome soon put him on the air as often as twice each day. In early 1941, Brown wrote August that he really enjoyed his new profession: "After 225 regular broadcasts.... I'm even more enthusiastic about it." In comparison with print work, he said he found the experience was as stimulating as writing for a newspaper, but he liked "the additional fillip that you feel because you are presenting your story to each listener individually." Like all successful announcers, Brown quickly grasped the fact that a quality newscaster needed to deliver stories as if he were talking to one person. He tried to picture August sitting in Pittsburgh listening to him. He would tell August, "Here in Rome tonight, Harry, the situation is this." He liked to anticipate listeners' questions then "answer them as we go along as a sort of conversation piece ... trying to explain and clarify and fit in one part of the jigsaw puzzle that we call Europe."[51] At the time, none of the members of the CBS crew knew they would become famous. They were just doing what Murrow and White expected of them in the only way they knew how. It had to be the same for all the boys, but especially Brown.

Like Murrow, he epitomized that distinctive American characteristic of being a "self-made journalist." Almost overnight, he was a broadcast star, his voice heard around the world. If the opportunity intimidated him, he did not let on. He had to be rejoicing in his good fortune. Before CBS hired him, he had not been a high-profile journalist whose work had appeared in major newspapers or large-circulation magazines. As a wire service reporter, he had been virtually anonymous. Nothing in his background had prepared him for the level of notoriety that his new position had thrust upon him, nor the responsibility he shouldered. Brown had fortuitously been "at the right place at the right time," but his good fortune was not just an accident. Like a Horatio Alger character, he had prepared himself to produce quality work when the circumstances presented themselves. In the years following this distinct set of circumstances, a fledgling journalist would never again be able to enter the broadcast news profession at the level Brown did. In the history of broadcasting, there would not be another break like this for a man with his limited background. Brown dedicated himself to take advantage of the special moment that his initiative had presented, but he could not have imagined how rough the road ahead would be for a radio correspondent in a foreign land.

◆◆ 3 ◆◆

A Correspondent's Rewards
Evicted, Strafed and Censored

After more than two years in Rome, the Italian Fascists knew Brown well, but broadcasting for CBS complicated the relationship. While impossible to scientifically measure how much greater impact radio could have on an audience than wire service reports, Brown speculated that "a radio story has thirty per cent more punch than a newspaper story." The Italian censors agreed that the impact was greater, because as soon as they learned of his new position they increased story censorship. Nevertheless, after securing access to a studio with a shortwave transmitter link, Brown was excited to prepare for his first broadcast as a fulltime CBS reporter.[1]

To gather information, he relied upon an aide to help him scrutinize as many as fourteen newspapers. Brown also talked to dozens of people, many official but also everyday Italians: "I often found important military information from casual conversation with a porter or a waiter."[2] It typically took about twelve hours to gather the materials necessary for a three-to-five-minute radio segment. In the hour before going on the air, he checked for late developments and re-read his script up to six times. The repetition was necessary to polish his delivery and time the segment. After censor approval, he could not change any words, but he could get an alert from New York to start his broadcast twenty seconds early or up to a minute late. That occurred when another correspondent's segment fell short or exceeded their specified time. Accordingly, Brown timed every paragraph, so that as he was reading he could adjust the script's length. He became adept at ending his broadcasts within a few seconds of the allotted time. Listening on headphones, Brown could hear the preceding correspondent finish his segment and verbally "throw" the broadcast back to New York. Brown knew how many seconds the announcer's introduction would take, so he could calculate how much time remained for him. Although he could edit his script for length, he could not adlib, because, as he spoke, sitting across the table from him with his preapproved script in hand, was a censor from the Italian Ministry of Popular Culture. Ministry officials were in charge of censoring all outgoing news.

Typically, Brown broadcast between three and twelve times each week. After preparing his script in his apartment, a cabby took him across the Tiber River to a small studio near Piazza Mazzini Square where he announced after midnight Italian time. When it was time to bring Brown in, the announcer would intone, "America calling Rome; come in Rome." Brown would answer, "Hello America, hello, this is Rome," sounding as if his voice embodied the city itself. The static-filled-shortwave transmissions were not high quality, but that reality encouraged listeners "to lean closer; to try to use your body to help pull him in yourself."[3]

One of his biggest challenges for Brown was learning to write to "time," instead of print "space." This meant he could not be poetic, so he strived to get his facts right and to convey them economically. In a typical segment, he employed sports metaphors to describe a meeting between Mussolini and German Foreign Minister Joachim von Ribberntrop. He announced, "According to the not-too-secret signals here in Rome, Hitler is about to toss another pass, a pass to the Greek and Turkish one-yard line, a pass to be caught by two Bulgarian ministers who are to take the ball over for the next Axis touchdown."[4] During the period he reported from Rome, Murrow provided limited guidance and Brown heard nothing from White about the quality of his work. Concerned, he cabled White for feedback, but he did not respond. Brown surmised, therefore, that his broadcasts were acceptable.[5]

Life in Rome for Martha and Cecil was difficult because of a British naval blockade. Martha described the experience as "weary and sometimes terrifying." They believed spies were everywhere, "the walls had ears" and telephone conversations were recorded. Rationing and the lack of accessible medical treatment left large numbers of the population undernourished and sick. The spaghetti Martha bought at the grocery was gray and the bread dark brown. The latter was comprised of chestnut, corn and potato flour and wood fiber. The Browns learned of several attempts by underground groups to overthrow the fascists, but because German troops supported them, all attempts failed.[6]

On June 4, 1940, Brown did a broadcast in which he said the Italians were mobilizing for war: "Mussolini and his Council of Ministers today passed some minor economic measures, but hidden within the documents was a reference to the council enacting 'some international accords.'" Brown said this meant Italy would join Germany in the war. He was the first correspondent to say so over an American network.[7] Six days later, Cecil stood with thousands of Italians at the Piazza Venezia—Rome's central hub—to hear Mussolini declare war on Great Britain and France. Following the speech, Brown dashed to his office, and with ten minutes to spare before having to broadcast, wrote what he considered his biggest story while in Rome. He announced the Duce's declaration three times that evening. In the initial broadcast he said the Italian people did not want war, but a censor cut that comment in later airings of the story.[8] Mussolini was taking Italy into war despite the fact it was poorly prepared, and he wrongly believed the war would last a short time. Brown labeled the hastily mobilized Italians "a comic-opera army preparing for slaughter under the order of a Duce with a titanic contempt for his own people."[9]

With Italy at war, censorship increased. The censors took orders from Reich Minister of Propaganda Joseph Goebbels in Berlin. Martha remarked that the Nazis expected her husband to play the role of radio's Charlie McCarthy (a dummy) to ventriloquist Edgar Bergen (Goebbels): "He was told that he wasn't the sort of Charlie McCarthy the Nazified Fascist propaganda chiefs could use."[10] Therefore, Cecil continually sparred with censors. If they blue-penciled items, he tried whatever means he could to circumvent the objections.[11] He was not alone in trying to outwit them, nor was he the only journalist who paid the price for attempting to get the truth out of Italy. The regime began restricting where reporters could travel, and a number of correspondents gave up and either left, or were kicked out for reporting stories that the ministry thought cast the regime in a negative light. Said Brown, "It must be remembered that constantly over every correspondent hangs the sword of Damocles of expulsion from the country, and other penalties for 'errors of judgment.'" Between 1936 and 1939 Italian authorities banished twenty-four correspondents.[12] More followed after Italy entered the war. Mussolini even restricted information from his own people. He ordered that they be fined 10,000 Lira and jailed six months if they were caught listening to a foreign broadcast.[13]

Brown had great sympathy for the Italian people but was contemptuous of Mussolini and his minions. During his more than three years in Italy, he "watched forty-five million people being deluded, traduced and consigned to horror and frightfulness."[14] A woman whose son was missing in Libya told him: "Believe me, *Signore*, the real Italian prays for a British victory." Brown estimated that of 45,000,000 Italians, less than 20 percent belonged to the fascist party. While many wore fascist emblems for protection against the Gestapo-controlled police, the same individuals belonged to subversive groups.[15] Although fascist leaders controlled the news, most Italians depended upon grapevine sources rather than official sources. People in the street considered the mainstream media merely propaganda outlets. Italians sometimes boycotted newspapers in a show of solidarity. An underground network circulated word of each boycott. One day, all 20,000 copies of the *Milan Corriere Della Sera* went unsold. Fascist officials were perplexed how such coordinated efforts could be surreptitiously accomplished.[16]

Brown, meanwhile, was fighting his own battle with censors. In April 1940 Ministry Director Telesio Interlandi summoned Brown. Interlandi was a "rough-looking man, with heavy shoulders and a broken nose, who wore the gray-green uniform, with yellow velvet collar, of an officer in the Italian artillery." Interlandi had before him on his desk several of Brown's scripts. He demanded, "What's the matter with you, Mr. Brown? Don't you believe our official communiques?" Brown pleaded innocence, so Interlandi read one of the scripts: "The Italian high command reported today that eight enemy planes were shot down." Throwing the papers across the desk, he asked Brown, "What kind of writing is that?" Brown said he did not understand the comment, "Isn't it perfectly correct?" Interlandi replied, "The facts are correct, but why do you have to qualify them by saying the high command reported them? Why not simply say eight planes were shot down? Just make it a plain statement of fact." Brown explained that he could not say something was fact unless he saw it personally. "Just show me the planes and I'll gladly say they were shot down," he said. "Otherwise I have to say it was only reported." He reminded Interlandi that newspaper reporters were following the same policies he was, and that censors had approved his scripts. "I know all that," Interlandi continued. "But the words sound different the way you say them." From that day on, Brown was in hot water on practically a daily basis with Interlandi.[17]

A few weeks later Interlandi became displeased with another story and he suspended Brown's broadcast rights for a week. Brown asked for forgiveness, pleading that he had not meant to convey anti-fascism in his newscasts, that he only had committed "an honest mistake. I very greatly regret the circumstances of my manuscript last Sunday night which has caused a series of unfortunate events." He said the suspension would not only create a financial hardship for him, but he was concerned that CBS would not be keeping America informed about Italian activities. "After two-and-one-half years in Rome covering news, it seems my record of objective reporting of fascism merits consideration. Most important, there were no repercussions abroad to this unfortunate statement," he stated.[18] Nevertheless, the suspension stood, and one-month later Brown was in trouble again. This time Interlandi accused him, ironically, of reporting the details of a meeting between journalists and Mussolini concerning what they could report. Brown defended himself: "I must convey to you personally my most sincere apologies and regrets for having reported on the air the projected plan of the Duce to receive the journalists." He said he had had to leave the conference early to broadcast and had missed the announcement that its details were supposed to be "off the record."[19]

In June, Interlandi again barred Brown from the air, this time for thirty days, because of a broadcast concerning an Italian Air Force officer's death. Marshal Italo Balbo's plane had crashed in Africa; his death was noteworthy because Italians considered him the heir apparent to Mussolini should something happen to him. The fascists said Balboa had "died a hero's death," shot down in combat. But Brown noted that the general's plane had been downed over Benghazi, and the censor passed the sentence. (Brown had learned, unofficially, that Mussolini had instructed Italian anti-aircraft batteries to shoot Balbo's plane down because Mussolini suspected him of plotting to overthrow him.) Brown could not broadcast that, but he found a way to inform listeners that Balbo's death had, in fact, been an assassination. The censor failed to recognize that since Benghazi was in the hands of the Italians, that Brown was letting Americans know, covertly, that his own troops had shot him down. Brown argued again that the censor had approved his script and, therefore, the penalty was overly severe. Consequently, the ministry reduced the suspension to seven days.[20]

But the censors made it more difficult for Brown to do his job. One way they did was by ruthlessly editing his copy. He no longer faced the problem of fitting all the details he wanted into a story because the censors were cutting them mercilessly. After they finished, there were not enough words left to fill his segments. He tried writing scripts that were too long, hoping the words left after the censor got through would fill the allotted time, but that did not work either. The more he wrote, the more they chopped. He complained to a censor, asking what he could do. "My only suggestion, Mr. Brown, is that you just talk more slowly." That was not a legitimate option.[21]

In January 1941, Brown was suspended again and he could no longer win his appeals. He sought a higher level of support by asking the counselor to the U.S. Embassy, Alexander Kirk, to intervene. Kirk met with Interlandi, who reinstated Brown, but with the proviso that he was on two months' probation. Kirk told Brown, consequently, "They don't want you here and it is foolish to stay." Thus, despite Martha's resistance, Cecil sent her back to the U.S. on March 6. Officials searched her bags as she attempted to buy her sailing ticket, and they confiscated two of Cecil's diaries. She suspected the contents played a part in her husband's subsequent banishment.[22] She sailed on the *Aquitania* via Portugal and France, and feared she would never see Cecil again. Upon landing in New York, a *Radio Mirror* reporter interviewed her. She said she knew her husband's work was dangerous but it was important to both him and America: "As long as he is doing a good job, nothing must be allowed to interfere with him, including her presence."[23] Because his probation was predicated on the abstractions of "good behavior and a greater understanding of fascism," Brown accepted that his days in Rome were numbered, and, indeed, on April Fool's Day the Italians expelled him "for life ... [because of] ... his continued hostile attitude toward fascism."[24] Three months later, the Italians banished all U.S. newspaper correspondents, and the following September all non–Axis correspondents were banished.

Thus, after three years in Rome, Brown asked CBS for a new assignment. Murrow decided he needed him in North Africa where the desert war was underway. Brown was excited about the opportunity to witness some real fighting, but he was on his own getting there. Forced to travel to Turkey by land around the Adriatic and Mediterranean Seas, he arrived in Belgrade on April 4 and checked into the beautiful Serbskikralj Hotel. His stay would be short lived, though, as two days later Italian planes bombed the city. The Yugoslavian Blitzkrieg had begun. Between bombing raids, he made one broadcast, telling the CBS audience: "There was no opposition to the bombers, which circled over the city like vultures and dumped their high-explosive eggs on the defenseless city."[25] It was the last time CBS would hear from him for two weeks because soon thereafter he was having tea in the hotel café when a bomb exploded just outside the hotel and shattered the windows. He spent the next two hours in the hotel's basement as bombs rained. No one was killed, but he and others with him were showered with splintered timbers, plaster and glass. He reflected, "The utter ruthlessness, the suddenness of the attack and the hopelessness of the situation had a terrible effect on my mind. It was my first experience under bombing. I enjoyed it thoroughly—I thought, My God, what a wonderful story this is."[26]

But his excitement turned to desperation when the hotel caught fire and Brown had to run for his life. Leaving his luggage, he headed for open country, thinking that outside the city the chances of being hit by a bullet or bomb would diminish. Unfortunately, he became a member of a group of thousands of refugees who had the same idea. As they alternately ran across open fields and hid in wooded areas, German planes strafed the crowd multiple times. Repeatedly, Brown jumped into ditches to avoid being hit, and along the way witnessed Italian soldiers lock Yugoslavs in their houses before setting them ablaze. The bombing leveled a quarter of Belgrade, killing 24,000 people. On his first taste of intimate warfare, Brown's commented: "There will [remain] be in my ears the scream of Stukas and always in my eyes the crash of bombs, and mangled bodies torn apart and streets splattered with blood."[27]

The following day, Brown found his way back to Belgrade where he encountered American attaché Louis Fortier, who had a 1930s'-era Buick sedan. They decided to join forces and make their way to Turkey. They drove from Belgrade to Uzice, before going on to Sarajevo. Brown called the second leg of the trip harrowing. The road descended 8,000 feet, blinding snow was falling and the roads were "as smooth as glass and the most intense cold." Part of the time, Fortier drove in reverse so he could keep the car from sliding into a gorge. Brown said the drive was so perilous he considered it "worse than the bombings and machine guns" he had survived.[28] He attempted to let CBS know where he was, but the Germans had cut all telephone lines and shut down shortwave facilities. For the next two weeks, Murrow and White would not hear from Brown and feared he had been killed.[29] In reality, Fortier and Brown were traveling without food or sleep. As they motored from town to town, Fortier gripped the steering wheel and peered at the road for patches of shoveled earth, which suggested buried mines. Brown stared out the side window, scanning the sky for Messerschmitts or Stukas. He kept his hand on the door handle so they could hurriedly jump out and into a ditch to escape strafing. But that was perilous as well: "If you got in the wrong ditch—they ship you home in a box."[30] The two Americans became convinced that planes were following them, but it was more likely they were just one of numerous moving targets. On Easter Sunday, April 13, Italian bombers struck the hotel in Sarajevo where Brown and Fortier were trying to sleep. They descended to the basement, but the hotel sustained three direct hits and began to collapse. Forced outside, they ran through the streets, dodging strafings, before escaping into the hills.[31] Brown commented, "The wanton destruction just made you cry. There was no way to retaliate."[32]

During their cross-country expedition, Brown observed a stream of German tanks rumbling through the countryside at forty-five miles an hour. In pathetic opposition, and slowly moving in the opposite direction, ox-drawn Yugoslav carts carried supplies through hub-deep mud to their army. The Luftwaffe overwhelmed the antiquated Yugoslav Air Force within two days. The Germans and Italians killed thousands of Yugoslav soldiers; thousands more surrendered or deserted. Another problem Fortier and Brown faced was that neither Yugoslav nor Axis soldiers trusted anyone, but they were not trying to avoid either. Brown and Fortier were caught in the middle of two warring nations. Their hope was that they could run into and through the Germans. America was not yet at war, but would the Germans consider them neutral observers? Yugoslav troops stopped their car nearly twenty times; just outside of Travnik two officers blocked the road. One put a revolver to Fortier's head; another aimed a rifle at Brown's ear. The lieutenant demanded: "What is happening … his voice almost hysterical.… We are ten men here. We have been cut off for two days. Our food is gone." Fortier updated them as best he could, before one said his men had destroyed the bridge ahead and they would have to go back. Fortier turned the car around, but after a short distance steered it onto a side road and they resumed their route toward Sarajevo.

The following day, Brown's ninth in Yugoslavia, the two encountered another group of Yugoslavs who warned them the Germans were just up the road, headed toward them. Fortier continued driving in that direction. An hour later, twelve Germans in four motorcycle cars screeched to a stop in the road and trained their machine guns on the Americans as they blocked the car. In the hope of not being shot, Fortier and Brown shouted: "*Amerikanische!*"

"*Amerikanische!*" Their cries, along with the American flag on a staff on the front fender, and Brown's offer of American cigarettes, stopped the Germans.[33] After the guns were lowered and the Americans and Germans conversed, Brown asked a lieutenant how close they had come to being shot. He replied in clear English, "Very close. You see, our job is to shoot first and afterwards see if we have made a mistake. I do not know how it is that I did not use my Tommy Gun." The Germans were an advance unit, and they let the two pass, saying they should have no more trouble. He told Fortier they would run into the main German column a few miles down the road, but he was wrong about trouble.

The Americans encountered the column, but the group, which included two Panzer divisions, was not hospitable. As a result, Brown became the first American journalist to report how Panzer divisions advanced.[34] Despite Fortier's protests, an officer accused the Americans of being spies and took them prisoner. Fortier had hidden a 45-caliber revolver under Brown's seat. The officer asked if they had a weapon, and when Fortier said they did, he demanded it be handed over. Fortier said he could not comply because it was U.S. property, but the officer insisted. Brown attempted to retrieve it but it was jammed under the seat. The officer pushed Brown's arm aside, but Brown shoved the officer's arm out of the way, saying he could handle it. The German's face became flushed, but he let Brown proceed. Brown retrieved it, and gave it to Fortier, who removed the clip before handing it to the German.[35] The officer ordered them to pull their car into the convoy.

The column proceeded through Bosnia, past thousands of German vehicles. The Germans first took them to Jajce. Brown described the scene as one of stark contrasts between idyllic beauty and harsh militarism. There was a beautiful waterfall nearby, and young girls were tossing flowers to Germans, who returned grins. As a band played the Horst Wessel song, Swastika flags fluttered from buildings while crowds lined the streets, each person's right arm outstretched in the Nazi salute they had been taught.[36] Fortier and Brown were unsure if they were prisoners, but after a General Stempel interviewed them, he returned Fortier's revolver. Stempel had the Americans fed and escorted to a hotel, where they slept. They stayed there for more than a week as the Germans repaired Serbian-destroyed bridges over the Danube River. Brown witnessed "Nazis shoot down Serbs the way you would not shoot a dog.... Bosnia [was] starving, dying and asphyxiating in the smell of death."[37] Brown said that during his tour of Yugoslavia he was strafed, bombed and threatened at the barrel of multiple guns, and "arrested three times as a spy and once as a parachutist."[38]

Brown met the *Chicago Tribune*'s Sam Brewer in Belgrade, who offered Brown the opportunity to join him and other Americans in a car bound for Budapest. Brown reflected that "it was one devil of a way to see the Balkans," but he expressed his gratefulness to Fortier for keeping him alive, and they parted company. Along with U.S. diplomat Cavendish Cannon, a Scotty dog and twelve pieces of luggage—Brown and Brewer made their way across the river via pontoon boat and beyond in an open-top Ford roadster. During the trip, armed Croats stopped the car three times; at one checkpoint, a Croat remarked, "Americans are our enemies," but he allowed them to pass after two hours.[39] From Budapest, Brown and Brewer drove themselves through Romania and took a boat from Constanta to Istanbul in six days' time. Brown was surprised by Turkey's peacefulness. Being involved in combat had left him in shock: "It felt unnatural, even from the boat to sense the peace of Istanbul. From those shores came no vibrations of fear, grimness and apprehension, and no odor of death." Brewer warned Brown that he would not "get out of Romania [or] ... into Turkey with the camera.... They will take away your excess money.... The trains to Ankara are always crowded." But he was pleased when none of Brewer's predictions came true.[40]

A day after arriving in Ankara, Brown exchanged cables with White, with the help of Winston Burdett, another CBS correspondent. White allotted nine minutes of airtime on the *Roundup*, the largest segment Brown had ever received, to tell his story. On Friday, May 2, he announced, in part: "I've just arrived from Belgrade; or rather I've just arrived from scenes of destruction, desolation, misery and starvation. In other words, I've come from a city occupied by the Germans." He saluted the brave Yugoslavs and alerted Americans that the escalating war could soon involve them.[41] Upon signing off at 2:30 a.m., Brown went to the Palace Hotel to have a drink with Burdett, but upon entering the hotel he collapsed.[42] Burdette helped get him into bed, where he stayed for two days, suffering from a cold and exhaustion. As he lay there, he was nagged by a feeling that he had not been earning his salary because he only had presented two broadcasts in three weeks. But he felt better when, upon coming down to breakfast, a clerk handed him a cable from White that read: "SPLENDID BROADCAST. NOBLE PIECE. GRAND REPORTING. EVERYONE DELIGHTED HEARING YOU. REGARDS."[43]

White's message buoyed him: "That cable from Paul was one of the greatest experiences of my life."[44] It helped Brown feel that he really belonged on the CBS team. He had never felt job security in the more than three years he had worked in Europe. Still, he admitted a lack of confidence: "After every broadcast I give, after every magazine piece I write, I feel somewhat sick. There is always that sentence I wanted to put in and didn't, always one word I have wanted to use and omitted, always an inflection I have wanted to give a phrase, and forgot."[45] Nevertheless, in August the *Saturday Evening Post* thought enough of Brown's work to publish a story about his Balkan experience. The events were over, he wrote, "but the memories are not.... And I knew ... that never again would I find peace. If ever I came to places where there was peace. I should feel ashamed and strange." He was also unsure if peace would return to the world during his lifetime.[46]

Burdett and his wife looked after Brown while he recovered. NBC's Martin Agronsky was also there, and he and Burdett vigorously competed to scoop one another.[47] After talking with Turkish authorities, Brown became concerned he would be detained in Ankara and miss the desert war. Ankara was expensive and he found the Turks unfriendly. He wanted to originate his next broadcast from Baghdad, so he befriended the first secretary of the Iraq legation, who cabled his foreign office about Brown broadcasting there. Brown also cabled White for permission to go to Cairo, fearing that the Turkish-Syrian border would close. On May 12, White gave Brown permission to go to Cairo, and he caught a train for Tripoli. That was the end of the rail line, so he hitched a ride in a car with French, English and Greek civilians. The vehicle took them into Palestine. British officials detained him there because his passport neither showed that he had exited Italy, nor that he had been in Yugoslavia. An officer asked him if he could broadcast from Jerusalem, but Brown insisted he be allowed to go to Cairo. He then asked Brown if he would talk to British intelligence about Yugoslavia, and Brown agreed. An officer took him to Haifa where a Lieutenant Temple interviewed him concerning his observations of German tactics. At 8:30 the next morning, Brown took a hot and crowded train ride to Kantara; sand blew in the windows, covering his clothes. He then crossed the Suez Canal on a ferry. In Kantara, a British officer took Brown's personal papers and refused to return them. Brown's anger grew over the treatment he received at each stop—he told the censor he was being treated like a spy. He threatened to report his conduct to the State Department and that he wanted an inventory of his papers before the official put them in an envelope. The officer did not provide the inventory but put the papers in a sealed envelope, on which he wrote: "Cecil Brown, Continental Hotel, Cairo." The officer put the envelope on the train to Cairo with Brown, which he shared with British, Australian, Indian and Yugoslav soldiers.[48]

The tight security perplexed Brown. As an American journalist in British territory, he had assumed he would be welcome, but that was not the case. Upon arriving in Cairo, Brown cabled White that he could do a broadcast regarding his experiences in Palestine, but White did not respond. It did not matter because the British would not permit him transmitter access. Both they and Egyptian officials said they had to certify his broadcast license, and the paperwork would take weeks. The following morning Brown walked to the American Ministry, where he surprisingly encountered Alexander Kirk, the counselor who had fought for Brown's right to broadcast in Rome. Brown observed that Kirk was his usual "svelte, groomed, massaged" self, but his pipe fell out of his mouth when he saw Brown. He was surprised that the newsman was in Egypt, but before they could exchange pleasantries they were cut off by two American correspondents who heatedly barged in. They were the *New York Herald-Tribune's* Edward Angly and the *Chicago Daily News'* Richard Mower. They called British censorship in Cairo "exasperating. What's the use of staying here?" Angly demanded.[49] Kirk attempted to defuse the newsmen's anger, telling them that if they could manage to get "one thought" out to America each day they would be providing a service. The correspondents departed unappeased. Angly was so frustrated that he returned to New York immediately.

It was a disheartening introduction to Egypt. Brown had assumed that the censorship he had experienced elsewhere would be absent in Egypt, and that he would enjoy press freedom. But he learned that the British command controlled foreign correspondents via their Public Relations Office. Journalists, Brown learned, were "unwelcome intruders." The attitude of the British military was that "this is our war and they didn't want to be bothered by us [journalists]." In addition, there was a long list of details correspondents were not allowed to include in their stories. They could not mention a soldier's name, unless it was provided in an official handout. They could not mention the names of military units or their location, unless officially announced; they could not mention the location of water nor personal stories taken from prisoners-of-war. Also off-limits were stories about civilian alarms or bomb-disposal methods. Stories could not mention anything about weapons or combat tactics. Furthermore, they could not mention the movements of high-ranking officials. That was only part of a longer list that was continually undergoing revision.[50]

It was brutally hot in Egypt in May: 120 degrees by day, and not much cooler at night. On May 19, Brown attended his first press conference, only to encounter another roadblock. Chief censor Captain Berick told Brown he could only accredit one correspondent from each news outlet, and there was already a CBS correspondent there. Brown was stunned that there was another CBS man in Cairo. But upon investigation, he learned that the other correspondent was Edward Chorlian, an Egyptian Broadcasting Network employee who was also a CBS stringer. When Brown encountered Chorlian, the Egyptian expressed fear that CBS had sent Brown to replace him. He attempted to dispel Chorlian's trepidation by explaining he expected to go to the front, and he would send stories back to Chorlian to broadcast. But because of Berick's statement, Brown was unsure if he could broadcast at all. To add to the confusion, White cabled Brown that he wanted him to broadcast twice each week. Brown replied that he could not provide broadcasts at all until White confirmed with the British that he was Cairo's sole CBS correspondent. Even before he was granted that right, however, Brown was making broadcast plans.

Shortwave transmission from Cairo had to be sent to London before being relayed to New York. There were no shortwave facilities in Palestine or North Africa, so Brown came up with the idea of securing a mobile transmitter. He believed the best way to cover combat was from is actual location. Brown located an unused transmitter that technicians could retrofit for truck mounting. It was a revolutionary idea—so revolutionary that neither the British nor White were open to it. Commander Ronald Tod was cool to the idea because he did not want to make a censor available in the field. Brown argued that he wanted to "make the farmers in Kansas, who are 1,500 miles from salt water, see and feel the desert and, to understand what Suez means, that he wanted to dramatize the war," but Tod remained opposed. Brown pleaded with White for backing. He said the transmitter would cost $5,000, and it should have a backup, raising the cost to $10,000. But his idea received no more support from White than it did from Tod.[51]

On May 24, both Egyptian and British officials granted Brown permission to broadcast, but then he needed a story. He thought he had one when he encountered "Jimmy" Roosevelt II at the American Embassy. He was just back from Iraq where Axis fighters had strafed a column of cars in which he was riding. Brown tried to get him to agree to an interview, but Roosevelt said he could not comply because he was on a secret mission on behalf of his father, the president. Fortuitously, and with his first broadcast scheduled that night, fortune smiled on Brown. He attended a press conference at which he learned from the British military attaché to Greece, J. S. Blunt, how he and King George II had escaped capture or death during the German parachute invasion of Crete four days earlier. The king had fled his residence near Canea when Axis forces overran it in April. Blunt had been assigned to protect the king, and he helped him escape to Egypt. After taking notes, Brown ran to his hotel room and typed the story while sweat poured from his brow. White had allocated him only three minutes on the *Roundup*, but in the cue channel before the broadcast Brown lobbied Murrow to give up a minute of his time so Brown could do a four-minute story; Murrow agreed.

On the air, Brown began: "The dramatic details of the German parachute invasion of Crete and how the King of Greece escaped into the hills while Nazi parachutists were shooting at them was told to me tonight." The German invasion of Crete was a disaster for British and Greek forces, but the story of King George's evacuation was electrifying. On May 20, German parachutists jumped from transports only 200 feet off the ground with tommy guns in their hands. The number of Germans was "so thick they almost blotted out the blue sky and white clouds." Some of them landed within 800 yards of the king. New Zealand and Greek troops engaged the Germans in hand-to-hand combat as the king's small party made its way into the mountains. They climbed nearly 8,000 feet to escape the Germans who were overrunning the

The April 1939 wedding of journalist Richard Mowrer of the *Chicago Daily News* (hat in hand) and Rosemund Emily Cole in Rome. Mowrer had just been expelled by Benito Mussolini for anti-fascist articles (he expelled Brown for the same offense two years later.) A few minutes before the deadline, the couple was hastily married with friends Cecil, behind the bride, and Martha Brown, as witnesses. Also in the wedding party are American consul John Jones, on the left, and a man identified only as Pepino. Then, as Brown wrote in his scrapbook, the happy couple "beat it to the border" (courtesy Wisconsin Historical Society).

island while German fighters strafed and bombed the route. Brown's report was the first radio account of the invasion, and the details of the king and his entourage's heroism constituted one of the most exciting early radio war stories.[52]

Despite this achievement, Brown was not feeling well; he still had a cold, his energy was sapped and his blood pressure was low. He received typhoid and typhus inoculations that precipitated a fever, his weight had dropped from 190 to less than 140 pounds, and he was homesick. Nevertheless, he pushed on. In his daily routine, British officers' nonchalant lifestyle flabbergasted him. They acted as if there was no war about which to be concerned. As he frequented hotel grounds and bars, he found officers playing polo and cricket, sipping whiskey and eating splendidly. They seemed unperturbed that the Germans had taken control of Crete and Iraq. This was the case despite the fact that the war was heating up nearby. On June 8, British and

3. A Correspondent's Rewards 47

Free French troops moved into Syria. Brown could not follow them because he had not been accredited as a war correspondent. He was stuck in Cairo and felt he was accomplishing little. The restrictive news situation was ironic. The British recognized the importance of bringing America into the war, so they wanted U.S. correspondents to disseminate stories. They understood that the more Americans learned about the Middle East situation, the more likely the U.S. would send materiel and troops. Yet, on a story-by-story basis, the P.R. officers were parsimonious in what they allowed correspondents to report. Brown's and British officials' definition of which news would encourage Allied cooperation differed significantly.

Brown prepared a story that cited the new British commander in charge, General Claude Auchinleck, as saying U.S. soldiers were needed to defeat the Germans and Italians. When British censors saw it, though, they had Brown meet with P.R. Director Philip Astley and Tod. They queried Brown about whether such a story should be broadcast. Brown did not understand their hesitation because he had directly quoted Auchinleck, and the need for U.S. assistance was clear to everyone. Tod agreed with Brown, "but I don't know whether the time is ripe to say so." Brown replied that he was getting suspicious that the statement Auchinleck was making was part of a British campaign "to inform Americans that our manpower is needed and is coming ... and [the propaganda] is being planted here and there by casual conversation." Tod and Astley said they knew of no such effort. Brown said he wanted to be certain the British were not using him as a mouthpiece to convey such sentiments without allowing him the ability to cite official sources.[53] After further haggling, the officers killed his story.

The incident was only the first of many run-ins Brown had with censors. In another story he said, "British and Free French forces have been offering one hand of friendship to the Vichy French and with the other firing guns and dropping bombs. One hand seems to have neutralized the other and there's no doubt Syria is a two-handed job." The censors thought the lines constituted commentary. They and Brown argued for several hours before, "In mutual exhaustion, I had to agree on a phrasing which changed the entire meaning I wished to convey." The approved version included only: "The British and Free French forces until now have been offering the hand of friendship to the Vichy French in Syria." Then, late in June, a censor killed a story he had written about the Syrian campaign, saying they did not know anything about the information. Brown suggested they should keep up to date so they could properly edit stories.[54] During a press conference, Tod told correspondents: "Now here is the line we want you to take in your stories." Even in Italy, the fascists had not told Brown the slant he was to present in stories. He did not know how other correspondents felt about Tod's directive, but he defined his job as reporting "the war on its facts and to report those facts up to the hilt without giving actual military information to the enemy."[55] He remained irritated that he could not get to the front, and he questioned if he was being of service to CBS: "Over here you seem cut off from everything and your work seems very insignificant. You report your story into a microphone and that's the last you hear of it. I've had no mail from Martha and no word from New York about anything."[56]

On June 17, the British finally accredited Brown as a correspondent, so he asked White if he could go to the desert. Brown had talked with a number of correspondents who had witnessed desert fighting. They seemed to return in what he termed "a state of A and D" (alarm and despondency). But instead, White surprised him when he responded that he wanted Brown to go to Damascus for the assault on the Vichy French position. Brown caught a train for Jerusalem, and after arriving in Lydda, rode in an officer's car to Haifa. After attending a press conference, he found a hotel room in which to write. It was the first story in which he was able to describe the severity of the fighting between the British and Vichy French. The underequipped British were fighting courageously, but he also gained "my first real insight into the amazing ability of the British command to commit one mistake after another."[57] The following day he convinced a Captain Huband to allow him to ride in his car to Damascus, despite the fact Huband cautioned Brown that they could encounter snipers. Brown was willing to take the risk. Ten miles outside Damascus, British troopers warned the two that if they valued their lives they should not proceed. Accordingly, they decided to spend the night there, and he learned that the British would not attempt to take Damascus that day. The Vichy French, with four tanks and machine gun nests, were holding out. Brown described the desert heat as "almost asphyxiating," with a wind blowing in from the Great Syrian Desert. Yet as he slept that night in the front seat of the car in the mountains outside of town, he shivered from freezing temperatures.

The next morning, Brown joined Australian, Senegalese, British and Free French soldiers as they inched their way toward Damascus. He spent part of the morning hiding on a stream embankment as the Vichy French fired at them. At 1:30 in the afternoon, on June 20, Brown accompanied the troops as they entered Damascus. The following day, he traveled to Safed, where he wrote until the wee hours of the morning, preparing a story about what he had witnessed. He collapsed into bed at 6 a.m. after having had four hours sleep during the previous forty-eight, but at 9 a.m. a hotel waiter awoke him with an announcement that Germany and Russia had gone to war. Brown was disappointed, because he knew it would divert attention from his story about Damascus, "America is not going to give a damn about Syria now."[58]

A week later, Brown received word that the British command wanted him in Cairo. He did not mind leaving Haifa because he had clashed with censors there who edited his observations to the point where he considered them unrecognizable: "The news staff at CBS must be scratching its collective head to make any sense out of those mutilated stories."[59] Back in Cairo, he was surprised to read a cable from White that read: "SUGGEST YOU MOSCOW POSSIBLEST HASTE." With the Germans invading Russia, CBS needed a reporter there, and Brown was eager to leave Cairo. He hoped his new assignment would provide readier access to information. But he soon learned that both his destination and his desire to report uninhibited would both surprise and disturb him in ways he could never have imagined.

✦✦ 4 ✦✦

Sounding the Alarm for Singapore

Brown had mixed emotions about his new assignment. He did not like cold weather, it would be difficult to get to Russia, and he feared the German invasion might be over before he got there. Regardless, he cabled White that he would travel as soon as possible. Kirk warned Brown not to try to get to Turkey across the Mediterranean because the Germans would sink any boat. So he arranged to fly to Tehran. He began making arrangements with the Iranian Embassy for a visa, but he was told it could take up to a month to process. Then on July 2 he received another cable from White: "FORGET MOSCOW. ERSKINE CALDWELL REPRESENTING US THERE. BROADCASTING DAILY." So Brown remained in Cairo for the time being.

On July 5, he did a broadcast despite feeling badly, suffering from flu-like symptoms. Egyptians referred to the illness as the "gyppy tummy," a malady that resulted from drinking contaminated water or eating spoiled food. Brown was running a fever and ached all over. Nevertheless, he said British officers were for the first time mentioning that they could not win the war without U.S. military assistance. The announcement represented a reversal from their previous stance in which they had held that if the U.S. supplied equipment than England could defeat Germany without American reinforcements. After the broadcast, he wrote in his diary how depressed he was. He had been away from the U.S. for nearly four years, and "was thoroughly fed up with being abroad." He wanted to go home, if even for a short respite, but there was no indication from CBS that that was going to happen. "Unless I get an engrossing story or go up to some front where there is a great deal to occupy my mind and energy, I shall not be able to endure this absence and these uncertainties."[1]

To take his mind off his downheartedness, he threw himself into his work more vigorously. He cabled White, pleading, "HOW GOING WESTERN DESERT FEW DAYS FOR LOOK SEE?" To his surprise, White approved of

4. Sounding the Alarm for Singapore 51

Brown heading to the desert within twenty-four hours. The following morning, he arrived at the Egyptian-Libyan border as a passenger in a car driven by Captain Sean Fielding. Brown did not have much with him, only a sleeping bag, blanket and portable stove. It was a forward position from which Brown through binoculars could see miniature Italian and German soldiers eight miles distant on the hillsides of Halfaya Pass. They were exchanging long-distance artillery rounds with the British. Brown quickly surmised that there could not be a worse location in the world to fight a war. He called it "the place God forgot. It's the place where man may sit down and realize for the first time how kind nature has been to other parts of the world.... There is only awful aloneness."[2] Nevertheless, strange as it seemed, Brown actually enjoyed what he saw. "The desert was the most vigorous and most thrilling place I have ever been. It seemed to command from one's deepest reservoirs every ounce of resistance and determination."[3]

He recorded his observations while seated in a command post. Periodically, German armored cars rumbled across the desert toward the British lines, and artillery near him tried to blast them into oblivion. Brown felt the sun on his head "like a sledge hammer." The heat was so intense that "fingers burn on the rifle barrel, your skin peels off on it and there's the odor of burning flesh." The British wore lightweight pith hats instead of steel helmets to moderate the heat. Flies were a constant irritation, and scorpions stung, "causing limbs to swell three or four times their normal size." Nor could they escape the "Khamsin"—the desert wind that left them "gasping for life." Saliva evaporated in the men's mouths, and blowing sand could break open their skin. Sores covered their arms and legs, which they painted with purple antiseptic. The cool nights, on the other hand, were a remarkable respite. On display were innumerable stars and the heavy dew made it feel almost as if it were raining.[4]

Occasionally, during his five-day foray, Brown joined Tommies as they dived into trenches when German shells exploded nearby. He calculated that he came close to being killed a half dozen times. He learned that the British avoided picking up any object from the roadside because it often obscured a mine. He experienced mirages and learned the necessity of keeping water—the most important resource in the desert—handy. Each soldier received one gallon per day for all purposes. An officer told him that "to be lost in the desert without water turns the strongest of men into a stumbling, babbling maniac in 48 hours."[5] It terrified Brown that in the desert, unlike in cities and forests, there was no shelter in which to hide from shelling or strafing. All soldiers could do when caught in the open was to lie spread eagle and hope they were not hit. When someone was hit in that position, his buddies said it was "jolly bad luck."[6] The remnants of battle lay scattered across the sand. Once, he came across a sight that distressed him: Thousands of Italian pith helmets lying in the sand, whitened by the unrelenting sun. There also were coats, guns and thousands of shoes. Brown recalled the faces of the men he had known in Rome: "Shivers ran up and down my spine.... I had watched their faces while Mussolini called them eight million bayonets," he remembered. Now, they were ghosts in the sand.

Upon returning to Cairo, Brown was more exhausted than he had ever felt in his life. When he dropped into a hotel bath, previously unrevealed mosquito and sand-fly bites made themselves painfully apparent. He recorded that he could now relate to the A & D he had observed in other correspondents after they had witnessed desert warfare. He wrote a 3:45 segment for the *Roundup*, in which he tried to cram in everything he had experienced. It had been an invigorating but dangerous expedition, and he was frustrated that White had allotted him less than four minutes to detail the experience. The following day he visited the *New York Times'* Hal Denny, and the *Chicago Daily News'* Mower, at a Cairo hospital. Almost all the correspondents were suffering from some ailment. Denny had contracted a virus and Mowrer had a heart condition.[7]

In December, *Life* published Brown's story about his trip to the desert titled "The Desert is Hell." Unconstrained by airtime, he went into detail concerning what he had learned from the Tommies. They had said that many captured Axis soldiers suffered from colitis or dysentery, and in their letters they found that the Germans hated Italians because the Germans believed they were in the desert because the Italians had botched the job. The British knew never to transport German and Italian prisoners together, or they would find the Italians dead when they reached their destination. Brown wrote that he was impressed by the British command's ability to bluff their way to victory. Because of the shortage of both men and materiel, the British employed a variety of strategies to convince Axis soldiers that they possessed more of both resources than they really did. For example, in Italy the RAF had sent a single bomber roaring over the frontier repeatedly to mislead spotters into thinking they had a force of planes. In the Sudan, they marched and countermarched 2,000 troops back and forth to give the impression the force consisted of tens of thousands of Tommies. The tactic confused and stopped 2,500,000 Italians from advancing. In an encounter with the Germans in the Halfaya Pass, ten Tommies split into three groups and while firing their rifles simultaneously ran to the right and left. The tactic confused the Italians to the point that they retreated. On the other hand, he found the phrase the officers at general headquarters used to explain prosecution of the war, which was "muddling through," a poor justification for the mistakes they too often made.[8]

Brown spent much of his remaining time in Cairo talking to officers in an attempt to learn British plans. They told him that because the Russians were holding out against the Germans, they believed the Germans would not try to invade Turkey until spring 1942. Ultimately, they never did. Tod did not think there would be more desert fighting until September, because of the summer heat. Consequently, Brown concluded there was not going to be significant combat in the desert anytime soon. Accordingly, he asked White for a reassignment, preferably to the Far East, before, he speculated, the Japanese invaded that region. But before he could make the request, White stunned him with a cable: "WOULD YOU WISH SINGAPORE ASSIGNMENT? ADVISE HOW LONG WOULD TAKE REACH THERE." Brown most certainly welcomed the opportunity. He quickly replied: "SINGAPORE SWELL."[9]

On July 30, he boarded a British Airways flying boat that lifted off from the Nile River, bound for Karachi. At each stop his papers were inspected, and some of them confiscated by British officials, especially the scripts that criticized British war policies. During the journey, Brown vomited, to the best of his recollection, at least fifteen times. Travel, regardless of the mode, was hard on him, but he tolerated it because he counted it as part of the price he had to pay for being a foreign correspondent. While overseas, he lost a lot of weight because of the number of times he regurgitated: "No wonder I'm thin."[10] As the pilot was attempting to lift the plane off from the water at Karachi it hit a swell. Brown was certain it was going to flip, but the pilot finally stabilized it. The passengers spent the next night in a Calcutta hotel before the flight proceeded to Rangoon. Brown noticed that at each stop of his five-day flight to Singapore, each port had a Union Jack flapping in the breeze. The trip took him through a seemingly endless expanse of the British Empire.[11] The plane made a final stop in Bangkok before heading to Singapore.[12]

Upon landing, Brown walked into the customs office at the Kalang Airport. The first official he encountered welcomed him by saying, "You're Cecil Brown, aren't you? We've been expecting you." Brown was taken aback by being recognized. He replied that he had "come for war," and asked if it was coming. The official responded by returning the question. But without waiting for an answer, the Malayan said he did not believe war was coming to Singapore. The new posting presented a huge contrast for Brown, after the barren desert. Singapore was an exotic location, and its name signified both the city and the island on which it is located. The population of 560,000 consisted primarily of individuals of indigenous Chinese ancestry, but British military and medical staff made up a large minority. About half the troops under British command were from India or Australia. Russell Braddon described 1941 Singapore as a "striking combination of blue sky, red earth and palm trees; and with its vibrant flowers and its almost overwhelming range of smells, from spices to the stench of drains and of fish drying on the streets."[13] The city was crowded, but the countryside was open, except for small, dispersed farms. The island was green and lush with tropical forests and mangrove swamps covering much of it. British soldiers on the island derisively called Singapore the city of "Chinks, drinks and stinks."[14]

Brown checked into the colonial-style Raffles Hotel. Located on Beach Road, the best of white Singapore society made the Raffles its home away from home. Potted palms lined its walkways, sun blinds—along with lazily whirling fans—helped keep the hot, humid outdoors at a distance. Five-course dinners were common, and even after the Japanese began bombing the city the following December the grand ballroom was crowded most evenings with well-groomed officers and fashionably attired nurses, dancing to orchestral music.[15] The Long Bar was famous as the 1915 birthplace of one of the world's most famous drinks, the Singapore Sling.

After dropping off his bags, Brown walked to the American Consulate to see if a cable had arrived, but none had. Reporters from the *Singapore Free Press* and the *Malaya Tribune* wanted to interview him immediately, which Brown found peculiar. But he soon realized why when they said he was the first American correspondent in the city. The interviews focused on what Brown knew about war coming to Singapore. He knew little, and he was surprised when he queried them that they knew even less about military circumstances in their part of the world. Brown would not be the only journalist on the island for long. Dozens of reporters from the U.S. and other nations descended upon Singapore during the latter half of 1941.

Occupying a vital tactical position, Singapore stood as the English embodiment of unchallenged power in the Far East. Imperial General Staff chief John Dill called Singapore "the most important strategic point in the British Empire." From the air, it appeared as if the island had once been attached to the Malayan peninsula, but somehow had broken off and drifted into the Straits of Malacca, where it guarded the primary route from the Indian Ocean to the China Sea. Between the first and second world wars it became the fifth largest port in the world, and in 1938 the British had built a huge naval base there. It was situated on the northeast corner of the island at the town of Sembawang. The King George VI Dock at Keppel Harbor covered twenty-one square miles, including the largest dry dock in the world. Defended by fifteen-inch guns, Tengah Airfield protected a base that housed enough petrol to support the entire British Navy for six months. Tethered at the dock were a hospital ship, interisland boars and internationally flagged freighters; giant cranes and machine shops lined the harbor. There was housing for 12,000 Chinese workers. No plans had been made to guard the base against a "backdoor" land attack. The British thought it inconceivable that the Japanese would attack through the dense jungles and unnavigable mango and peat swamps that covered the island to the north.[16]

Singapore's importance far exceeded its dimensions. The island is only

4. Sounding the Alarm for Singapore 55

about twenty-five miles from west to east and fourteen miles north to south, but it was symbolic of United Kingdom power, and enjoyed an important position in its finances and imperial communications. It served as the eastern gate for the defense of India and the northern gate for the protection of Australia.[17] As he explored the city, Brown noted that the inhabitants acted as if there was no war going on, or that Singapore was threatened. Piers Brendon agreed that Singapore was a "fool's paradise ... [and that] the British community in Singapore had been softened by imperial self-indulgence. They dwelt in a world of servants ... two-hour siestas, lazy afternoons of golf ... [and] cocktail parties."[18]

Brown enjoyed his first meal in the aromatic flower-laden Raffles garden courtyard. He thought it was a wonderful place to stay, but suffocating heat and humidity would play havoc with his health. Nevertheless, after what he had experienced in Yugoslavia and the desert, he considered his accommodations more than acceptable.[19] He spent several days learning what he could about the military situation. He met with British Commander William Burrows, director of the Services Public Relations Organization (SPRO). Burrows' office distributed press releases, and oversaw censorship and correspondent activity. Burrows was a man in his mid–50s, red-faced, largely built, with a gruff demeanor. Brown found him cordial, but pompous. Brown next talked with Ken Tsurumi, the Japanese Consul General. The general's view of relations with Far Eastern countries and the U.S. was "bizarre." Tsurumi "was a short, compact, thick-chested, English-speaking diplomat, who had the air of a good-fellow and the eyes of a cut-throat." He told Brown the Japanese had ventured into Indo-China only as a defensive act. When he asked Tsurumi about relations between Japan and the U.S., he replied, "The situation between our two countries is very tense. Your Mr. Sumner Wells [under Secretary of State] makes criminal statements." Brown left the encounter convinced that he had arrived in Singapore in time to cover a war.[20]

He next visited Eric Davis at the Malaya Broadcasting Corporation to arrange for his broadcasts. The facilities were underwhelming, but Brown provided Davis with a list of fifteen-minute periods during the week he would need to participate in the *Roundup*. He learned that his broadcasts would be transmitted to Bandoeng in Java, before being re-transmitted to San Francisco, or would be relayed through Manilla via radiotelephone to California then on to New York. No international telephone lines were available for broadcasters in Singapore, as the British restricted their use to military traffic.[21]

Brown's interviews with British officials secured assurances that they were ready if Japan attacked Singapore. But they were convinced the Japanese would not attack anytime soon. Even if they did, the officers expressed no doubt that the multinational force could repel them. However, lower-level officers voiced doubts about their ability to defend Singapore.[22] Brown found many of them bored by the lack of action. They were eager to go to Thailand to fight if the Japanese invaded. There was a handful of U.S. military men in Singapore, advising the British on naval tactics. Brown asked one of them, Captain Archer Allen, what he thought about Japan starting a war. He said he did not believe the Japanese were that stupid. "If she did that Japan would commit national *hara kiri*."[23]

A Chinese tailor made Brown a white dinner jacket soon after his arrival; guests were required to wear one in the Raffles dining room. He wore it the first night, but it was the last time anyone saw him in it. Most of the time he dressed in his reporter's unofficial "uniform." Brown had lost most of his clothing in Yugoslavia, and during his time in the Egyptian heat the only clothes he had worn were a short sleeved bush jacket, khaki shorts and trousers. He dressed in the same attire in Singapore. Shortly after his arrival, Major C. R. Fisher, who was in charge of the correspondents' facilities, told Brown he was "the most un-militarily dress[ed] correspondent of this war." Brown agreed that he was probably right.[24]

On Monday, August 11, word arrived from New York that White had scheduled Brown to make his first broadcast. It was to last two-and-one-half minutes. But before he could present it, British censors had to clear his script. The process took two-and-one-half hours, during which Singapore Governor Shenton Thomas's censors, named Duckworth and Burrows, poured over every word multiple times. Afterward, Brown decided that if it had not been his first broadcast, he would have called the whole thing off. "It was the most maddening, energy-sapping experience I had ever encountered with a censor anywhere in the world. The censorship was petty, suspicious, absurd in the extreme," he judged. Nevertheless, the broadcast went off on August 17, and Brown introduced American listeners to what he had learned about British preparedness for war in the Far East: "The British in the Straits Settlements consider themselves on the verge of war with Japan. Reinforcements of troops and aircraft have been pouring into Singapore." He continued, "This island fortress is bristling with guns and noisy with aircraft overhead. It is now in a state of unofficial emergency." He added that the only way to stop the Japanese from invading Thailand was for the Allies to threaten a declaration of war, if Japan invaded. He probably shocked many listeners when he said there was a real possibility of war coming to that part of the world, and that if that happened there was a likelihood the War Department would call upon U.S. soldiers and sailors to fight there. He also informed them of the fact, which few Americans knew, that U.S. merchant ships regularly docked in Singapore to load cargo bound for the States.[25] The U.S. was the world's largest user of rubber and three-quarters of its tin came from the Far East. Consequently, the U.S. was economically interested in what happened in Singapore.[26]

4. Sounding the Alarm for Singapore 57

In late August, he and several other correspondents ventured into the Malayan jungle, near the Thai border, accompanied by Tommies. The purpose of the trip was to get a sense of the terrain and to gauge the ability of British troops to repulse a Japanese assault. Brown gathered material there that he used in subsequent broadcasts and later turned into an article for *Life* magazine. Upon returning to Singapore, Brown received a letter and a check from the Malaya Broadcast Company's Program Director, A.T. Lay, thanking him for his first broadcast. Offering him remuneration confirmed that officials in that part of the world were unaware of American journalists' ethical standards. He returned the check along with a letter in which he said that as an American journalist it was contrary to his values to accept compensation from another nation for broadcasts. During his spare time, Brown tried to keep up with what was going on in America by reading two-month old copies of *Time* and the *Saturday Evening Post*. He also attended American movies, and saw such fare as *Meet John Doe*. He liked to see U.S. films because "I have been away so long I am afraid of forgetting how Americans talk, and what makes them laugh and cry."[27]

During the last week in August, White cabled Brown that CBS was having trouble receiving his broadcasts. The Malayan transmitter was decrepit and sending out a barely audible signal. The revelation upset Brown because of the realization that what he considered important insights were not reaching the U.S. He asked Davis about securing a new transmitter or reserving a telephone connection. Davis was curt, which also was the experience of NBC's John Young, who had joined Brown and also was having trouble with transmissions. Brown quickly grew to respect Young. So they jointly met with the head of the British Ministry of Information, Robert Scott, about securing a more reliable transmission facility. Brown said CBS was going to make him leave Singapore if the connection could not be improved. In response, Scott instructed Young and Brown to submit a letter to the British Colonial Secretary in London, a solution that both broadcasters deemed a waste of time. Afterward, Brown told Young, "Singapore undoubtedly has the greatest concentration of stupid, vapid, uncooperative officials we have ever encountered."[28]

The censor's office in Singapore was an odd situation that prohibited correspondents from having direct access to the men who wielded blue pencils. A floor to ceiling hurricane fence divided the office, on the other side of which sat the censors. Their supervisors and the correspondents rarely had access to one another. Rather, the censors took script issues to their superiors, without involving the correspondents. "[The correspondents] could be seen clinging to the hurricane fence—their wailing wall—pleading for someone to listen," noted *Chicago Daily News*' reporter George Weller. When not engaged in his own battles with the censors, he became fascinated with

Brown, in particular, because of his reaction to the obstructionism. He characterized him as "looking like a Russian Wolfhound," who would cry out, "Can't someone come to the screen and talk this over in a friendly way?" When none of them obliged, Brown exclaimed to other correspondents, "It's no use ... forty million listeners don't matter."[29] Weller called the censorship "ferocious; a particular practice was to cut the leading paragraph off a narrative then send it ten-thousand miles away to enter the newspaper office headless, its statement of topic, place and circumstances amputated, a victim of amnesia." He said "little of what he or other reporters experienced and wrote filtered through in any authentic form to their newspapers, magazines or radio broadcasts.... It is, ultimately, a frustrating profession that one way or another can destroy many of its bravest and most honest practitioners."[30]

On the last day of August, White informed Brown that CBS had scheduled him to broadcast the following evening. Unfortunately, in the same stack of mail was a letter from Davis, which said the shortwave transmitter would not be available for his next broadcast because entertainment programming was scheduled during the time period. Brown was appalled that Davis would consider fiction more important than the facts he sought to deliver to the U.S. Consequently, he sent Davis a seven page, single-spaced letter to remind him of the commitment he had made upon Brown's arrival in Singapore. He said he found the "attitude of the Malaya Broadcasting Corporation toward my efforts to present to the American people ... the dangers besetting Great Britain in the Far East totally incomprehensible." He argued that CBS had built a strong record of cooperation with British authorities around the world during its war coverage, which was not completely accurate. "Neither CBS nor myself have found elsewhere any stinting of the British officials to cooperate with us."[31] But Davis was unmoved.

He cited Singapore's change to Daylight Savings Time, and the importance of a Mandarin program that Davis had scheduled for broadcast during Brown's requested time slot as reasons for the denial. Brown's appeal to Scott was similarly unsuccessful. Consequently, Brown cabled White, asking him to lodge a protest with the Ministry of Information in London and the British Embassy in Washington.[32] In response, White instructed Brown to send his scripts as cables to New York so an announcer could read them. Word of the impasse quickly leaked to other media in Singapore. The *Strait-Times* editorialized that Davis' refusal was wrongheaded: "It seems preposterous to suggest the programme cannot be revised ... to allow a provided friend of Great Britain and her Allies to broadcast a three-minute news review with a Pro-British bias to an audience of at least twenty million."[33]

On September 10, a new Minister for Far Eastern Affairs, Alfred Duff Cooper, arrived in Singapore. He had formerly held the post of Minister of Information in Churchill's Cabinet. The prime minister had sent him to

Singapore to investigate the litany of problems that both British and non–British subjects were relaying to London, including the CBS protest. Churchill had charged Duff Cooper with establishing a Malayan War Council to resolve local issues. Because of his reputation for getting things done, Young and Brown were hopeful Duff Cooper would solve the transmission issue. Soon after he arrived, they met with him. During the session, he was sympathetic to the correspondents' problem and said he would look into the matter. He was open and friendly with Brown and mentioned that he knew CBS Chairman Bill Paley well. Brown responded that he knew Paley better than he did, because he had never met him.

Absent Duff Cooper, a group of foreign correspondents and British officers met a few days later in a building at the naval base in an attempt to improve press relations. More than a dozen correspondents from the U.S., Australia and Britain sat down with Air Marshal Robert Brooke-Popham and Admiral Geoffrey Layton. After initial cordialities, Young stood and spoke: "You people ... have the chance to use us. NBC and CBS reach eighty million Americans. We have the perfect pulpit. Speaking for NBC, I'll put on the air anything you give me to use.... [But] instead of using us you hinder us." In reference to his colleague, Young said Brown had had to fight with the Italians and Germans elsewhere to get news out, and now he had to fight anew with the British, America's supposed ally.[34]

Other correspondents voiced similar sentiments before Brown spoke. He said they all were anxious to cooperate in helping the British, but they continually butted heads with men who reported to Burrows. His office, Brown said, "is a bottleneck. Due to the situation here, some of our best correspondents have gone away in disgust. I cannot over-emphasize to you, gentlemen, the importance of getting the story of the Far East across to the American people." The *London Daily Express*' O'Dowd Gallagher spoke next: "As a British citizen, I agree with every statement made by Mr. Brown." While listening to the correspondents, the officers became increasingly annoyed. Brooke-Popham's face turned red and Layton—the elevated pitch of his voice revealing irritation—responded: "This is the thing that happens when there isn't much news and the journalists get bored and blame us.... We can't build a bonfire just to make news for you people."[35] As the officers lectured them on the necessity of supporting British strategy, it became clear to the correspondents that they were wasting their time. The commanders had no intention of coalescing to the correspondents' wishes. The meeting ended without securing a mutually agreeable policy. This was the first occasion on which Brown had encountered Brooke-Popham, and he was unaware of a directive the air marshal had issued regarding information the British command would permit concerning Singapore's defense. He believed only in publishing statements that gave the Japanese "an exaggerated impression of our strength, and of our confidence in our security. He thought they had to maintain public calm by making highly optimistic pronouncements and heavily censoring all media for "negative or alarming news."³⁶

Brown later reflected that the encounter at the naval base signaled the beginning of the end of his ability to broadcast from Singapore. When his comments at the meeting were reported to Burrows, he used every profanity he could muster to criticize Brown. Burrows decreed that Brown would have no further access to broadcast facilities. Brown was unsure why the British singled him out for retribution. He was not alone as a critic of press relations; nor had he been the most vocal at the naval base. Irrespective, because he had been in Singapore longer than the other correspondents, British command had tired of what they considered his excessive tactics, and he had become notorious for arguing with censors. Burrows saw him as the ringleader of the "foreign complainers." Brown and the other correspondents continued their argument for facilities' access, but on September 20 Young left for Batavia, saying he had convinced NBC there was no use in staying. After urging Brown to do the same, he cabled White, asking for permission to leave. He proposed moving to the Dutch Indies, Bangkok or Chungking.

While waiting for a response, Brown composed a 160-word cable to White, which the censors had to approve. Upon reading it, they held it because Brown had made serious charges against British officials. For example, "I find the tactics here similar to those employed in Rome and Berlin to make the inquisitive American correspondents as uncomfortable as possible." Yet, in a surprise development, Duckworth allowed the cable to go out in its original form.³⁷ Two days later, White cabled Brown that he needed to stay put. There was a possibility that he could reassign him to Manila in early December and that Brown would need to arrange for a successor in Singapore. A week later, White sent another cable, but this one contained a different tone. Brown's complaining had not only aroused the ire of the British, but had cast him in a bad light back in New York as well.

White's cable said, in effect, "Cool it." He began, "THIS IS A HARD LETTER FOR ME TO WRITE." Nevertheless, he had written it, despite the fact he acknowledged not having all the facts. White explained that Duff Cooper had sent a cable to Paley in which he characterized Brown's behavior at the conference with Layton and Brooke-Popham in most "unflattering" terms. White agreed that Brown had the right to protest the availability of facilities, but that they also had the right to restrict information. It would be preferable, White wrote, if CBS correspondents in areas of the war were allowed to report everything. "[But] WHEN A COUNTRY IS AT WAR, THE OFFICIALS OF THAT COUNTRY NECESSARILY HAVE TO CONDUCT THAT WAR IN THEIR OWN WAY." White understood that no correspondent liked censorship, but in an area where a foreign government controlled information, there was "BOUND

4. Sounding the Alarm for Singapore

TO BE REPORTORIAL UNHAPPINESS. UNFORTUNATELY, FREE JOURNALISM AND WAR DO NOT SEEM TO BE COMPATIBLE." White instructed Brown to stop criticizing British officials. It is unknown if Duff Cooper acted on his own in writing Paley, or if he had been ordered to do so.

Shifting his tone in the second part of the cable, White became personal in commenting on Brown's comportment as a correspondent. "MAN TO MAN ... I THINK THAT YOU MIGHT DO WELL TO REORIENT YOURSELF ON QUESTIONS OF THIS KIND." Other correspondents had told White, apparently in a friendly way, that "'CEC IS A SCRAPPER AND A DAMN GOOD REPORTER, BUT THE TROUBLE WITH HIM IS THAT HE FEELS EVERYBODY IS OUT OF STEP WITH HIM.'" White was concerned that Brown's haranguing was hindering his ability to secure the news CBS needed from Singapore. He counseled Brown that an approach that ingratiated himself to a greater degree with British officials would accomplish more. White concluded by saying he did not accept the other correspondents' comments regarding Brown as completely accurate, but he was passing them along for "PROPER MEDIATION AND INTROSPECTION."[38]

In his reply, Brown expressed gratefulness for White's candid advice. He explained that he did not feel his efforts to report activities in Singapore had compromised military secrets, but he expressed regret for his comments at the naval base. Brown acknowledged that his expectations had been unrealistic that he should receive access to information in Singapore in as open a manner as he had in Egypt. Nonetheless, he felt a moral obligation to keep Americans informed about events that could affect them. He understood he had a responsibility to represent CBS professionally wherever he was, and that he appreciated the reminder that he needed to "MEASURE UP AT ALL TIMES TO YOUR AND MY OWN STANDARDS."[39] He also informed White that four British correspondents had cabled the London War Office, complaining about the inadequacy of correspondent access in Singapore. Brown said they had invited him to add his name to the cable but had declined to do so. He included copies of the cables the correspondents had sent,[40] and he sent a letter of apology to Layton.

Unfortunately, between the date Brown received White's reprimand and when he replied, he had submitted a script to meet a noon deadline for a broadcast he wanted to give the following morning. Ill-advisedly, the content of the script succeeded only in demolishing any possibility he had of broadcasting. Duckworth read it and said, "I will have to submit this to higher authority. There is too much in here that is untrue and undesirable." He telephoned Brown at the Raffles within the hour to say Governor Thomas had cancelled the broadcast altogether. Brown asked if he could rewrite the script, but Duckworth said that regardless they would not allow him to broadcast it. Brown should not have been surprised. Included in the script were correspondents' complaints about censorship. He characterized the situation as similar to what he had experienced in Rome. He added that the British had threatened him with expulsion because he had sent a cable to CBS reporting the correspondents' protest. He charged that the authorities were attempting to drive the correspondents out of the country, and he was the only remaining American broadcaster. After Duckworth and Thomas rejected Brown's script, he went to see Duff Cooper, who read the script and said he would not have held it up, but that he did not possess the authority to approve it, either. As a result, Brown scheduled an appointment with the governor.

Brown had little hope he would make much progress with Thomas, but he was determined to exhaust all possibilities. Peter Thompson described the governor as a "cocky, rotund, red-faced former schoolmaster" who refused to accept the reality that the Japanese were a threat to Singapore, and he was "in over his head."[41] To Brown's dismay, the governor greeted Brown with criticism regarding his story. Labeling Brown's words "untrue and libelous," Thomas told him: "You can't abuse us from here." Brown asked what was libelous about it, but Thomas would not tell him. Brown said the Italian Fascists had treated him better that the British in Singapore, but Thomas responded, "You seem to fight with everyone." Brown replied that the governor's remark was surprising because he had enjoyed good relations with many British officers and soldiers. He concluded by telling Thomas, "Every broadcast in the future is going to report facts about Singapore as I find them and see them."[42] The meeting ended as badly as it began. Brown summarized his view of the governor afterward with, "He lives in a dream world where reality seldom enters, and where the main effort is to restrict the entrance of anything disturbing."[43]

Six days later Brown took his appeal to General A. E. Percival, commander of British troops in Malaya. He had Brown's killed story on the desk in front of him and flatly stated that he could not transmit it. Brown told him he did not understand why the British were censoring it because he was only reporting what Percival's own officers had told him. But Percival said Brown's approach was not the way British journalists did their job: "They go out and get the material so that their editors can write leaders [editorials]." Brown "almost fell out of [his] chair at that remark." He attempted to provide a short course in U.S. reporting methods, but Percival was uninterested. Seeing that he was not making headway, Brown remarked, "With all due respect to you, General, you and your people here have no conception of how the American press and radio work. You are paying a heavy price for that, just as you paid a heavy price for it in London and Cairo." As he left the office, Brown told himself he was certain the only thing the British wanted communicated was propaganda. "If you didn't do as they wanted," he thought, "then there was no story to report."[44]

4. Sounding the Alarm for Singapore 63

Although he was now having trouble getting any news out, Brown continued working his contacts. He regularly talked with a Japanese man who said he was a journalist, but whom Brown was certain was a spy. Johnny Fuigi worked for the *Singapore Herald* (which the Japanese Foreign Office operated). Its stated purpose was to "counter anti–Japanese sentiment, disseminate propaganda, and proclaim Anglo-Japanese amity." Fuigi tried to pry information out of Brown, but Brown also interviewed him, while editing his own comments. Fuigi, conversely, was blunt about the Japanese attitude regarding Singapore. On October 12, he told Brown, "I don't see how war can be avoided here."[45]

Brown wrote a letter to Martha on October 20 while seated at a desk on his hotel room veranda, a fan, the size of "an airplane propeller," circling over his head. Thirty feet below, on the Palm Court, he could see flame-colored lamps on tables, and people dining and laughing. Even though he was wearing shorts, he was, as always, sweating. He typically changed his shirt four times each day. His hotel room was unbearably hot at night, making it difficult to sleep. Adding to his misery was the fact that it was monsoon season.[46] He was depressed, which was sapping his energy and his will to report. He had trouble writing, felt homesick, yearned for a good story, and wanted to be anywhere other than Singapore. Weight loss demonstrated that his health was deteriorating, and he caught one cold after another. A version of the dengue fever regularly visited him, a disease characterized by fever, headache, muscle and joint pain, and a measles-like rash. A British doctor told him the climate was not agreeing with him, and that it appeared he was also suffering from the symptoms of typhus and typhoid. He prescribed six Vitamin B pills per day, but also advised that he either needed two weeks' rest or should go back to the States.[47] He was distraught over his inability to broadcast, and White's refusal to relocate him. He also felt a sense of impending doom regarding Singapore. He concluded, "Casualness, thy name is British."[48] He was certain the Japanese were going to attack, and that the arrogant British and unprepared Singaporeans would suffer. Each day, he talked with officers, enlisted men and local residents, and cabled CBS about what he was learning concerning island defenses. In one, he noted: "[THE] PEOPLE IN SINGAPORE ARE DEPENDING SO MUCH ON SOMEONE ELSE."[49]

Near the end of October, he interviewed Tsurumi, asking how war could be avoided between the U.S. and Japan. Tsurumi replied, "There is only one way. Draw a line from north to south down the middle of the Pacific. You stay on one side and we will stay on the other." Brown concluded there was little chance America was going to evade war.[50] A number of British and Australian journalists continued to complain about the facade of false information British command foisted upon them. An incident within their own ranks added fuel to their indignation. British journalist Leonard Mosely wrote an exasperating story for the *London Daily Sketch* that the *Singapore Free Press* reprinted. Mosely had toured Singapore in September and upon returning home wrote, "There is no need to worry about the strength of the air force that will oppose the Japanese should they send their army and navy southwards." He said British planes would easily defeat Japanese land and sea forces. The other correspondents were outraged at the story's absurdity, but when Brown encountered Burrows, the commander gushed about it: "That's cracking good stuff. That's the kind of thing we want out of here." Then he asked Brown, "Why don't you use that in a broadcast to America?" to which Brown responded, "I think that is as fine a piece of fake and dangerous writing as I have ever encountered."[51] Brown's cynicism was confirmed by a personal experience the following month.

On November 6, Brown hitched a ride in one of eleven British airplanes that made up a patrol that flew from Singapore to within five miles of the Thai border. They were vintage Vildebeestes, open-cockpit, single-engine biplanes, and they were all that was available to British pilots. Brown was issued a flight suit, signed a waiver that relieved the British of liability should he be killed, and was shown how to put on a parachute. Twenty-four-year-old pilot Jack Lyle asked Brown if he had ever jumped out of an airplane with a parachute. Brown replied that he had not, and he doubted that he could, because if the time came he believed fear would incapacitate him. He crouched behind Lyle's seat in the plane, which also carried a radioman, as they lifted off. The wind rushing through the open-cockpit was terrific, and the planes flew with no more than fifteen feet separating their wings, which made Brown nervous.

After an hour-and-a-half, the Vildebeestes circled to land at the Kuantan Aerodrome. As he looked down, Brown noticed water covering the field. This was typical of most of the Malayan jungle airfields. Nevertheless, the planes landed safely, with water spraying into the cockpit as the plane plowed down the runway. On the ground, Lyle asked Brown when the U.S. was going to send troops to help defeat the Germans. He asked why Lyle wanted to know, and Lyle said he believed that when the U.S. joined with the British that the Allies would invade Europe. The pilot's confidence dismayed Brown, and Lyle was surprised at Brown's reaction. He cautioned Lyle about being overconfident, but he responded, "That's taken for granted.... [It's] not arrogant but just confident of victory."[52]

The return flight hugged the coast for nearly 400 miles. They flew over dense jungles and level with mountain peaks. It was growing dark as they neared the British aerodrome and Brown enjoyed the brilliant red sunset. As they touched down, however, the landing want awry. The plane's wheels bulldozed through water and mud, and the plane bumped up and down. As it neared a camouflaged gun mount, its wheels slipped into a ditch and it came to a jarring stop with its nose pitched into the mud. The crash ripped off both wings and gasoline began pouring out of them. The pilot and radioman jumped out, but they had to help Brown because the crash wedged him in. As he slid down a wheel strut, he lost his balance and ended up face first in the mud. All three were taken to an infirmary, but none of them were seriously injured. Back at the Raffles, Brown was surprised he had felt no fear. The following day, however, he could barely walk, a result of stiffness and bruising. And three days later, he sustained additional injuries when the driver of an army truck in which he was riding lost control and crashed into a hillside. One of the truck's seats landed on top of Brown, and he suffered bruises on his head and near his kidneys. The pain persisted for a week; so Brown visited his doctor, but he assured him there was nothing seriously wrong.

On November 14, White sent Brown a cable in which he advised him not to make any plans until CBS Far Eastern Manager Bill Dunn arrived in December. It was the first Brown had heard from White in six weeks, and British authorities had not allowed him to broadcast during that time. The following day he replied via cable and opined, "MALAYA LACKS LEADERSHIP. THOSE AT THE TOP ARE CONSPICUOUSLY DEFICIENT IN BOLDNESS, BREADTH OF VISION AND INSPIRATION." He was surprised when it avoided censorship.[53] Yet, four days later the censors killed another cable he composed, which included the comment: "IF WAR BREAKS OUT THE BRITISH FAR EAST COMMAND IS PREPARED IMMEDIATELY TO JOIN IN WITH ANGLO-AMERICAN STRATEGIC PLANS WITHIN THE FRAMEWORK OF BRITAIN'S ABILITY AND PREPAREDNESS IN MALAYA." He had no idea why the censors blue-penciled it: "Either they are prepared to do something or they are not prepared."[54] Adding to his downheartedness was a feeling that the war was passing him by. But two days later, while suffering through another cold, he opened a cable from White that made him feel better. The CBS chief was congratulating him on winning the 1941 Sigma Delta Chi award for Best Radio Reporting from Abroad. It was for the story he had broadcast from Cairo in which he had described King George's rescue.

As November ended, British officers kept telling him they did not believe the Japanese would attack Singapore. But Brown noticed subtle indications that they were simultaneously taking steps to prepare for exactly that eventuality. They put Chinese laborers to work fortifying Keppel Harbor, troops in the city were carrying weapons for the first time, and soldiers were occupying pillboxes and batteries along the coast twenty-four hours each day. On December 1, Brown notified White that Singapore had proclaimed a state of emergency and was calling up Malayan volunteers for the army, air force and navy. A week later, all Malayan troops went on full alert.

Suddenly, at 4 a.m. on Monday morning, December 8, war arrived in Singapore with a bang. Fisher awoke Brown with a call that he was to come to press headquarters for an announcement. No sooner had Brown hung up the phone, when he heard a loud boom outside. Japanese bombs had begun falling. He believed he knew what the announcement would be, but he had trouble getting to headquarters. He could not talk a coolie into pulling his rickshaw toward press headquarters because explosions were occurring in that vicinity. The usual fare for the distance was thirty-five cents, but Brown had to pay two dollars to get him moving. Following the briefing at 4:45 a.m., he cabled CBS that the Japanese had invaded Malaya and were bombing Singapore. Brown's fears regarding the unpreparedness of Singapore had been borne out. Fighter Control Operations had received a report of unidentified aircraft 140 miles from the city thirty minutes before the attack began, but no one had been available at the air-raid headquarters to receive the alert. Even worse, under a full moon with the city's lights on, Japanese pilots had no trouble spotting targets. Many Singaporeans milled in the streets, thinking the planes were British. Some of them learned they were not, with deadly consequences. The attack killed sixty-three and injured 133. According to one eyewitness, "People hid in the deep ditches beside the roads during the attack, were peppered with shrapnel, and the water ran red with blood."[55] The attack shocked Singaporeans because the British had been saying war was not coming to their city.

Returning to his room, Brown learned for the first time over the radio of the Japanese attacks on Pearl Harbor, the Philippines and Hong Kong. Along with the landing of Japanese troops on the shores of Malaya that same day, the battle for Singapore was underway. Later that morning, Brown met with British correspondents who commented, "Well, now you Americans are in." Brown agreed that they were.[56] What he did not realize was that not only was America now in the war, but he would soon be a participant in it himself.

♦♦ 5 ♦♦

Reporting History Up Close and Personal

Early in the war, Winston Churchill had assured New Zealand and Australian officials that defending Singapore would take precedence over the United Kingdom's Mediterranean interests, but the situation changed as the war unfolded. His advisors said it would take additional battalions of soldiers, tanks and hundreds of up-to-date planes to defend Singapore. But without telling British personnel in Singapore, Churchill decided he had to sacrifice the island to the Japanese. Not only did England need all the materiel and troops it could muster to defend the British Isles, but the prime minister had committed planes and tanks to help the Russians ward off the Germans, and in the Middle East England had to defend its oil fields. As a result, Churchill could not spare what was needed to save Singapore.

Churchill decided that the best he could do was to send a naval force to Singapore that might dissuade the Japanese from invading it. On December 2, 1941, Churchill's declaration regarding the defense of Singapore arrived in the form of Force Z. Much of the island's inhabitants turned out to welcome what they believed would be their salvation. Force Z was the code name for a convoy that consisted of the battleships *Prince of Wales* and *Repulse*, and four destroyers: *Electra*, *Express*, *Tenedos* and *Vampire*. At 35,000 tons, the *Wales* was one of England's most formidable vessels. The British admiralty said it included the best of everything in anti-bomb and torpedo protection. Its deck featured four to six inches of armor, and there was a sixteen-inch armor belt at the waterline. Its armament consisted of ten eleven-inch guns, along with anti-aircraft pom-poms and a variety of other guns. It also had the latest in radar technology; unfortunately, it was not fully operational. Captained by tall and stylish John Leach, the *Wales* had been part of the fleet of ships that the previous May had sunk Germany's *Bismarck*. In August, the *Wales* had carried Churchill to meet with Franklin Roosevelt in Newfoundland for the Atlantic Charter signing.[1] Churchill told Stalin that the *Wales* was capable of destroying any Japanese ship.² First utilized during World War I, the older *Repulse* was a 32,000 ton ship that recently had been retrofitted and updated with stronger armor and more powerful guns. During more than two years of World War II maneuvers, the *Repulse* had sailed more than 53,000 miles, but it had not seen any combat.

The aircraft carrier *Indomitable* was supposed to accompany the group to Singapore, but it had run aground as it was entering a Jamaican harbor, and had to go into dry dock in Norfolk, Virginia, for repairs. Richard Smith, a nineteen-year-old *Repulse* sailor, said that during the sail to Singapore the officers drummed into the men that Force Z would easily defeat the Japanese. "Everybody was told that the Japanese fleet was absolutely useless and that it was just a lot of rice paper and string.... It would be a walkover and we would enjoy ourselves."³ Admiral Thomas Phillips commanded Force Z. At fifty-three, Phillips had been a naval officer for thirty-seven years. Colleagues called him the Tom Thumb of the Navy because he stood only five-feet-four-inches tall. Although he had seen considerable action during World War I, he was yet to participate in World War II fighting, yet he was confident of British superiority over the Japanese.

Brown was among the reporters that witnessed the arrival of the fleet, but British leaders prohibited them from reporting any details. But the following day, Brooke-Popham invited thirty correspondents, including Brown, to a press conference. Brooke-Popham expounded broadly about Japan coming into the war, which he asserted would be foolish because the U.S. would join the conflict if Japan took that step. His comments were noteworthy because they signaled the first time an officer had acknowledged the possibility of war coming to Singapore. Brown cabled a story to CBS under the lead, "Informed quarters whose reliability unquestioned asserted Japan now virtually certain to engage in military operations and direction will be southward." But the censors blue-penciled his copy so it read, "Informed quarters asserted Japan not certain engaging in military operations."

A week later, at noon on December 8, Brown was having lunch with Gallagher and the *Sydney Telegraph*'s Tom Fairholl at the Raffles Hotel. Their discussion focused on how they could get to the front to cover the fighting they were sure was coming to Malaya. As he was about to finish the conversation, a clerk approached and told Brown he had a phone call. He went to the front desk and heard Major Fisher's voice on the other end of the line, wanting to know if he was interested in going on an "unknown [four day] assignment." Brown asked about the nature of the opportunity, but Fisher was mum concerning the details. Fisher insisted that he needed an immediate response. Accounts differ as to what happened next, but according to Brown, after hesitating, he told Fisher he would go. He returned to the table and told the others what had happened, but the three agreed that the most important developments were going to be in Malaya, if not Singapore, soon. Then Gallagher was called to the phone. He received the same invitation, but in response, he asked a "guarded question and received an evasive answer." Putting two and two together, Gallagher surmised that the opportunity could only be an invitation to sail on the *Wales*. This is where the account varies. According to Gallagher, Brown had decided to reject the offer, and when Gallagher returned to the table, he had to "beg and bully" Brown to accompany him.[4] Regardless of which account was accurate, both men accepted the offer. Gallagher exclaimed that they were the only correspondents the British command was inviting to be on the *Wales* as it ventured into the South China Sea. What neither of them knew was that the same offer had been made to at least five other correspondents before them, all of whom had turned it down.[5]

Phillips had learned from British intelligence that the Japanese were landing troops at Kota Bahru, the northern-most port in Malaya. Reportedly, no less than a Japanese battleship, five cruisers and twenty destroyers were supporting ground troops in the Gulf of Siam. Phillips decided to take Force Z north to stop the Japanese. Before sailing, Phillips radioed Air Vice-Marshal C.W. Pulford, asking if he could provide air cover. Pulford replied that he wanted to help, but the Japanese had already overrun his airfields in northern Malaya. He told Phillips he could provide reconnaissance flights the following day but could made no promises for December 10.[6] Admiral Arthur Palliser warned Phillips that it was dangerous to proceed without air cover. Palliser told him Japanese bombers in Indochina could reach the planned route of his fleet. But Phillips dismissed the warnings, as he believed it would be "shameful" if his ships failed to support British troops engaged in fighting in Malaya.

Meanwhile, Brown ran upstairs to his room, grabbed his camera and some film, and threw an extra shirt and pants into a bag. When he arrived in the lobby, correspondent liaison Lieutenant Brian Reynolds screamed at Gallagher and Brown that they needed to leave immediately because the ships were waiting for them. Nevertheless, Brown scribbled a cable to White: "OUT TOWNING FOUR DAYS SWELL STORY. BROWN." In the car, he told Reynolds that if anything happened that his belongings were in his Raffles' room and he should send them to CBS in New York. Reynolds assured Brown he would be back in a few days because little was going to happen. When the correspondents arrived at the *Wales*, Leach informed them that a launch would transport them to the *Repulse* instead. They were disappointed and exclaimed that filing their stories from the *Wales* would carry more weight than from the *Repulse*. Leach understood, but there was no more room on the *Wales*. Gallagher and Brown thought about returning to shore, but after discussing it, accepted the transfer.

Just after six p.m., Force Z weighed anchor and made its way into the Straits of Johore. It was a beautiful evening, with a bright red sunset descending over the ocean. Marine Lieutenant Halton took the correspondents on a tour of the ship and introduced them to its officers, including Captain William Tennant. He had distinguished himself in June 1940 when he oversaw the evacuation of Dunkirk. During their limited conversation, Brown sized up Tennant as a man of about fifty who was "smiling and courteous, and seemed confident that we would encounter action." Tennant told the correspondents: "You may make history on this trip—and then again, it may not be very important." Tennant asked them where they would like to be located. After looking around, they said they would prefer to be in the after-mast control tower where they could see best. Brown added, "There's a lot of armor protection up there that I would kinda like to have around me." But Tennant responded that they could see more if they were on the flag deck, so they could move from port to starboard and back. Tennant said they would try that, but if they were dissatisfied, he would arrange for alternate positioning.[7] An Admiralty photojournalist joined the two reporters on the ship. He was Press Officer Horace "Tubby" Abrahams, who had been assigned to document the voyage for the Royal Navy.

As the ships took a northeasterly heading, Gallagher and Brown joined some officers in the mess where they spent much of the evening discussing how little they knew about the mission. The only information anyone on ship possessed came from Tennant's bulletin board memo: "We are off to look for trouble. I expect we shall find it." He said they should be on the lookout for surface ships and aircraft. The captain urged everyone to keep on their toes, stay calm, concentrate on their jobs and keep their life-saving gear nearby. "However, I don't think anything is going to happen to the ship—she is much too lucky."[8] On the *Wales*, Phillips thought the mission would be successful because they held the element of surprise. He believed the Japanese were unaware Force Z intended to intercept the Malayan invasion. Regardless of the odds, he said, "honour and the operational imperative dictated that he confront the enemy despite the risks of air attack." Unfortunately, Phillips' overconfidence and directives would prove disastrous.[9] What he did not know was that the Japanese had been tracking Force Z even before it arrived in Singapore. On November 28, Japanese reconnaissance had spotted the British ships in Sri Lanka, then followed them to Keppel Harbor. The appearance of the fleet had surprised the Commander-in-Chief of the Japanese Fleet Isoroku Yamamoto. He viewed it as a threat to landing troops in Malaya and capturing Singapore. The Japanese had no ships powerful enough to win an engagement with the battleships. Therefore, Yamamoto decided an air attack was the best strategy to neutralize the British threat.

Some of the enlisted men on the ships not only shared Tennant's pre-

5. Reporting History Up Close and Personal   71

monition they would encounter trouble, but were more anxious than the captain about their chances of surviving it. Maurice Edwards, a *Wales* seaman, said, "I had a terrible feeling of foreboding we just didn't know what we were going to encounter, but one thing I do remember is being convinced that we'd never get back to the colony in one piece." A rating named Smith said, "Sending us out there was absolute folly, a terrible thing to do. It was like sending a lamb to the slaughter."[10] Others were more optimistic. In the mind of the *Repulse's* Bert Wynn: "I still remember the feeling of absolute confidence running throughout the ship. Everyone was eagerly awaiting the kind of action we'd trained for ... the outcome of such an engagement was felt to be a formality."[11]

Meanwhile, Brown was spending an uncomfortable first night onboard. In his cabin, it was "like a steam bath.... I never sweated so much in my life."[12] Thus, he and Gallagher were up at 5:15 a.m. the next morning, and a seaman escorted them to the flag deck. The position made them uneasy, because it was the ship's most exposed area. The *Wales* was cruising one-half mile ahead and the four destroyers were positioned a mile on either side. First light appeared at six o'clock, and at 6:20 lookouts cited what were later identified as three Japanese reconnaissance planes far off the starboard side. The lookouts were unsure if they were Japanese, and that they might not have spotted the ships. The correspondents joined some seamen for breakfast in the wardroom and listened to a BBC broadcast in which Roosevelt announced the U.S. was at war with Japan. Brown was relieved his country was finally in the war, and thought about shouting, but decided not to when he observed that the sailors seemed unexcited about the development.

At midmorning, he and Gallagher went to the captain's cabin to interview Tennant. Glass enclosed the cabin front, affording Tennant an expansive view. He paced, looking out as he informed them that the ships were headed around the Malayan coast toward Patani. Tennant said he was pleased an American was onboard. He was interested in hearing Brown's perspective on the U.S. entering the war, which he supplied. The captain said the convoy might see combat that day if planes spotted the Japanese. Gallagher asked if Tennant would summarize any action for the reporters afterward. He replied that he would as best he could. Afterward, Gallagher and Brown returned to the wardroom and talked about strategies for covering the war. "Well, are you going to be a propagandist or are you still going to be that objective reporter?" Gallagher asked Brown. "I'm still a reporter, Gal, and I still reserve my democratic right to criticize," Brown replied. "Okay," Gal said, "but we'll see how much your American censorship will let you do."[13]

In conversations with crewmembers, Brown learned that because the *Repulse* had yet to see action its men were eager to prove themselves. Throughout Wednesday afternoon, clouds diminished the possibility that

Japanese planes would sight them. Nonetheless, shortly after five o'clock, spotters saw what they thought was a reconnaissance plane four or five miles away. Leach and Tennant now believed the Japanese had seen them. The British later learned that they were wrong, but the captains were correct that their presence was not a secret. Even before the lookouts had seen the aircraft, a Japanese submarine had observed the ships at 1:45 that afternoon. The sub's captain alerted the Japanese cruiser *Yura*.[14]

At dinner that night, Brown ate with a dozen officers. The discussion focused on what they knew about Japanese strategy in the Far East. One commented: "Those Japs are bloody fools" for using small forces to attack in a wide span. Another chimed in: "Those Japs can't fly.... They can't see at night and they're not well trained." After listening, Brown replied, "You British are extraordinary people. You always underestimate the enemy." He then provided a litany of instances in which they had done so in Norway, France, Greece and Crete. He argued that it would be better if they began overestimating the enemy's abilities, which would allow them to be better prepared. The officers initially met Brown's comments with silence, followed by rejoinders from some who claimed they were not overconfident, but "we just don't think the enemy is much good."[15] Later that evening, after the group broke up, Lieutenant Halton entered the wardroom and spoke with Brown. Force Z had increased its speed to twenty-six knots, and Brown asked Halton if he thought they would encounter the Japanese in the morning. He replied that now that they were certain the Japanese had spotted them they were planning to engage them as soon as possible.

Just before ten o'clock that night Tennant's voice came over the loudspeaker. To everyone's surprise, he said the convoy was turning around and heading back toward Singapore because they had lost the element of surprise, and Phillips believed Force Z would come under air attack before they could engage Japanese ships. The *Repulse*'s crew expressed displeasure with the alteration in plans. Pom-pom gunner Woods said, "There was tremendous disappointment onboard as we felt cheated out of a rightful confrontation." The following morning the orders changed again. Phillips was ordering them to steer toward Kuantan on the Malayan coast. A message from British intelligence had informed Phillips that the Japanese were landing troops there. He had decided to attack the landing barges as well as the destroyers escorting them. Phillips believed he had regained the element of surprise, and that the risk justified the possibility of catching the Japanese unawares. It was later learned that the report was erroneous.

That night was another uncomfortable one for Brown. After sleeping three hours, he arose at four a.m. and went onto the pitch-black flag deck. He was thirsty, but upon searching the galley found nothing to drink. Unbeknownst to him, another Japanese submarine had cited the ships forty-five minutes before Brown arrived on deck, and had fired four torpedoes at the *Repulse*. None of them hit their mark in the dark. Nevertheless, the submarine captain had radioed Japanese command that he had cited the ships for which they had been searching. Until this time, Japanese intelligence was unsure where Force Z was. They had thought it might still be in Kepple Harbor, but now they realized it was in the open sea, and dangerously close to where Japanese troops were landing. As a result, the Japanese 22nd Naval Air Flotilla, based near Saigon, took off at 6 a.m. to locate them. The flotilla included thirty-four twin-engine Mitsubishi G3M Nell and G4M Betty bombers, and fifty-one Mitsubishi Type 96 single-engine torpedo bombers.

After eating breakfast, the *Repulse* crew reported to their stations. A seaman gave Brown and Gallagher coveralls, anti-flash hoods and helmets as the ships moved within eight miles of the Malayan shoreline. For three hours they zigzagged south then north and both the *Repulse* and *Wales* launched catapult planes in an attempt to locate the enemy. Brown was awestruck as he observed the grandeur of the ships with water spraying around their hulls as they plowed through the pea-green waves at twenty-four knots, and the orderly choreography of the crew's activities. The *Repulse*'s guns were at the ready, but the crews played cards as they waited for an alert, which soon came.

The Japanese pilots had about given up the search and were running low on fuel, when at 10:45 a.m. they spotted the fleet. The sky was clear, and a few minutes later word came over the ships' loudspeakers that a squadron of enemy aircraft was approaching. Brown cited them astern and counted nine planes flying single file; they were the Bettys, the likes of which British sailors had never seen. At a speed of 250 miles-per-hour, their torpedoes carried a 330 pound warhead. Once in the water, the torpedoes ran for more than 2,000 meters at forty-one knots."[16] As the Japanese made their initial pass over the *Repulse*, its gun crews opened up with pom-poms and high-altitude guns but failed to bring down any fighters. From Brown's position on the flight deck, slightly sheltered by an air funnel, but eight feet from a pom-pom battery, the sound was deafening. The gun flashes nearly blinded him and the stench of cordite filled his nostrils. Standing open-mouthed, looking up, he saw the second run of planes was dropping bombs. The sight so mesmerized him that he did not duck or seek shelter. The first bomb landed in the ocean ten yards to the port side and sprayed him with water. A moment later, he felt a dull thud under his feet, the ship shuddered and a shower of paint chips covered him. It was seventeen minutes after eleven. Brown had not seen it hit, but an announcement alerted him that at least one bomb had struck the *Repulse* and set it aflame below decks. The Japanese planes dropped additional bombs, but most of them were landing in the water. One of the pom-poms finally brought down a plane, which crashed about one-half mile away, and a cheer went up from the gunners.

Brown scurried about, noting the damage as well as the crew's actions. Their "extraordinary calm" astounded him. He heard one of them shout, "Bloody good bombing by those blokes." As Brown returned to his original position, he was stunned to see there was a three-inch hole in the air funnel about eighteen inches above where he had been standing. He thought, "My number isn't up yet," but he learned that the attack had killed about fifty men, and he watched as four stokers were brought onto the deck with skin hanging from their hands and arms "like tissue paper." At twenty minutes before noon, he looked across the water and noticed that the *Wales* had been hit and was moving slowly. He tried to discover how badly the damage was to the sister ship, but no one on the *Repulse* knew. Gallagher, Brown, and a number of sailors lit cigarettes and inhaled deeply in an attempt to calm themselves. But they had only five minutes to do so before a bugle blew and the loudspeakers blared that another formation of planes was headed in their direction.

Brown sighted nine torpedo planes on the horizon as the *Repulse's* guns barked into action. The ship vibrated and shell casings clanked onto the deck as the gunners fired. Paint blistered on the gun barrels, their gunners moving at a frenzied pace, soaked in sweat. Brown heard one of them shout, "Look at those yellow bastards come!" Brown suddenly realized that amid all that was happening his only weapons were a fountain pen, a notebook and a camera, yet he felt no fear. Reportorial instincts had taken over. Glancing from side to side and up and down, he tried to catch as much action as he could, all the while scribbling details for the story he was composing in his head. He later reflected that at a time like that "you have two choices. You can either get panicky and lose your head, or keep you head and do your job.... I was no more heroic than anybody else who's been bombed, but if you start getting too worked up about those things, you miss the story."[17] As they came closer, the planes descended to 300 feet above the water and 300 yards to either side of the *Repulse*. They were so close Brown could see the pilots' faces. After they released their torpedoes, they machine-gunned the ship's deck as they roared upward. Three men fell dead ten feet away from Brown while gunners fired into the exposed bellies of the planes as they banked overhead. Brown realized that "it's difficult to comprehend sudden death" as it occurred around him. He witnessed one of the planes glide "beautifully," as he perceived it, away from the ship, before crashing into the sea and exploding. When he first saw the plane overhead, he did not think there was anything wrong, but then he noticed it was not regaining altitude. He wrote, "Tracers are plowing into it ... it struck the water and immediately burst into flames. It burned fiercely, a twenty-foot circle of orange on a blue sea." A short time later, he ran to the starboard side and snapped a picture of another plane no more than 200 yards away. He was puzzled why it was not dropping its torpedo until he noticed it had a huge hole in its side and was on fire. The plane buckled in the middle "as though stricken with a cramp, the bomber dove, shapeless, flaming, and seaward. It's just a pillar of fire until it hits the water and spreads out into nothingness."[18]

The torpedo attack was over in six minutes, and Brown observed on his shipmates' faces "a mixture of incredulity and a sort of sensuous pleasure, but I don't detect fear. There's an ecstatic happiness, but strangely, I don't see anything approaching hate for the attackers." One officer commented: "Plucky blokes, those Japs. That was as beautiful an attack as ever I expect to see." But there was no time to reflect as yet another attack was already beginning. At one minute past noon, a second wave of twelve torpedo bombers attacked the *Wales*. By this time, the ship was an easy target because a previous torpedo had jammed its rudder; the helmsman had lost the ability to steer. The ship was moving in a uncontrollable circle and its speed had diminished to fifteen knots. On the *Repulse* bridge, Tennant was directing his helmsman to zigzag so the ship could evade torpedoes. Tennant's tactic probably helped the *Repulse* avoid sixteen torpedoes, but others found their mark.[19] Word spread that the next attack might include a crash dive, and Brown knew the flag deck was a prime target. The coveralls, anti-flash hood, and tin helmet made him sweat ferociously. His ears ached from shell blasts, and his mouth felt as if he had cotton in it. If the scene were not so horrific, he thought he would have deemed it awe-inspiring. He found the obliviousness of the Japanese pilots to the sheet of bullets and shells the ships' gunners were firing at them simultaneously courageous and suicidal. They simply flew through it. He scribbled on his pad, although he had pushed so hard on his pen that he had bent its tip. He heard and felt bullets hitting close by. He glanced upward to see a line of holes in the funnel two feet above his head.

At twenty minutes past noon, yet another wave of ten bombers arrived. This time, one of them dropped a 550 pound bomb barely 300 feet above the *Repulse*, and it struck the deck forty feet behind Brown. The concussion threw him off his feet, and the ship began listing. On the bridge, Tennant realized the *Repulse* was doomed. He told the men to grab their lifebelts, abandon ship, and "God be with you." Brown ran to his cabin for his lifebelt as the order came to move to the ship's starboard. The *Repulse* was kneeling so far over to port that that side of the deck was nearly under water. Gunner Woods said it was so close that it was appealing to enter the water there, but "we were being warned away from that route of escape as the submerging superstructure could easily drag you down with the ship."[20] Altogether, thirty-five torpedo bombers and eight high-level bombers had attacked the *Repulse*, but only one bomb had struck her. The planes had launched more than twenty torpedoes at the *Repulse*, and ten had found their mark. Two 1,100 pound bombs had struck the *Wales*, and eight torpedoes had scored hits.[21] British gunners had brought down only four enemy planes.

As he returned to the deck, Brown encountered Gallagher who was inflating his lifebelt. He attempted to do the same, but the heat had rendered Brown's incapable of retaining air. They agreed to stick together when they left the ship, but in the confusion they became separated. Around him, Brown observed that none of the crewmembers were panicking as they methodically moved toward the quarterdeck. An officer told him to get into a lifeboat that was hanging by its davits, but the only way he could reach it was to do a hand-over-hand cable crawl through ten feet of open space. He accomplished the feat, but once he made it to the boat, a lieutenant told him he had to get out because it was overloaded. Brown stepped back over and fell several feet onto the deck, which was slanted more than ever. He slid ten more feet and crashed into a bulkhead. The impact left him dizzy, but he grabbed a cable and pulled himself up the slippery deck.

Men were throwing any floatable object they could find off the ship before leaping toward it. A few were jumping from control towers into the water on either side of the ship, but misjudged their leap and injured themselves when they hit the ship's side. Oil and debris cluttered the water. At the stern, the ship's screws were still turning, and some men who leaped there were sucked in. Brown sat on the deck watching the action around him as if he were not a participant. Nearby, a chaplain—- unconcerned for his own survival—was administering last rights to a dying gunner. Elsewhere, those who were able were helping wounded shipmates into the water. As Brown slipped off the new shoes a Chinese cobbler had made him only days before in Singapore, he was apprehensive about how to escape. For a moment, he thought, "Cecil, you are never going to get out of this," but he knew he had to try. After pausing, he slid down to a porthole, and braced himself while taking off his helmet and anti-flash hood. He was not afraid, but felt as if he were glued to the hull. Looking at the clutter of men and wreckage in the water, he was uncertain about leaving the seeming security of the *Repulse*, but he also realized that his refuge would soon be sliding from beneath him.

While Brown was making up his mind, elsewhere on the ship Tennant and his officers were arguing over whether he would join them in abandoning ship. He was insistent on going down with her, but they would not hear of it. Finally, they forcefully pushed him into the water and followed. Brown remained still until he witnessed a man slide down the ship's side to a three-inch bulge of steel that extended around the hull. The sailor then executed a perfect swan-dive into the sea. His flawless plunge nudged Brown into standing up in the porthole, from which he dove twenty feet into the sea. At first, the water seemed unusually warm, but he quickly realized he was swimming more in oil than water. His decision to jump had an impact on a sailor who likewise was having trouble deciding how to abandon ship. Seaman D.W. Avery recounted that he was sitting on the ship's bilge hole, trying to muster

5. Reporting History Up Close and Personal 77

courage to jump. As he pondered, Brown came alongside him, took off his shoes, and sat them carefully beside him. "He then stood up, turned to me and said, 'Good Luck, pal,' dived into the water and swam for the nearest destroyer. This, and the fact that the ship was getting lower into the water, made my mind up for me and I dived off."[22]

After jumping, Brown remained stationary a few minutes until he noticed men around him swimming away, and he decided it would be a good idea to follow. He looked at his left hand and saw that the wedding ring Martha had bought him in Italy was loose on his finger. He was afraid he was going to lose it, so he clenched it and began stroking with his right one. The oil quickly saturated his clothes and lifebelt, making swimming ponderous. The strings of the lifebelt tightened around his neck to the point he feared they were going to strangle him. This was the first moment of fear he had felt during the ordeal, mainly because it reminded him that throughout his life he had been terrified of strangling. Looking around, he calculated there were 500-to-600 men in the water nearby. For several minutes he was not making much progress, when suddenly a whooshing sound fifty feet behind startled him. He peered over his shoulder and saw the *Repulse* rising vertically into the air to begin its death dive. Suddenly he was aware of a tugging on his legs, so he paddled furiously to escape the suction. Some of the men closer to the doomed ship were unable to paddle, and the ship's pressure pulled them under with it. Brown felt as if the force was pulling his legs out of his hip sockets, but he fought the force of the submerging ship. As its bow went beneath the waves, the ship sent a huge wave of oil across the water. With his mouth open, gasping for air, Brown ingested some. It tasted like dirty castor oil, and it made him sick. The time was 12:33. The *Repulse* had sunk within eleven minutes of sustaining its first torpedo hit.

Brown could not recognize the men nearby because of their oil and blood-covered faces. Many were unable to swim because of their burns. He looked for Gallagher but could not identify him. During the next few minutes four or five of the men close by were too weak to continue, and their hands slipped from whatever item they had been hanging onto and disappeared beneath the waves. One man called: "Are you all right, War Correspondent?" As Brown attempted to answer, he swallowed more oil, so he decided that if another sailor asked that he would just wave. As he attempted to swim, he became fatigued, so he grabbed onto a small wooden table. It was too slick to hold onto for long, but at least it gave him a short rest. One man cried that an eel had shocked him. Survivor Ted Matthews said he observed sharks thrashing around. At first, he thought they were attacking the men, but then he realized that was not the case. They were dying from the oil. Matthews also saw "bright yellow and red objects darting across the water." He recognized them as sea snakes, which typically would lie on the surface. But they were swimming wildly, apparently frightened by the noise or being poisoned by the oil. From experience, he knew "if you were bitten, then you would swiftly and painfully die."[23] This probably occurred with some of the crewmembers, but Brown was one of the lucky ones who somehow survived the marine threats.

He scanned the horizon and spotted a raft about three-quarters of a mile away with men on it and a destroyer about two miles farther, but he was certain he had no chance to reach either. He told himself he needed to remember these details for the story he would write, but then he reminded himself that there was little chance he was going to survive to write it. But if by some chance he did, he wanted to be certain to emphasize the men's extraordinary courage. He had witnessed it onboard minutes before as they attempted to fight off the attacking planes, and he was seeing it again as they struggled to survive in the sea.[24] An investigation later concluded that the oil ingestion was probably the cause of death for more of the men than the attack itself.[25]

Brown's clothes continued to impede him; they felt as if they weighed a ton. He discarded his socks, which provided some relief, but he could not hang onto the table while ridding himself of clothing. The lifebelt cord and camera cable continued to choke him, but he gave up getting rid of the lifebelt and he was adamant he would drown before discarding the camera. Eventually the tide took him toward a fifteen-by-ten foot Carley float. A marine, whom he later learned was twenty-year-old Morris Graney, stretched out his hand as Brown floated by. For several minutes, they had difficulty clasping one another's hands, but eventually they did and the muscular Graney pulled Brown onto the raft. There really was no room, but Graney cleared some space. Now the destroyer was a mile away, and the men on the float were trying to paddle the raft in that direction, but there was only one paddle. Others hanging onto it in the water were kicking to propel it. Graney was urging the men on, telling them repeatedly they were going to survive. To lift their spirits, he led them in "When Irish Eyes Are Smiling." Within a few minutes, two men on the raft died and sailors pushed them over the side to make room for others. Brown was delirious from the oil he had swallowed and his weakened state. A couple of times he told Graney he wanted to get back into the water because it was too much effort to remain upright. But Graney would not hear of it—he held Brown up, and at one point slapped him to wake him.

Soon thereafter, a half-dozen Japanese bombers made another run over the survivors. They feared they were sitting ducks, but the bombers did not attack. Japanese pilots later said they were under orders only to fire on the ships. Because they respected the sailors who opposed them, they did not strafe them.[26] As the minutes passed, some men believed the destroyers were moving away because they were was making such slow progress toward them. A few were ready to give up, especially when a second group of planes roared over them. But those were British Brewster Buffaloes. When the Japanese attack had begun, Phillips had radioed the Singapore squadron to help fight off the Japanese, but they arrived too late. Even if they had been in time, the antiquated fighters would have been no match for the Japanese. Meanwhile, Graney kept urging the men with "We'll soon be there."

His optimism was rewarded within the hour when the float and destroyer *Electra* converged. A seaman tossed a looped rope over the hull toward the raft. Graney grabbed it and shouted, "We have an American war correspondent here." He asked Brown if he could grasp it. When he nodded, Graney yelled to the men above to "heave up." The *Electra* sailors yanked Brown off the Carley and dragged him through the water for about ten feet. He felt like he was plowing through "a solid wall. The pressure pound[ed] at my head like a great rubber hammer." From the deck, a sailor yelled for Brown to grab onto a wooden ladder that extended down the side, but its lowest rung was four feet above the water, out of Brown's reach. He floated for a minute, while the sailors yelled, "Hurry—you'll have to help yourself." Suddenly, a wave elevated him enough so he could reach the bottom rung. Although weak, he climbed slowly until four ratings grabbed him and lifted him over the taffrail.

Brown did not know if Gallagher had survived. The overweight British correspondent could not swim. Before jumping from the *Repulse*, Gallagher had paused on one of the torpedo blisters and lit a cigarette. Tucking his notebooks into his shorts, he jumped and paddled to a lifebelt onto which two sailors were already hanging, but they soon disappeared. In his semiconscious state, Gallagher was unsure where they had gone, and he felt terribly alone. Eventually, he made his way to one of the floats, but he had to hang on to a rope trailing it because he was too weak to lift himself into it. Neither could the men haul him in because of his weight, which had become greater because of his oil and water-saturated clothing. But after a few minutes, two sailors jumped into the water, and with the help of others onboard, boosted him in. As they administered artificial respiration, they found that Gallagher's stomach had swollen so much that his pants were nearly cutting his belly in half. Unable to help himself, the sailors unfastened his pants to relieve the pressure, and probably saved his life.[27] Photojournalist Abrahams was a stronger swimmer than Gallagher, and likewise survived. Unfortunately, the pictures he had taken of the attack did not. Before jumping, he knew he would not be able to stay afloat with the weight of the Speed Graphic camera and four-by-five inch slides. He placed the camera and slides in a locker, and kept the most important slides on himself. Unfortunately, as Abrahams surfaced, a marine wearing hobnail boots jumped and landed on him. The collision punctured Abraham's life-vest, injured an eye and sent the slides to the deep.[28]

The *Wales* sank at 1:20 p.m. Despite sustaining more strikes than *Repulse*, it stayed afloat longer because of its stronger hull. That fact allowed more of its men to survive. However, Phillips, Leach and most of the *Wales*' officers went down with her. Brown was barely on the *Electra* when the *Wales* began to slip beneath the waves. When he stepped onto the deck, he felt his feet burning. The *Electra*'s ratings stripped off his clothes and threw a woolen parka over him, which left only his khaki shorts underneath. Regaining his senses, Brown asked for a dry camera so he could document the *Wales*' sinking, and a sailor scurried off for one. Brown opened the notebook in which he had recorded an account of the attack. The pages were oil-soaked and wet, but legible. Around him, others were having their wounds tended.

When the seaman returned with a camera, Brown took as many pictures as the roll of film would allow. He hopscotched from one side of the deck to the other, onto a hatch, then back, as the heat blistered his feet. A rating later remembered what he described as "an almost naked man dancing up and down screaming for a camera to photograph the *Wales*' sinking. Whoever it was [apparently Brown] never got his picture and neither ship's sinking was photographed."[29] It is unclear whether Brown was jumping up and down because his feet were burning or because he was crying for the camera. Subsequently, chief engineer Frank McLeod found a pair of shoes for him along with a logbook. He put on the shoes so he could scurry about the ship, taking notes as he interviewed survivors.

An hour after his rescue, Brown sat with forty-to-fifty of the sunken ships' officers in the hot wardroom as they drank tea and tried to make sense of what had happened. Several of them sported bandages; they were all naked to the waist. One of them said to Brown, "You told us not to underestimate the enemy." "Yes, I know," Brown replied, "but I take no satisfaction in that now." Brown asked if anyone had seen Gallagher or Tennant. The officers said they had not seen Gallagher, but one said he thought he saw Tennant floating face down. *Wales*' survivors said they witnessed Phillips and Leach disappear. Phillips had gambled and lost that Force Z could halt the Japanese invasion, without air cover, before the Japanese airplanes could attack him. Ironically, the landing he sought to stop did not take place.[30]

It had been a harrowing experience for the journalists and ships' crews. Brown was alive but changed. He later sought to reassure Martha by writing: "Health reasonably satisfactory. In October, the air force crashed me. November an army truck plunged over a hill with me. In December, the navy tried to sink me. Since no additional branches of the force remain, don't worry about the indestructible Mr. Brown."[31] Weller—who would win a Pulitzer Prize in 1943—wrote that the combat reporter occupies "a peculiar position. [His task] is to get as close as possible and report as much as possible while surviving as long as possible." Brown's experience certainly met those requirements."[32] He would

5. Reporting History Up Close and Personal

This photograph was taken by a British sailor minutes after Brown was rescued from the sinking of the British battleship the *Repulse* in the South China Sea, only three days after the attack on Pearl Harbor. He is standing on the deck of the destroyer *Electra* in a woolen parka the crew has thrown over him after stripping him of his water- and oil-soaked clothing. He is in his bare feet, which quickly became painful because the ship's deck was blistering hot. Soon thereafter, the crew found a pair of shoes for him to protect his feet (Library of Congress).

continue to experience those extremes as he returned to Singapore. Back on dry land, he would make one of the most dramatic reports of the young Pacific War, but his rescue only led to yet another battle with British leadership.

✦✦ 6 ✦✦

Out of the Sea but into Hot Water

The news about the sinking of the British ships reached the U.S. at five a.m., New York time, December 11, from, ironically, Japan. A CBS employee who was monitoring a Tokyo broadcast heard an announcer claim their planes had sunk the *Prince of Wales* and *Repulse*. But neither he nor anyone else in the newsroom took the announcement seriously. The reaction was that it was just "another fantastic claim" meant to spread confusion, while lying on White's desk was Brown's pre-sinking cable. At that time, no one at CBS thought the two communications related.[1]

Meanwhile, the destroyers hurried back to Keppel Harbor at thirty-one knots, arriving at half past midnight December 11. Many of the survivors were in a bad way. Dockworkers carried them off the ships on stretchers to the previously unused barracks. A number of survivors had died while in route and were buried at sea. At the gangway, Brown encountered *Repulse*'s Captain Denby and asked if he knew what had happened to Gallagher. Denby told him Gallagher was all right; that the *Express* had picked him up and that he was ashore. Brown began worrying that Gallagher would get his story out before him. He boarded the *Express* and in the wardroom encountered Tennant. He and Brown hugged, with Brown saying, "You gave us quite a story." Tennant agreed. He arranged for a car to take Brown into Singapore, but the ride took an hour and a half because of a torrential downpour. Brown kept urging the driver on, but he kept replying, "I no want get kill." As they drove, Brown attempted to mentally compose the story he would write. He was exhausted and sick, still suffering from ingested oil as well as the shock of the loss of the *Repulse* men he had befriended.

He went directly to the cable office so he could get his story out quickly. His typewriter had gone down with the *Repulse*, so he hoped he could use one at the cable office. As he stepped out of the car outside the office, a spine-tingling shriek startled him. A bayonet appeared close to his face, followed by a bright light in his eyes—it was a Chinese guard. Brown responded with a stream of expletives. The impact of Brown's words was accentuated by his appearance: He had on the parka from the *Electra,* and he had replaced his shorts with trousers that stopped six inches above his bare, white ankles. Three other guards soon arrived, and after additional arguing in a mix of English and Mandarin, finally allowed Brown to enter the office. Inside, he spied a typewriter, but clerk Cuthbert Donough would not allow him to use it, saying its use was limited to employees. Brown pleaded an exception, but to no avail. Exasperated, he asked for a handful of cable sheets and, using the pen fastened to the chain on the counter, began handwriting the story in segments. Because the counter was chest height, and he was weak, it was an arduous task. As he scribbled about 200 words on each sheet, he handed them to Donough. Finally, at 4:30 a.m., Brown finished the story, which ran approximately 700 words. He asked Donough to send it to New York via Manila, the cable route Brown had been utilizing for weeks.

He got back to the Raffles at 5:30 and fell into bed. When he had passed the front desk, he had asked if there were cables for him—but was told there were none. However, a clerk awakened him three hours later to say he had four cables—White had been trying to reach him. One message said he should file his stories through London instead of Manila because the Philippines' communication link was unreliable. That message shocked him out of a half-awake stupor. He threw on some clothes and raced back to the cable office. He instructed Donough to resend his cables via London. Consequently, almost twenty-seven hours after the CBS employee had heard the Tokyo announcement, Brown's cable recounting the maritime tragedy reached New York. CBS broadcast his account four times that day: at five and eight a.m., and at 3:45 and 8:16 p.m.

Brown went to the SPRO Office where he encountered Gallagher, who was thrilled to see him because he thought Brown had gone down with the *Repulse*. He borrowed a typewriter there so he could compose a longer story, but his hands trembled as he typed. He experienced flashbacks to the catastrophe, and the loss of men haunted him: "It is hard to believe that death can be so sudden and final. One minute a man is beside you on deck and a few hours later he is not there or anywhere else in life."[2] The *Repulse* had suffered the greatest loss of life because it had sunk so quickly. Out of 1,309 men on her, 513 had died. Fewer had been lost on the *Wales,* with 1,285 of the 1,618 rescued. The *Electra* had pulled nearly 900 men out of the water; the *Express* more than 1,000.[3]

As word reached Singapore and London of the tragedy, shock engulfed the British Empire. An officer in Singapore wrote that it was a "catastrophe of gargantuan proportions ... [and] we felt completely exposed." In London, the news devastated Churchill. When Fleet Admiral Dudley Pound awoke

Churchill to inform him of the calamity, the prime minister hung up the phone, stunned: "I was thankful to be alone. In all the war I never received a more direct shock." In addition to his grief over the ships' loss, was the realization that not only was Singapore defenseless, but both the Indian and Pacific Oceans were completely open to the Japanese. The news had a similar effect on the public. England's populace had not yet recovered from Dunkirk, when the bleak naval news arrived. The sinking was "perhaps more dramatic than the attack on Pearl Harbor," wrote Arch Whitehouse. "[The] effect was complete and final.... The full details of the success [at Pearl Harbor] were not admitted for several months, where the sinking of the *Repulse* and *Prince of Wales* was announced immediately by friend and foe."[4] At the same time that the sinking destroyed the illusion of England's Far East dominance, fear of Japan's ability to prosecute the war soared around the world.[5] Occurring so soon after Pearl Harbor, the Japanese had accomplished even more than score major victories over its two foes. Japan had also proven that the Allies' battleships, which they thought were dominant weapons, could be so easily vanquished. In warfare history, it was the first time airplanes had sunk two capital ships on the open sea, and "the sinkings were the Royal Navy's greatest loss as a result of a single engagement," according to Alan Matthews.[6] Those three days in December 1941—with the disasters at Pearl Harbor and in the South China Sea—were among the most devastating in naval history.

The impact on Brown personally was similarly far-reaching. On December 11, he began receiving cables from the U.S. White wrote, "OVERJOYED ABOUT YOUR RESCUE.... FILE YOUR STORY VOLUMINOUSLY.... YOU MAKE GOOD YOUR BOAST ABOUT WONDERFUL STORY." He also received a cable from Bill Paley, his first message from the network head since becoming a CBS employee: "ALL OF US OVERJOYED TO LEARN OF YOUR RESCUE. [Your story] STIRRING INFORMATIVE ALL ROUND GREAT REPORTING." He also received cables from *Newsweek* editor Joseph Phillips, and *Collier's* Gervasi. Both asked him to write stories for them. Another, from Random House's Bennett Cerf read: "WE WANT TO PUBLISH YOUR BOOK WHENEVER YOU WRITE IT. WOULD APPRECIATE LETTER." Cecil cabled Martha to meet with Cerf to draw up a contract.[7] Cerf's request not only acknowledged the importance of Brown's account, but the attention his broadcasts had been receiving in the U.S. Cerf said two of his friends, playwright Howard Lindsay and his actress wife, Dorothy Stickney, and many others in New York were devoted Brown listeners. Lindsay had written the Broadway play *Life with Father*, in which Stickney played the role of Vinnie. After coming home from the theater each night, they enjoyed Brown's broadcasts.[8]

Undeniably, Brown was lucky to be alive, and the fact that he could tell the story in the first person, also was remarkable. If reporters had not been onboard during the attack, the British Navy would have controlled how the news was disseminated. Censors could not manage this story. "We were able to tell the truth because we had seen for ourselves what had happened," said Gallagher. "There were no public relations officers to gum things up, because the Royal Navy was in such a mess no one had any time to think about correspondents and their stories." Dunn, Brown's bureau boss, said he was pleased Brown had survived and that CBS had scored a "world beat." On the other hand, "I would be less than honest if I didn't admit a little salt in my own wounds. There can be no situation tougher for a reporter than to find himself just barely out of reach of the most important story of his career." Dunn had planned to meet Brown in Singapore in early December to discuss a reassignment, but he had been unable to get a flight out of Burma.[9] He may have been even more envious if he had known of another communication White sent Brown: "HAVE NOTIFIED YOUR BANK YOU DID ONE GRAND JOB." White had veiled his meaning because he was uncertain how British tax regulations might affect the transaction. What he was saying was that he was authorizing a $1,000 bonus for Brown. Brown got the message, and responded, "My God! A thousand-dollar bonus."[10]

On December 12, he took his first bath since the rescue and scrubbed the oil off his body. Afterward, he was pleased he no longer smelled badly, but his body felt even worse. His muscles, lungs and ears ached; he could not lift his arms above his shoulders, he shook continually, had difficulty concentrating, could not sleep, and his systolic blood pressure was at 104. Nonetheless, the following day he broadcast at 7:23 a.m. (6:53 p.m. New York time), but because of transmission problems, he was unsure if the broadcast had reached New York. In it, he mentioned that the Japanese success in sinking the ships was largely due to the lack of fighter protection. The censors had previously expunged that information from his cables, but for this broadcast he worked with Captain O.K. Fearon, whom he initially found a more reasonable censor. Fearon made only minor changes to Brown's copy. It was the first broadcast British Command had allowed him to make since early September. Although no one had said his broadcast privileges were reinstated, Fearon told him he could transmit this story. Brown assumed they were allowing him back on the air because his celebrity status made it difficult for officials to explain why they were not allowing him to originate stories. But it was a public relations' decision, not a signal that the commanders viewed Brown more favorably.

Now, as he moved around town, Brown noticed that the British military and Singaporean apathy concerning war coming to the island had disappeared, and voluntary evacuation was underway. Nonetheless, he continued meeting resistance in obtaining information about what the British were doing now that Japanese forces were moving toward Singapore from Thailand. On December 16, he shipped his story off to *Collier's*, for which the magazine paid him $750, and he had dinner with Graney. Brown expressed gratitude to Graney for saving his life by not only buying dinner but by presenting him with a gold watch. Just after nine o'clock the air raid sirens went off, and he and Graney spent at hour waiting out more bombing. The two ran to an open field just off Beach Road, which was a safer place than in the city. Brown was exhausted, and Graney told him he needed to "take care of himself and get some rest." Brown said, "I'll rest when the war is over," to which Graney replied, "I guess that's the way it will be for all of us."[11] Unfortunately, Graney died the following February off the coast of Singapore while attempting to evacuate civilians when Japanese forces captured the city.

On December 18, Brown learned that the Japanese had overrun Alor Setar and Sungei Patani in Malaya, putting them only fourteen miles from the Penang Peninsula. They had advanced seventy-five miles, and the revelation shocked Singapore's inhabitants. The threat was now less than 450 miles away. In a script, Brown wrote that the advance threatened Singapore. But this time he argued with Fearon for nearly an hour to secure approval because Faron considered it "overly pessimistic." Brown insisted that it was factual and would help get Allied reinforcements into Malaya. Nevertheless, Fearon would not allow him to announce that the British were at a disadvantage because of a lack of fighter protection. The following day, rumors were rampant in the streets that Singapore would fall within days, and morale in the city correspondingly fell. At the Raffles, evacuees were filling the rooms. Brown learned that American military personnel were leaving for Batavia. He interviewed General C. A. Lyon, who had been commander of the British Penang Fortress, over a drink at Raffles. Lyon was in Singapore because command had ordered him to evacuate Penang, and the Japanese now occupied it. Brown wanted to report the news in his next broadcast, but Brooke-Popham stopped him out of fear it would panic the population. Brown thought this only the latest in a long line of flimsy excuses for not permitting reporters to tell the public the facts, about which it already had a considerable idea. The Malayans and Chinese were particularly afraid, fearing the Japanese would target them for abuse, and there was no indication that the British were stopping the Japanese anywhere in Malaya.

Three days before Christmas, two other U.S. newscasters joined Brown. One was NBC's Agronsky, and he and Brown shared a drink at the Raffles. He asked Brown how he could arrange for broadcast facilities, and Brown said he would introduce him to the people in charge and show him how to originate broadcasts. Brown's willingness to assist Agronsky surprised him. "You mean," Agronsky said, "you are willing to help me? ... After all, we are competitors." Brown responded: "Listen, Martin, I haven't got time to worry about your getting an exclusive story or me getting an exclusive story. We are trying to cover this war and report it to the American people, and when bombs are dropping you don't have time to worry about scoops; you just do the best job you can." Reacting with disbelief, Agronsky replied, "Well, that's fine, but that isn't the way we correspondents worked in Ankara." Brown responded: "That's the way I feel like working here, and if you want to go out and scoop me, go right ahead." Agronsky accepted Brown's benevolence, saying, "All right, fine…. I will give you what I know and you can give me what you get." However, Brown—indicating his collegiality did not extend that far—set Agronsky straight: "No, it won't work that way." He would introduce him to sources and those in charge, but they would not be sharing stories.[12] That same day, Dunn arrived. Brown hoped his boss' appearance would mean he could head north to cover the fighting, or leave altogether. He asked Dunn if he would stay in Singapore to cover developments while Brown went to Malaya. However, there was no transportation for Brown, so Dunn told him to sit tight while he flew to Batavia. He would try to return in a few days and then Brown could go to Malaya.

On Christmas day, he awoke at 7 a.m. and wrote a script for broadcast at 11:20. He was stunned when censor Duckworth, seemingly caught up in the Christmas spirit, edited little of his copy and confided: "All of your efforts here did much good. They woke a lot of people up." Brown told American listeners that in Singapore it was a "grim Christmas, with not much joy, and people knowing they may hear the whistle of bombs at any moment." He said the greeting "Merry Christmas" had an empty sound to it. "Singapore is fighting for its existence, and with great odds against it." He said the Japanese were too close to celebrate "peace on earth. Most people know that this Christmas Singapore is reaping the terrifying fruits of wishful thinking and unpreparedness. In some respects, Singapore is a confused man walking about as in a dream, knowing something terrible might happen and not quite sure how to meet it." But the Christmas spirit ended quickly. Two days later, he spent ten-and-one-half hours with Fearon going over 6,100 words in "Malay Jungle War," which he wanted to send to *Life*. Fearon referred portions of the content to higher authorities, but in the end, most of the article survived.[13]

On December 29, the Japanese resumed night bombing. Brown joined others in diving into twelve-inch wide, three-foot deep ditches. It was another moonlit night before the bombing, but then he heard airplanes, and searchlights punctuated the sky. He thought about going to a shelter but they stunk. His alternative was the ditch, but after a short time he climbed out and laid on the sidewalk. He used his tin hat as a pillow: "The ditch smell was almost too overwhelming and there were all kinds of things crawling around. I just thought to myself, 'You're a big boy now and lying around in ditches! What a civilization this is. A man has to lie around on the sidewalk.'"[14]

The following day, the British declared martial law in Singapore. Duckworth wanted Brown to broadcast the entire 400-word statement, but he refused, saying it only deserved passing mention. Subsequent decisions indicate that if he had agreed to broadcast it, Brown may have improved his ability to continue broadcasting. He and Agronsky moved their belongings into the country, about 100 yards from the radio studio, so they would be safer from the targeted city. Growing impatient with Dunn, Brown asked White if he could go to the front, but he responded that he wanted him to keep CBS informed on developments in Singapore. Brown countered by asking if he could leave permanently, but White told him to stay put as long as broadcast facilities remained operational. In a broadcast on the thirty-first, Brown said the U.S. supply of tin and rubber would be evaporating for the next several years because Malaya was in Japanese hands. Fearon attempted to kill the story, but Brown got it through when he appealed to British diplomat George Sansom. He had just arrived in Singapore after a stint in Washington as an adviser for the Royal Navy. In Singapore, he became the sole civilian member of the War Council.

Unfortunately, no sooner had Sansom helped Brown than he made his job more difficult. The first week in January, Brown and Agronsky met with Sansom to complain about censorship. Brown said all they wanted was the opportunity to work more closely with the censors to discuss changes, instead of them capriciously cutting words. But instead of reacting agreeably, Sansom said the War Council had decided to begin treating their newscasts as "local broadcasts." Sansom said the reason for the change was that "because of the effect on morale, they are to be censored." Brown argued that the decision was illogical because the reporters worked for American networks, not local stations. But Sansom responded: "Objective reporting and the local morale situation are irreconcilable."[15] The correspondents left the meeting shaking their heads.

As disheartened as they were by that decision, the news only got worse on January 8. In Brown's box at the SPRO building, he found a note from the Malayan Broadcasting Corporation: "We have just been advised by the Director of Publicity that your broadcasts are to cease after tomorrow. We are very sorry to be informed of this because we have been happy to give you every possible facility." Dumbfounded, he hurried downstairs to ask Sansom what the note meant. Brown said it did not make sense, but Sansom responded that it was accurate. "I am sorry but you can't broadcast anymore." Brown asked who was responsible. Sansom said he could not go into the reasons, but that Command had made the decision. Brown argued that taking him off the air deprived 7,000,000 Americans of news from Singapore. Sansom replied, "Yes, that's why."[16] This led Brown to meet with the Deputy Director of Military Intelligence, Colonel Leonard Field.

Field explained that the military had taken the action because of local complaints about Brown's newscasts. "One woman wrote in from Kuala Lumpur that your broadcasts are Fifth Column." Brown asked if he was making the decision based on one woman's complaint. Field responded: "Oh no ... but I have read the broadcast [transcripts] and I agree." He added that Brown had attempted to circumvent censorship by arriving at the studio without a copy of the script for the censor to check. Brown responded that Field was misinformed, but Field cut Brown off: "A large part of the defense of Singapore depends on local morale. It is very bad. It's my job to see that nothing happens which depresses that morale." Exasperated, Brown replied, "But I am not broadcasting for or to the people of Malaya. I work for CBS and my broadcasts are designed to inform the American people." Field countered that his newscasts were heard locally.[17] Brown asked Field to cite instances where he had reported incorrect facts. Field said, "I don't question any of the facts in your broadcasts, but it is the organization of them and the choice of words." He asked Brown if he could change the way he wrote stories. Brown responded that his integrity would not allow him to compromise. He asked if he could send a cable to White, explaining that "due to extraordinary local morale conditions" he was no longer permitted to broadcast "accurate, honest reporting of local and military situation. Please advise." Field said he would approve such a cable. Brown left the meeting still hopeful that Field's superiors might reverse the decision, but when he arrived at the Raffles a message was awaiting that dashed any such optimism. It was from Fisher: "I have this day sent a communique to the War Office, informing them that you are no longer an accredited war correspondent and asking them to cancel your license. I am satisfied that the evidence in favor of taking this step is overwhelming." Brown recorded in his diary that "this action is the same as an expulsion, because they know very well that if I can't broadcast and am not an accredited war correspondent I can't carry out my functions for CBS."[18]

Brown wrote White: "I AM CONVINCED THE FACTS AND CIRCUMSTANCE FULLY JUSTIFY WASHINGTON TO MAKE THE STRONGEST REPRESENTATION TO THE BRITISH FOREIGN OFFICE." He said the order denied him the opportunity to cover the war from the American perspective, which should be a concern because the U.S. was a British Ally. He told White that his license revocation was a "SERIOUS REFLECTION ON MY WORK WITH CBS, [AND] MY LONG ASSOCIATION WITH THE BRITISH.... I AM WILLING ... TO STAND THE MOST SEARCHING INVESTIGATION." Two days later, he turned in his license and asked if he was entitled to a court martial. Field said, "No," because he was not an enlisted man. Brown also learned that Duckworth had stopped his cable to White as well as those of other correspondents who were trying to relay the news of Brown's dilemma. He called Duckworth, who said he needed to talk with Sansom before allowing his subordinates to send the cables. Later that day, Duckworth called back to say Sansom would allow the cable to be sent as long as Brown assured him it would not be used as news, but only as correspondence.

The next part of the conversation became even more infuriating. Duckworth told Brown that Sansom had decided that the scripts Brown had been submitting "show[ed] a state of mind that makes you *persona non grata*." Brown asked Duckworth if he fully understood what he had said: "You mean it is what I attempted to say in my broadcasts that led to this action?" Duckworth replied that he was well aware of his meaning. Brown asked if this was the actual reason they were censuring him. Duckworth said it was. Brown hung up the phone, convinced that because Field, Sansom and Duckworth had made disparate charges they simply wanted him off the air and out of Singapore. He penned in his diary: "I never thought a time would come when the British would say to a correspondent: 'You must write copy which requires us to cut nothing out. Anything that we have to cut out will be held against you.' In other words, the British here now demand control of the thoughts of correspondents."[19]

In his January 12 broadcast, Agronsky told his NBC audience what had happened to Brown. "He is regarded by his colleagues as an objective, truthful and conscientious reporter whose belief in the democratic cause has been proved on any number of occasions." Agronsky said all the correspondents were concerned because they thought the precedent the British had established with Brown could be applied to them, too.[20] Two days later, Brown received a cable from White in which he said CBS had disputed the action. The network had asked the Roosevelt Administration and the State Department to intervene with the British in Washington and London, but without success.[21] He urged Brown to meet again with officials in an effort to achieve reinstatement. He told Brown, the "CURRENT WORLD SITUATION AND NECESSITY OF ALLIED UNITY EVEN, IN CONNECTION WITH EXCHANGES OF NEWS, MAKE SUCH EPISODES REGRETTABLE FROM THE STANDPOINT OF ALLIED MORALE." He added that CBS was counting on him to resolve the situation in a way that was best for everyone concerned.[22] Brown took the cable to Sansom, but Sansom said he was being transferred to Java and there was nothing he could do. In its next issue, *Time* noted that Brown's "silencing in Singapore ... was the first case of an Allied reporter of known integrity being denied the use of the Allied radio."[23] Gallagher wrote an explanation of the case for the *Daily Express*, in which he chastised his nation's representatives.[24] Conversely, Giles Playfair, an Englishman who was working for the Malayan Broadcasting Company, said Brown had been banned because of "plain speaking—and quite rightly, I think." Playfair noted that the London newspapers who denounced the action were "badly out of touch." He added that there was nothing wrong with Americans hearing what Brown had the say, but the problem was that Malayans could as well, "and that just isn't allowable in present circumstances. I can't imagine the Russians letting Cecil Brown loose at one of their microphones."[25]

6. Out of the Sea but into Hot Water   91

Brown was not the first journalist against which the British had taken action. They had jailed a correspondent for the *Sydney [Australia] Daily Telegraph*, Thomas Fairhall, earlier in the month after he wrote a story that officials said contained secret information. They ordered him to reveal his sources, but he refused. Regarding Brown, there was only speculation regarding what he had done wrong. Weller thought he had "pressed a little too hard on the weak spots to be popular with the authorities." In other words, an accumulation of incidents had caught up with him. Specifically, Weller thought Brown had been overly outspoken about British overconfidence concerning Singapore's defense. When Brown's observations began coming true with British defeats in Malaysia, they were considered bad for military morale. It also appears Brown's article in *Life* in January 1942, was the final straw. In "Malay Jungle War," he repeated many criticisms regarding British passivity, with which he coined the phrase: "Singapore Mentality." He charged that the British were "unprepared, physically and mentally, for war," adding that they practiced a "walking death ... an apathy to all affairs except making tin and rubber, money, having stengahs between 5 and 8 p.m., keeping fit, being known as a 'good chap' and getting thoroughly 'plastered' on Saturday night." It had presented a thoroughly pessimistic view of the ability of the British to hold Singapore.[26] Some other correspondents felt that if Brown had self-censored himself he could have continued broadcasting, but restraint was not part of Brown's makeup. They believed the censors increased restrictions on their work, too, as a result of the Brown episode.

One week later, one of the most devastating air raids yet struck Singapore. More than 100 Japanese planes were involved; the attack killed 300 and injured 550. The following day, Brown read a story in the *Singapore Free Press* concerning a question a Reuters' reporter had asked of the British Minister of Information, Brendan Bracken, in the House of Commons about Brown's censure. Bracken had responded, "While there was no dislike of civil free criticism, it was felt that in the abnormal conditions prevailing, Mr. Brown's comments passed the bounds of fair criticism and were a source of danger."[27] The article spurred Brown to not wait to hear from White to authorize departure. He wrote in his diary, "I cannot broadcast, cannot cable stories, nor do any work. I haven't even a gun to fight back, and the way things look now it means just staying here and waiting to be taken prisoner or shot."[28] He booked a flight on British Airways out of Singapore on Friday, January 23. It turned out to be the second to last civilian flight to leave before the airport closed. Japanese land and air forces were so close it was no longer safe for airlines to use Kalang Airport.[29]

When Brown arrived at the airport, he saw that bombing had blown all the windows out of the aerodrome the preceding day. Before he could board the plane, a customs' inspector detained him. Brown noticed that in the inspector's passenger list his name was circled. The official questioned him concerning his bags' contents: "Show me what you have ... it will make it easier for both of us." Brown produced copies of his cables and broadcasts, which the official cleared, but he noticed a black notebook—it was his diary. Fortunately, it was empty because Brown had removed nearly 900 pages and placed them in the bottom of one suitcase. He had anticipated that officials might confiscate them. The inspector examined the book and did not scrutinize the entire suitcase. He straightened up and leaned over to Brown, who braced himself for trouble. Instead, the inspector quietly said, "I know all about you Mr. Brown.... I hope you publish the whole story about Singapore.... Close up your suitcase," and he cleared Brown to board. After takeoff, the place flew only 500–1,000 feet off the ground or water throughout the flight. There were twenty-eight passengers on the seaplane, which made it overloaded, and slowed its airspeed. The pilots hoped that flying low to Batavia would help the unarmed aircraft avoid Japanese fighter detection, and their judgment was correct.[30]

Unfortunately, the rough air at low altitude left Brown nauseated. "I still get air sick, car sick, sea sick and train sick. Some guts I got for a furrin [sic] correspondent," he wrote.[31] Brown's ticket permitted him to fly to Calcutta, but he wanted to make his way back to the U.S. via Australia. There was a phone circuit in Batavia that allowed him to call New York, and he hoped he could convince White to permit him to return Stateside because he was exhausted. Despite Brown's pleadings, White told him CBS needed him in Australia. White also said he was making six-minutes available for Brown the following Sunday morning during the *Roundup*. He wanted him to do a wrap-up on the status of Singapore. Brown went to see a Dr. Reitmann, who was in charge of Dutch press affairs. Reitmann greeted Brown by saying, "So this is the famous Cecil Brown, that international scoundrel." Brown acknowledged that he was the CBS newsman, and asked Reitmann if he could arrange for a broadcast. Reitmann said he would have to check with the Director of Military Intelligence for the Far East, Colonel Field. Brown immediately realized this would result in a denial, and within a few hours Reitmann informed Brown he could not broadcast from there because Field considered him "an outlaw."[32] Brown informed White that he could not broadcast. So White encouraged him to fly to Melbourne where he believed the Australians would allow him to transmit.

On February 3, Brown took a train to Surabaya. He arrived the next morning and contacted the American Naval Headquarters to see if he could arrange for transport on a U.S. Navy plane to Australia. After being assured that he could, he bought some souvenirs in a shop. As he exited the establishment, sirens went off, and he found himself in the midst of the first Japanese attack on Java. He spotted a pile of dirt in a field nearby where a shelter was under construction, and he plopped down beside it—the only partial protection in the area. He saw the bombers overhead and the payloads they were dropping. As bombs exploded upon hitting the ground, each one came closer. "What a rotten way to die!" he said to himself. "And just when I was on my way home…. [I] prayed as I have never prayed before." He stuffed a handkerchief into his mouth so as to not bite his tongue from the concussions. The ground heaved—it felt as if he were in an earthquake. But as certain as he was that he was going to perish, the bombing ended, and he was unharmed. Seventy-to-eighty planes had been involved; thirty-one people died and more than 100 were wounded. The planes destroyed four flying boats and four B-17s on the ground. Antiaircraft fire brought down two fighters and one bomber. Brown decided that regardless of where he went, bombs seemed to follow him.[33]

He got up and headed to the Oranje Hotel, where he had lunch with three American naval commanders. Brown was struck by how much more open they were in talking about naval operations than the British. The Americans were pleased to encounter a U.S. reporter because they felt the American press was ignoring them. To demonstrate their sincerity, they offered to introduce Brown to Rear Admiral William Purnell at naval headquarters. When, a few hours later, an orderly ushered Brown into Purnell's office, the admiral exclaimed: "We have stories for you…. Our boys have done a job that the whole world should know about." It was music to Brown's ears. Purnell introduced him to Captain John Wilkes, commander of U.S. Submarine Forces in Asiatic waters. Purnell asked Wilkes to show Brown Lieutenant (J.G.) Wreford G. "Moon" (nicknamed for his facial shape) Chapple's diary. When Wilkes pulled the diary out of his filing cabinet, Brown saw it was marked Secret and Confidential. He asked if it was permissible to use the contents in a story. Wilkes replied that he had no objection, and added that he would be reading "one of the greatest operations of the war thus far." As Brown took notes, Wilkes drew a map of the Lingayen Gulf off the coast of Luzon. It was where Chapple's submarine had encountered a convoy of Japanese destroyers and transports.[34] The following morning Brown met the tall, husky Chapple, and told him that although he had the rough details of his experience he needed "color, atmosphere and dialogue" before he could write. But Brown did not have time to interview him because his plane was about to take off, so he typed several dozen questions. He asked Chapple to mail the answers to him in Sydney, and Chapple replied: "That's about the toughest assignment ever given to me, but I'll try."

As Brown was finishing the questions, the PBY pilot was yelling that they needed to take off before daylight to avoid Japanese fighters. They hurried to the dock, boarded, and the plane lifted into the sky at 5:30 a.m. The pilot was Lieutenant (J.G.) Elwyn Christman; six additional men comprised the crew. They scanned the sky throughout the flight, looking for enemy planes. Christman told Brown there was a fifty-fifty chance they would encounter them, but the flight proceeded unmolested. The trip was rough as the plane flew through rainstorms. As usual, Brown became airsick, then seasick, as the plane landed on rough water in the Darwin, Australia, harbor. A Navy launch ferried Brown to the U.S.S. *Langley*, and a few hours later the shore patrol took him to air headquarters. With few amenities, hut-like houses, and flat land with constant wind, Darwin seemed like the end of the world. The flyers said he could hitch a ride to Sydney on a bomber the following morning. In the barracks' recreation room, they provided him with a spot on the floor with about three dozen flyers to sleep. But before he did, he interviewed six around a table under a hanging light bulb. They related stories about their encounters with Japanese fighters, but they said he really needed to interview twenty-eight-year-old Texas Lieutenant Hewitt Wheless about his extraordinary engagement, which he did.[35] During the interview, he learned about Wheless' mission. After losing two of his plane's engines during a bombing run over Luzon, Wheless had nursed his Flying Fortress—with 1,200 bullet holes in it—back to base despite being hounded by Zeroes, losing most of his crew, and crash-landing. Brown had a great story, and in May, *Life* published it.[36]

The following morning, Brown was a passenger—along with nine crewmembers—in a B-18 that took off at 7:40 a.m. on a "milk run" across Australia. The pilot seated Brown in the glass-enclosed nose so he had a great view. After stopping at multiple towns over two days, the plane landed in Brisbane. From there, on Sunday, February 8, Brown caught an Australian Airlines flight that took him the four remaining hours into Sydney. On Monday, Brown learned Japanese troops had crossed the Straits of Johore and landed on Singapore Island Saturday night. Meanwhile, he arranged with the Australian Department of Information's Richard Boyer to broadcast. Brown said he hoped Boyer would not kick him out of Australia before he made some broadcasts. "Oh, no, you will be very welcome here. We are just as regretful of what happened in Singapore as you are."[37]

Regrettably, the assurance was premature. He was prepared to make his first broadcast on February 11. But, upon reading the script, which included comments that Singapore would fall to the Japanese within one to three days due in part to British incompetence, a censor named Wilson, called Brown's script "destructive." Brown argued that the Sydney newspapers were publishing similarly critical comments, but Wilson remained unmoved. The argument lasted for five hours, and included a phone discussion with chief censor E.G. Bonney in Canberra. Ultimately, Brown convinced them that only minor script changes were necessary. CBS listeners heard Brown at 6:51 p.m., New York time. He intoned: "The picture in the Pacific is very far from optimistic.

6. Out of the Sea but into Hot Water 95

At no point are the Japanese being held by the Allied forces." He concluded that "the tragic story of Singapore is not all one of Japanese numerical superiority.... The Japanese are at Singapore also because of what the British authorities failed to foresee, prepare for and meet at the crucial moment."[38]

Two days later, Brown did his first broadcast concerning Australia. He said the population was alarmed by the pending fall of Singapore, and that the Japanese could target Australia next. In concluding, Brown commented, "Australia is at one of those points in history that comes once to every country—to be great or to be mediocre. It remains to be seen whether it will measure up to the role of greatness reserved for it and the Unites States in the Southwest Pacific." Afterward, New York and London newspapers reprinted his scripts, along with supportive editorials in several. One example appeared in the *New York Post*: "Australia is to be congratulated on allowing Mr. Brown to broadcast the truth. His broadcasts are a great service to the Allied cause." Nonetheless, he feared that the long arm of Whitehall would extend to Australia and curtail further broadcasts, but he was hopeful the Australians would not capitulate.[39]

To his surprise, Brown did not hear from London, but once again White was troubled by his comments. He cabled that he was concerned about Brown's bluntness regarding Australia: "SOMEWHAT AFRAID YOU UNWITTINGLY TAKING CRUSADING ATTITUDE YOUR BROADCASTS.... FEEL IN VIEW SINGAPORE BAN GENERAL PUBLIC WILL FEEL YOU ARE PAYING OFF OLD DEBTS." White cautioned Brown to exercise restraint "REGARDING FAULTFINDING EXCEPT WHERE IT IS NECESSARY." He told Brown it was easy to criticize military leaders anywhere at that time, but if he did not restrain himself it would "EVENTUALLY DETRACT YOUR WORTH AND PLACE IN PUBLIC CONFIDENCE." Once again, White had felt obligated to caution Brown about anti–British crusading. Part of the reason was that several New York newspapers had printed Brown's newscasts word-for-word under headlines such as "Tragic Singapore Fiasco," "Australia Takes up Critic of Britain," and "Bungling Lost Singapore."[40] In a response, Brown thanked White and assured him he would tone down the rhetoric. "HEARTILY AGREE OVERDOES HARSH CRITICISM UNWISE AND NOW IS MOMENT TO PROFIT BY EXPERIENCE. PLANNING TO DO CONSTRUCTIVE SUNDAY BROADCAST."[41] He was true to his word. On Sunday, he announced, "An honest report on what preceded the war against Singapore, how it was fought and how the Japanese got there, must contain recriminations. But recriminations will not win this war. Once the mistakes are known, fault-finding deters the job of getting on to victory." Yet, he could not help but mix conciliatory comments with some chastisement: "That is one of the great lessons of Singapore—that suppression of a reasonable account of the progress of the war provides every facility to the Fifth Columnists to destroy confidence."[42]

Chapple's notes arrived, and between broadcasts Brown went to work chronicling the submariner's exploits. "Take 'er Down" appeared in *Collier's* in mid–May. It was a morale-building story that Americans needed to read after five months of negative Allied news from around the world. Chapple was an archetypal, humble, young American from Montana. He had been skipper of a submarine that had sunk a Japanese transport—one of the first Japanese ships the U.S. sunk in the war. In an attempt to exact revenge, the Japanese sent destroyers after the submarine. Chapple settled the submarine to the bottom of the harbor in fifty feet of water, where the crew sweated for thirteen hours while the Japanese launched dozens of depth charges in the area where the submarine was submerged. After nightfall, Chapple navigated the sub out of the harbor, over razor-sharp reefs, past more Japanese warships, and into the open sea. The War Department awarded him the Navy Cross, and Brown wrote, "It's proud they are out in Billings." It was an exceptional accomplishment, but according to Brown, "you'd never think, though, from reading Moon Chapple's diary, that he did anything extraordinary." In the 1950s, the writers of the TV series, *The Silent Service*, acknowledged using Brown's story as the foundational concept for their pilot script.[43]

On Sunday, February 15, Singapore fell to Japanese forces. Australian journalist Phillip Knightley told readers that a disorganized British Army with ample munitions had "surrendered to a Japanese force barely one-third its strength and down to its last hundred rounds of ammunition per man." He added that "[British] correspondents must accept some of the blame for the shock that the fall of Singapore caused" because, unlike Brown, they had lied about the charade the British military and politicians had foisted on the public.[44] When Brown heard the news, he said, "It felt as though I had lost my best friend." The Japanese took more than 130,000 Allied prisoners—the largest military incarceration in the British Empire's history. American journalist John Gunther called the fall of Singapore "a disaster to the cause of the United Nations at least as great as the fall of France."[45] On February 17, Brown broadcast, "The Australians ... love action. They have a great fondness for energetic sports, and Britain's way of fighting the war has been too static." He said Australians were traumatized by Singapore's demise because the Japanese made up to 15,000 Australians prisoners of war. As a "subject people," they had given loyalty, workers and materiel to Great Britain, but Australians felt they had received little in return.[46]

On February 19, Japanese planes dropped bombs on Australian soil for the first time, at Darwin. They sunk ships, destroyed aircraft, and strafed the military base, killing approximately 250 American servicemen and Australian civilians. The incident stunned Australians because up until then they had felt they were safe from attack. They were surprised the Japanese were moving so far so fast. An enemy had never attacked Australia, but it became a foregone conclusion that the Japanese would soon seize control of Java, with Australia next. That same day Brown received a cable from White that informed him that the Overseas Press Club had named him their 1941 recipient of their Best Radio Reporting award.[47] White said he needed to write an acceptance speech, which he could broadcast via shortwave to the Press Club at the Waldorf-Astoria in New York the following evening. It was only a closed-circuit speech, but when he went to the studio to prepare, censor C.A. Rorke deleted segments of the script that he considered inappropriate. Brown's initial comments, in which he thanked the Press Club, and said he was accepting the award, not for himself, but on behalf of the "entire corps of American radio correspondents.... They have done and are doing their utmost to keep the American people informed," seemed harmless. However, Rorke took his blue pencil to portions thereafter, in which Brown saluted his colleagues for overcoming "pressures and intimidations in most foreign countries in which they operate ... fighting and winning in the job of doing factual reporting for America." Brown said Americans' right to "know the facts is our guiding star in radio reporting this war." In another section of the report, Rorke deleted "To conceal from the people a reasonable report on what is going on makes freedom of speech something more dynamic than an academic phrase." Brown had concluded his remarks by saying, "The freedom to report that within the bounds of reasonable censorship is one of the greatest guarantees of victory."[48]

Rorke's censorship appalled Brown because his comments were solely for members of the Press Club. Brown called Bonney and told him the censorship made him suspicious of Rorke's motivation and that he was going to report the incident to Washington if it continued. Bonney asked Brown to read the script over the phone. After doing so, Bonney agreed the deletions were unwarranted and fired Rorke.[49] Meanwhile, Brown began making arrangements to return to the U.S. In his diary he wrote, "I have not been feeling well.... By night, I was so tired and my nerves are so ragged that I can hardly see straight.... I have difficulty sleeping, and I can't relax.... I feel on the verge of collapse, and not able to do much about it."[50] Brown was suffering from what today is called "post-traumatic stress disorder." On the last day of February, he cabled White, asking if he could leave Australia, and White responded that he could.

In a broadcast that same day, he discussed the preparations Australians were making for war: "The eyes of every Australian are turned toward the United States.... [And] the affection of the people here for America has reached the greatest warmth." During the weeks he was in Australia, Brown spent time studying the lifestyle of the indigenous people. He observed: "[They] are easy people to like. They are eager fighters and have the courage to die." Months later, and back in the U.S., he wrote more concerning the

Australians in an article for *Life*. At the time, Americans knew relatively little about Australia, nearly 10,000 miles away. But as the U.S. sent troops and equipment there to fight Japanese incursions in that part of the world, American interest in Australia intensified. Brown told *Life* readers that he felt he understood the Australian character after seeing their soldiers in action in Libya, Malaya and Java, and living in their homeland for four weeks. He wrote that Australians "did not like to rush, liked to bet on horse races, and liked to drink." He said one could track Australian soldiers in Egypt by following the trail of beer bottles left behind in the sand. If someone pressed an Australian to move too fast, he would respond: "What's the hurry? The day's a pup." He also found military decorum more informal than that of either British or U.S. soldiers. Although Australians generally disliked foreigners, they showed an affinity for Americans and their way of life. He judged that Australia was patterning itself more after America than its mother country. Australia represented, he thought, the antipathy of England's "stodginess." He perceived the vision of the country "down under" as "dynamic," like America, and anything but boring, like England. He found Australian criticism of England common on the street and in the newspapers. Brown said he liked Australians because of their forthrightness, their gratitude for American assistance, and their ability to enjoy life. On the other hand, he characterized them as "laid back." He did not believe they took the Japanese threat seriously enough, and that the nation was unprepared to defend against invasion. He thought Australia's leadership was nearly as inept as that of the British in Singapore.

Although there was a lot in Brown's article that was complimentary, many Australians did not appreciate the criticisms, especially when he implied that relations between England and Australia were problematic. The reaction substantiated another comment Brown had penned regarding Australians: "He resents criticism of his country by an outsider."[51] An editorial in *The [Brisbane] Sunday Mail* was representative of the ire Brown roused. The editor said Brown had not been in the country long enough to make such assertions. He argued that relations among America, England and Australia "had never been more willing." The editor said readers should consider the source of the comments: "Brown's article caused no surprise in journalistic circles here, as his comments have been similarly unhelpful in every country he has visited."[52]

Fortunately, Brown was safely back in the U.S. before his article stimulated Australian indignation. On March 6, Brown boarded the Australian freighter *Moormacstar* to sail back to the U.S. The ship crossed the Pacific unescorted and made it safely to San Francisco in twenty-three days. During the voyage, he speculated about what would be next. His overseas' experiences had convinced him that it was his job not only to report the news, but to analyze and interpret its meaning, regardless of the consequences. Radio had transformed him into a respected celebrity correspondent; he was armed with self-assurance. But he wondered how he would pick up the pieces of his life back in the States after being away so long. He was unsure how he would fit in, or if he would, at CBS: "In many ways my relations with them [CBS bosses] have been strange and I am much puzzled by my status."[53]

It was the end of a long, tough journey in which Brown had learned much about war, radio, and dealing with the differing views of friends and foes regarding proper reporting. He was ecstatic to be getting home: "My trip around the world took four years, five months, twenty-five days and nineteen hours." He had broadcast well over 200 stories. He admired the soldiers and civilians in the nations at war from which he had reported. He wrote, "Patriots in the occupied countries are fighting for us. Stealth is their lot, murder their duty and death their fate. But they are the ones who want no finer epitaph than this: He died for freedom."[54] Brown was also a freedom fighter—for freedom of the press. He had left America an unknown, inexperienced journalist. He was returning, armed with confidence that he could handle any assignment. He was ready to begin a new phase of his career. Unfortunately, he did not leave trouble behind in the South Pacific.

♦♦ 7 ♦♦

Welcome Home to Accolades and Controversy

When the *Moormacstar* docked in San Francisco, Martha met Cecil. He was so excited to be home that he dropped to his knees and kissed the earth. She was thrilled to have him back in the States but shocked to see his appearance. "He looked so gaunt.... I hardly recognized him." His lined face and emaciated body were testaments to the hard miles and stresses he had undergone. He would take many more trips abroad during his career, but never again would he be away so long, nor would the journeys be as hard on him—Martha made sure of that.[1]

What would his next assignment with CBS be? He did not know, and neither it seemed initially did White. After Brown regained his health, would he return to foreign correspondence? In an interview a few days after his return, he told a New York reporter he was looking forward to going abroad again.[2] The man who had left the U.S. in 1937 as an unknown freelance journalist was now eminently familiar to the American public. He may have been *persona non grata* in Singapore, but in the U.S. he was well known and respected. MGM Newsreel reporter Adelaide Hawley said the names of American journalists like Brown had become "household words." In particular, "those whose dramatic accounts of the war come into our homes at the twist of a radio dial are the most celebrated of them all. Foreign correspondents are the celebrities of modern times."[3] This was especially true of the CBS team: "[They were] the hottest commodities in journalism—wordsmiths inventing a new medium.... The Murrow Boys weren't reporters as much as seers, urbane commentators who dined with prime ministers one day—and parachuted out of planes the next," wrote Timothy Gay.[4] Americans felt a special kinship with broadcasters because hearing their voices in their living rooms made them seem "as familiar as one's neighbors."[5] But for the correspondents, this was new ground, and they were not prepared to handle the sudden fame.

"In a time when public perceptions were shaped by the written and spoken word, war correspondents were often as influential as politicians and as celebrated as movie stars," according to scholar Hynes.[6] Douglas said Brown, like the other Murrow Boys, found themselves "hounded by autograph seekers, reporters, and photographers, all pumped up by CBS press agents' tales of hair-raising adventures and brushes with death ... that made him [them] sound like Superman" when they returned to New York. The experience was heady stuff for a formerly unknown wire service reporter like Brown.[7] Of course, what was good for his image was also good for CBS's prestige. The *New York Times* added to his aura when it named him to its "1942 Radio Spring Honors List." The *Times'* announcements said Brown's reporting of the *Repulse* sinking "will take its place in Radio's Hall of Fame: a dramatic, vivid, factual piece of work. Even more important, one suspects, was his insistence of telling the truth as he saw it about the Malayan campaign."[8]

The intent of CBS's war coverage was not simply to keep the public informed, but to increase the network's audience, which would result in attracting more advertising. On an average day during the war, listeners tuned in to CBS news four-and-one-half hours to hear their favorite foreign correspondents report. The Sinclair Oil Company—first sponsor of the *Roundup*—paid each reporter a seventy-five-dollar bonus every time he was on the air. Murrow cooperated—if unintentionally—in building the image of his team as "daredevil[s] with nerves of steel" who defied danger to get their stories.[9] He had set the standard by reporting the London Blitz in 1940 as German bombs fell and buildings collapsed around him. He later flew more than two-dozen B-17 missions over Europe. In August 1943, Sevaried bailed out of a stricken C-46 transport on a mission over the Himalayan Mountains, and hiked 100 miles to escape headhunters and the Japanese. Richard Hottelet and Charles Collingwood later risked their lives to cover the D-Day invasion. "Physical courage was of utmost importance [to Murrow] ... who expected it of his newsmen and praised it on the air," noted Douglas. CBS promoted the team as "tough, competitive individuals who did what it took to get the story.... [They were] defiant, too, taking on censors, border guards, [and] military police." It had not been part of the job description when Brown had applied to become a correspondent, but he had fulfilled all these qualities. Douglas called CBS PR "ruthlessly efficient" at promoting its radio correspondents as heroes.[10]

During a press conference after arriving in New York, Brown described the greater challenge of being a radio reporter as opposed to reporting for INS. The radio correspondent abroad has a tougher job, he claimed. "In both Rome and Singapore the official view was that the power of the spoken word was so much greater than that of the printed word that a radio correspondent could not be allowed the same 'freedom' as a newspaper man." When questioned about censorship, he replied, "If you're asking people to die, and they have the courage to die, they have the right to know why they are dying." He said that had not been the case because the British and Italians had suppressed his stories.[11] Concerning the occasions when his life had been threatened, Brown claimed he did not consider being a foreign correspondent such a dangerous job: "As far as getting bumped off is concerned, you can get bumped off here in New York just as easy."[12] He added that as soon as he recovered, he hoped CBS would again send him abroad.[13] Brown reported to the draft board within a few days, but he received a 4-F classification, apparently because of his emaciated condition, the fact he was taking medication for typhus and typhoid, and because of the aftereffects of hernia surgery (post-operative hernias were a common reason for 4-F classifications).

Brown was an easy subject for CBS to promote. Writing about him upon his return, the *Washington Post's* Isaac Stone said that for Brown "reporting is not a profession, but a vocation." The correspondent, he said, did more than merely transmit news; he was a "crusader for truth." It was the first time someone had employed the phrase to describe Brown, and it stuck, often being employed thereafter on posters and in advertisements for his speaking engagements. Stone added that Brown "is avidly eager to be everywhere, to see and to hear all, and report the truth as he sees it. These instincts have been fortified by indomitable courage, an adventurous spirit, an unquenchable curiosity and a capacity for hard work."[14] CBS scheduled a cross-country speaking tour for him and, of course, he had a book to write. He and Martha bought a penthouse apartment in a co-op complex at 25 West 54th Street, just north of the Museum of Modern Art. The Browns paid $77,000 for the apartment, which occupied the top two floors of the building; it served as their home for much of the next twenty years.[15]

On April 13, Cecil began a thirty-eight city speaking tour, during which he spoke on "The War in the Pacific." The circuit began in New Jersey, worked its way through the South, then the Midwest and ended along the West Coast. In Spartanburg, South Carolina, the *Herald-Journal* reported that as soon as word got out that Brown would be lecturing "every available date on his schedule had been filled." It added, "Bookings for Brown's lecturers have set a record in the annals of the lecture business." An *Ohio Jewish Chronicle* story billed him as the "ace Far Eastern correspondent and the only top-flight correspondent to return to America from that part of the world since our entry into the war."[16] CBS promotional advertisements said Brown had experienced so many narrow escapes that his friends sometimes referred to him as "the indestructible Mr. Brown," and declared, "He has as many lives as a cat."[17] On April 28, he spoke in Richmond, Virginia. There, he criticized news censorship, arguing that it was the duty of every correspondent to report as much as he could about the situation he had witnessed as long as it did not compromise military security. The next night, in Williamsburg, he spoke at the College of William and Mary. The college newspaper described him as "tall, slow-spoken and looking rather thin after his harrowing experiences." He told a reporter that he was having trouble accustoming himself to "the plentifulness of food in America" after having had to deal with the lack of it in the places where he had served.[18] It was not the first time since his return that the subject of food had come up during an interview. When he first arrived in New York, reporters had asked him what he had missed most while overseas, and he replied "popcorn." He said he often thought of peanut butter sandwiches and milkshakes, too. "I didn't drink a glass of milk during the four years I was away. I never wanted to take a chance with it [being contaminated]."[19]

In Ohio, he warned an audience that the threat of the war was much closer at hand than they imagined. "We are in the biggest crisis of our national history. The next three months will decide the war," and that thousands of American boys would have to die in combat. He said it was difficult for most Americans to appreciate the severity of the situation because they were isolated from the risks, and that the only way to win the war was for all Americans to sacrifice and to support the United Nations. "Nothing else matters.... Politics, class struggle, and everything else interfering with the one supreme purpose is OUT [his emphasis] for the duration."[20] The tour represented the first significant public speaking Brown had done since college, but he was a hit with audiences. Consequently, speaking on news coverage of foreign affairs became an avocation that he practiced for most of the next thirty years. Commenting on the popularity of his speeches, Martha said, "The crowds were thrilled on the tour because he was good at speaking, and he gave them lots of inside information that they didn't know."[21] Yet the public did not appreciate some of his frank comments.

In Indianapolis, Brown aroused Hoosier anger when he accused members of the audience of being "apathetic and unconcerned" about the war. He said, "Out here in Indiana residents are betting ... that the war will be over by Christmas—and they mean this Christmas, not Christmas, 1946." He chastised them for disputing the federal call for gasoline rationing. He said they were not making the sacrifices he had observed in other states, and they were suffering from "the existence of hang-over propaganda from the non-interventionists." He based his conclusions on discussions with local residents and newspaper articles he read. Reporters printed his comments and inflamed rebuttals resulted. Editors countered that Indiana was leading the nation in the sale of war bonds, and that the state's percentage of armed forces volunteers was among the highest nationally. Eugene Pulliam, chairman of Indiana's war bond drive, angrily responded: "I don't know to whom Mr. Brown could have been talking here unless he was talking to himself in his room." Brown offered a partial apology after returning to New York, but the offended Indianans were not appeased. It was a stateside-episode that was reminiscent of the backlash Brown had received in Singapore when he criticized British policies.[22] Yet, at the same time he was alienating Hoosiers, he sought to rebuild the bridges he had burned in Australia. In August, Australian newspapers reported that Brown was designating all the proceeds from his lectures to the Australian War Relief Fund. In an article about Brown's donation, the editor of *The Charleville [Brisbane] Times* said he believed Brown's comments regarding Australia were actually placing his nation in a more favorable light: "The lecture tour should do much to help America understand Australia's needs and outlook."[23]

After completing the tour, Brown set about writing his book for Random House. Cerf was in a hurry to publish it because Random had barely weathered the Depression, and after December 7, 1941, Cerf and partner Donald Klopfer wondered, "If people who were preoccupied with the war, and deeply disturbed by the way it was going, would still read?" The answer came when they published several war-related books that became best sellers,[24] including *Guadalcanal Diary* and *Thirty Seconds over Tokyo*. Brown's effort added to their list of "hits." In 1943, Cerf said that by then publishers were coming out with a number of books about war experiences because "they are giving the American public stark facts, without any sugar-coating, that have been overlooked sometimes by the press and barred by the radio. Their wide circulation is assurance that after this victory is won the country will know what it wants when the peace treaty is drawn up." Cerf added that books like Brown's were important because they "blast[ed] away at the blunders of brass-hat incompetents.... [And] record and interpret history at the moment of its making.'" He said they are "weapons in the War of Ideas" that were necessary to win the war.[25]

To write the book, Brown relied to a great extent on the diary he had kept overseas. As he wrote, Martha saw to it that he got enough food to regain some weight. She also kept him on a regimen of taking a variety of pills five times a day so he could overcome the aftereffects of the diseases he had contracted. He dove into the task with a passion, putting in eighteen hours day after day; he finished in six weeks. "I had to drag him from the typewriter so he'd get enough sleep," Martha complained.[26] Having signed the book contract while Cecil was still in Singapore, she was fully engrossed in the process. She reviewed every page, helping him piece together elements of the diary account with details from his memory. Numbering nearly 550 pages when finished, the book was largely a blow-by-blow, first-person account. The American public had heard his reports, now they would learn about the behind-the-scenes tribulations of one of the first radio correspondents as he provided personal insights into what he had experienced. He did not depict himself as heroic, but rather as a correspondent just doing his job. Others, such as Vincent Sheehan, in *Personal History*, had written about the challenges of being a foreign correspondent, enduring perilous travel, and living each day as if it might be their last, but Brown's account ascended to a new level, especially his meticulous descriptions of confronting censorship.

After the writing was finished, Cerf and Brown went back and forth for more than a month trying to agree on a title. They kicked around a number of ideas, including *Cecil Brown: Under Fire in the Far East*. But Cerf thought it lacked the pizzazz necessary to make it a prospective movie title. Brown disapproved of it because he did not feel it encompassed the entire experience, and he felt uncomfortable making his name the first element of the title. Finally, he came up with *Suez to Singapore* as encompassing the geographical elements of his reportorial journey. When he proposed it, Cerf said everyone at Random was "crazy about the title." To demonstrate his faith in the commercial possibilities of the book, Cerf sent Brown a check for $7,500, a significant amount of money in 1942 (he received additional royalty checks that amounted to $17,500 during the following year).[27]

At the time Random published it, the U.S. was at war, so censors in Washington had to examine *Suez's* contents to ensure it did not violate military restrictions. The Office of Censorship called for twenty-seven changes, objecting, in particular, to references to Allied troop size and technology. The rumors' clause of the Code of Wartime Practices also stated that publishers had to eliminate comments that might cause division among the United Nations. Saxe Commins, the book's editor, responded to the critique: "We have made every possible effort to comply with your suggestions. In the very few instances—two or three out of almost thirty—where we were not in complete accord, we have tried to give definite and concrete reasons for adhering to direct quotations which have been previously published elsewhere and have, therefore, passed censorship."[28] Cerf told Brown that *Suez* caused "the biggest headache" with U.S. censorship of any book Random published during the war. But the bigger headache occurred when Commins sent the manuscript to the United Kingdom's Washington ambassadorial delegation. When Lord Halifax read it, "he hit the ceiling and wanted to tear the book apart," according to Cerf. Fortunately, the censorship office pointed out that Random House had been cooperative in reworking questionable parts of the book, and that "all his [Brown's] statements were direct quotes made in the presence of witnesses. The British did not challenge its publication further."[29] Nevertheless, because of their reaction, Cerf and Brown agreed that Random would not market *Suez* in England or Australia.[30]

After clearing Washington's obstacles, Radom prepared to release *Suez to Singapore* in October 1942. Cerf vividly remembered the night of the twenty-fifth of that month when he and his wife Phyllis, along with Martha and Cecil, ate dinner at The Stork Club. Cerf said it felt like opening night for a Broadway play. The couples were waiting for the *New York Times* to hit the street late that evening with the first review. They had to walk from near 52nd Street and Fifth Avenue over to Third Avenue and 59th Street to find an open newsstand that late. Cerf said, "We bought the *Times* and it contained a rave review. I remember that the four of us danced down the street!"[31] In the review, Frank Adams wrote that Brown "was at his best when he narrates the history which he saw made." The most exciting part of the book, in Adams' estimation, was in the chapter where Brown recounted the sinking of the *Repulse* and the *Prince of Wales*. The book's overriding theme, in Adams' estimation, was "a reporter's account of the impact of war on people who were not ready for it."[32] Other reviews were equally positive. *Newsweek* called it "action reporting at its best" and recognized Brown for his willingness to admit when he was wrong.[33] The *Boston Globe* noted that Brown "is a big fellow indeed when it comes to appreciating human nobility under stress, and no weakling himself in a tight place."[34] The *Chicago Tribune's* William Shinnick said the book was "ruthless" in its authenticity and in helping readers understand that the war was witnessing "the passing of an era—the era of the superior white man ruling the yellow and brown races of the orient."[35]

Those who panned it said Brown devoted too much space to conflicts with censors. In *The Nation*, Keith Hutchison criticized Brown's first-person-singular writing style by penning a parody: "I took my typewriter to a British store to get the capital 'I' renewed on Saturday afternoon. They told me it couldn't be done till Monday, because people stopped work on Sundays. What abject, nauseating nonsense. Don't they know there's a war on?"[36] Others said Brown was merely repeating what other correspondents had written upon returning from warzones. *Foreign Affairs* magazine judged that "after reading this very forthright book the reader will conclude that the author must have inherited some of the characteristics of that other Brown [the abolitionist] known as 'God's Angry Man.'"[37] For some reviewers, however, the focus on censorship was the most insightful part. The *New York Herald Tribune's* Lewis Gannett wrote, "To every believer in a free radio ... this portion of the story is not only the most interesting, but also the most significant." Gannett added that some readers might decide from *Suez* that Brown was "anti-British ... [which] he might be," but his admiration for the courage of British soldiers overshadowed his disdain for "the arrogance, stupidity and blind self-assurance of higher officers."[38] With censorship also imposed upon U.S. media, some reviewers disparaged Brown's patriotism. The *Saturday Review of Literature's* Murray Harris thought Brown's criticism of the British could hurt the war effort. "As a promoter of that unity which is so essential to the

Allied cause, Cecil Brown ranks very low among his confreres of the press and radio.... He has abandoned first principles of reporting—the recording of facts—and has taken to think pieces."[39] Among his colleagues, Murrow commented in a letter to Sevareid that he thought *Suez* was "a mess." A bit of competitive spirit may have fueled the statement. Murrow had written a book himself in 1941 in which he described his experiences during the blitz. *This is London: Witnesses to War* had not been well received. In a letter to Brown, Sevareid wrote that he enjoyed *Suez*, but "Murrow, Shirer and I all went through the same kind of experience. We fought [censorship] constantly, but somehow none of us thought it was of world-shaking importance."[40] Regardless of whether the critiques of *Suez* were positive or negative, Brown thanked them for their review.[41] He also sought to rebut some of the criticism. During a speech to an Overseas Press Club luncheon, he asserted, "The citizens of this country are entitled to a reasonable and honest report of what is going on abroad, and while it is fresh." He said he could not understand a government that sent its sons off to die but then did not "trust its citizens to have the courage to hear a reasonable report."[42]

Klopfer, was a member of the Army Air Force during the war, stationed in England. But Cerf kept him informed about *Suez*. Klopfer read a rough draft, and told Cerf that Brown's one-sided views and "know-it-all" attitude marred it. Cerf responded, "I agree that all the worst sides of Brown's personality crop up in the manuscript and mar it to a considerable extent. We took out what we could in the editing, but you can't change a leopard's spots entirely." Nevertheless, he added, "I think it's going to be a wow of a best seller," and he was proven right. The public devoured the book at $3.50 per copy, and it remained on the *New York Times'* Best Seller list for more than a year. In early October, Cerf informed Klopfer that Random had printed 40,000 copies, and that the company had sold second-serial rights to newspapers in New York, Philadelphia, Boston, Detroit, Akron and Miami. He said the *Philadelphia Inquirer* had paid "the unbelievable sum of $1,200 for second serial rights and the *New York Post* $1,400."[43]

Brown continued to be in the public eye that spring when *Life* published his article, "How Japan Wages War," in May. It was the first feature in a mainstream American magazine that analyzed Japanese military tactics. Brown's research for it resulted from interviews with British officers and his own observations during forays into Malaya. He explained that the Japanese had been successful in the Pacific because "they haven't met really effective competition." He called the Japanese military structure simplistic but effective because Japanese soldiers were disciplined and had an "infinite capacity for detail," making them easy to command. In addition, "the Japanese are taught that it is a sacred honor to die ... [they have been] ordered never to surrender." He explained that the attacking Japanese soldier "is uncontrollable, shows no mercy and takes no prisoners," and his officers, he wrote, did not attempt to control their men's brutality. He added that the officers had armed their soldiers with a "mental vitamin" that made them ferocious, which was "contempt for the white man." For these reasons, he believed the Japanese would be difficult to defeat, and that the war could last seven to ten more years. He estimated that the conflict with the Nazis would last another four years.[44]

On April 11, Dr. Steadman Sanford, chancellor of the University System of Georgia, heightened Brown's broadcast status when he conferred upon him the second annual George Foster Peabody Award for Best News Reporting. Established one year earlier by the National Association of Broadcasters (NAB) and the University of Georgia's Grady School of Journalism, broadcasters consider the award the equivalent of the Pulitzer Prize for print journalists.[45] The citation noted that Brown's "dispatches from Cairo, Singapore and Australia were remarkable for their accuracy and courage. He was frequently in hot spots, and his eye-witness account of the sinking of the *Repulse* and the *Prince of Wales* was the most dramatic single story of the year. His news sense, his coolness under fire and his insistence—even under censorship—that the truth must get home sets an example for reporters everywhere."[46] CBS analyst Elmer Davis had won the inaugural Peabody, and, interestingly, Brown's award preceded by one year the one the committee awarded to Brown's mentor, Murrow.

With the accolade added to his growing reputation, Brown figured it was a good time to ask White for a salary increase. It seemed to Brown that he and White had an "amicable one [relationship] in which White treated him with respect and kindness."[47] So at the end of May he asked for a raise retroactive to January 1; Brown made the request by letter while on tour. White's response, however, was not the one Brown expected. It contained an irritated retort. White told Brown he believed his request was "preposterous" and outlined why he thought so. He told Brown that if had he remained overseas he would have increased his salary by $50 per week, which "would have been the highest single raise that has ever come out of this department." But Brown wanted to come home. He loved being a foreign correspondent, but his body had suffered from the rigors. White said CBS's expense of paying for Brown's transportation home had been substantial. He also noted that since Brown's return to the States that his services to CBS had been limited. He calculated that Brown had worked for the network only a month since the first of the year, although White recognized the network had been "getting value received because of the promotional work you have been doing on your lecture tour."

White reminded Brown that he had secured New York magazine article commitments on his behalf while Brown was in the Far East. The result had been several hundred dollars in income for Brown, but White had received no remuneration. "I actually peddled, as though I were an Armenian rug dealer, your various scripts and your talent, and this was done with no thought of personal gain on my behalf." White added, "I don't ask and never have asked anything for this activity on your behalf, except loyalty and friendship." White finished his curt letter by reminding Brown that salaries of $10,000 or more a year in the broadcast news business were uncommon. Yet he softened his denial when he added that he would increase Brown's salary to $7,500, with incremental raises taking him up to $10,000 within two years: "I don't know of any other sustaining salary arrangement in the department that is as generous."[48] Although neither man mentioned it, and contrary to Brown's public comments that he yearned to continue as a foreign correspondent, he and White had quietly agreed that he would remain Stateside for the foreseeable future. But it was not the last time Brown would ask for a raise. Although he and Martha lived comfortably and traveled widely, throughout his career he believed he was underpaid.

By the fall, with his first speaking tour concluded, his health restored, and weight regained, Brown was back on the airwaves. Although neither he nor White explained it, Brown's days as a member of the Murrow Boys had ended after three-and-one-half years. It is unclear why; perhaps it was because foreign correspondence had been so hard on his health, or perhaps White thought CBS could better profit from his notoriety by utilizing him Stateside. Whatever the reason, by the fall White had installed Brown as a daily newscaster that at the time was one of the higher CBS newscaster salaries of the time: $7,500. In one of his first broadcasts, in September, Brown saluted the Russian Army as it fought to repel the Germans: "Those incredible Russians actually are counter-attacking at Stalingrad. The city is burning, most buildings are wrecked, dive-bombers are over every hour, and the Germans are pouring in reinforcements of men and tanks. But the Russians are fighting for every house, and even fighting inside houses, from room to room." In another broadcast that month, with the war in the Pacific turning in favor of the Allies, Brown told listeners that Japan was beginning to have doubts about winning the war. "The Japanese are now showing more obvious evidence that they see the handwriting of defeat on the wall. Tokyo radio tonight is broadcasting dark predictions of the future, even suggesting that there's a possibility that Japan could be beaten. And that's quite an admission for a people who think that their victory is inevitable and predestined."[49]

As British forces made progress against the Germans in North Africa in December, he let it be known that he missed the action. "I wish I could have been there. I saw the way free men fight and die, and what I saw makes me proud to ... not only to be an American, but to be part of the United Nations. Watching the British fight, I've often thought they have more courage than any nation has a right to expect of its sons." In between war stories, Brown commented on what he thought was an unfortunate electoral victory for the Republican Party when it wrested eight U.S. Senate seats from the Democrats in the 1942 elections. "Some observers here say many people cast votes, not for [pro-isolationist] Republicans, but against Democrats. They pointed out the irony of that, too. In voting against some Democrats, voters returned to Washington some of the dunderheads, those men who before December 7, [1944], voted in a way that would have made America a pushover for the Axis."[50] The comments made his political allegiance apparent to Americans for the first time.

In December, when the Allies launched Operation Torch in North Africa, U.S. and British leaders made a series of compromises with the Vichy French to gain intelligence about Axis troop movements. The negotiations set off alarms with the war's most respected reporters. From London, Murrow asked, "Are we fighting the Nazis or climbing into bed with them?"[51] Scripps-Howard's Ernie Pyle—known more for esteeming the enlisted men—remarked, "We have left in office most of the small-fry officials put there by the Germans before we came.... Our fundamental policy still is one of soft-gloving snakes in our midst."[52] Brown joined them in criticizing the negotiations with those who had collaborated with the Nazis. He also took up the gauntlet of military censorship in that theater of the war. This time his comments targeted the U.S. military: "American censorship in North Africa ignored years of experience, our own as well as others. It was and is repressive. But it is incredible for anyone to think that censorship can go on hiding the truth. It may for a time but events catch up with censorship. And when they do catch up repercussions start."[53] On another occasion, Brown wrote that "the time is past when the military are a thing apart, immune to criticism, self-sealed from change, repeating the same mistakes time and again." George Weller, with whom Brown had fought against British censorship in Singapore, concurred: "The American and British peoples were fighting to be informed.... They could take it. It is through knowing the truth that the people discover their hidden will."[54]

Brown continued the attacks on U.S. censorship the following month when he criticized the Navy's reluctance to release information to the public: "It has created excessive and unnecessary worry among many people." He said it appeared the Navy wanted to hide combat news until it could balance its wins and losses. "That would indicate the Navy isn't yet sure that the American people can take it," he argued. In March, he reported that the AP "says the smoke of battle hides a situation," but, in his words, "it is more accurate to say, not smoke, but censorship conceals. Correspondents are restricted to reporting bare communication mutations which are remarkable for their brevity ... reports will not be issued until it's decided whether we are beating the Germans or getting beaten."⁵⁵ His outspokenness continued to result in recognition. In May 1943, Union College awarded him an Honorary Doctor of Letters degree. It was the first such degree the college had awarded a broadcaster. In conferring it, Union President Dixon Ryan Pox said the college chose Brown because "he is the outstanding exemplar of the ideals and the competence which should mark this new profession.... [And because he is] a passionate believer in the single principle of reporting the news 'exactly— as I [Brown] see[s] it.'"⁵⁶

The following month, and without forewarning, fate continued to smile upon Brown. In mid–June, Roosevelt appointed Davis director of the new Office of War Information (OWI), a friendly term for the government's "official propaganda agency." White named Brown to replace Davis in the prestigious prime time slot of 8:45–9:00 p.m., Monday–Friday nights. Originating from the network's Studio 9, White called it "the most prized spot" in the network radio schedule.⁵⁷ During the first ten minutes of the new *Cecil Brown and the News*, sponsored by Johns-Manville, he objectively presented stories. But during the last five minutes he voiced commentary, or "analysis," as White preferred to call it. It was one of the few times CBS allowed one of its newscasters that kind of editorial latitude.⁵⁸ The time slot had become nationwide appointment radio with Davis and it continued so with Brown in a way that is now unknown to American audiences. "Lots of people looked forward each evening to hearing news and opinions from a favorite commentator, a span of 15 minutes that put an exclamation point on the day," according to Irving Fang.⁵⁹ Brown repeated the fifteen-minute program at 11:00 p.m. The position carried with it a salary of $58,000 per year. It was one of the highest salaries for a broadcaster of that era.⁶⁰ Only Murrow, who would return to New York in 1945 at a salary of $125,000, would collect more than Brown as a CBS journalist during the 1940s.⁶¹

With the loss of the popular Davis, who at the time many considered America's "most esteemed journalist" Brown's naming was a move intended to capitalize on his popularity and to maintain the nightly audience of more than 12,000,000.⁶² At the time, CBS considered only two forms of experience sufficient for naming one of their reporters a commentator: Either he had reported from Washington, or he had served as a foreign correspondent. Mitchell Charnley noted that commentators, or "oracles," as he termed them, were paid more because they were "a select kind of performer." He "had to be a thoroughly competent newsman ... whose special distinction [from previous experience] gives their comment on current affairs public standing."⁶³ With his appointment, Brown had jumped ahead of dozens of CBS journalists who were more experienced, but Brown possessed the qualities that successful commentators had to demonstrate: "A presentable radio personality—not necessarily one characterized by a golden voice and broadcast glamour, but at least one that carries conviction and has the ring of authority. And it doesn't hurt if he has a touch of the crusader, and at least a modicum of showmanship," according to Charnley.[64] In Brown, CBS and Johns Manville were getting all those qualities. Roosevelt was so enamored with the influence of radio commentators that he once said, "I know what I'll do when I retire. I'll be one of those high-powered commentators."[65] Scholar William Frayer affirmed Roosevelt's opinion: "The voices we know best are the voices of the commentators, the men who untangle for us the tangle of an ever-growing web of news, to analyze and interpret. While their interpretations are frequently open to question, their influence upon the public mind is certainly great."[66] Louise Benjamin wrote that commentators were "one of the most colorful groups of journalists in history. They enlivened, enlarged, and personalized the public debate ... as they made radio a major force in the political perceptions of millions of listeners."[67]

Brown's appointment to prime-time newscaster further cemented the observation of a number of outsiders that he was the network's "white-headed boy among American foreign correspondents and news broadcasters."[68] With his experience abroad and knowledge of foreign affairs, the public respected his opinions on military and international matters. Even government leaders tuned in to his broadcasts. Six months after assuming the position, and while in Washington, Brown met Secretary of State Cordell Hull. When he entered his office, Hull got up from his desk, walked across the room and warmly greeted Brown with "I am very happy to see you and to see that you are all right. Mrs. Hull and I have heard your broadcasts with the greatest interest. We always listen to them."[69] Not surprisingly, the attention added to Brown's self-esteem. Conquering the various challenges he had faced, further emboldened him. He had always been aggressive, but now he had a highly visible radio forum that allowed him to be more influential. His self-assurance rubbed some of his colleagues the wrong way. Douglas Edwards described Brown as "headstrong." Others granted that Brown possessed the qualities of a good reporter, but those attributes also made him appear excessively confident, even obnoxious, in their eyes. Assistant CBS News Director Everett Holles considered Brown "contentious—a guy who never wanted to agree with anyone else and who always had a chip on his shoulder." Shirer pointedly said, "Of all the people who came up in those days, he [Brown] had the most swelled head of anybody."[70]

From Martha's perspective. her husband's success made some at CBS "jealous"[71] for what he had accomplished in such a short time, and for the accolades he was receiving. Although this was a wife's subjective view, there probably was some truth to it. Within the Murrow group, competition was conspicuous. It already had been apparent in Europe, as each man had lobbied Murrow to gain as much airtime as possible. Now, as they began returning

7. Welcome Home to Accolades and Controversy   113

to the States, they all were ready to capitalize on their notoriety. Hottelet said that in that regard Brown was not much different from the other members of the team: "We all had big egos. We all wanted to be the star.... There was great feeling about it, a sense of intoxication." From the time Murrow had hired Brown, he had largely been on his own, as had the other members of the team. Neither Murrow nor White exercised much supervision over them unless they crossed a line that White had drawn regarding personal viewpoints. The British had reprimanded Brown for crossing that line, but Sevareid had traversed it, too. After one or his broadcasts from France, White cabled Sevareid that he had gotten "furthest limbward," which in the vernacular meant that he had gone as far as any CBS correspondent dare venture with personal views before White would censure him. Sevareid said he learned the hard way that he "could not impose his opinions on listeners, [even] through choice of words or alteration of vocal tone. A CBS newsman must not display a tenth of the emotion that a broadcaster does when describing a prizefight," White had mandated.[72] Murrow had recommended each correspondent because of the quality of his work and then turned him loose to produce it. If they had failed to fulfill their duties, they would have heard from him, but the aggressive opposite was typically the case with the members.[73] Brown expected the same independence in New York that he had enjoyed overseas, but he was mistaken to assume that amount of freedom would remain available.

Years later, Brown acknowledged that he believed he was in "kind of a special category," and was embarrassed to say he was "one of the first prima donnas [in broadcast news]." As a result, he never felt he was truly "part of the team" at CBS, and that "some of the guys thought I should have gone back to the war instead of staying in New York."[74] Of course, Brown's listeners were unaware of the strained relationships. A month after taking over the evening newscast, *Billboard* magazine evaluated how Brown was doing. Keeping in mind that Davis had been extremely popular, the article noted that taking Davis' place was "sufficient to give any smooth-running mind an aggravated case of jitters. However, Brown holds his own quite nicely. Editing, selection of news and good straightforward delivery are much on the plus side."[75] If the position intimidated Brown, he did not let on. Soon after assuming the timeslot, he said, "Assignment to this news period on CBS is not altogether a new job for me. After all, it means reporting the news objectively and accurately, and that is the aim of every reporter worth his salt."[76] *Motion Picture Daily* selected Brown as one of the Top Radio Stars of 1942, along with Bing Crosby, Dinah Shore and Guy Lombardo.[77] That same year, a *New York World-Telegram* reader poll named Brown the best news broadcaster in America.[78]

What he did not seem to appreciate was that his appointment carried with it network expectations for self-censorship that were similar to those the British had imposed upon him overseas. He believed the First Amendment protected his candor. What he failed to respect was that—like the British—the U.S. government was vigilant about the impact news could have on American morale and military security. Tension between Washington and the networks had been mounting since before the U.S. entered the conflict as isolationist and interventionist sentiments clashed. Most broadcasters reacted with self-censorship out of fear that the government might become more restrictive if they did not limit programming deemed detrimental to the war effort.

In July 1939, the NAB had issued a statement regarding news that the networks and a majority of station executives ratified. It said, in part, "News ... shall not be colored by the opinions or desires of the station or network management, the editor or others engaged in its preparation, the person actually delivering it over the air, or, in the case of sponsored news broadcasts, the advertiser." Sol Taishoff, *Broadcasting* magazine's publisher, commented that if it kept the FCC from imposing regulation on radio, "it will be worth the price.... From where we sit, it's not solely a question of self-regulation. It amounts to self-sacrifice."[79] The Overseas Press Club (OPC) issued a statement that said the NAB's procedures gave "an intelligent commentator all the freedom he needs" in analyzing war news. The OPC acknowledged that the hardest task for journalists was to keep their emotions under control, and that every commentator had opinions and prejudices, but he should not "flaunt them." The document also addressed the unique precautions newscasters needed to take: "Every word must be weighed. Even the tone of one's voice must be watched. Microphone manner is just as important as microphone matter."[80]

But Washington was not satisfied that self-regulation alone was adequate. White House Press Secretary Stephen Early put broadcasters on notice when he warned that radio was a "rookie and had yet to prove its capacity for self-discipline without government control over its dissemination of news" and must behave as a "good child." To reinforce the administration's oversight, Roosevelt had FCC Chairman Lawrence Fly travel to New York to meet with network executives about news coverage parameters. Fly told the executives to avoid "horror, suspense and undue excitement" in reporting wartime events.[81] Then, in January 1942, the Office of Censorship took the government's strongest step yet concerning news content when it published its Code of Wartime Practices for American Broadcasters. The directive said radio needed to be concerned with broadcasts that "might provide information helpful to internal spies and saboteurs, or external military and naval commanders." The office called for "voluntary censorship of news, ad-lib talk and game shows, and foreign language programs. Proscribed from such programs were references to the weather, fortifications, war-related experiments, troop or materials movements, [and] casualty lists." In an effort to dispel fear among broadcasters that the office intended to take more extreme steps, the directive stated that "free speech will not suffer during this emergency period beyond the absolute precautions which are necessary to the protection of a culture which makes our radio the freest in the world."[82]

The Office of Censorship statement alerted Paley that stricter regulations could be forthcoming if the networks did not restrain themselves. He reacted by instructing Vice President of News Ed Klauber to ride close rein on CBS analysts. In consultation with his counterparts at Mutual and NBC, they generated a policy to guide news analysts for the duration of the war. The statement said analysts were to restrict themselves to "explaining and evaluating facts, rumor and propaganda." They were not to "express personal editorial judgment" or to attempt to "influence action or opinion of others."[83] The guidelines extended beyond script content to on-air demeanor. Klauber told his newscasters to "read calmly, without showing emotion or prejudice. The task of news analysts would be to help the listener understand, to weigh, and to judge, but not do the judging for him."[84]

It was not surprising that government and network leaders were cautious about what radio commentators said. "A strong case can be made for the thesis that American opinion made by the radio ... out-performed the sector of the printed word. There were more than 65,000,000 radio sets when the U.S. entered the war," noted James Martin.[85] Polls found that members of the audience said they trusted radio commentators more than newspaper columnists. Fang believes this was because "the personal presence of a warm and thoughtful voice speaking directly to us really mattered.... [And] it was comforting to listen to someone who thought the way you did, understood your problems and your feelings, got the inside scoop, and explained it so that it made sense."[86] But, for Paley, commentators represented a conflicted entity. They brought in the audience, which boosted profits, but they also created headaches, especially if they were liberal. Paley realized that public affairs programming was important, and could elevate the network's image, but simultaneously it constituted programming that was "dangerous.... [It would] be an area filled with controversy, dispute, pressure, anger and possibly even lawsuits." Thus, he proclaimed the network "must never have an editorial page."[87]

Publicly Murrow said he agreed with Paley's editorial standard. Nevertheless, he repeatedly evaded it. As early as 1938, he, along with all the members of his team, because they were witnesses to the Nazi blitzkrieg, employed language that called for American intervention in Europe; so did Davis at home. On the other hand, all of them were cautious in never directly calling for a U.S. declaration of war against Germany. For example, in a story nine months before Pearl Harbor, Murrow announced, "The idea of America being more help as a non-belligerent than as a fighting ally has been discarded even by those who advanced it originally. Maybe we should hear some frank, forthright talk across the Atlantic instead of rhetoric, but I doubt it." Murrow got away with such comments because he was 3,000 miles away, and he recognized that "subtle, guarded advocacy, coupled with an awareness that the quiet, informed, objective voice was often the best persuader."[88] American public opinion was gradually shifting in favor of preparing for the day when the nation would enter the war, and comments like Murrow's played a role in helping Americans overcome their isolationist disposition.[89] But such comments also raised red flags for those who believed news reporters should not advocate a course of action; they were to remain objective. Audience members, including congressional leaders, who opposed European intervention before December 1941, objected to a reporter who crossed that line. *Newsweek's* Raymond Moley (formerly Roosevelt's speech writer) said journalistic opinion made it difficult for listeners to differentiate between fact and fiction. He accused members of Murrow's team with "frequent snap judgments, sensational and unjustified deductions and, I regret to say, a good deal of raw propaganda favoring one side or the other in the European struggle."[90] Yet, on December 7, Pearl Harbor convinced the majority of Americans that staying out of the war was no longer an option.

Thus, with the U.S. at war, commentators no longer felt any compunction to maintain neutrality. Most of them became flag-waving militarists. Some radio observers thought the networks would end news commentary and analysis, and confine themselves to purely objective news, but they did not. On the other hand, network programming fell into three distinct categories: "vital information, the boosting of home-front morale, and the selling of the war itself."[91] Radio and the U.S. military formed an alliance. Commenting on network radio's close relationship with the war effort, NBC's Niles Trammell said, "Radio in the United States shouldered arms.... Every wartime effort found its support in radio.... American radio proved itself a mighty weapon in the nation's service."[92] Paley and Sarnoff both enlisted as communications' officers.

Americans were hungry for news from the various fronts, but once the U.S. was involved they wanted the analysis of knowledgeable commentators to help make sense of complicated developments. "The mass public is a lay public. It is inexpert in chemistry and physics, economics, politics, medicine, social welfare, psychology. It cannot understand the interrelations and impingements—*the meaning*—of news without more help than mere information gives it," Charnley said.[93] The International Press Institute found that among the Allied populations, "media consumers were bewildered by the 'deluge of unrelated and uninterrupted' spot news stories about places and

7. Welcome Home to Accolades and Controversy　　117

events of which they had no background knowledge."[94] That was a gap a radio commentator could fill. OPC representatives maintained that with the world embroiled in conflict the context in which news was reported had changed. The public needed journalistic help to comprehend world affairs. "There are deep meanings under the surface of events which the present-day correspondent must dig into and interpret." The OPC said it was no longer adequate for a correspondent to be courageous, and to be able simply to write a story: "He must be aware of the social movements, the ideologies, the economic forces operating around him. Millions of Americans today are frankly bewildered by events in Europe." Although the public read newspapers and listened to broadcasts, "most of them felt that these are not enough," added the OPC statement. "They want someone who has studied the situation more thoroughly to interpret the news."[95] Newspaper editors had recognized the need several years before radio, but broadcasters now needed to step up because of their increased influence. With the world becoming more complicated, depersonalized and threatening, and the role of the U.S. in it uncertain, it became imperative that newscasters interpret the day's events.

In terms of reporting the war, the networks attempted to respond to the need for comprehensive coverage. Before the war, less than 3 percent of the networks' daily schedule had been devoted to news, but by the second year of the war the percentage had grown to more than 25 percent. During the war, local editions dominated newspaper readership. Consequently, radio brought the nation a sort of "national newspaper" for the first time.[96] A 1939 Roper poll found that before the war 25 percent of Americans had said radio was their primary source for news. But by the end of 1942, "a survey of ninety-five localities showed that seventy-three percent of the respondents received most of their news about the war from radio, while only forty-nine percent listed newspapers as a major source for such information." Not only was radio's influence growing but so was its credibility. By the end of the war, "an overwhelming majority felt that radio news was more objective than newspapers and that radio commentators were preferable to newspaper columnists and editorialists."[97]

This meant that within the radio news hierarchy, the commentator was elevated to an esteemed position. Reporters could not editorialize; only the commentator was granted that privilege. The challenge for the commentator was that he had "to be able to instantly evaluate the news as it comes to him, to decide whether it needs explanatory material to show its meaning or its relationship to other news." Charnley added that commentary "is generally taken to be explanation of a news event in the light of the speaker's personal knowledge and judgment."[98] Brown's experience as a member of the Murrow team had prepared him for this expectation. Regardless of his personality quirks, White valued that Brown was intelligent and fearless, and analyzing war news required a person with integrity and spunk. Demand spawned increased excellence delivered by a new breed of "thinking" journalists. In the words of the OPC, "The intellectual level is unavoidably higher [among journalists] because the ignoramus and the fool are at a disadvantage in reporting."[99] In Gay's words, the Murrow Boys felt comfortable in the analytical role because they had become accustomed to being more than just the writers and readers of news that characterized most radio correspondents. "They dissected it, putting it into bold historical context, giving events a passion that print journalists—even A.J. Liebling and Homer Bigart at their best—were hard-pressed to match."[100] Gerald Nachman described the commentator as "a professor at large in a global classroom."[101] This is how Brown positioned himself.

Charnley outlined the traits a radio commentator had to display to be successful: He had to "take hold of the dial-twisters in his first sentence, or forever lose them." He had to "avoid sensationalizing, sentimentality, and over-emotionalism … [to] avoid becoming a special pleader … [and] ought to try to avoid confusing him/self with God."[102] Brown understood that he occupied a distinguished position, and he took it upon himself to begin providing advice on how the War Department should prosecute the war. In April 1943, he announced that the U.S. should "start a spring offensive to achieve a better understanding with Russia. Each day that is becoming more imperative. Russia shows many signs that she has very deep suspicions of the United States."[103] The following month, he argued: "For the future peace, it is essential that the German cities should be destroyed and there's a good chance the American and British Air Forces will achieve that before the end of the war."[104] As these script samples indicate, his commentaries were anything but restrained. Of course, by its very nature, many of a commentator's statements could arouse disapproval. And although Brown made it clear that the opinions he expressed were his own, and not the network's, White became increasingly concerned about the possibility of "guilt by association." Therefore, it did not take long for Brown's sometimes provocative content to catch up with him. Paley was familiar with this dangerous territory—he had been there before with Kaltenborn and Davis. In August, after occupying Davis' time slot for only two months, White decided that Brown had stepped over the line with his questioning of U.S. policy. The result would be a controversy among network executives and commentators that Brown unintentionally precipitated. The issue would call into question network news policy, and would cast Brown—unfairly or not—as a martyr for undefined broadcast press freedom.

❖ 8 ❖

A Cause Worth Quitting For

The most estimable word historians have employed to describe the Murrow boys is that they were "idealists." The term certainly described Cecil Brown. Because of the revealed power of radio journalism and how the public embraced it, Brown and others believed they could change the world. Like Joseph Pulitzer in the New Journalism era fifty years before, they thought radio news could play a role in addressing the plight of the underdog, and exposing the powerful when they abused their privileged position. Because of his Jewish heritage, Brown sympathized with the plight of society's downtrodden. He embraced the notion that by enlightening them he could help improve their situation. His experiences in Europe and the Far East had exposed him to how the politically and militarily powerful ignored or even created the issues that kept the disenfranchised in the dark. Uniquely, radio is a democratic medium—free to all in society who possess a receiver. The oral presentation of news could help the illiterate and the poor understand the world in a way that newspapers and magazines had barred them from doing. This set radio apart as a medium that could provide everyone—regardless of their status—with enlightenment and understanding.

Between the time Brown had headed overseas and when he returned to the States, the government and the public's perception of the importance of journalism had changed. The Murrow Boys were not alone in grasping the influence news could have. As the *New Republic* observed, "Back in 1935, foreign correspondents were merely tolerated by the great men of the world, but by 1940 they had become political powers capable of influencing their nations and helping to determine the outcome of the war."[1] While correspondents could be independent voices before the U.S. entered the war, now the expectation was that they support the Allied effort. This meant "that while they saw, they rarely reported war's casual brutality, its incompetence, its vainglorious seeking after honors," according to Bernstein and Lubertozzi.[2]

Censorship, official or self-imposed, dictated this. The president had charged OWI, under Davis, with making sure that network radio served as "the major propaganda arm" of the government.

But Murrow's team, especially Brown and Severeid, rejected such restraint. Brown utilized his airtime to discuss the meaning and effects of the war's activities. In April 1943, after word got out of the execution of two of the surviving aviators from the Doolittle raid over Tokyo, Brown described the effect on the home front: "A hot wave of burning hate for Japan is sweeping the United States. The execution ... is giving a new vigor to fighting the war. Some men in the street urged the extermination of the Japanese people from the face of the earth. The executions boomed the investment in war bonds."[3] The following month, concerning news from the African desert, Brown told his audience that although the Allies were claiming victories there, Americans needed to understand that winning the war was going to be difficult. "The Germans fought well.... They make us pay a heavy price for victories.... On the approaches to Tunis and Bizerte there are hundreds of dead British and American boys. In Tunisia, the Germans were beaten because they were outnumbered, outsmarted and outfought.... Those are the ingredients for victory, and we shall have to make use of them many times again."[4] Brown's experience as a foreign correspondent had demonstrated how a citizenry unprepared for war, because its leaders had hidden the truth from them, equaled disaster. He believed the same thing could happen in the U.S., and he was not the only one at CBS who held that view. Because of their news-gathering activities, the Murrow Boys became privy to a great deal of classified information. They saw America as fighting not just for military victory, but for freedom itself. That knowledge led to a dissatisfaction that although they could report on political and military decisions regarding prosecution of the war, they could not alter those decisions. It was a frustration, in the words of Bernstein and Lubertozzi, which "at times expressed itself in calls for a tougher war, a war fought for better-articulated ideals."[5]

None of the team members attempted to hide their views, but Murrow was more adept then some of them when expressing them. His restrained delivery avoided the "appearance of trying to shape the news," according to Barnouw, but there is no doubt that like Brown and the others his rhetoric had encouraged America to join the fight. Archibald MacLeish said as much in 1941 at a dinner honoring Murrow: "[You] destroy[ed] the belief that what happened 3,000 miles away was not really happening. You burned the city of London in our houses and we felt the flames that burned it. You laid the dead of London at our doors and we knew the dead were our dead—were all men's dead."[6] Murrow also read stories from British newspapers that made the points he could not make as his own. He was well aware of what he was doing. In a letter to his parents, he wrote, "I am preaching from a powerful pulpit.

Often I am wrong, but I am trying to talk as I would have talked were I a preacher. One need not wear a reversed collar to be honest."[7]

Murrow's group had to tread carefully. Paley would not tolerate editorializing, or what White labeled "foisting." An analyst who moved into that realm of communication, crossed an impermissible line, and Brown did not enjoy the same tolerance Murrow did in pushing against that line for a number of reasons.[8] He was not as adept in replicating the veiled advocacy Murrow practiced; he was within "arm's reach" in New York, unlike Murrow, he was not a personal Paley friend, and despite White's tolerance of Brown's missteps with the British, he had put White on alert with his lack of delicacy in reporting overseas.

During the summer of 1943, White allowed Brown to originate his broadcasts from affiliate stations and deliver speeches nationwide, while he was also completing an assignment for *Collier's*. For the latter, he traversed the nation, asking no less than 2,000 individuals twenty-two questions regarding the circumstances of the war. The responses were of a grassroots' quality, and not just achieved by, in his words, "sitting in an ivory air-conditioned tower in New York." He believed the undertaking would pay off in a number of ways, including content for a second book.[9] The underlying intention of the interviews was to determine if Americans really knew what they were fighting for. This related to the charge from *Collier's*, which was to ascertain if Americans grasped the meaning of the word "fascism." It was a legitimate question because the Roosevelt Administration had been using the word as a rallying cry to marshal public support for entrance into the war for nearly a decade in advertisements and public service announcements. Motivation for the campaign was that knowledge of the term would serve as a "psychological aid in prosecuting the war … by presenting some clear and unified picture of the nature of the enemy."[10] In his nightly broadcasts, the transcripts of which numerous newspapers reprinted, Brown told listeners what he was learning. Surprisingly, few respondents could define fascism with any specificity. The responses left Brown dismayed, and he arrived at the conclusion that Americans either were not taking the war seriously or did not understand the true reason why America was fighting.

A Kansas radio executive told Brown, "A fascist is usually a radical type of thinker such as a New Dealer." A female office worker responded, "Fascism means being ruled by a government and having part of your salary taken by the government. We just about have fascism in America now." Brown was alarmed that none of the individuals were prepared to describe how much effort or sacrifice they would expend to help win the war. A Dallas advertising man said the U.S. was fighting the war "so that I can have the privilege of calling the president whatever I like." Brown was disheartened that everywhere he went he found individuals who wanted something from the war for themselves, instead of asking what they could contribute to the effort. In Kansas, a man told him: "I wouldn't know a fascist if I saw one." In the Deep South, a black field worker commented: "The word doesn't make any impression on me. It doesn't strike any reaction whatever."[11] Although White did not upbraid Brown when he heard the negative recounting on the air, Brown's negative comments regarding Americans' lack of knowledge about fascism and commitment to the war served as the first of three strikes White complied against Brown. The pessimistic tenor of Brown's commentaries did not constitute the patriotic rhetoric Paley or federal officials wanted to hear.

At speaking engagements, Brown espoused his views on how he believed the media should report the news. A Louisville newspaper quoted him as saying he was "'a passionate believer in the single principle of reporting the news exactly as I see it.' Cecil Brown has consistently fought for the right to present the facts without the sugar-coating of propaganda."[12] During a speech in Syracuse, he helped raise money for war bonds, something he did on multiple occasions. His efforts drew the attention of First Lady Eleanor Roosevelt, who, in her March 30, 1943, column, "My Day," noted that tickets to Brown's speech were limited to those who bought bonds. The sponsors of the lecture said they raised $187,000 that night, including $102,000 donated for the speaker's autographed copies of *Suez to Singapore*. Mrs. Roosevelt concluded, "I think this is a pretty good record for a speaker in one evening."[13]

Brown's reaction to the lethargic attitude of Americans toward the war was predictable, given comments he had written in *Suez* about his experiences as a foreign correspondent. He related that he had seen too many innocent people killed. He said, "This is a war of every man, woman and child. If you wish to be a spectator, that is no longer your choice." He argued that the Axis powers threatened everyone, regardless of where they lived. He called the choice simple: "It is either freedom or slavery." He attempted to impress upon both his radio and speech audiences that "the soldier at the front is not any more a soldier than the man or woman working behind the front, ten miles in the rear or ten thousand miles. We all face death before victory comes to us."[14]

As he had repeatedly proven, Brown's speaking and reporting approach typically was "damn the torpedoes." He was incapable of moderating his comments, regardless of the potential fallout, even referring to himself as "headstrong." In an article about him in *Time*, a reporter characterized Brown as "combustible ... [an] honest but emotional reporter."[15] Unlike Murrow, Brown lacked the sensitivity to be subtle in his writing and speaking. His vocal style was fast-paced, often with an elevated pitch and unequivocating. The second strike against him occurred in early August 1943 when he encouraged radio listeners to see the film *Mission to Moscow*. Almost immediately, the Johns-Manville Company, his program's sponsor and one of CBS's largest advertisers, threatened to cancel its contract. Although the Russians were allies, the film had become controversial because of its pro–Stalinist communist agenda. Ironically, the OWI had commissioned Warner Brothers to produce the film because Roosevelt was seeking support for Stalin as his troops sought to repel Germany's invasion. Regardless, the rightwing press vigorously attacked the film, and the Left, which loathed Stalin because of his cultural purges, also attacked it.[16]

White did not immediately inform Brown—who was in Indianapolis—that Johns-Manville was threatening to cancel its sponsorship. But he was so displeased with Brown that he was auditioning other newscasters to take his place. (In this era, advertisers, more than network personnel, determined which talent would be in programming they sponsored.) Johns-Manville's first choice to succeed Brown was Trout. The advertising agency representative who interviewed Trout told him the company wanted to distance itself from Brown because he was "putting in little cracks from time to time that they felt were against their best interests as a corporation." But, notwithstanding his own reputation for objectivity, Johns-Manville did not select Trout. He believed company executives changed their mind after he refused to reveal his political allegiance.[17] Eventually, Johns-Manville accepted Bill Henry, a conservative columnist for the *Los Angeles Times*, who had also been covering Capitol Hill for CBS, to succeed Brown.

Already poised to replace Brown, White checked off the third strike against him on August 25 when Brown criticized the first Quebec Conference between Roosevelt and Churchill in a broadcast. Despite his admiration for the president, he was critical of what he considered Roosevelt's nebulous comments about the Allies' plans for prosecuting the war. He said the president "had missed a tremendous opportunity ... to give new surge and power to the people to fight the Axis and fascism." He went on to say that Americans were "tired of the vague words" that came out of the conference, and that they "are in need of words which present a vision of the future in understandable terms." He added that, as a result, Americans were becoming less willing to sacrifice and that "enthusiasm for this war is evaporating into thin air."[18] What Brown did not know, because the details of the conference were top secret, was that Roosevelt and Churchill had actually laid long-range plans for concluding the war. They discussed the buildup for D–Day, cutting off Japan's resources prior to an invasion of that nation, and agreed to share technology to develop an atomic bomb.[19] If Brown's comments were hard-hitting, they were no more so than those he had made before and they expressed sentiments that other columnists and radio commentators, including Sevareid and Murrow, had expressed. In fact, they were not afield from Murrow's philosophy regarding analysis. "Occasionally, in reporting this war, the reporter is obliged to express his personal opinion, his own evaluation of the mass of confusing and contradictory statements, communiqués, [and] speeches by statesmen."[20]

Nevertheless, two days after the broadcast, White sent Brown a memo in which he charged him with voicing, instead of "analysis ... nothing but an editorial." He called Brown's commentary, "Defeatist talk that would be of immense pleasure to [Nazi Propaganda Chief Joseph] Goebbels and his boys." White added that Brown's broadcasts of recent weeks, in which he had asserted that Americans were not supporting the war, were erroneous. He argued that U.S. factories were breaking munitions' production records, that the public was exceeding expectations in buying war bonds, and that battlefield eyewitness accounts confirmed that military morale was high. White added that regardless of Brown's forty-day national interview trip, it was impossible for him to "gather sufficient information about the temper and spirit of the American public" to arrive at the conclusions he was making. He ended by charging, "It illustrates to me what I previously suspected, that you undertook the tour of the country with preconceived notions and merely looked for the things which would support your theories." White accused Brown of violating CBS's standards of objectivity. He said Brown's comments were merely his opinions, and represented his attempt to say what he would do if he were president instead of Roosevelt: "The people did not elect Cecil Brown but did elect President Roosevelt." White concluded by saying that if Brown could not adhere to CBS policies regarding objective analysis: "I will be glad to consider affording you relief from your contract with us."[21]

The final sentence was an indication that the option existed for Brown to mend his fences with White. Nevertheless, Brown was so adamant about the rightness of his analysis, and that he could easily find employment elsewhere, that he was not about to alter his perspective. Elsewhere in White's memo, he had counseled Brown that his script would have been acceptable if he had framed his comments more delicately. "If you had written, 'I have just talked with Americans all over the country and from information I received in those interviews, I gathered the impression that Americans are losing interest in the war.'" That, White said, would have been good reporting, but because Brown offered no proof for his assertions, that made them editorializing.[22] But Brown was unwilling to accept White telling him how he should express his findings. He believed his statements were accurate, and that as an experienced journalist the network should trust his judgment in delivering them.

Instead of responding to White, Brown believed he had built enough capital with the network that he could communicate directly with Paley. Therefore, he wrote the chief executive about White's charges on September 2. While stating that he hoped to continue his personal relationship with Paley, he told him that in light of White's memo, he "hasten[ed] to accept his [White's] suggestion." He asked that his contract with CBS be cancelled no later than September 24, because it "undoubtedly [is] something which White and I would like to have over and done with." He informed Paley that he rejected White's "conclusions, his insinuations, and his version of the facts." Brown said he wrote him because White was far down on the corporate ladder and did not make network policy. Therefore, Brown wanted to "acquaint the head of the network with facts and circumstances of which he might not be aware and of consequences he should contemplate."[23] But if Brown thought Paley was going to encourage him to remain at CBS, he was mistaken. Paley responded in a succinct memo five days later that it was up to White to accept Brown's resignation, and that he was notifying White that Brown had requested that CBS accept it. While Paley assured Brown that he was "appreciative of the very fine work you have done for us over the years. You have made some valuable contributions to the American people," he did not urge Brown to reconsider.[24] Years later, Paley summed up his feelings about his clashes with a number of outspoken news analysts with which the network had parted company, when he said, "They were all alike. They claimed to be objective, but none of them really were. Had to watch them all. They all wanted to make personal comments. Had to fight with them all."[25]

Within a few days of the memo exchanges, and without any face-to-face discussion, Brown's tumultuous tenure with CBS came to a sudden end. But the parting represented only the first blow in a larger episode that would play out over several months. And it was not only sponsor influence and CBS policy that had influenced the decision. Paley was concerned that the White House would follow up on the warnings it had made concerning additional restrictions if broadcasters failed to patriotically support the war. For his part, Brown had proven in numerous ways that he was a patriot. He supported the war and hated the Axis powers, but he believed it was his duty as a journalist to reject blind acceptance of Washington's official line or agree with the popular perception that the public wholeheartedly understood and supported the war.

In reality, Brown's pessimistic view of Americans' commitment to the war was, although incomplete, largely accurate. His unscientific sample had correctly discovered that Americans were uninformed about the reasons for the nation's involvement in the war. Ironically, the fault for that situation lay largely with the Roosevelt Administration. Before 1941, the administration— with the acquiescence of the nation's newspapers and broadcasters—had cooperated in stifling debate regarding U.S. entrance into the war. What Brown had told the CBS audience about events in the Far East that would draw America into the war, Roosevelt had downplayed. The president "was convinced that controversy tended to undermine the public confidence necessary for him to conduct the nation's affairs as he deemed appropriate. In short ... the issue of war and peace was too important a subject for debate," said Richard Steele, who added that the president was more interested in raising morale than discussing issues. Steven Casey agreed. He argued that Roosevelt was slow to alert Americans to the emergency nature of war preparations. "Rather than initially seeking to manipulate and arouse a lethargic public by exaggerating the danger Germany represented, Roosevelt's information campaign was always highly cautious." Casey added that the "cozy, consensual atmosphere often portrayed in popular histories" as existing during the World War II, did not in fact exist.[26] Not all Americans understood what the war was about or unequivocally supported it. Liebling reached the same conclusions as Brown when he returned from Europe. "The apathy and ignorance of friends stunned him," wrote Gay. "Despite his best efforts, Liebling couldn't wake up America. Whether liberal, conservative, or agnostic, Americans deceived themselves into thinking that the spread of fascism was somebody else's problem."[27]

It seems that Brown's estimation of the American public's unpreparedness for war arose in part from his experience in Singapore. His jaded perspective emanated from his witness of the British being so unprepared and unwilling to acknowledge the Japanese threat. He was fearful the same thing could happen in the U.S. Although home-front calamity was avoided, historians who have studied World War II news coverage agree that Brown's findings were accurate. Robert Desmond said, "[There] was a softening of adverse aspects of the news, leading to a complacency about the war," and Fletcher Pratt concurred, "It was very nearly the worst reported war. Most Americans ... remained ignorant 'of the larger issues of the war, of the way it was fought, of what actually happened both on the home and the military fronts.'"[28]

While Brown was ready to move on from CBS, he could not have imagined that his actions would become a nationwide *cause celebre* among fellow commentators and newspaper journalists. They believed he had a First Amendment right to broadcast his views. The issue for them was free speech, and CBS's attempt to suppress it. The fallout from the disagreement quickly became, in the words of Alexander Kendrick, "a small civil war."[29] Based on Kaltenborn's own unhappy departure from CBS, as well as a number of other incidents involving network commentators, in 1941 he had helped found the Association of Radio News Analysts (ARNA). One of the primary reasons for formation of the organization was to explain the purpose of commentary and to defend its members when employers attempted to gag them.[30] Kaltenborn was aroused when White said he would stop all CBS reporters from expressing opinion. At the Waldorf Astoria on September 15, at a NAB luncheon, Kaltenborn told attendees that he had a "deep and passionate conviction that it is both my right and duty on proper occasions ... to tell listeners what is on my mind." He said "every news analyst 'worth his salt' showed editorial bias every time he selected or rejected which news to report, or by the mere matter of shading or emphasis [in his announcing]." He continued that every commentator worth listening to caused "some controversy even if the subject he discusses is not considered controversial." Kaltenborn acknowledged that no analyst should veer too far to the right or left politically in his opinions. Nonetheless, "it is altogether too easy for timid broadcasters to go too far in catering to the sensibilities of special interests of a squeamish or powerful minority."[31] White was seated across the table when the analyst made the comments, but when pressed for a response he said he was not prepared to make a statement. But newspapers widely reported Kaltenborn's comments, which made it necessary for White to respond soon thereafter.

He did so in a letter to Kaltenborn. White wrote that there was a difference between a news "analyst" and a news "commentator." He believed that an analyst "was a newsman who analyzed the news but promoted no view," but "a commentator was an opinion-pusher—[and] not wanted at CBS."[32] He argued that no analyst "should he be so privileged, could parade his personal opinions in the guise of analysis." He said he understood that it was impossible for newscasters to display complete objectivity, but it was not their job to "crusade ... harangue ... or attempt to sway public opinion." Rather, it was an analyst's job to "point out the facts of both sides, show contradictions with the known record. The analyst's function is to help the listener to understand, to weigh, and to judge, but not to do the judging for him." He argued that CBS's policies helped ensure, "in its broadest meaning, freedom of the air."[33] Kaltenborn reacted by marshaling a group of twenty-four commentators from the three networks who voted to support Brown. CBS's Shirer was the lone dissenter. On September 23, White further elucidated the CBS policy when he addressed an ARNA luncheon at New York's Hotel Algonquin. He told attendees that the network's schedule was open to partisan speakers on controversial issues where the battle of opinion could be waged. "This is most important because it eliminates the camouflaged propaganda that opinionated reporters could otherwise insinuate into a field which we think should remain simon-pure, honestly objective, and utterly non-editorial."[34]

Kaltenborn responded that it was ironic that this controversy was taking place less than two years after Roosevelt had outlined his Four Freedoms in the 1941 State of the Union address. The president had said everyone should be permitted to enjoy "freedom of speech and worship, freedom from want, and freedom from fear."[35] Yet, in Kaltenborn's eyes, a radio commentator could not enjoy the same freedoms as any U.S. citizen. He argued that no news analyst had ever developed a large and loyal following without expressing his opinions, and never would. Kaltenborn said it was impossible for an analyst to be completely objective; that the words he selected or discarded, the way he used his voice to emphasize copy, and "every exercise of his editorial judgment constitutes an expression of opinion." He added that the analyst was not worth listening to if he did not generate disagreement. "Controversy is the lifeline of democratic freedom. Democracy gains when men, all men, are permitted to speak what we feel, not what we ought to say," he concluded.[36]

From London, Murrow reacted in a letter to White in which he asked, "What happened?" but White did not respond with any specificity. Murrow was shocked that the man who had done a quality-reporting job wherever he had been was resigning. Over the cue channel, during conversations with CBS personnel, he kept asking for a fuller explanation, but he never received one. It was left to Shirer to do that, but he was not about to defend Brown. In a letter to Murrow, Shirer displayed his sardonic view when he speculated that Brown "may try to make plenty of trouble." As an analyst himself, he did not think the issue would change the way he did things. He told Murrow: "The whole question of whether a guy should be allowed to shoot off his personal prejudices about anything on the air still puzzles me.... I can't see that it has ever prevented gents like you and me from expressing ourselves about such things." He claimed that he could say about whatever he wanted, and that no one at CBS had looked at his scripts in months.[37] Murrow responded that "one of the many things I like about you is that you are puzzled and unsure about such important matters."[38]

Murrow, on the other hand, was concerned that CBS was allowing advertisers to determine what commentators could say. Program sponsorship by a single advertiser was a relationship that concerned Murrow because it allowed them to have *de facto* veto power over how journalists reported the news. Halberstam characterized the conflicted relationship in which U.S. broadcasting attempts to function as "curious.... It is the most powerful instrument in the world for merchandising soap, and it is potentially the most powerful instrument in the world for public service."[39] Regrettably, network executives have consistently prioritized the profits soap can generate instead of the light news can shed on issues and the actions of society's elites. Privately, Murrow believed the Brown affair raised serious concerns. In a letter to her family, his wife, Janet, made it clear that she and Ed had discussed it and found the situation alarming. She thought the confrontation "seemed very stupid of White and a very weak position for him to take.... It won't do broadcasting any good in the long run."[40] A few years later, Murrow became involved in his own dispute with management over news content in which, based on the appearance of obvious facts, he objected to management's insistence that he present both sides of a clearly unjust situation. He said he was "appalled ... by growing pressure to balance out viewpoints for the sake of an artificial fairness[; he] compared this with balancing the views of Jesus Christ with those of Judas Iscariot."[41]

For his part, Brown did not attempt to make trouble, as Shirer had predicted. He was uninterested in generating coverage of his side of the story until he believed White misrepresented his position. For several weeks, White was widely quoted in newspapers because he became the target of virtually every columnist who believed press freedom should extend to radio as well as newspapers. At each venue where he appeared, White defended the network's position. Speaking to a gathering of the AP's managing editors, White said the network had "recently got[ten] rid of the last one" of what he called "gossip spielers." CBS also placed full-page advertisements in the *Washington Post* and *New York Times*, which declared: "We will not choose men who will tell the public what they themselves think and what the public should think because without such a policy it is easy to see that a powerful and one-sided position on serious issues could be created for a small group of broadcasters.... [By doing so] freedom of speech on the radio would be menaced."[42] The network conducted an on-air discussion of the situation on September 25 on *The People's Platform*. Moderator Lyman Bryson asked White if Americans had the right to receive the "best possible kind of information?" White said all he insisted upon was the "elimination of camouflaged propaganda that opinionated reporters" might employ. He considered it appropriate for analysts to "bring the news into focus via special or common knowledge and background, but 'haranguing' was taboo." Representing the ARNA was NBC's John Vandercook, who contended that CBS was attempting to put itself in the position of determining what constituted "truth." This, he charged, was "an untenable position" because "CBS was taking on the high duty of deciding for the good of the people what the people shall hear." Vandercook added that he thought it should be up to the listener to "decide what he shall choose to hear." He contended that control of opinion should occur "at the point of outlet in radio not at the point of origin [or corporate control]."[43]

Billboard editorialized that the Brown-White dispute had elevated a controversy to the level of public debate that had been percolating within radio newsrooms for several years.[44] Winchell devoted his entire *New York Daily Mirror* column for several days to analyzing the disagreement. In one, he wrote, "Hey CBS! Has it struck you gents that a radio commercial is an opinion?" In another, "Aside from being a dangerous rule [banning commentary], it's a silly one. Any reporter worth a damn can outwit such a nonsensical rule in an hour. But that way lies vicious and irresponsible reporting. Radio has committed many sins, but its record on news has been swell.... If it reduces news reporting to the level of some executives, then it'll be time for the air to be purified."[45] The public generally could not understand why the disagreement was such a big deal. For a time, CBS appeared to "be a lone wolf surrounded by persons and things with greater fangs than it ever suspected," noted *Billboard*. It and other publications wrote that CBS was losing the public relations' battle by making "a mountain out of what might have remained a molehill." On the other hand, they rejected allowing Brown to "slide into the easy chair of martyrdom" because he was not innocent.[46] In the *New York Times*, John Hutchens offered: "A listener does not tune in CBS's ... Shirer ... Murrow [or] Quincy Howe ... only to hear a fact stated or to enjoy their rhetoric. Respecting their background and knowledge, he is interested, and rightly so, in their enlightened opinion." He said CBS was effectively eliminating the editorial page from radio, which, he added, "underrates the public's intelligence, [and] its ability to distinguish between competent and incompetent opinion."[47]

Billboard later invited a commentator from each of the four networks to comment on the controversy. Mutual's Sydney Mosely said censorship was not necessary during peacetime, but that the time called for special restrictions. He added that the best kind of censorship is "self-censorship. This is war.... Probably over 90 per cent of those on the air don't need to be reminded, [but] a few do." He said some commentators should be off the air because they were causing "confusion, disunity and mischief." Two NBC network commentators, however, offered less conservative perspectives. H.R. Bukhage said, "I expect to be able to give my listeners my opinions.... Such opinions ... will be my own ... and not those of any solicitous ax-grinder." Upton Close said, "The public wants opinion on the air and the more wishy-washy radio gets, the less it will be worth its time relatively, to the advertiser." CBS's Howe wrote, "I wish it [CBS] had laid the emphasis on the integrity rather than the neutrality of the analysts," but that CBS had never censored his scripts.[48]

Several columnists noted that the incident called for the networks to scrutinize thoroughly how they presented news. Newspapers had been offering editorial opinion for decades, and, as the new kid on the block, radio was different, but it should not be pandering to the government or advertisers. "Brown, it appears to us, has the best of this argument. When CBS hired Brown ... they must have been impressed with his personality and insight. Brown was thus encouraged to have strong confidence in his own judgment. It must have been a shock to him to learn that he was to be edited," noted the [*Newark, New Jersey*] *Star-Ledger*.[49] *Time's* editor argued that he found the case ironic because CBS news had never been "impartial nor without principles. Its accounts of the outbreak of the war were instinct with editorial views of the dangers of totalitarianism. If radio becomes guilty of making its commentators take sides—or pull their punches—in order to curry favor with advertisers, it will have much to account for."[50] Dorothy Thompson, who had been the first American woman to head a European news bureau, was the second most influential woman in America after Eleanor Roosevelt. In a *Time* article titled "Is Thinking Dangerous?" she wrote, "If CBS is not buying their [analysts'] capacities to think and to form opinions out of background, insight, clarity of thought, what in the world is it buying?" She added that if commentators were not allowed to express their views, then who should Americans look to for interpretation of daily events? "Only politicians, party machines, businessmen and their promotion experts? ... [Commentators] have no financial or political power or ambition. They can influence only through knowledge, reason and logic. In the end, the pubic, with the chance to listen to all of them, decides every issue. It is not nearly so easy to influence as Mr. White fears."[51] The *St. Louis Post-Dispatch* noted said it was ironic that the very same Brown had proven the value of voicing opinion in Singapore. In that situation, Brown's opinion, "the view of a skillful, alert, impartial observer—was tremendously important; and if it had been heeded the history of the Second World War might be different, and somewhat less bloody."[52]

Even the FCC's Fly, who had warned network executives to tread cautiously, disagreed with White. Fly had no issue with newscasters offering opinion as long as the networks labeled it as such. "It's strange to reach the conclusion that all Americans are to enjoy free speech except radio commentators, the very men who have presumably been chosen for their competence in the field." He said it did not make sense for radio analysts to quote the opinions of newspaper and magazine journalists but not offer their own thoughts.[53] If the radio industry did not allow editorializing, he added, it put it at a disadvantage as a news source. Fly said, "In lodging that power over the whole output of news analysis and opinion are we not well-nigh setting up both a censorship over the very company editorial policy which some have sought to avoid by curbing independent commentators?" He echoed Murrow's view when he added that "it might well be that there ought not to be any sponsorship of news or comment."[54] *Editor & Publisher's* Arthur Robb judged that radio could not "prosper ... [as] an intellectual eunuch.... If radio can hand out the news of the day only in terms that the listener cannot discern the viewpoint of the speaker, then radio cannot last in the business of purveying news. News and editorial cannot long be divorced."[55]

White countered that radio and newspaper editors could not treat commentary alike because the mediums were dissimilar. The issue was not about freedom of speech, he insisted, but about journalistic fairness. He said a finite number of channels made it "dangerous for a handful of commentators to become 'pulpiteers' for a cause." He declared that "the threat of such unbalanced power is inimical to a democratic and free radio and to democracy itself."[56] NYU Professor Charles Siepmann countered that the CBS policy represented an unrealistic ideal. He maintained that other CBS journalists had been doing exactly what White had charged Brown with: "Men like Murrow and Sevareid ... are too intelligent and socially responsible to forego an occasional stab at interpretation of events. They recognize how all but invisible is the line dividing 'objective' explanation from 'subjective' interpretation."[57]

Until September 22, CBS had attempted to position the situation as an in-house, personnel issue, with only the network's side of the controversy elucidated publicly. But on that date, Brown ended his silence. He was still a CBS employee, but was only a day away from leaving the network permanently. Brown said he was miffed that White had raised the issue of editorializing over his script because editor Henry Wefing had cleared Brown's copy on the broadcast in question. On the afternoon of the 22nd, Brown invited reporters to his apartment to tell his side of the story after reading White's statements in *PM*. He shared the content of letters he had sent to White and Paley. He told Paley: "It was not my desire to enter into a discussion over the acceptance of my resignation, especially since I am most appreciative of your very gracious letter to me. Yet, White's [inaccurate] remarks in ... this morning's *PM*, compel me to answer." In a letter to White, he disputed his statement that Brown's resignation "was in no manner connected with the present censorship row." He called that a "misstatement," and said he found it impossible to continue to work under White's policy, which he felt made him a "mere messenger boy" for his version of the truth. Brown added, "It is no part ... of my sense of duty to the American people as a reporter and analyzer of the news, to forsake my honesty, experience and judgment in order to become the propagandizer of your notion of what constitutes 'non-opinionated' news." Brown argued that what White had considered Brown's personal opinion in the newscast in question, "a thousand pages of notes and quotations from the American people themselves, from coast to coast, in all walks of life" had supported.[58]

The following night, Brown made his last CBS broadcast, but even that became controversial. The initial version of his script read: "This is my final broadcast over the CBS Network. I have resigned." But Paul Kesten, the new vice-president of news, did not like Brown's ending and told him to change it to "With this broadcast I end my series for Johns-Manville. This is also my final broadcast for CBS." However, upon seeing it, the J. Walter Thompson Advertising Agency representative objected to linking the company's name with Brown. Brown refused to change the lines again without Kesten's approval, but by then he had left the building. So another staffer contacted Paley by phone, and he approved yet another version. Though, by the time Paley's revision, scribbled on a sheet of paper, was rushed to the studio, it was too late. Brown was already on the air with the second version.[59] As far as some of Brown's colleagues were concerned, he could not depart quickly enough. Douglas Edwards said there was "no great weeping or wailing or gnashing of teeth ... [or] Gee! What a terrible thing to do to Cecil Brown." Trout said Brown's leaving resulted in "no loss at all to the CBS newsroom morale," while Everett Holles commented, "It couldn't have come too soon for me."[60]

8. A Cause Worth Quitting For

The public's view was somewhat different. The night after his broadcast an incident in a New York taxicab summed up how many listeners regarded Brown. Cecil and Martha were talking in the backseat about an expensive chair she had bought. Cecil chided her about spending money when he was losing his job. As they were about to exit the cab, Brown tried to hand the cabby the fare, but he responded, "That's alright, Mr. Brown. I won't take the money. I used to listen to you every night. I'm all for you."[61] As an ironic postscript to the dispute, in March 1945 the War Department issued an Orientation Fact Sheet to U.S. troops overseas. Its purpose was to ensure that soldiers could define fascism. The department instructed soldiers that Brown's discovery that many Americans did not know how to define the term should serve as a warning. "If we don't understand fascism and recognizing fascism when we see it, it might crop up again—under another label—and cause another war," the document warned.[62] White, meanwhile, said he could hardly wait for D–Day so breaking news would overshadow the Brown row. He continued to enforce editorial constraint as Murrow and his colleagues prepared to cover the European invasion. He issued a primer for them to follow as they reported the assault. "Keep an informative, unexcited demeanor at the microphone," he directed. "Give sources for all reports. Use care in your choice of words. Don't say 'German defenses were pulverized'; say 'German defenses were hard hit.'"[63]

Meanwhile, Brown moved on, confident that he would have little difficulty securing employment with another network. "I was hot stuff," he said. Mutual Broadcasting System did indeed hire him, but it took more than four months for that to happen. In the meantime, he busied himself writing articles and a second book, and speaking. Martha said he had no trouble filling his days: "Cecil even hates to stop to eat; he thinks it's a waste of time." He countered, "It breaks my train of thought. I'd just as soon Martha sent out for a couple of hamburgers."[64]

In December, *Good Housekeeping* published an article he had written. It was about the 20,000,000 women who had gone to work during the war. He wondered what would happen to them once the conflict ended. His research had come from his coast-to-coast trip. He wrote that no one in Washington seemed concerned about what women workers would do when the men came home. He said the women he interviewed were proud of the work they were doing: "[They] have found a new kind of life ... a 'thrill,' and a sense of creative achievement." He thought it would be difficult for them to return to mere homemaking because "you don't easily forget or forsake a sense of achievement." In addition, he found both men and women who thought the female employees needed to resume homemaking after the war. One woman said, "I don't think women look very lovely in slacks." A male Colorado judge commented, "This whole thing of womanpower has broken down American home life. There is chaos in the American home today, and the very roots of American existence are threatened." Brown concluded that politicians who failed to address the issue would do so at their own peril at the voting booth. Otherwise, he did not make any specific recommendations because "I am confident CBS women will decide when they want to put away their working clothes, and they won't put them away except on their own decision."[65]

He continued to speak to college and civic groups, and on behalf of the Red Cross and war bond drives. He addressed the meaning of war, U.S. chances, and warned against a negotiated peace, saying the enemy would "negotiate peace only to their benefit." He argued that the Axis nations had to be unconditionally defeated or the U.S. would be fighting them again in a few years. Typically, when he approached the dais after being introduced as a commentator, he said he preferred an introduction as "the man who resigned from CBS." Cerf sent him an advance for a second book, the content of which he planned to glean from the interviews he had conducted about the meaning of fascism. Brown set about organizing the comments he had received, the same ones that had gotten him in trouble on the air, into a volume that he hoped would wake America up to the dangers of taking the Axis threat too lightly.[66]

During an interview with columnist Elsa Maxwell a couple of months after his resignation, she asked him why he was willing to throw away a $58,000 a year job. Brown replied that it was about principle, not money. "If the air doesn't belong to the public, what does? Truth is not absolute." Maxwell wrote that Brown had "moved Independence Day up on the calendar from July 4 to September 25," and she wondered, "How did this mild-mannered man get that way?" She answered that it was "because Cecil Brown has certain definite convictions about truth, the war, and the freedom of the air waves." She added that he said, "Everyone has their prejudices. I admit I have mine. I'm prejudiced in favor of the little man ... the man who supports his family on little over a thousand a year. He's entitled to the truth as near as we can give it to him."[67] No one at the FCC or the networks responded to his question about the airwaves belonging to the public then, or the years since. Brown believed one of the ways to achieve the promise was to provide opposing points of view during newscasts, then allow the public to make up its mind about the truth. Although he did not employ the terminology, he was advocating for a radio "marketplace of ideas," the ideal that had guided the Founding Fathers when they made journalism the one profession mentioned in the Bill of Rights.

As for White, CBS fired him in 1946 because of alcoholism, but he resurrected his broadcasting career in California. In a twist of fate, he became a commentator at KFMB AM and TV in San Diego. In 1954, when Murrow exposed Wisconsin Senator Joseph McCarthy for his reckless anti-communist campaign on his *See It Now* program, *Newsweek* recalled that during the White-Brown episode such a program as Murrow's would have been impossible. White responded with a letter in which he wrote, "An eleven-year old quotation on the emasculation of commentators' opinion on radio or television has returned to haunt me. I have since changed my mind and have recanted publicly on several occasions." He said his nightly broadcast, in which he did exactly that for which he had chastised Brown "is proof that I no longer subscribe to that 1943 viewpoint." He added that at the time he also thought the "Soviet Russia was a valuable ally, that nuclear fission was impossible and that, after the war and with rationing and control removed, steaks would be plentiful and cheap."[68]

The Nation's William Sommers lauded White for his transformation in philosophy: "He is always attracted to a lively scrap, likes to take a lost cause and give it a whirl." Sommers noted that in the 1950s the FCC's new Fairness Doctrine allowed White to produce "bold and factual" editorials. His efforts had succeeded in getting a sixty-two-year-old man's job restored after he had lost it because the Navy had accused him of being a Communist. When the PGA refused to allow black boxing champion Joe Lewis to play in a San Diego golf tournament, White mounted an on-air-air protest. The PGA surrendered, Lewis played, and area golf courses opened their links to black players. Sommers concluded that White "is a refreshing editorial radio breeze."[69]

Although several of the Murrow Boys had distanced themselves from Brown during the 1943 controversy, some of them, including their namesake, would find themselves similarly sanctioned in subsequent years when Paley felt their insistence upon editorial independence threatened the network's relationship with advertisers. The CBS journalists had made radio news mandatory listening for the World War II audience by defining what constituted excellence in broadcast news, but the network's executives and federal government were only willing to allow them to determine news content within limits. After VJ Day, federal censorship ended, but in the years thereafter unofficial censorship continued in the form of sponsor influence. Brown's confrontation was only the first of a number of incidents that fractured the idealism that he, Murrow and the others had shared regarding the grand possibilities of radio news. Regardless of their public statements regarding Brown's squabble with CBS, "through many subsequent years, when ethical crises loomed, Murrow, Shirer and the others had occasion to recall that act of courage—characteristic of those stricken with integrity," according to David Levering.[70]

The golden age of radio news was unceremoniously over. While many of the Murrow team continued working for CBS for decades, others departed. The most esteemed broadcast news team had disbanded. Twenty-five years after the 1943 controversy, Brown reflected on what took place at CBS during his last days there. He saluted the network for what it had accomplished in the intervening years in broadcast news, but he added, "I believe CBS also must bear the scar of the events of 1943. In that case, I am pleased to think that CBS came out second best in the matter of integrity and respect for the First Amendment."[71] For Brown, leaving CBS turned out to be a career setback, but it was far from the end of his broadcast career. The ending provided a new beginning. He would persevere and continue to deliver his insights on the news to nationwide audiences for many years. Brown said he carried a grudge for several years about his parting with CBS: "The case seemed important at the time, and it was, but it has faded."[72] Indeed, in the earliest days of truly professional broadcast news reporting, Brown's case foreshadowed the unresolved question that to this day has yet to be resolved at CBS or at the other networks. Just how should broadcasters define the parameters of the news they deliver to the audience? Brown would spend the remainder of his career at other networks attempting to help the industry answer that question.

◆◆ 9 ◆◆

Exercising a Liberal Voice

The Mutual Broadcasting System (MBS) was thrilled to welcome Brown as a member of its news team. A broadcaster with his reputation enhanced the status of a network that trailed CBS and NBC in audience reach and advertising impact. Notwithstanding its disadvantages, when Brown joined the network in early 1944 Mutual had established a reputation for providing trendsetting news, including extensive international coverage. The network's news department was not at CBS's comprehensive level because Mutual did not possess the financial wherewithal to challenge the Murrow team. But among the networks Mutual employed more commentators than any of the others, and their views stretched from one end of the ideological spectrum to the other. Among them were moderate Raymond Gram Swing, and conservatives Upton Close and Fulton Lewis, Jr. With his employment, Brown counterbalanced them.[1] Mutual provided an ideal situation for Brown. Then, as now, conservative talkers dominated the airwaves. While Lewis was an isolationist and outspoken Roosevelt opponent, Brown was an internationalist and New Deal proponent. He sometimes was critical of Roosevelt's war activities, but he consistently supported the president's social initiatives and international vision.[2] The network claimed that it did not censor its commentators and presented a "completely balanced schedule of news analysts."[3]

This more than likely was one of the prime reasons Mutual hired Brown. In addition, the financial stakes were not as high as they had been at CBS, and there were limited attempts by management to manage his commentaries, an assurance Mutual provided Brown when he accepted the position. Upon joining the network, Brown said, "I have no censorship, no dictations, let alone even a suggestion, as to what I use or don't use. And if I did there would be a new war."[4] Like the other networks, Mutual had created policy regarding what commentators could say, but the statement was not as restrictive. It included only three qualifying points: (1) the commentator had to be experienced in analysis, must know his subject, and needed to exhibit high journalistic standards; (2) his comments could not epitomize those of a particular group, but had to represent his own viewpoint; and (3) he could not "engage in special pleading ... [and had to be] factual ... accurate and fair." The imprecision of the guidelines meant that of all the networks, Mutual was laxest in enforcing the NAB's wartime guidelines.[5] One of the network's most powerful stations was WOR in New York, and from there Brown originated most of his broadcasts. The CBS incident had not hurt Brown's reputation with the public. If anything, it had accentuated it. He became a popular "crusader for truth," a catchphrase he proclaimed from coast to coast in public speeches as well as on Mutual for the next twelve years. Brown's tenure at Mutual would turn out to be the longest period of time he would spend with one news organization.

Between the time he left CBS and began at Mutual, Brown wrote several hundred pages of a book. He intended to title it *Report on America*, and it would include his critical assessment of Americans that had cost him his CBS position. Based on his thinking that the public's morale and resulting actions constituted the biggest home-front story of the war, Cerf had paid Brown a hefty advance. When word leaked out that Brown was working on a new book, the press wondered when it would appear. But, with the book almost complete, he had Martha read the manuscript. Her response was not what he expected. She told him, "If Random publishes this book it will be the last one you ever write because it is so depressing." Based on her feedback, he backtracked on the definitiveness of his findings. He told a *New York Times* reporter that he now doubted the conclusiveness of the findings. He claimed that "much more time and evidence-gathering would be necessary" before he completed the book.[6] Shortly thereafter, he quietly returned the advance to Cerf and filed the manuscript.[7] Then, after a short vacation in the Caribbean, Brown began a three night per week news and commentary show on MBS from 7:30 to 7:45 p.m., on February 6, 1944, sponsored by Phillies Cigars. The network billed him as "probably the most talked about radio reporter of World War II ... [and upon returning to radio commentary, said he had] developed a genius for being on the spot when great events happened."[8]

His nightly program replaced one hosted by Sam Balter, whom Mutual had fired. According to industry hubbub, the network dismissed Balter after he criticized *Chicago Tribune* publisher Robert McCormick. The *Tribune* owned Chicago's Mutual affiliate WGN. McCormick was an isolationist and an outspoken opponent of the New Deal. McCormick—along with William Randolph Hearst—were part of a group of publishers that Roosevelt labeled the "divisionist press." McCormick believed a protracted war in which Roosevelt insisted upon unconditional surrender would take too long and be too costly.[9] Mutual denied that McCormick had influenced Balter's firing, but the dismissal demonstrated that even at Mutual powerful corporate influences could curtail a commentator's outspokenness. The title of Brown's new program was *Sizing up the News*, and soon after he began at Mutual, the Voice of America (VOA) started retransmitting his broadcasts overseas. The VOA subsequently broadcast several commentaries that he did with other analysts under the program title *What American Commentators Say*.[10]

Outside the acoustically treated studio walls, Cecil and Martha were popular in New York society. As one writer noted: They were welcome at New York's "best tables" because, they were, in Martha's words, "VIPs." In addition to the Cerfs, the Browns counted among their friends Lindsay and Stickney, playwright Russell Crouse and his wife, and future *Tonight Show* host Jack Parr and wife Anna. They also socialized with Frederick March and his wife; writer Rex Stout, *Nero Wolfe* mystery novel writer, and his wife, fashion designer Pola. In addition, they partied with Mr. and Mrs. Frank Loesser; he wrote the music for *Guys and Dolls*.

Yet, while the Browns were respected in New York society, anti–Semitism continued to be an issue across the nation. A 1945 Roper Poll found that 58 percent of the respondents believed that Jews had "too much power in the United States.... Only 39 percent of Americans felt Jews should be treated like other people." Other 1940s' surveys showed that Americans believed "Jews were ... a greater threat to the welfare of the United States than any other national, religious, or racial group."[11] But Martha claimed that anti–Semitism never touched the Browns. Their friends knew she and Cecil were Jewish, but it did not matter, she said. They were more impressed with Brown's persona than they were concerned about his genealogy. "It was not, 'Oh, he's Jewish, or he's that.' You were just judged on what you were," Martha said.[12] If Brown's radio or speaking audiences knew of his heritage, which many did, there is little evidence, save a handful of letters that mentioned it in passing, that it concerned them. Brown's friends extended beyond the well-known of New York to journalists and broadcasters. He gained a reputation among working class journalists for helping those who were unemployed find their next job. His connections with influential people and empathy for what it meant to be an experienced, but out-of-work journalist, made him willing to help ameliorate their situation. As a result, unemployed reporters often dropped by their apartment to see if he could help them. He would tell them: "Come back tomorrow, I will look into this and make an appointment," which he often did.[13]

The Browns also were friends with a Russian immigrant by the name of Leon Moore and wife Sonia, a French actress. His real name was Lev Borisovich Helfand, and Brown played a role in the Helfand's defection. Cecil had become acquainted with the Helfands when they were in Rome. Leon was the Russian Embassy's First Secretary as well as head of Rome's KGB station. During casual discussions, Helfand asked Brown questions about U.S. life, such as the cost of New York taxi fare, rent, food and salaries. One day, Helfand confided that because of the Russian purges of 1936–37, he believed the KGB would execute him if he returned to Russia. In July 1940, the Helfands left Rome on a train scheduled to take them to Moscow, but a short distance outside Rome they disembarked, boarded a plane to Portugal, and made their escape to the U.S. Operatives in the U.S. intelligence community were pleased when Halfand volunteered to provide insider Russian information. By 1943, Helfand (then Leon Moore) became an informant on the top-secret Venona Project, which decrypted Soviet intelligence messages.[14] New York theatrical producers recognized Sonia for her acting ability, and she eventually founded the Center for Stanislavsky Theater Art. There is no evidence that Brown assisted the Halfands in their defection, but the couples remained close after the Moore's took up residence on Park Avenue in Manhattan.[15]

Contrary to his on-air penchant for controversy, friends found Brown to be a mild-mannered man with whom they could spend a stimulating evening. Because he was knowledgeable about current events and traveled extensively, he had an opinion about all the major issues. People considered him an excellent conversationalist who shared interesting stories about his adventures. Martha said, "Everyone wanted to talk with him whenever we went out to dinner or were at a party."[16] Others commented that he had a "charming sense of humor" and was "wryly self-deprecating."[17] Nephew Jonathan, who became a 1960s civil-rights activist, characterized conversations with Uncle Cecil as extremely convincing: "Most of his talking was about what he thought. He didn't have a lot of casual conversations. You did not often feel that you had won an argument with Cecil. You had survived it, and sometimes you had maintained your position. He was extremely persuasive." Jonathan added that during conversations about issues his uncle often became "excitable.... He was sometimes like a little child, making himself known." Adding to his persuasiveness was the fact that he was physically imposing, "a large person ... very striking looks, [with] a deep, assertive voice."[18] Part of this impression resulted from the fact that Brown remained physically active at a time when most professional men did not. He played tennis and swam throughout his life, and he learned to be a dancer after Martha bought him lessons at an Arthur Murray Studio for their tenth wedding anniversary. He did so, even though he had to undergo a second hernia operation during the late 1940s.

Brown remained on friendly terms with Murrow after the war, and Sevareid occasionally came up from Washington to attend the same parties as the Browns. Otherwise, Brown did not maintain friendships with other members of the CBS wartime team. Although they had shared time on the same broadcasts, Brown had not been geographically in close proximity to them. Thus, they were never close. Providing news to the same network and

This undated photograph shows Brown doing two of the things that often occupied him during the 1940s and '50s, scanning a teletype machine for breaking news and smoking, as almost all newsmen of the day did. During his forty-year career, he became one of the few, if not the only, broadcast journalist to work for all the major commercial networks, culminating with his introduction of news commentary to the educational television (PBS) audience in Los Angeles (courtesy Wisconsin Historical Society).

Murrow coordinating them was all they had in common. While he and Murrow remained friends, Martha said Murrow team members did not like Cecil because "he was not like them—not at all."[19] His lifestyle was significantly different. Murrow "enjoyed fine clothes, a good address, fast cars, and the best restaurants."[20] He was "virile and magnetic ... a man who could make smoking a cigarette seem like the height of romance," according to Smith.[21] Several of the boys, like most journalists of that period, engaged in hard living. Murrow—and some of the others—were involved in extramarital affairs, and most of them, in Martha's words, drank "like fish," including their namesake. She recalled a time when Murrow spent an evening at the Browns' penthouse and "finished off almost a quart of scotch all by himself." Brown was not much of a drinker, sipping only a bit of wine. Martha claimed he could become inebriated at the smell of liquor. His one vice was that he smoked heavily, but almost all journalists of that era did. Both Martha and Cecil quit in the 1960s. He stopped smoking after a doctor noticed he was becoming breathless with minor exertion. He told Brown that if he wanted to dance with his wife and breathe at the same time, he would have to quit smoking.[22]

As he settled into broadcasting for Mutual, Brown continued to press a number of agendas he had begun at CBS. For example, he felt the Roosevelt Administration had to share the blame for Americans not being more aware of details for prosecuting the war: "The objectives of this war have not been presented to the American people in straightforward, acceptable terms. The result is nationwide confusion in the[ir] minds … neither the administration nor the opposition has presented the people with a concise, dynamic, and all-embracing picture of where this nation wants to go and why."[23] Now that Brown was at a network where advertiser and management pressure was less intense, he broadened the range of his commentaries; nor did he limit them to political analysis. He demonstrated that, when given time, he could reflect and provide metaphorical perspective. On Christmas day 1944, Brown reminded listeners that they needed to be thankful for the sacrifices American-fighting men had made so civilians could enjoy Christmas. He congratulated Americans for sending GIs a number of presents that year: "Big beautiful bombers—the better to burn down Tokyo…. Heavy, practical invasion barges—the better to get on the shores of Normandy…. Big field guns … [and] speedy fighters. All the parts were there and they worked very well…. Every day and every night, we sent our fighting men what they needed." As a result, he said, the public had received so much more in return from the men in combat. "They sent you a tiny dot in the Pacific [Saipan]. A rather expensive gift—it cost sixteen-thousand casualties…. Here's another gift to put under your tree tonight. It is the Atlantic Wall…. Be careful with the pieces…. So that you could have them, 200,000 Americans fell on the battlefield." Later in the piece, he reminded listeners not to become overconfident, even as the war appeared to be going well. He used the occasion to remind them that the military still needed their sacrifices. "The road has been hard and expensive, but it is false and dangerous Christmas cheer to pretend that the road ahead is going to be any easier. There has been too much fake optimism, that downright, stupid underestimation of the enemy, that irresponsible desire of some people to keep the customers happy, despite all the facts to the contrary. One gift we can send to our men at the front is determination that we are ready and anxious to tighten up our belts for the job ahead."[24] He was not ready to quit reminding them that they needed to sacrifice for the men who were dying for them.

Brown did so many stories during the war concerning his abhorrence of the Germans and the need for the U.S. to achieve total defeat of the Nazis, that listeners and sponsors complained about how often he pounded on those themes.[25] In 1943, while still at CBS, Brown had announced, "There is no need to manufacture German atrocities. The brutality of the Germans is beyond comprehension. Those who have witnessed them ... understand the innate bestiality of the Nazis." Three months later, he was unequivocating in what the Allies needed to do: "It is essential that the Germans should be smashed. Their army must be ripped to shreds on battlefields." He opposed any form of a negotiated peace with the Axis powers, for which some U.S. commentators and politicians were calling to shorten the war. "It would be unfortunate for the future peace if the Germans were to surrender in France or Belgium or in the Balkans. Germany must be invaded," he argued.

In other commentaries, Brown condemned not just Nazi leaders but the German people as well. His experience with the Germans in Europe had led him to think the worst of them. After positioning himself behind the Mutual microphone, he disputed the perceived innocence of German civilians. "There might be a few good Germans, but the so-called good Germans who might have objected are too few to affect German history."[26] A view that he was unyielding on was that the American people were mistaken to differentiate between the Nazis and German civilian culpability. In September 1944, Phillies Cigars' advertising agent Near Ivey wrote Brown that Phillies' representatives had calculated that his condemnation of Germany had occupied "74 percent" of his newscasts during the previous month. "Mr. Brown seems to have an obsession on Germany and the German people, and we feel that everybody who listens to him knows that Mr. Brown thinks the Germans are barbarians, so why keep on telling us that every night," a Phillies manager had written to Ivey. Ivey urged Brown spend more time on domestic affairs.[27]

Part of the reason for the American view of Germans had to do with the fact that Germany "had operated an active propaganda organization in the United States since 1933" that clearly influenced many Americans' view of that nation. To keep the U.S. out of the war in the 1930s the Germans had stoked isolationism and in 1940 had campaigned against Roosevelt's reelection.[28] Scholars have since confirmed the validity of Brown's criticism of Americans for being overly conciliatory toward Germans. Many in the U.S. were willing to grant German civilians the benefit of the doubt because of the friendly German-Americans they knew who were their neighbors in the U.S. Americans did not hold a similar view regarding the Japanese. Popular opinion played a role in the federal government incarcerating more than 127,000 Japanese-Americans out of fear that they would remain loyal to their homeland. Brown was not one of the commentators who supported that questionable action. Casey noted in *Cautious Crusade* that throughout 1943 and 1944 "a clear majority [of Americans were] still content to blame only a few leading Nazis for all the aggression and brutality."[29] As the war news improved with Allied victories, Brown cautioned his audience not to prematurely celebrate. The Battle of the Bulge confirmed that they needed to heed his warnings. He told listeners that only when German civilians protested the continuation of fighting in large numbers and German soldiers refused to fight and turned their guns on the Gestapo would the war end.[30] In the winter of 1945 when the Allies discovered the extent of the Holocaust, Brown insisted that all Germans had to share in culpability. As news about the atrocities uncovered in the death camps made headlines, opinion polls showed that Americans finally acknowledged that they could not lay the extent of the carnage solely at the feet of the Nazis.[31]

As the war news improved in the spring of 1945, Brown was able to deliver good news on April 9: "Tonight we are fast reaching the moment that the world of decent people has prayed for, and fought for. And that moment is the destruction of the German war machine."[32] Only four days later, though, his encouraging voice became somber when he announced that Roosevelt had died in Warm Spring, GA. Brown asked, "Why did he have to die when we needed him so much?" He declared his admiration for the four-term president by referring to him as a "dear friend [to Americans]," and the "people's champion." Although Roosevelt's relationship with the press could best be termed "stormy," Brown admired him for what he had done for the average American. He believed average Americans were sorrowful about the death because Roosevelt had been so much like Abraham Lincoln in that he had suffered because he fought for the "common man." Brown reflected: "Roosevelt raised the so-called ordinary people to a new sense of dignity, of self-respect, of importance, not only by his words and promises to them, but because he put into practice [referring to opponents of his policies] the rights of men.... And anyone who does that is going to run into trouble." Roosevelt had helped Americans overcome fear, Brown stated, and had broadened their perspective of the world. He speculated that the American people were ready "to face an uncertain future ... [because] Roosevelt gave us a new sense of world responsibility, one that we are not going to refuse to accept. And he gave us a stirring vision of a world where the four freedoms are going to be practiced."[33]

Then, in August, after Japan capitulated, Brown reflected on the end of the war: "It is strange and wonderful to be in a world of peace. There's a happy emptiness. The days and nights of death of our finest young men are gone, but not forgotten. For some children, this is an entirely new and unreal world. For they have never known a time when bombs did not fall, and guns crack, and broken bodies were not scattered over streets and sidewalks." No doubt, the comments reflected the memory of his own experiences in Yugoslavia, Singapore and elsewhere earlier in the war. He continually tried to find meaning in the passing parade of events, and to place them in context, not only as they related to political and military leaders, but to civilian soldiers and innocent bystanders.[34] The verdicts handed down by the tribunal at the Nuremberg Trials in October 1946 fell far short of his expectations. While the jury convicted nineteen Nazis, it acquitted three officers and sentenced twelve to death. When the verdicts were announced, he said, "The surprising part of the verdict was that only 12 of the criminals were sentenced to die.... The shocking surprise was the acquittal of three of the notorious criminals of Germany.... [And] it is beyond comprehension that such men as [Hjalmar] Schacht and [Franz] von Papen should be able to walk out of the international court as free men." Clearly, Brown was not satisfied that the jury had delivered justice upon the men he referred to elsewhere in the story as "gangsters."[35]

With the end of the war, the OWI had ceased to exist, and the federal government and network executives' concerns about the impact of commentary on the war effort ended. Big shifts were taking place at the networks; program schedules were changing, and executives sought a better understanding of the role commentary would play on the peacetime airwaves. In the fall of 1945, the Hooper Company found that the average man listened to radio nearly three hours each day, and the average woman almost four. Clearly, radio played a major role in the average American's life. In early 1945, *Variety* published the results of a study in which 46 percent of those surveyed said they did not want news commentators to take sides on issues; 37 percent wanted them to take sides. Sixty-five percent thought a commentator should express his opinion, while 43 percent thought commentators expressed personal opinions during commentaries. Surprisingly, 15 percent thought a commentator should express his sponsor's opinion.[36] This latter finding would have violated the standards of objective journalism as well as one of the ethical principles of the ARNA.

CBS President Frank Stanton—who held a Ph.D. in Psychology from Ohio State—was not satisfied that the findings of surveys such as the one *Variety* conducted were statistically reliable. Therefore, he encouraged the NAB to research the topic in a more scholarly manner. Thus, in the fall of 1945, the NAB contracted with the National Opinion Research Center, under the direction of Paul Lazarfeld at Columbia, to obtain a more precise sense of the public's perceptions of news and commentary. After conducting nationwide interviews, Lazarfeld's team found that only 12 percent of those surveyed said they could identify bias in news programs. Eighty-one per cent felt that "most radio stations make serious efforts to be fair to all sides." Respondents said in comparison they thought newspapers fairly represented all the aspects of an issue only 45 percent of the time. Lazarfeld thought the results were surprising because he anecdotally believed there was an imbalance in the opinions radio commentators expressed. He remarked, "It is very unlikely, for instance, that an individual listener has the background to judge whether news broadcasts and commentators give a fair and balanced picture of current events." The researchers added, on the other hand, that "a variety of surveys have shown that the people who read these [news] magazines [*Time* and *Newsweek*, *Look* and *Life*] are also the people who are most likely to listen to commentators and to read more than one newspaper." Clearly, the researchers doubted their findings. Therefore, Lazarfeld recommended that the networks conduct a "periodic sampling of commentator scripts to study the expressed opinion on a variety of matters," in subsequent years.[37]

This analysis work was taking place alongside scholarly studies that were seeking to confirm that commentators' opinions affected listeners' views. A University of Wisconsin study concluded that "a voice amplified by radio [presenting news or otherwise] had persuasive powers."[38] In the days before television, and in the aftermath of a war that had transformed both American and international affairs, the public tuned to radio to make sense of a more complicated world. Commentators had the ability to "call attention to a condition, make some people care where they did not care before, make the already committed care very much, and mute a few who are opposed," according to Fang.[39] Martin later elucidated the impact of journalists who made their living commenting on public issues. He asserted that they were more influential than public officials: "People in office come and go, but ... columnists and newscasters, [and] commentators ... remain, and frequently enjoy careers of 35 to over 50 years, while politicians have gone into oblivion or their graves."[40]

In May 1947, President Truman affirmed federal officials' perception of the power of commentators' sentiments when he hosted members of the ARNA at the White House. Kaltenborn, Brown, Davis, Sevareid and nearly two-dozen others attended. Truman greeted them by saying, "As I have told you on several occasions, there is nothing much that I can tell you. You are always telling me what to do!" Of course, Truman was kidding, and the laughter that resulted from the opening continued when he added, "I think every one of you has given me the right advice ... on internal and foreign affairs. If I don't get those things right, I can assure you gentlemen it won't be your fault!"[41] The cordial meeting represented Truman's affinity for the press, which he believed could help achieve his goals. In his memoirs, he said he saw the role of the media as "primarily educational. It would tell the public why he had done what he had done in the hope that they would understand and support his initiatives." Truman understood that he needed public opinion on his side if his policies—considered drastic by many Americans—were to succeed.[42] Brown was initially uncertain of Truman's abilities as chief executive, but after the thirty-third president rolled out the Marshall Plan and condemned Russian aggressiveness in Europe, Brown became a Truman supporter.

That same year, Lazarfeld's team again surveyed the national audience, investigating more in-depth listener newscast and commentary perceptions. They found that 79 percent of the respondents thought newscasts and commentary were fair and balanced. They found an increase of ten points in the percentage of respondents who felt newspapers were presenting fair and balanced columns. Lazarfeld speculated that the change could be explained by the fact that many of the nation's newspapers had not supported Roosevelt's policies, but now that he was dead the public believed newspapers had become fairer. Lazarfeld believed the change also resulted from the renewed importance newspapers enjoyed in the postwar years in comparison to the dominance of radio during the war. The radio audience still held commentators in higher esteem than newspaper columnists. However, 10 percent of those surveyed also "chided [radio news] for being unfair, for being 'Communists,' [and] for not always presenting the truth." Apparently, these results related to the investigations regarding suggested communist sympathizers in the radio industry that had made headlines in the intervening two years. The researchers also asked respondents who they felt was responsible for unfairness in newscasts and commentaries. Thirty-two percent said advertisers were at fault, while 26 percent blamed radio ownership. Only 18 percent said commentators themselves were responsible. In comparison, 53 percent said that in the case of newspapers, ownership was responsible, only 16 percent said the columnist, and only 7 percent believed advertisers were to blame.[43] The studies seemed to indicate that the public was more perceptive about the dynamics of influence within the media industries than executives believed. The results also were good news for radio commentators in that they unofficially provided statistical evidence to support their latitude to continue voicing their opinions.

Regarding his own ratings, Mutual executives were pleased with Brown because he brought with him a built-in listenership that boosted Mutual's audience. Complete ratings of the period are unavailable, but a March 1946 *Billboard* ad touted: "Cecil Brown ranks high as a listening favorite. His 1945 rating average, according to Hooper, was 6.2; [and] went as high as 7.8. Brown's recognizable name and reputation as a crack reporter has made him a success with advertisers as well."[44] A Mutual affiliate salesperson in Texas wrote MBS, "We are writing to tell you of the splendid results our client, Richter's Department Store, is receiving from the morning newscast by Cecil Brown. The results are far beyond our highest expectations."[45] The commentator receiving the highest Hooper ratings during this period was gossiper Winchell, who was in a league of his own, with ratings in the 22 range.[46] Nevertheless, Brown's ratings were solid in the heyday of radio commentary, which by 1947 had upwards of 600 "oracles" on the air.[47]

Such findings flew in the face of the expectations of many industry observers who believed that with the war over, commentators would become unpopular. MBS's Program Director Bertram Hauser told *Broadcasting* in 1947 that his network did not believe that was going to be the case. "It all boils down to the fact that news commentators and news programs in general still have great appeal to the audience—and they're still doing a real job for advertisers."[48] His emphasis of the latter point made it clear that satisfied sponsorship was the key element in a commentator remaining on the air, but though Hauser did not say it, commentaries provided an important public service. MacDonald said commentators did two important things: (1) they "offered their own reasoned, but subjective interpretations for listeners to consider" and (2) they provided an "educative effect ... [that] allowed listeners to test the validity of their own conclusions, to confirm or refute those interpretations, and to learn in the process." He concluded that, rather than "condemn American radio for presenting a cacophony of opinions, ... broadcasting should be commended for tolerating the varieties of the Truth." This, he added, "compelled [listeners] to learn for themselves the correct position from which to understand the news of the world."[49]

In the years just after the war, a regiment of journalists returned from covering the conflict on multiple fronts. Like Brown, "they had seen what happens when an independent press and people abdicate responsibility and cave in the face of ignorance and intolerance," noted Gay. Because of the censorship they had endured, they were ready to flex their muscles at home where the Constitution purported to ensure freedom of the press. But *New Yorker* writer Liebling, one of those journalists, called the U.S. press "the weak slat under the bed of democracy." It had to become—from the returning correspondents' perspective—bolder and more relevant. Liebling and the others wanted to make American journalism "more inquisitive, more worldly, more informed," and they did. Gay asserted that the post-war journalistic "call to arms," spawned "the greatest era of press independence and integrity in American history."[50] Throughout the remainder of the 1940s, according to McDonald, "The liberal crusading spirit that emerged from the war was notable in radio journalism."[51]

Brown and the other members of the Murrow team were determined to perpetuate that sprit at the networks. But Paley, Sarnoff and other executives were unwilling to turn their airwaves over to liberal journalists who were set on, in the journalists' words, "correcting" or "improving" American society. Media scholars have labeled the Murrow-styled approach "advocacy journalism." According to the method, a journalist presents a story in a manner that recommends social or political change. He is clear about the set of beliefs from which he is framing the opinion. The tactic is not propagandistic because the journalist employs facts and a reasoned argument to support a logical point of view. This style of journalism, in the hands of a conscientious, public-service-oriented journalist, has as its purpose the greater good of society, although critics of the strategy consider it manipulative. They believe it puts an excess amount of influence in journalists' hands. *New York Times* editor Lester Markel argued that because of their special access and commitment to fairness, journalists needed to share their perspectives to help the public understand events and issues: "Opinion, which is the *sine quo non* of a sound public opinion is, in large part, the assignment of the mass media," but too many in the fourth estate did not grasp that mission, or, in the case of radio, were prevented from exercising it.[52] Martha Brown said, "Everybody [1940s' journalists] agreed that if you were a good newsman you expressed an opinion because of the knowledge you gleaned from reporting."[53]

Nevertheless, entertainment programming increasingly dominated network programming, and even after Congress would require the networks to wrest editorial control of their programs from sponsors in the 1950s, advertising pressure continued in the form of refusals to buy time during programs that featured content that conflicted with sponsors' agendas. Although not singled out for its efforts, with its broad range of commentators Mutual seemingly was fulfilling the goals of the FCC to a greater degree than that of its more powerful competitors. Fang agreed: "Mutual and ABC [the two least financially powerful networks] ... tried to offset bias by balancing commentators on both the right and the left." But, he added, "they did not always try very hard."[54] But for radio journalists, particularly those with a liberal bent, which meant most of the Murrow team, other events would short circuit their dreams of elucidating the nation's problems.

Even before the war's end, as early as 1943, the moderate *Atlantic Monthly* wrote that the networks were replacing liberal commentators with conservative ones. CBS' Howe wrote the article only two months after Brown left the network. In it, he argued that advertisers were readily sponsoring programs that featured a conservative commentator and that liberal commentators' programs were less popular with sponsors, especially those that favored the New Deal. Although the liberal social agenda secured achievements throughout the 1930s and 1940s, it failed to realize many of the goals that would have fundamentally transformed America. The New Deal propelled the growth of the welfare state, the labor movement, the replacement of an isolationist worldview with an internationalist one, and the emergence of the civil rights movement. Yet, the liberalism of the post-war period, especially after Roosevelt's death, turned out to be tamer than the version for which the New Dealers of the 1930s had aimed.[55] This was disappointing for Brown. Like many journalistic brethren, the ideals, both for the common man, and broadcast news, were not realized. Several factors short-circuited them.

With the growth of radio's popularity, advertising became more expensive, thus limiting to major corporations the number of companies that could afford to buy commercials. Noted Howe: "It is the big-money sponsors who pay top prices to put news analysts on the largest networks at the most desirable times." In addition, the U.S. economy boomed following the war. The consumer economy replaced the wartime armament economy as the public raced to buy products that rationing had prevented them from purchasing during the war. In the public's eyes, a plentiful number of jobs at good wages diminished the need for many of the New Deal's provisions, and convinced many Americans that government's role in their daily life should be limited. The 1946 national election, in which Republicans won both houses of Congress for the first time since 1928, further exemplified the national mood.[56] With this evolving trend in America and American radio, Brown became one of a minority of commentators who provided Mutual's audience with a voice for the Democratic administration, first of Roosevelt, then Truman. This sentiment was otherwise seldom seen in newspapers, the majority of which had consistently opposed Roosevelt's election.[57] McCarthy further diminished liberal credibility when he "castigated liberals for being unpatriotic, not harsh enough in their anti-communist statements, [and] too supportive of the socialist legacy of Roosevelt and the New Deal legislation."[58]

Howe did not draw any relationship between the Brown-CBS incident and the demise of on-air liberalism, but he did discuss the growth of sponsor influence regarding commentary. He noted that radio was more susceptible to advertiser manipulation because, unlike newspaper advertising plus subscriptions, program sponsorship constituted radio's sole means of income. This resulted in an abridgement of freedom of the air, in his mind. He said the networks needed to clarify whether an analyst was presenting commentary that represented the views of his sponsor versus an analyst who presented views that "sets the public interest higher than" a sponsor or interest group's agenda. Howe charged there is no such thing as "responsibility, tolerance, diversity, and honesty on the air.... [Because] the sponsor tends to judge news shows largely on the basis of audience appeal—which in turn puts a premium on sensationalism." His solution to the quandary was for the networks to "develop a new feature—the unsponsored, non-sensational, news analyst [program].... His network or station would vouch for his accuracy, taste and judgment."[59]

However, with the end of the war, and Brown's outspokenness, he became the center of attention again, along with a number of other high-profile, progressive commentators. Beginning in 1945, fear grew that communists were undermining American society. The House of Representatives Un-American Activities Committee (HUAC) began investigating suspected communist infiltration within influential institutions. These included network radio and Hollywood motion picture companies because the committee suspected that the content of radio programming, especially news, and motion pictures contained subversive messages. In writing a critical expose on the committee's work in 1948, Kahn depicted the committee's focus as characterized "by one salient feature: the attempt to stifle freedom of expression among the American people. Nowhere was this underlying objective more apparent than in the measures taken by the committee in the field of public communication."[60]

In October 1945, HUAC demanded that the networks or stations at which five so-called "progressive commentators" worked submit seventy-five of their scripts to the committee. In justifying the action, Representative John Rankin declared, "Whenever things go on the air that are dangerous [to the safety and welfare of the American people] we are going to investigate them."[61] The remark reflected a generally held impression that commentators possessed an inordinate amount of influence over public opinion. HUAC charged that "these men became known by voice and mannerism as no reporters of the printed press had ever been known. They became public personalities.... Commentators are in the best position to 'propagandize.'"[62] The suspect commentators the committee identified were Johannes Steel, Swing, Hans Jacob, William Gailmor and Brown. In issuing the order, Representative Hugh De Lacy noted why the committee requested their scripts specifically: "The commentators whose scripts are sent for are plainly warned that they are under government surveillance.... The radio stations and sponsors ... are thus put on warning that if they wish to stay out of the center of the smear controversy, they had better get other commentators."[63] De Lacy said the committee was acting in response to listener complaints. When the networks and several stations failed to fire the commentators immediately, Chairman John Wood proposed legislation that required the broadcasters to list the commentators' birthplace, nationality and political affiliation, but the bill failed to garner sufficient votes to pass.[64] A number of newspaper editors came to the defense of their radio brethren, arguing that just because the men were working in a younger medium did not diminish their free-speech rights. More than one editorial noted that by calling for the scripts the committee was damaging the commentators' careers, because no advertiser would be interested in sponsoring a program on which a commentator whose name the committee had linked with Communism was affiliated. "If the Un-American Affairs [sic] Committee succeeds in smearing these newsmen, it will have forged a weapon that it can hold over the head of every broadcaster," noted one editor. The investigation featured arguments on the House floor in which several Democratic representatives charged HUAC members with attempting to "influence and intimidate" the analysts.[65]

Brown probably had been included for circumstantial reasons. The committee had linked his name with support of *Mission to Moscow*, and sentiments in his scripts during the war that celebrated the Soviet Army. In one of his 1943 newscasts he had said, "Whether you adore Russia, are indifferent or antagonistic, the fact remains that Russia is the miracle of the war.... Her part in winning this war cannot be ignored."[66] Other commentators had similarly extolled the Russians, as had members of the administration, because Russia was an ally during the war. The committee could have pointed to them as one of a number of comments Brown had made in which he saluted the Russians for their courage against the Germans and their role in helping the Allies defeat the Nazis. Nevertheless, committee members charged that some of the comments of the five correspondents bore a striking resemblance to those in the *Daily Worker* newspaper. The committee may even have used Brown's previous employment with CBS against him. Conservative congressmen viewed the Murrow Boys' views during the war as so liberal that they sometimes referred to CBS as The Red Network.[67] Ultimately, HUAC did not call any of the commentators to testify, and of the five whose scripts they reviewed, only Steele lost his job. Nevertheless, the threat of congressional action had a definite chilling effect on the radio industry, and other commentators were not as fortunate as Brown in keeping their jobs.

In early 1947, in an article in the liberal *New Republic*, former network commentator Bryce Oliver charged that CBS, NBC and several major market stations had fired as many as two-dozen left-leaning newscasters the previous year. The reason he gave for the dismissals was "sponsor pressure." According to Oliver, "Radio's resistance to ideas seems mainly opposition to liberal ideas. Pressure to 'tone down' news which is sympathetic to organized labor and to Russia has increased rapidly in the last few months."[68] In December, a *Variety* article charged, "A quiet but effective campaign to drive from the airwaves every radio gabber ever-so-slightly left of center was seen shaping up during the last week." The trade publication went on to say that it was obvious that "a plot" to eliminate liberal commentators—which HUAC had started more than a year ago—was underway. In addition to Steele, *Variety* documented the "decapitation of Jacob, Sidney Walton, Lisa Sergio, Estelle Sternberger [and Frank Kingdom] just in New York—and the firing of a half-dozen prominent gabbers on the West Coast." Newspapers were reporting the occurrence of similar incidents at Chicago stations. Radio executives denied that there was a coordinated effort to get rid of liberals, saying "purely economic forces" were the cause of the dismissals.[69] But in 1948, *Variety*, along with noting that the number of liberal commentators continued to diminish, also judged that "those who remain are 'not only conservative, but what's worse, not intelligent.'"[70]

Brown saw the campaign as an attack on free speech, and the mention of his name as a suspect did not dissuade him from saying what he thought about HUAC. In October 1947, he announced, "It seems to me that this House Committee on Un-American Activities is further evidence of the rising fear over the country of ideas, of things of the mind. There is a rising intolerance of a difference of opinion in our nation." Nor did the congressional call for his scripts stop him from reporting developments in Russia, and there was a lot to report. Obviously, the friendliness between the Soviet Union and the U.S. deteriorated after the war. Russian expansionism in Eastern Europe, Stalin's campaign to promote socialism, repression of his own people, and his dispute with Allied leaders over the division of Berlin dominated the headlines. Stalin's initiatives added to American fears that Russia could not be trusted and that it was becoming a threat. Although Brown had admired Russian courage during the war, there was never any evidence that he embraced Soviet ideals. Anyone who would have read his overall body of journalistic work, dating back to 1928, would have seen that. Following the war and throughout the remainder of his career, he solidified an anti-communist position. While he criticized what he termed "hysterical commentators," such as John T. Flynn and Dan Smoot, who drummed up Russian fear, simultaneously Brown announced, "The stakes are too high for the United States to desert our friends [Free Europeans] in their hour of need."[71]

The Soviet Union further exacerbated tensions between the two former allies in 1947 when it formed the Cominform. The initiative's purpose was to unite all of Eastern Europe in a campaign to destroy anti-communist elements in countries behind the Iron Curtain. "No one can mistake that it will be confined in Europe. The Soviet brand of tyranny has its eye on the entire world.... Russia has declared political war on the United States," said Brown. Although he encouraged the U.S. to negotiate with Russia to maintain peace, he refrained from celebrating Russian actions during the remainder of his years as a commentator.[72] When he did a broadcast that same year that signified the importance of the VOA beginning to broadcast into the Soviet Union, Assistant Secretary of State William Benton wrote Brown. "May I congratulate you on your broadcast dealing with Russia?" "You did the best editorial job, in my opinion, of any commentator or newspaper." Benton added, "You treat the subject as it should be treated, a most important development in the handling of American foreign affairs and you treat it with sympathy and insight."[73]

Although the networks did not join in the local station campaign to rid the airwaves of liberal commentators, their executives did become fearful of advertiser or government pressure to deal with perceived communist influences. In the spring of 1947, three former FBI agents formed the American Business Consultants. The group's purpose was to identify and expose supposed communist infiltration at the networks. They launched a weekly newsletter, *Counterattack*, which listed the names of suspected Communists, especially newscasters. The networks and major advertisers subscribed to it. CBS sponsors soon became alarmed about having their products associated with anyone suspected of being a Communist, and they let Paley know about it. He and the other network heads were intimidated not only by advertisers that they would withdraw sponsorships but also by fear that HUAC could convince the FCC to threaten the networks' station licenses. One committee member, South Dakota Representative Karl Mundt, said he liked CBS's "no-opinion policy, [and] warned the other networks that they might be taken over by the government unless they mended their ways."[74]

Those who found themselves in the line of fire were appreciative of Brown's comments on their behalf. In November 1947, several motion picture executives instituted the "Hollywood blacklist," which banned ten writers and directors from employment that HUAC had found in contempt of Congress. The so-called Hollywood Ten refused to confirm committee allegations that communist sympathizers were planting propaganda in film scripts. Brown did not openly defend the Hollywood Ten on the air, but he called for them to get their day in court as Americans whose right to do so was guaranteed under the Sixth Amendment. Unfortunately, anti-communist crusaders were commonly trampling such rights during that period. In one of his commentaries, Brown left no doubt where he stood on the HUAC investigation, calling the House probe "a farce, a circus, a joke, a vaudeville act." He said the committee's activity "is further evidence of the rising fear over the country of ideas, of things of the mind. There is a rising intolerance of a difference of opinion in our nation."[75]

Screenwriter Ernest Pascal wrote Brown that he appreciated his perspective, uncommon among national commentators, to ensure film-industry personnel of their constitutional rights. "You did us all a world of good last night, and contributed more than you'll ever know to the job that we are trying to do of revocalizing the liberal voice of Hollywood." He thanked Brown for encouraging listeners to investigate the evidence before jumping to conclusions: "As you know a voice can't be clear and won't be listened to very long unless the thinking back of it is clear, and it is only people like yourself who can help us in that primary and most vital consideration."[76] Brown's utilization of logic, historical facts and an ability to cast accusers as individuals who were excessively trampling citizens' rights, resonated with his audience. Despite voicing broadminded commentaries in a period when many in Congress and the public interpreted such comments as communist-inspired,

Brown was able to express himself in a way that successfully kept his name out of *Red Channels*. That was the list of 151 suspected broadcasters, journalists and creative artists the American Business Consultants published. The consultants charged network newsmen Shirer, Robert St. John and Howard K. Smith of having communist connections.[77]

Although Brown escaped further congressional investigation, the taint of communist-affiliation continued to pursue him. A January 1949 letter from David Mitchell to Mutual executives chastised the Yami Yogurt Company for sponsoring Brown: "He may not be a communist card holder but he certainly talks like a Moscow stooge." Mitchell sent the letter after Brown defended two Oregon State University professors that school administrators had dismissed following accusations that they were Communists during the height of the effort to expose academics suspected of such affiliation. The University of Washington had fired three professors for the same reason. Most of the Oregon State faculty supported the firings; at the time, the Pacific Northwest was less tolerant of liberal thinking, but Brown was not ready to join the bandwagon in condemning the professors.[78] Mitchell asserted, "[The professors] are losing no more academic freedom in being fired than Cecil Brown would be if he were fired from radio, which, I believe, would be the best thing that ever happened to radio."[79]

Mitchell's complaint prompted Brown to threaten to sue Mitchell for libel. In a direct response to Brown's threat, Mitchell said, "Radio is a wonderful invention ... it must be very comforting for the commentator to be able to ram his opinions down the ears of the public, without the risk of argument." Mitchell asserted that he had the right as a listener to dispute Brown's claims: "That, my friend, is the commentators' occupational risk, and he shouldn't cry for mama when someone hands back a little of the same medicine."[80] Brown did not follow through on his threat to sue Mitchell, but there is no evidence that he softened his stance on defending Americans whom he believed were falsely accused of being Communists. Brown's personal response to Mitchell was only the first of many he made to listeners. He was not about to let them get away with unfounded allegations.

Later that year, Marguerite Pratt of Santa Monica wrote Mutual that "it has been my observation that Mr. Brown has been opposed to any investigation that tends to expose communistic activities in this country."[81] In response, Brown wrote, "Your letter, frankly, suggests such a superficiality of thought that I am puzzled whether you object to my recognition that times do indeed change [the focus of his broadcast had been that times were changing in the U.S. regarding the view that HUAC's charges were legitimate]." He said he condemned HUAC, under the leadership of J. Parnell Thomas, because of its "totalitarian operations and its willful disregard of American rights. Your letter questions my loyalty and integrity." His righteous indignation over again being called a Communist prompted him to charge her to either prove her allegations or, failing to do so, retract them in a letter to Mutual.[82] She did not reply, and more accusations followed. A February 1950 letter from a Minnesota listener to Mutual management asked, "What did the Communists pay Cecil Brown for his broadcast ... [yesterday] entitled 'Interview with [Spain's Francisco] Franco from Madrid'? It was the rankest expression of bigotry and typically communistic in spirit."[83] But Brown did not equivocate, especially regarding his view of McCarthy. On the air a month later, he announced, "When, as McCarthy seems anxious to have us do, we embark on a program of mass accusation without proof, a program of guilt by association, then, as in no other field that I can think of, we have adopted the totalitarian technique."[84]

Such comments kept alive suspicions about Brown's communist sympathies. In October 1950, his agent booked him for a speech at California's Redlands University. But Redlands President George Armacost wrote the agency that Brown was not welcome because "he has shown sympathy with communist causes, has communist leanings, and perhaps at some point had been a fellow traveler." Upon receiving the letter, Brown's agent wrote Armacost: "[Brown's] opinions are known to millions of listeners and how anyone could interpret anything he had been saying to indicate sympathy with Communism is utterly beyond belief." When Brown saw Armacost's letter, he was outraged, saying he would not speak at Redlands unless he received an apology from Armacost. He wrote the president: "I will not dignify stupid and vague insinuations with any detailed answer of my fervent opposition to ... Communism ... [or] countenance on this or any other occasion such ridiculous assaults on my long-established reputation for honor, integrity and Americanism." He demanded to meet his accusers face to face. Two days later, Armacost apologized, claiming he could not find the accusers and urged Brown not to cancel his speech. Brown did indeed keep the engagement.[85]

The volatile letters Brown exchanged with listeners were illustrative of the communications that appear to have been distinctive among radio commentators. While other commentators received a lot of mail, some of it unpleasant, Brown's correspondence indicates how diligent he was about replying, regardless of the tenor of the listener letters. And, unlike some of his contemporaries, he did not employ form letters. Some of his responses ran up to seven single-spaced, typed pages, addressing each individual point a listener had made. Such responses indicate that he took listener letters seriously, and that he was determined to either set the record straight, or drive home the validity of his position via additional evidence that he had not included in a story. Other letters he received prior to 1950 also indicate that Brown was ahead of other commentators, and in the minority, in defending public figures whom he felt were being unfairly accused of being Communists.

Such commentaries during the late 1940s also demonstrated that he was willing to risk his reputation and job to speak out. Regardless of the consequences, he believed it was his duty to oppose those who sought to silence him. In March of 1949, he commented on his program, "For those of us who are at all interested in democratic rights, we are now witnessing in this country, more than ever, a kind of scatterbrained demand to suppress free speech."[86]

Brown's position with Mutual remained solid during these years, mainly because sponsors backed him in the face of listener complaints. In May 1950, Victor Van Der Linde, president of Dolcin Corporation, and one of Brown's sponsors, responded to a complaint from a Mrs. Engs. He wrote, "We have every reason to believe that Mr. Brown is unbiased, intelligent and capable ... but, of course, it is always possible to get an incorrect impression of what anybody says if you are really looking for opportunities to impute motives which as not present."[87] To Brown, he wrote, "This mastery presentation [Brown's response] should convince her that you are not the devil she accused you of being."[88] The Brown reply to which Van Der Linde referred, included Brown's comment that "I feel confident that we can discuss these issues with open minds, searching for facts and accepting differences of opinion. I don't expect to say things and get universal agreement, but please Mrs. Engs, let us never destroy the American system of freedom of opinion—your opinion and mine—even if we disagree."[89]

The Red Scare had received an infusion of credibility in early 1950 from McCarthy. On February 9, he made a speech in Wheeling, West Virginia, in which he waved a piece of paper in the air that he said contained the names of more than 200 State Department employees whom he claimed were known Communists. His speech vaulted the Wisconsin politician into national prominence and aroused the public's paranoia regarding communist spying in the U.S. Coming on the heels of Mao Tse-tung's takeover of China, Russian detonation of its first atomic bomb, and charges against the State Department's Alger Hiss of spying, it created a new level of Cold War hysteria in the U.S. Brown was among the first journalists to expose McCarthy, in 1948, for what he really was: a demagogue who craved publicity more than the truth. He began doing reports critical of McCarthy's tactics soon thereafter, joining Drew Pearson and Elmer Davis (who was presenting commentary at ABC) as the earliest national journalists to criticize McCarthy. Pearson's sponsors abandoned him, after which NBC cancelled his show. Because most American political reporters were practicing "pure objectivity," McCarthy successfully manipulated their stories. Setting aside what their instincts and even observations told them about McCarthy, they reported only what they saw, what quotable spokesmen told them, or what written sources provided. Brown did not observe such limitations.[90]

ABC, conversely, which trailed all the other networks in audience ratings, was granting Davis more freedom than he had enjoyed at CBS. Like Brown, he argued against the prevailing mood of "fear of intelligence, fear of thinking, [and] fear to trust your own opinion." Both Davis and Brown called for reason, courage and caution against allowing McCarthyism to hysterically mobilize the public.[91] Brown continued his criticism of McCarthy throughout the subsequent months, even though numerous politicians and conservative journalists jumped on the senator's bandwagon in accusing, without evidence, creative artists and journalists of being Communists. Brown saw McCarthy producing a chilling effect on public speech, progressive education and scientific innovation. Four years later, Murrow joined Brown in exposing McCarthy's campaign as the work of a manipulator of facts who had harmed numerous Americans' rights and reputations. Murrow's noteworthy 1954 *See It Now* program, in which he documented McCarthy's unsubstantiated tactics, is often heralded for having constituted the beginning of the end for McCarthy. But Brown, along with Davis, had exposed McCarthy repeatedly in the years before. That historians identify the *See It Now* episode more vividly speaks to the attention television was attracting in the early 1950s in comparison to radio as well as Murrow's notoriety.

As the Army-McCarthy Senate hearings—which got underway in March 1954 to consider conflicting charges about communist infiltration of the Army, Brown said McCarthy and his supporters were trying to "reduce free people into frightened people." He charged that McCarthy's accusations presented a greater danger within the U.S. than the threat of communist attack from without. He identified the danger as "a growing fear to speak, write, to have free discussion and free inquiry—this eagerness to confuse disagreement with treason." He asserted that McCarthy's charges were helping the Russians defeat the U.S. without firing a shot.[92] Brown continued to disparage the House un-American Activities Committee at the same time, citing a summer 1954 incident in which the committee sought to bar a beauty contestant from visiting the U.S. as a participant in the Miss Universe pageant. Immigration officials had denied Greece's beautiful Rita Diallina a visa so she could compete in Long Beach. Officials charged that she once had designed a book cover for a communist writer. "We can hardly permit such a designer—however beautiful she may be—to come over here with designs on our government. It could imperil the very survival of the United States," deadpanned Brown.[93] And as the Senate was about to censure McCarthy in 1955, Brown commented: "[He] is the haven and refuge of the racial bigots, the soreheads, the isolationists, the make-war-now crowd, the anti-foreigners, anti-intellectuals, anti-allies, and anti-United Nations."[94]

In response to Brown's statements against McCarthy, listeners were divided in their reactions to him. "At a time when reason and decency and truth have been drowned out by un–American reactionaries like Senator McCarthy and his ilk, it is vital that the millions of thoughtful people in this nation who still believe in democracy stand by a vigorous adherent of honesty such as yourself," wrote a listener from California.[95] But others charged Brown with traitorous comments regarding McCarthy, whom they viewed as a true patriot. But subsequent events validated Brown's criticism. In a five-page response to one critic, he remarked, "I find no evidence whatever to revise any of my observations about Senator McCarthy. I consider him irresponsible and reckless…. I consider him dangerous. I hope you will continue to listen to my broadcasts, giving to them your critical analysis, recognizing that if we differ … [that each broadcast] is genuinely and intelligently concerned with the welfare of our country."[96] When McCarthy died in 1957, Brown said McCarthy had proved two things: "That one senator could frighten the entire U.S. government, from the president on down; and second, that one senator, if he conducted himself vigorously could condemn the image of the U.S. all around the world." In concluding his commentary on McCarthy, Brown said a man's death is supposed to produce kind words about him, but all that he could say about McCarthy was that "he was the victim of forces within himself that he himself may not have understood…. Driven by hates and fears, he became a man to be pitied."[97]

Brown certainly provided an example in his body of work in Kaltenborn's statement that a network commentator knows he is doing a good job when he pleases as many people as he offends. As Kaltenborn had put it, "I am constantly accused of being pro–German, pro–Japanese, pro–Communist, or pro–Roosevelt. So long as I get an equal number of letters telling me that I am anti–German or anti–Roosevelt, I feel reasonably certain that I am being neutral."[98] Brown's correspondence reflects that his commentaries definitely generated respondents who agreed and disagreed with him. In March 1950, Hollywood produce Sam Goldwyn wrote Brown, "I want you to know that I listen to your broadcasts from abroad every morning at 8:00 Los Angeles time, and I found your reports on England, Austria and all the other countries most interesting. You … gave me a liberal education as to what is going on the other side."[99] Another member of his audience wrote, "We have been listening to your news and comment over the radio for a long time and we surely enjoy every minute of it. If all the commentators would give us the real thing like you do Mr. Brown I think this would be a better place to live in. You sure have the courage to give it to us straight from both the Republicans and Democrats regardless of what they think or like." And from yet another, "Every morning I hear your broadcasts. I especially welcome your fearless, comprehensive, and clear-cut way of putting things."[100] Brown claimed that favorable mail regarding his broadcasts comprised 85 percent of the letters he received.[101]

Among network commentators, both the public and broadcast brethren consistently classified Brown as a liberal. He agreed with the assessment in a letter in March 1948 to Seniel Ostrow, president of the Sealy Mattress Company, which sponsored a Brown programs. "I consider myself a liberal and a progressive and I attempt to reflect those views in my broadcasts." Yet the next part of Brown's response indicates that he was not speaking strictly in political terms. "It seems to me that a liberal must be concerned with the basic rights of the human being. In addition, he must recognize and attempt to deal with the expanding needs in the hearts and minds of individuals."[102] Given his Jewish immigrant family's background as persecuted underdogs, Brown's positions can be categorized as favoring human decency and calling for leadership accountability. He remained true to these ideals, regardless of where those positions took him along the political spectrum. This made it increasingly difficult to pigeonhole Brown, especially with shifting international alliances after World War II and U.S. policies that seemed to him to be inconsistent and sometimes less than principled during the 1950s.

Without a doubt, during the second half of the 1940s and into the '50s, Brown's positions on a number of issues aligned him with the liberal perspective. One could say the same for most of the Murrow Boys. Brown was like most journalists in the 1950s who believed the U.S. had to be a worldwide police force to contain Communism. He supported Truman's military buildup, but today Republicans claim that position as a mainstay of their legislative platform. His anti-communist position was more conservative than liberal. He was a champion for civil rights and free expression, issues that Democrats favored, and he criticized the policies of big business, with which Republicans aligned themselves. The GOP also favored the status quo when it came to civil rights and tolerated the anti-communist campaign. Traditional conservatives were critical of New Deal (and Truman's Fair Deal) initiatives, such as strengthening unions, increasing the minimum wage, and global involvement. Brown supported all of those strategies to uplift the livelihood of everyday Americans. These positions add up to Brown exemplifying what political scientist George Wright has classified as a "modern," or "corporate-liberal." This placed Brown close to the popular political center during the period that extended from just after World War II until the end of the Lyndon Johnson Administration.[103]

In a letter to one of his sponsors, Kraft Foods, in 1956, Brown depicted himself somewhat differently. "My broadcasts and my approach to them do not represent a liberal, radical, conservative, left-wing, right-wing, middle-of-the-road, Democratic or Republican label. They are designed ... to be an intelligent, balanced and tasteful examination of the facts and circumstances of the issue." He observed that it had become popular to label everyone as either rightwing or leftwing, Communist or anti-communist. He said too many Americans tossed around such labels too easily, and that his principles were "not the prisoner of political parties, and they are not captive of an unawareness of events. If my work needs definition, I should say it is actuated by such propulsions as these: The American Constitution, the Bill of Rights, a recognition of evolutionary events, a compassion for human weakness, and a respect for character, integrity and decency."[104] Jonathan Brown said he did not view his uncle as consistently liberal: "It never appeared to me that his opinions were ideological. I think life would have been easier for him if people could have said, 'Well, Cecil Brown was a leftist.' Then all the leftists would have rallied around him, but he wasn't. Nor was he conservative. He never lost the idea that journalists should be truthsayers. He looked for the truth wherever he found it, rather than following the line of the left or the right. I think that's fairly unusual. [And] he suffered for that."[105] For Brown, issues that began simmering in the 1940s would dominate the headlines and alter American society and the world throughout the 1950s. He examined and commented on most of these throughout the Eisenhower years, which helped create a new set of problems.

♦♦ 10 ♦♦

Fighting for Unpopular Causes

Scholar William Frayer, who analyzed Brown's radio delivery, commented that he sometimes sounded "overwrought," but that he "identifies his own point of view with sanity, progress and a solicitous concern for all mankind. He is effective in jolting his listeners to an awareness of important issues."[1] There is no doubt that Brown's announcing demeanor disseminated his conviction that political and military dangers were ever-present internationally and domestically, and that listeners needed to be vigilant in guarding against the threats.

On the air, it often sounded as if he were delivering an after-dinner speech. In fact, there seemed to be little difference between the manner in which he delivered speeches and radio commentary. But after a decade at Mutual, both listeners and critics learned to overlook his speaking style in deference to the quality of his message. Walter Goodman, writing in the *New Republic*, exemplified an appreciation for Brown's abilities when he compared him to his Mutual colleagues. "A few of the minor attractions [commentators] seem primarily concerned with reporting the news. Cecil Brown ... [is] by no means apolitical ... a quiet liberal ... [but he does not] grind his ax so furiously that you can't see the news for the sparks.... [His work is] a calling, which distinguishes him around MBS."[2] Others found Brown's announcing, while often excitable, assuring. Hollywood producer Alfred Nadel wrote of Brown: "His manner and strength ... never failed to give me great comfort." Another 1940s era listener said listening to his broadcasts "even in the grimmest of times, was always a morale booster. He gave us the facts and the necessary background to interpret them and to see them in a world perspective. His confident and well-modulated voice was reassuring."[3]

The quality of his commentaries kept Brown in demand as a public speaker. Nationwide audiences respected his knowledge and forthrightness, and they were willing to pay to hear him. In October 1944, he told an audience in Lewiston, Maine, that they should view America's part in World War II as "an historic mission which may never come to us again." A reporter said

10. Fighting for Unpopular Causes 163

Brown's presentation was "frank and intense."[4] In his diary, Brown recorded that during 1945 alone he spoke at such diverse locations as the Carl L. Norden Company in Indianapolis (manufacturers of the Norden bombsight), at multiple locations on the Four Freedoms Tour to raise support for war bonds, and at military installations, such as Fort Hamilton in Brooklyn, where he was asked to help boost the soldiers' morale. He also spoke on college campuses. He was in such demand he could have spoken somewhere practically every night, but his broadcast schedule was also becoming more demanding.

In September 1945, MBS moved Brown's news and analysis program to the 11:00–11:15 a.m. Monday through Friday time slot, where he would remain for the duration of his years at the network. The following June, he began a new one night per week five-minute commentary program. Then in September 1947, MBS began another Brown commentary program, fifteen minutes in length, on Sunday afternoons at 1 p.m., sponsored by State Farm. In July 1953, he would add yet another five-minute commentary slot to his schedule of broadcasts at 5:55 p.m. each day, sponsored first by Johnson Wax, and later by Kraft Foods. By 1955, 220 stations were airing his morning broadcasts, which the network retitled *The Real News of the Day*, and 540 affiliates aired his afternoon commentaries. It was a busy schedule, but his ratings were strong, which attracted advertisers. Brown believed that it was his job to debunk mainstream opinion as well as cut through what he perceived to be political doubletalk. He increasingly viewed himself as a commentator who wasn't "looking for abject agreement from his listeners[;] he hoped rather to tease the not-interested into being interested." What pleased him the most was that the longer he worked at Mutual the more inquiries he received from listeners regarding overseas' developments.[5] He believed this was a good sign that he was helping his audience become more educated about world affairs. When Kraft executives cautioned him in the mid–1950s that they were concerned about his liberal views, he responded: "My broadcasts have a long and honorable record of premature recognition of events which, while producing a mature examination of those events, were upsetting at the time the reports were made."[6] He referenced his stories about civil rights and Joe McCarthy as examples in which he had been out front with stories, the importance of which was confirmed later. Despite misgivings, Kraft stuck with him.

Brown relied on wire services only for small portions of his news updates or as leads to introduce commentaries. In most of his copy, he utilized his own research, gleaned from reading more than a dozen daily newspapers and magazines, and personal interviews. Typically, he began each commentary by presenting a problem, building a case for or against particular solutions, offering evidence for the solution(s), then concluded with two to three sentences that encouraged the audience to agree with his recommended course of action. An analysis of his writing reveals that Brown often employed anecdotes, figurative and literal analogies, and comparisons, supported with testimonials drawn from his and others eyewitnesses' accounts. He utilized inductive reasoning to establish the credibility of his premises, and then built deductive arguments to support his positions. He painted word pictures to make the stories vivid, often seeking to appeal to listeners' emotions, including pride, shame and patriotism. Brown sometimes unambiguously advocated a perspective, but sometimes indirectly urged listeners to take action by marshaling statistics, quotations and examples of historical precedence.

He commonly inserted loaded words into his scripts, such as fascist, Communist or isolationist, and utilized stereotypes as a shorthand device. He likewise relied upon a variety of sentence forms, such as repetition, parallelism, amplification, imagery, contrast, and rhetorical questions to accentuate important points. He cast himself as the authority on the issue he was outlining.[7] Brown was, after all, a persuader, whose job it was to convince the audience to agree with him and even carry out a course of action. He fulfilled the duties that latter-day CBS and NPR producer Jay Kernis said a commentator should fulfill. They "should provoke thought. 'That means airing commentaries that are provocative and original even adventurous—opinion and analysis that you will hear nowhere else.'"[8]

Brown's communication strategies helped him achieve what Walter Lippman had identified in 1922 as news that generated a worldview by creating "pictures of reality in their [listener's] heads."[9] Brown's depictions domestically and internationally created their perception of reality in audience members' minds. It was what a commentary needed to do, especially in the years after World War II, to help the audience understand an increasingly complicated world of evolving alliances and cultural change. Throughout his career, Brown executed Murrow's directive regarding the proper blend of intellect and understandability in presenting the news. "You are supposed to describe things in terms that make sense to the truck driver without insulting the intelligence of the professor."[10] In this sense, Brown did not employ references to philosophers or intellectuals, but he utilized historical benchmarks to locate events in a larger context. He understood that many in his audience lacked the background to understand that world and domestic activities were not occurring without precedence or in a vacuum.

Beginning in 1945, as the war was ending, multiple events occurred that influenced Brown's own worldview. The first was the April organizational meeting of the United Nations in San Francisco. Based on what he had witnessed during the past seven years, he believed the organization provided the best hope for the world to achieve peace. In July, Stalin, Churchill and Truman met in Potsdam, Germany, to plan Europe's future. Simultaneously, hearings were beginning in the Senate to ratify the U.N. Charter. The events put Brown in a hopeful mood. "Edward R. Stettinius, the first U.S. Ambassador to the U.N., told the Senate committee that the San Francisco meetings prove that the Big Five know how to cooperate. That is quite true. So the success at San Francisco shows that prospects are rather good for success at Potsdam as well."[11] The second event occurred August 6, when a U.S. B-29 dropped the first atomic bomb on Hiroshima. The day after, though Brown was unaware of the extent of the devastation and loss of life, he said the Japanese had to decide whether they wanted all of their cities destroyed unless they agreed to an unconditional surrender. "This is a wonderful and amazing day in history, and it is also the most frightening man has every faced," he concluded. Several of Brown's commentaries in the days thereafter indicate that he was as surprised as anyone that the U.S. had used such an incredible weapon, but he also was dismayed that other countries would soon be able to utilize it to wage war. "This discovery is bound to affect the world as much as the discovery by ancient man that he could make a fire with stone, or the discovery of gunpowder, or the invention of the printing press or the steam engine," Brown commented.[12]

He believed the U.N. provided the best, and perhaps only, solution to preventing a cataclysmic world war. After John Hersey's "Hiroshima" appeared in the *New Yorker* a year later, Brown stated: "[E]ither we do away with war or we engage in an atomic bomb race here in America and elsewhere."[13] He voiced intolerance with Republicans concerning their opposition to the U.N.: "The Republican Party is still in the midst of trying to make a decision it can't quite make. It can't decide yet whether there's anything worthwhile to this idea of world cooperation."[14] Over the next decade, as relations between Russia and the U.S. deteriorated, he often revisited the threat of nuclear war and championed the U.N. as the solution to preventing a conflict that could destroy civilization. In 1948, he explained that if Russia launched a nuclear attack on the U.S., the weapons would wipe out twelve of the nation's major cities and kill 26,000,000 Americans within the first twenty-four hours.[15]

The third event that affected Brown's perspective began to unfold in 1947. The president became embroiled in international controversy when he failed to publicly support the establishment of the nation of Israel. The Israeli story was one that struck close to home for Brown because, given his family's genealogy, it was personal, and the president's restraint diminished Brown's admiration of Truman. The British had controlled Palestine since the end of World War I. The Palestinians considered it their home, but Jews had been immigrating to the area since the 1920s and '30s, saying it was rightfully their homeland, which resulted in recurring trouble between the two. The Holocaust had encouraged even more Jews to immigrate to Jerusalem. British forces attempted to restore peace but soon found themselves caught in the crossfire. Throughout 1946, with the British waffling on their next step, and Truman failing to take a proactive role, Brown criticized both. He said the British had become experts in stopping 100,000 Jews from entering the country. He argued that the British "record is filled with broken promises to both peoples [Arab and Jew]" because the British did not want to give up Palestine. He called for partitioning of Palestine and said Truman should send U.S. troops to undergird the Israeli cause.[16]

In March 1947, the president asked Congress to provide aid to Greece and Turkey to stop communist forces from overrunning those countries. The statement—later labeled the Truman Doctrine—signaled a new era in U.S. foreign policy. It also signaled the unofficial beginning of the Cold War, as Truman declared that the U.S. would take steps to contain communist aggression around the planet. Brown approved of the policy, saying, "The stakes were too high [for the U.S.] to desert its friends in their hour of great need," but he continued to be upset that the president did not take proactive steps to secure Israel what he labeled its "rightful place" in Palestine.[17] What Brown did not know was that within the administration a struggle was taking place concerning the risks of the U.S. supporting Israel because of apprehension that the nation would be drawn into an unwinnable Middle East war.[18]

The crisis came to a head in July 1947 when the British Navy intercepted the *Exodus*, a ship loaded with 4,500 Holocaust survivors, bound for Palestine. None of the Jews possessed proper immigration papers, and before the ship could dock in Palestine, British destroyers rammed it and towed it, first to Haifa and then France. The French refused to allow the Jews to disembark, and they had to remain in the ship's cargo hold for twenty-four brutally hot days, without adequate food and sanitary facilities. The British then transported them to detention camps on Cyprus, while the world press depicted the British as cruel and heartless. The English Parliament, looking for a way out of the catastrophe, asked the U.N. to partition Palestine. On September 1, Brown broadcast a commentary in which he supported establishment of the nation of Israel. In addition to being a humanitarian solution, he believed the initiative would open the Eastern Mediterranean to economic development and Western-style democracy." He said Jewish farms would make "the desert wastes grow where once there had been nothing but sand." He argued that "the Jew can do that, and the record shows that the Arab either cannot or will not."[19]

The creation of Israel took another tumultuous year to become reality. Throughout the crisis, Truman failed to publicly support partitioning until it became a foregone conclusion. The president's inaction disappointed Brown, which he believed would have added urgency to the process. He chided the White House for its inaction and failure to comprehend what its indecisiveness was doing to the reputation of the U.S. around the globe regarding human rights.[20] In September 1947, Brown called the British-appointed Mufti, who was in charge of governing Palestine, an "opportunist ... [whose] opposition to partition and threat to align themselves with the Soviets was an attempt at oil blackmail." In February 1948, Brown accused Truman of failing to support partitioning with military force, which he strongly advocated. Brown told his audience that he was convinced Palestine was the "number one issue before the world. How the United States handled the crisis would determine the future of the U.N. and ultimate control of the West's most strategic outpost." On March 20, Truman told the U.N. he believed Palestinian partitioning was not viable. Brown said the president's position "mortally wounded the United Nations and reflects America's gutless fear of Russia." He added that the decision meant an "abandoning of our moral position as the champion of democracy." Two months later, in the midst of combat with Palestinian forces, the Israelis took matters into their own hands by declaring the land they had acquired as the independent nation of Israel on May 14, 1948. During the intervening time, Truman and the U.N. had waffled on what position to take, but after May 14, they both recognized Israel's sovereignty.

In the aftermath, Brown called American policy toward Palestine "notable for its amateur approach, [and] its incredible unawareness of what we ourselves were doing."[21] He declared that "the dream" of an Israeli homeland had become a reality "not because big powers were honorable, [that they] kept their promises or [that they] were wild about justice." The new Jewish state, he added, had come into being only "because the world still prefers to depend on force of arms rather than understanding or decency." Brown and the other members of the pro–Israel-U.S. press had played a role in mustering popular sentiment for Israel.[22] But his inexorable support did not sit well with all his listeners. "I know that you are Jewish, but that is still no reason to lose your objectivity," wrote Presbyterian minister Thomas Kirkman, Jr., of Wisconsin, who added that in Brown's commentaries "there was only praise for Israel.... Once again, Israel was a god and the Arabs were the devil."[23]

Two years later, in February 1950, Cecil and Martha visited Israel on one of what had become numerous multi-nation journeys. The previous November, the United Nations had voted to "internationalize (*corpus separatum*) Jerusalem," in which both Israel and the Arabs claimed it as their capital. The U.N.'s vote did not, of course, please Israel's leaders, nor Brown, and he made his view known. He said Russian diplomats had assured Moshe Sharett, Israel's Foreign Minister, that it would support Israel against internationalization at the U.N., but had "double-crossed" Israel. He said Israel was merely a pawn in the Cold War struggle between the U.S. and Russia. He speculated that the Truman Administration was treading carefully because

Soviet leaders were prohibiting three-million Jews in Russia from immigrating to Israel. He explained that Russia was one of the biggest landowners in Jerusalem. It was an unusually long commentary, more than six minutes in length, and its purpose was to educate the American audience about the reasoning behind the U.N. vote. Brown concluded by saying, "With straight faces, the Communists in Israel said, 'When we called for a National Jerusalem, we meant an International Jerusalem.' It's clear that the Communists in Israel are the same as those in the U.S.: the total stooges of Moscow."[24]

In the years after the founding of Israel, Brown made his support of the Jewish nation quite public and substantive. In January 1951, he spoke in Pittsburgh, at the YMCA before the Hadassah Builders' Donor Rally. The purpose of the really was to raise funds to build a new medical center in Jerusalem, and a poster for the rally billed Brown as a "fearless commentator" who was unafraid to speak on behalf of Israel.[25] Three months later, he spoke at the kickoff dinner of the Federated Jewish Welfare campaign of Bridgeport, Connecticut. Organizers targeted the money raised that evening to benefit Israel as well as local, state and national Jewish organizations. Between the two occasions, Brown personally visited Israel again. He interviewed Premier David Ben-Gurion and surveyed conditions in the tent cities. He said he also had "evaluated the social, political and economic problems there."[26] He told the Bridgeport audience how impressed he had been with Israeli developments during the previous four years. In a later radio commentary, he told listeners: "If all through the Middle East there was the same energy and drive—the same determination to give new birth to a parched and ignored soil—as there is in Israel—then most of the problems of the Middle East would evaporate."[27] And in yet another speech he gave on the topic in 1951, he called Israel "the most exciting country I have ever been in."[28]

A month later, he spoke in Massena, New York, at a Jewish Appeal fundraising dinner, and soon thereafter gave an impassioned speech before the Women's Division of the United Jewish Fund in Columbus, Ohio. At that gathering, he told the women, "Nothing you have read, no picture you have studied could prepare you for the stirring experience of seeing Israel right now." He related how he and Martha had traveled the full length of Israel, talking with people who lived in a variety of circumstances. Holding a small jar with sand in it from Israel in his right hand and a stone from the Negev Desert in the other, he said, "There are three things in Israel, this dry sand, these stones that cover the fields, and if these were all, there would be no future for Israel. But there is a third thing: the people. The dedicated, stubborn people, more stubborn than this dry soil, more stubborn than these hard rocks. These are the great resource of Israel." He called Israel "a promise that must be fulfilled,"[29] and his speech helped raise $40,000 for the new nation.

During the next few years, he continued to champion the call for Israeli support in speeches across the U.S. In March 1953, he was the featured speaker at the Temple Beth Israel Mobilization Rally in San Diego. A poster for the rally said Brown would answer the questions "How can I stop persecution of Jews around the world, particularly behind the Iron Curtain? How can you help maintain a strong Democratic Israel?" Brown told the audience they could help answer the questions by "support[ing] national and local [Jewish] agencies." His comments addressed the heightening crises created by communist aggression around the world, which was threatening Jews in Europe and the Near East.[30]

Throughout the late 1940s and into the '50s, many of Brown's speaking engagements highlighted his knowledge of international affairs. In October 1950, for example, Brown addressed students and faculty at Central Washington College, where his topics were the Cold War and Korea. He called American foreign policy "timid" and that the U.S. had "abandoned moral and ethical principles" when it supported tyranny in Yugoslavia, Spain and Western Germany. He charged that the U.S. was "in the position of trying to hire any thug or *gangster* [emphasis mine] that would help it in achieving international aims ... for reasons of expediency or because it is the realistic thing to do." He warned that employing such a strategy was "like committing the first murder. It is easier after that."[31] Following a speech in New Mexico that fall, in which Brown stressed similar themes, Methodist Minister Will-Matthis Dunn wrote Brown an appreciative letter. The pastor said he was sending only the second fan letter he had ever written, but Brown had impressed him in Los Alamos on October 30. "I wish to thank you for your keen analysis of the contemporary problems facing us.... We need more men like you, sir. I pray God's blessing will attend you, and that you may reach many people with your message."[32]

To obtain firsthand knowledge about international situations, beginning in 1947 Cecil and Martha embarked upon a series of overseas trips so he could gather facts and conduct interviews. They had unsuccessfully attempted to have children, so they were free to travel extensively. Because Martha had worked in public relations during World War II and published her own articles, she knew her way around journalism. She and Cecil were devoted to one another, and she was committed to helping him with his work. Because both of them had already traveled extensively, they enjoyed visiting other nations and meeting the indigenous people. She also helped maintain his health and deal with the various modes of transportation better than he had on his own during the war. The trips were important in helping him better understand the people of the world, including his enemies. "A free flow of information aids in understanding the hopes, aspirations and desires of others. The better you know a person the less desire you have to punch his nose," he said.[33]

In the summer of 1947, they spent two months in England and France, where Cecil reported on those nation's post-war status. In July 1949, he planned to travel without Martha but with a group of journalists to the Far East. On the thirteenth of that month, the plane he was supposed to be on, a Royal Dutch Constellation, crashed three miles from Bombay's Santa Crus Airport in a monsoon. All eighty-four passengers and eleven crewmembers were killed, including thirteen journalists. Only a last-minute snag in connections had caused Brown to miss the flight. The journalists had been on a tour of Southeast Asia and were on their way to interview Indian Prime Minister Jawaharla Nehru in New Delhi. Among the dead were WOR's H.R. Knickerbocher and Mutual's Elsie Dick.[34]

A month later, the Browns began a ten-nation journey to France, West Germany, Czechoslovakia, Austria, Yugoslavia, Switzerland, Italy, Israel, Spain and Portugal. As they were boarding their flight at LaGuardia, Brown told a reporter he was determined to "picture in sound the voice of the people of Europe, to bring home to Americans an understanding of what the people of Europe think and believe." He said it was important for him to help Americans understand the state of mind of Europeans who were attempting to pick up the pieces of their nations and lives in the aftermath of the war's devastation. He was the first U.S. correspondent to visit Europe after the Russians had made their initial nuclear test on August 29, 1949. He said U.S. "security is tied up in the stability and prosperity and the survival of Europe. I intend to find out how the individual people in these countries feel about us."[35] During their travels, the Browns exercised a proclivity for collecting ceramics, paintings and dolls (especially Asian art) that represented the various nations they visited, and they enjoyed sampling a wide variety of cuisine. In broadcasts after the trip, Brown called upon the U.S. to provide aid to underdeveloped countries, saying it constituted the best prescription to defeating communism. "Always in history there have been the poor and miserable, but historians might agree, never before has there been such a burning desire of so many people to get away from that poverty and misery," he said.[36]

The following year, the Browns embarked upon a five-month, 40,000 mile around-the- world tour. On these late 1940s and early 1950s expeditions, he carried with him one of the first portable reel-to-reel tape recorders, which weighed a hefty sixteen pounds. Mutual advertised the excursion to help promote sales of the Ampex company recorder, saying that tape recording, which was barely three years old, was revolutionizing radio programming. "Were it not for the dramatic rise of television in the postwar era, the tape recorder would now be the most talked about development in the history of broadcasting," claimed Ampex. Brown airmailed the recordings to New York for broadcast. Mutual promoted the fact that he could make recordings in airplanes and autos, and "out in the field interviews with farmers, in homes with

10. Fighting for Unpopular Causes 171

housewives, with heads of state as they relax in their garden, with troops in the field, and workers at their job."[37]

Between July and December 1951, the Browns spent twenty weeks traveling around the world to Greece, the Philippines, Yugoslavia, Korea, Japan, Pakistan, India, Germany, Turkey, Israel, Taiwan, Hong Kong, Tokyo, Manilla, and London. He made six recordings each week from the various locations and shipped them to New York. It was the first time a radio journalist had pulled off the feat of recording and having a U.S. network air audio reports from such a broad range of locations. Brown's Mutual sponsors underwrote the trips. The most humorous highlight of the 1951 excursion was when Japan's Emperor Hirohito granted Brown an interview. Brown almost sabotaged the opportunity, however. Because he was six-foot-four-inches tall—substantially taller than the average Japanese man—he could not locate formal clothing that such an occasion required. Brown feared his inappropriate attire could cost him the interview, but he showed up anyway in a navy blue suit. When he arrived at the Emperor's Palace, and an aide saw his attire, he told Brown to be seated and excused himself. While Brown waited, he wondered if when the aide returned he would tell him that that the emperor would not see him. But after several minutes, the aide returned and ushered Brown in to meet the Emperor. To Brown's surprise, the emperor was wearing striped trousers and a blue business jacket. Brown later learned that Hirohito had discarded his cutaway suit to make Brown feel more comfortable during the interview.[38]

At another stop, he conducted the last interview with Pakistani Prime Minister Liaquat Ali Khan before an Afghan national assassinated him. Exiled Nationalist Chinese leader Chiang Kai-Shek also agreed to be interviewed by Brown. It turned out to be the longest interview any U.S. reporter had achieved up until that time. The Generalissimo told Brown that he had six-million men available in Taiwan to re-take mainland China "if and when he [Chiang] mounts one." He added that guerilla forces in mainland China were already active and would join his troops in attacking the communists. When Brown asked if he needed U.S. military assistance to mount the invasion, Chiang replied that he did not require additional troops, but that he needed "military aid and equipment and ammunitions, plus some technical advisers." Major U.S. newspapers reported the Generalissimo's comments to Brown in the following day's editions.[39]

Upon returning from the journey, Brown composed a fifteen-page summary for State Farm, one of the trip's underwriters. Brown wrote that the U.S. was the strongest nation on the planet, but that it could not financially support the rest of the world. He added that Americans were facing an international crisis "never before equaled in its demands on finances, courage, sacrifice, manpower and spirit." The latter statement was particularly interesting, given his experience a little more than a decade earlier during World

War II. In a subsequent broadcast, he warned: "No young man can now look forward to what is known as a state of peace. The United States must become strong, must acquire discipline and accept the meaning of duty to this country and to our allies."[40]

Brown's jaunts around the planet pleased Mutual executives because it allowed them to boast that he possessed a determination for getting facts first hand, and that he did his own research and reporting for each of his commentaries. One of the network's newspaper advertisements crowed: "His extensive travels throughout the world—he's actually become an around-the-world commuter—have given him inexhaustible contacts that permit behind-the-scenes explanations of each day's headlines."[41] A later press release said, "'If Cecil Brown goes around the world one more time,' a fellow reporter has remarked, 'he'll qualify as an artificial satellite.'"[42] In 1954, the couple was off again. This time, Brown met and recorded interviews with a variety of leaders as well as everyday people, in England, France, West Germany, Brussels, Belgium and the Netherlands. The couple concluded their around-the-world newsgathering junkets on behalf of Mutual three years later, when they visited the Soviet Union, Poland, Germany, Denmark, Sweden and France.

Sometimes Brown did not have to travel overseas to secure international news—sometimes it came to him. Such was the case in 1951. That year, a historic disagreement prompted Brown to voice commentaries that caused almost as much controversy as the historic dispute he was addressing. The commentaries dealt with the Korean War power struggle between General Douglas MacArthur and Truman. MacArthur insisted that Truman allow him to direct U.S. troops to invade North Korea and to launch bombing raids on China. MacArthur was confident that China would not retaliate, but Truman was not as confident, fearing such aggression would bring China into the conflict, thus turning it into another global war. Truman and MacArthur had disagreed on military strategy for several months, with MacArthur publicly contradicting what Truman was saying. The day before Truman made a public statement about what he would do regarding MacArthur's recalcitrance, Brown urged the president to reign in the flamboyant MacArthur. Brown understood that a constitutional mandate was at stake regarding who was in charge of the military: the president or the commander in the field. Criticizing MacArthur was not a popular position to take as far as the American public was concerned. The majority of Americans believed the U.S. had defeated the Japanese in the Pacific because of MacArthur's leadership, and that his earlier Korean War strategies had saved South Korea from a North Korean invasion. They believed the World War II hero knew more about how to win a war than Truman. Nonetheless, the Founding Fathers had written Article II of the Constitution, which established the president as the commander in chief. They had done so to ensure that the military could never mount a dictatorship, as early Americans had witnessed in Europe. Brown said a "very fundamental matter" was at stake in the dispute, in referring to the constitutional nature of MacArthur's challenge of Truman's authority. "It's an odd thing, but those Americans who say they fear military control of the United States, now seem to want to give MacArthur what they call a free hand." Brown lamented the public's failure to recognize what they were risking: "On the face of it, it's incredible, that suddenly, a segment of the American public should want to abandon the customary processes of our government and our political system."[43]

Truman fired MacArthur on April 11, 1951, but the majority of Americans continued to support MacArthur. Historians have called it the most famous civilian-military confrontation in U.S. history, and it established a precedent that presidents could fire military commanders for publicly disagreeing with official policy. Brown's rejoinder to the opposition to Truman was to say the Russian's "devout wish" was to get the U.S. involved in a war with China, which he said would lead to World War III. Brown reflected, "I can't recall when so many people, ordinarily considered responsible, were so strongly in favor of this form of military dictatorship." He said those who thought Congress should impeach Truman were only wrong in that he should have been impeached if he had failed to fire MacArthur. Brown told listeners that a groundswell of popular opinion did not mean that the majority possessed the truth. "It would be well for us to recognize," argued Brown, "those who consider it more important to 'get' Truman, than to stop Stalin." In criticizing conservative journalists who supported MacArthur, Brown added, "That is also the aim of the extreme ring-wing commentators."[44] Of course, when MacArthur returned to the U.S., he received a Caesar's-style welcome and delivered his "Old Solder's Never Die" speech before a special session of Congress.[45]

Brown's position on the controversy provoked dozens of listeners to express their agreement or disagreement with him. He said on no other subject on which he did broadcasts during his career did he receive a larger number of letters. He was gratified by writers who recognized the value of his dissent from popular opinion. Evelyn Bing of Las Vegas wrote, "Your analysis of the MacArthur incident is the most penetrating I have heard." Mrs. Walter Power of Albany, New York, told Brown, "In all the hysterical uproar that has swept our poor country these last hours. Your voice has emerged as the most truly realistic and rational. You did not wait as did so many 'name' commentators to sense [sic] whence blew the wind." Mrs. R.J. Trumpfer of Berkley, California, called Brown's comments "courageous and enlightened." An anonymous writer told Brown: "If all the commentators would give us the real thing as you do.... [But] all the other commentators ... carried on so over the radio that it made us nervous."[46] Helen Eberhard of Artesia, California, wrote, "Thank you for your two very fine broadcasts of yesterday and today. McArthur has played God long enough." Another, from San Francisco, read: "Your forthright and courageous logic on the MacArthur situation is a godsend in these emotional times. Without men of your caliber, even those of us who try to think straight would find the comfort of the easy path almost too appealing to resist when faced with overwhelming opposition such as is being demonstrated around us here today."[47]

Concerning the war itself, Brown was as frustrated as most observers regarding the stalemate in Korea. A month after the war began in June 1950, Brown had been hopeful the conflict would help U.S. leaders become more sagacious in dealing with the new realities of the post–World War II world. "As tragic as the Korean War is, it can serve a worthwhile purpose. It can reveal American weaknesses in dealing with the facts of the world as it is," he concluded. But Red Chinese involvement and the surreptitious support of Russia only made Korea a more complicated and troubling conflict. Brown thought the war could be lost if China decided it wanted to push the U.S. out of Korea. He said the U.S. Army had overextended itself, and he cautioned listeners that communist forces were now a threat in Eastern and Western Europe, too. He believed that Russia's actions in both areas demonstrated that it "intends to conquer." Therefore, Americans could not continue to bask in the afterglow of victory from 1945, but had to prepare themselves for "rigorous living." He praised the Truman Doctrine and the Marshall Plan, saying Western Europe would be in peril if not for U.S. military and monetary aid. But he added that if Americans wanted European gratitude for all the aid they had shipped there, we should not expect it. Rather, Americans should be thrilled with "the concrete fact that it stopped the western tide of communism. And after you've seen what communist control does to a people, how it makes people outright slaves, stopping that tide is something to be grateful for."[48] He cautioned, on the other hand, that "the peace of the world is at the mercy of an incident."[49]

In only five years, the U.S. had gone from celebrating unconditional victory over Germany and Japan to a conditional impasse in Korea. During several commentaries, Brown said the only reason the two sides had not reached an armistice was that Russia wanted to see the war go on so it would occupy and drain America's military resources.[50] Following a 1951 tour of the fighting in Korea, he was unsure if the U.S. should carry on the fight there: "If Communist China wants to extend its land power there it has the full capability of throwing us out." He could not see "how we can furnish sufficient reinforcements to hold, since we had to strip ourselves to conduct the operations against the North Koreans alone." He believed it would be a disaster to get bogged down in a protracted war with Communist China because it would strain the ability of the U.S. to defend itself elsewhere.[51]

10. Fighting for Unpopular Causes 175

He concluded about the situation, "If we had not gone into Korea than all Asia today would be lost to us, or untenable to the free world. Also, I doubt if we would have many friends in Europe. Asiatics are impatient for more American commitments out there." He judged that the "strongest defect in American foreign policy is lack of firmness ... [which] comes from shortage of American strength ... difficulty of finding able people for government service, [and a] lack of sufficient understanding by American people of issues and circumstances in various countries."[52] In July 1953, after officials from North and South Korea agreed upon an unsatisfying truce, Brown reflected on what American GIs thought about the outcome. He said he was sure they were asking why 25,000 of their buddies had died for an unsettled cause. "He is disturbed. He, an American soldier—not defeated on the battlefield—was not able to defeat the enemy. That never happened to an American soldier before. And it upsets him.... He knows one thing: His job is not finished in Korea, or anywhere else. And he figures the people back home better understand that, too."[53]

During these years, while U.S. leaders attempted to construct a consistent and effective strategy that would meet the communist challenge around the globe, trouble of another sort had been bubbling at home since the end of the previous war. Some students of civil rights have overlooked the fact that Truman took the first federal steps to reverse racial discrimination in 1946. It was a domestically progressive initiative that Brown applauded, and he spent the better part of the next two decades championing it. Racism in America was an issue that dated back more than 100 years, and every few years tensions between the races exploded because of lack of progress regarding racial equality. The 1940s was no exception as black soldiers died for their country overseas but upon returning to America faced second-class treatment. In the summer of 1943 race riots in a number of American cities had made the news. Between May and August, African Americans had confronted whites in a number of cities over a variety of racially motivated issues; including military, housing and employment discrimination, and police brutality. In Los Angeles, Mexican-Americans and whites battled in the so-called Zoot-Suit Riots. Three-dozen people died in the confrontations and nearly 700 were injured across the nation. Nevertheless, neither federal nor local governments instituted changes to address the uneasy relationship between white and minority Americans. The year after Truman became the nation's chief executive, he proposed federal legislation to redress the second-class status of minorities, particularly African Americans and established the President's Committee on Civil Rights. In October 1947, the committee issued its report, titled "To Secure These Rights." In February 1948, Truman became the first president to send to Congress a special message on civil rights. In it, he asked that the Department of Justice classify lynching as a federal crime. He also called for an end to poll taxes as well as statutory protection to ensure that every citizen could freely vote, and he requested legislation that would end workplace and labor union discrimination. McCullough called Truman's proposals "a brave, revolutionary declaration." Although southern congressional opposition blocked most of his civil rights initiatives from becoming law, he ended segregation in the federal government and armed forces by executive order.[54]

Even before Truman's proposals, Mutual had been the first radio network to make its airwaves available to African Americans. Beginning in 1942, a program produced by the Rev. George Lake Imes at the Baltimore Mutual affiliate, *My People*, had aired over the Mutual network. Imes paid for sponsorship of the program himself. It was more-than-likely the first network radio program entirely written, produced and sponsored by blacks in America. A year later, Mutual aired *Fighting Men*, in cooperation with the Negro Newspaper Publishers Association, which featured episodes of an all-black U.S. Coast Guard unit as it conducted rescues at sea.[55] Given his Jewish background and empathy toward the disenfranchised, it was not surprising that Brown actively supported racial equality. That he would vigorously do it on the air as early as the 1940s, had at least in part been motivated by his admiration for Truman. Just as important, was the fact that with Mutual's record for giving a broadcast voice to blacks, Brown was working for the right network. Regardless of his reasons, he, in the estimation of more than one scholar, was either the first, or among the first, to become "a supporter of racial integration in the days when it was not popular to favor integration."[56] In January 1949, Brown put the situation in international perspective. He intoned: "Civil rights is one of those essential but very difficult matters that we will have to resolve if we are going to be effective in the worldwide fight against dictatorships." As this indicates, he not only was concerned about the abuse whites were inflicting upon blacks, but he saw racism as a stain on America's reputation that would harm the nation's ability to occupy the high moral ground in comparison with communist or dictator nations. He revisited his concern for America's reputation abroad, given its negative racial record, numerous times. In the coming years of the racial struggle, he argued: "It's mandatory that the western world undertake a gigantic and genuine crusade for individual human and economic rights.... We are committing suicide if we continue our policy of racial discrimination and arrogance, and if we help to deny other people what they want most—a dynamic program of social and economic reform." In February 1954, he commented, "All the money we spend in the Far East has a terribly hard time winning friends for us in Asia, for one simple reason: the racial policies that exist in the United States." And in 1960, during a speech in Detroit, he told the audience, "The violent segregationists in this country ... people like that have done more good for the communists ... than 100,000 Red agents working day and night in Asia. Now that's quite a gift to give to the enemy."[57]

Brown's commentaries alienated some Mutual-affiliated radio managers, especially in the South, as segregation became a more volatile issue with each passing year. One of the first incidents occurred in July 1949. The trouble began when a white woman accused four armed blacks of molesting her in Groveland, near Orlando, Florida. Deputies arrested three of the men and were seeking the fourth, but a white mob attempted to intervene and take justice into its own hands. The mob burned three black-owned homes and was threatening other blacks in Groveland. Governor Fuller Warren called out the National Guard, police and sheriff's deputies to protect blacks' homes, but the mob was determined to lynch the three men who were in custody. In his broadcast Brown said, "In Groveland, a group of anti–American gangsters tried to act like super-patriots, and end up as worthy exponents of tyranny." Gainesville's WRUF Station Manager Garland Powell, in a letter to Mutual, charged Brown with "an injustice to the people of the great state of Florida" with his comments. Brown responded, "If you wish to make a charge of prejudice against me, I will accept it only on the basis of the prejudice against gangsters, which the white mob is, and a prejudice against tyranny, which the mob was practicing."[58] It was only the first in a long line of incidents in which Brown would exchange disagreeable sentiments with southern radio station managers or owners who objected to his calls for equality.

Brown's position on this and other national issues made his forum more difficult in the 1950s. The continuing fear of communist infiltration, Dwight Eisenhower's election, and southerners' opposition to integration increasingly cast liberalism as unwelcome, radical thinking. Acting as an unofficial spokesperson for liberal viewpoints did not put Brown in popular company. Joseph Mankewitz, who in 1951 was president of the Directors Guild of America, said, "As much as the Negro or Jew ... the American liberal is being 'slandered, libeled, persecuted, and threatened with extinction.'"[59] He was referring to the work of HUAC and other communist-accusing groups who continued their campaign to silence creative minds, especially in the popular arts. Thus, Brown found himself under fire from segregationists, political conservatives and anti-communist demagogues.

The evolving mood of the country troubled Brown. While he campaigned for reform, the majority of Americans yearned for a break from men who called for critical analysis and change. The American middle class was ready for a respite from war and turmoil. The economic boom that World War II had initiated benefitted more Americans as the 1950s progressed. Consumerism propelled increased, secure employment, the baby boom, suburbia, flashy automobiles, electronic conveniences, a reliable health-insurance plan, and escapist entertainment on that most welcome and cherished of all home appliance of the era: television. White middle-class Americans benefitted greatly during the decade, but they were largely uninterested in public service, or the fact that minorities and the poor were not getting to share in the benefits of the post-modern American Dream. Bubbling under the surface were a number of issues that would rip the comfortable society apart a decade later, but for the present they were out of site and out of mind. The middle class largely ignored or criticized men like Brown—and others who attempted to raise public awareness about what the Eisenhower Administration and Congress were ignoring—for rocking the boat and not enjoying the status quo. Representative of the naysayers was John Kenneth Galbreath, who disputed the "conventional wisdom," that "maximization of economic growth [was] the answer to all problems."[60] He joined with Brown in debunking the administration's PR that promoted People's Capitalism as fact.[61]

Against this backdrop, Brown opposed Republicans. He was particularly perplexed when they failed to implement a number of the elements of the Truman Plan, which Brown believed were vital to bring equality to the nation's underclass. Then again, he was not entirely pleased with Truman's strategies. In 1950, he said the Marshall Plan and the formation of NATO were positive steps, but "we went in only up to our ankles and did not go all out." Then he added, "This is not time to chase scapegoats ... it is true that the Administration has made mistakes, but on its own record, the opposition is even less dependable."[62] An especially troubling representative of that opposition, as far as Brown was concerned, was Ohio Senator Robert Taft. This is not surprising, given that Taft, who served in the Senate from 1939 until 1953, was a consistent opponent of Roosevelt and Truman, which meant he disagreed with Brown on practically every White House initiative during those years. As one of the most powerful men in the Senate, Taft was devoutly partisan. He opposed the New Deal, labor unions, and was an ardent isolationist. During several 1944 commentaries, Brown criticized Taft for the bill he introduced to stop the military from distributing books, films and other publications that contained what Taft considered political propaganda. Brown labeled it an inappropriate extension of censorship.[63]

Because of his strong conservative views, many in his party called Taft "Mr. Republican." He sought the Republican presidential nomination three times and supported MacArthur in his confrontation with Truman. Brown believed Taft was unwilling to face international reality and the role of the U.S. in it, and he was particularly upset that Taft wanted to make the MacArthur-Truman conflict a political issue. In April 1951, Brown voiced, "Taft has a consistent and easily provable record of not understanding what goes on in foreign affairs."[64] In February 1952, Brown followed up that statement by charging that Taft was "dangerous ... [and] utter[ly] irresponsible." The occasion for the accusation was when Taft said American foreign policy made the Soviet Union a threat. Brown commented, "I can think of no statement that could be made by any American today which exhibits more than that one, a more thoroughgoing misunderstanding of the nature of communism."[65]

Many of Brown's listeners agreed with his assessment of Taft. A Pasadena, California, listener wrote: "Thank you for stating so clearly the record of Sen. Taft's bad judgment in world affairs. We all are inclined to forget that 9 out of 10 of his predictions have been proved wrong."[66] When Taft died of cancer, though, in 1953, Brown laid aside their differences and fashioned a tribute that saluted the senator for, ironically, his opposition to Brown's favorite men and policies. He said Taft had served an important purpose in the democratic process. Brown's tribute demonstrated that although he opposed the late-senator's politics, he respected him professionally for the role he played in government checks and balances. The word that most appropriately characterized Taft, said Brown, was an "againster," a Brown-invented word. "Senator Taft served a notable function…. Both FDR and Truman needed a traffic cop to blow the whistle on them. Taft compelled the people in power to justify what they were doing. He forced them to prove and sell their case. [Taft] also fought strenuously for the rights of individuals—sometimes harder and more intelligently than did liberals," said Brown.[67]

Regarding the celebrated soldier who won the presidency in 1952, Brown initially expressed optimism that Eisenhower would successfully deal with the issues facing America. In the summer before the election, Brown commented that Eisenhower "was a refreshing breeze in the political storms because he was the one candidate who had the capacity to say three simple words: 'I don't know.'"[68] Other candidates did not possess the self-confidence, noted Brown, to utter the phrase out of fear it would cost them votes. Although he—like most journalists who had experienced global war and Cold War politics—were pessimistic about the possibility of politicians achieving peace, he held out hope with Eisenhower. On December 6, he reminded his audience that they were on the eve of the anniversary of the day the Japanese had bombed Pearl Harbor. He said the U.S. had bid farewell to "peace and normalcy" in 1941, and it had not returned since. The U.S. was now in "a continuous state of post-war jitters … [and] it is rather, more of a dull and expensive pain."[69] On December 8, he asked his audience, "Do you remember the song that offered 'the sun will come out tomorrow?' Of course, the sun of peace is not yet shining over the world, but a big break in the dark and menacing heavens is visible tonight." He based his hope on the president's U.N. speech, scheduled for the next day. He believed Eisenhower was about to end a quiet first year in office by announcing important initiatives. "From all appearances, the presidential year of reorienting the ground, estimating his friends and evaluation his enemies—after a year of study and patience—

a year of action and leadership is about to begin for President Eisenhower." Brown surmised that the president's speech would help set a path for "the people of the world to stop murdering one another," but he also speculated that it was unlikely the speech could achieve that lofty goal.[70]

But Brown's hopefulness that Eisenhower would accomplish great things dissipated over his years in office. It appeared to Brown that in too many cases the president truly did not know what to do, or was inept in dealing with issues. In comparison to Roosevelt and Truman, Brown found Ike lacking in leadership abilities, and he let his audience know it. Political observers agreed with Brown, referring to Eisenhower's two terms in office as "the bland leading the bland." Brooks said the president "was often oblivious to the most consequential emerging historical currents of his time—from the civil rights movement to the menace of McCarthyism."[71] On June 6 that year (the tenth anniversary of D-Day), in a broadcast from Normandy, Brown said, "Eisenhower was to give us a crusade toward peace and security—morality and wisdom. What has come is neither firmer peace nor stronger security—neither higher morality nor greater wisdom." He did not hold Eisenhower wholly responsible for the lack of progress, but he declared that Eisenhower was accountable because it had occurred on the president's watch.[72]

Just as troubling to Brown was the relationship that Eisenhower and his press secretary, James Haggerty, established with the press. After nearly twenty years of mutually beneficial relationships with two Democratic presidents, the open door policy slammed shut on reporters. Eisenhower had many friends among the national media, but they were not journalists. He counted a number of powerful media owners, including Paley and *Time's* Henry Luce as acquaintances. But Eisenhower could not understand why they allowed their reporters to be so aggressive, especially commentators like Brown. The president's opinion was that these "minion reporters, who operated in a safe haven, did not seem to possess any extraordinary talent, and had obtained their jobs through happenstance." They were, Eisenhower believed, merely "interlopers who clogged the communication channels." He could not afford such interference as the leader of the free world.[73] Paley, who had been a lifelong Democrat, converted to the GOP after Eisenhower took office. In an era of accusations by communist hunters about the networks harboring them, and a president who believed journalists were incapable of understanding his administration, Paley understood that he needed to maintain a friendly relationship with the White House to keep CBS free of federal oversight.

The president's awkward relationship with the press made it difficult for journalists to gauge accurately the effectiveness of the presidency. Brown—steeped in the Roosevelt and Truman years of comfortable press relations—and considering the issues facing the nation, believed Americans needed strong, active, vocal leadership from the White House. It became clear to him over time that Eisenhower was not providing that. He believed the president was "abdicating" the duties of his office. He criticized Eisenhower for not speaking out against McCarthy's campaign and the damage it did to the national psyche. Although he blamed the president's silence on his advisers, Brown held Eisenhower accountable for accepting the counsel. In fact, close friend Swede Hazlett had urged Eisenhower to criticize McCarthy, but the president "flatly refused, calling the affair a '"newspaper trial. When you have a situation like this,' he declared, 'you have an ideal one for the newspapers, the television and the radio, to exploit, to exaggerate and to perpetuate.'" Exemplifying his disrespect for journalists, he judged: "Reporters needed confrontation," but he was not going to provide it.[74] The president and his aides believed McCarthy's bellicosity would help Republican candidates win votes in the 1955 elections. "The result is well known. McCarthy's power went right on increasing. He showed disdain for the president himself," charged Brown, who added that the president in March 1954 is "now making an agonizing reappraisal."[75]

Adding to Brown's disappointment in Eisenhower was the fact that he twice defeated the candidate that Brown saw as the most promising candidate during the 1950s: Adlai Stevenson. Brown typically was careful not to campaign overtly for candidates on the air or in speeches, but with Stevenson—whom he considered a man of remarkable foresight and astuteness—he made an exception. The Illinois Governor's no-nonsense, unpretentious eloquence was striking. His open support of civil rights and nuclear disarmament, and opposition to McCarthy resonated with Brown. As he did with many in the American intelligentsia, Stevenson's liberal ideals and speaking style appealed to Brown's intellect in a way Eisenhower did not. Eisenhower may have been Columbia University's President before winning residency in the White House, but as the former general's years in the presidency progressed, he failed to impress Brown as a man with the erudite ideals that could lead the nation to new heights. Stevenson, on the other hand, captured Brown's imagination; he provided Brown with the vision that he embraced. Many of the nation's intelligentsia agreed with Brown. Stevenson "was the voice of a reasonable, civilized, and elevated America. He brought a new generation into politics, and moved millions of people in the United States and around the world," noted Schlesinger, Jr.[76] Unfortunately, mainstream Americans were not ready for his cerebral vision or innovative brand of politics. Stevenson was "the first to articulate some historic initiatives—including education and housing aid, federal medical assistance, and a nuclear test-ban treaty," but these were not enacted until years later," noted Martin.[77]

Unfortunately for those like Brown, Stevenson was a reluctant candidate who conducted poorly orchestrated campaigns. Brown understood that he was sabotaging his own campaign: "Stevenson is ignoring almost every one of the hard and fast rules of politics. He is ignoring party officials, he didn't whistle stop [tour], and he refused to adapt his speeches to specific audiences, or make concessions to sectional interests." Adding to Stevenson' slim chances to win was the campaign of designated Eisenhower "saboteur" Richard Nixon. He worked to turn Stevenson's erudite appeal against him, calling him the man "who got his Ph.D. from Dean Acheson's College of Cowardly Communist Containment." In a notable October 1952 speech, Stevenson argued that government "should be an umpire, denying special privilege, ensuring equal rights, restraining monopoly and greed and bigotry ... creating an economic climate in which creative men can take risks and reap rewards ... [and] has the duty of helping the people develop their country."[78] But by that month the nation had already made up its mind, and Eisenhower won a landslide victory. Despite the results, Brown reiterated his regard for Stevenson: "Most people would agree—that is, the fair-minded folks who agree—that Adlai Stevenson, in his campaign, exhibited great intelligence, courage, gallantry and statesmanship—and all these are qualities which our country can use."[79]

Two years later, as Stevenson began a second presidential run, Brown commented on the candidate's grasp of the American mood. Brown said, "Of all the figures on the American scene, the best at putting into words what beats in the hearts of men and women, is Adlai Stevenson." The commentator said Stevenson had the ability to cut through the confusion of the Red Scare and the "all-is-well façade" that the Eisenhower Administration was promoting. "There is a great moral and human vacuum within us.... That vacuum has produced a national neurosis of fear and doubt.... Ignorance begets fear—the most subversive force of all," charged Brown.[80] Following a campaign speech, Brown commented that Stevenson's frank assessment of the American mood was what the nation needed to hear. "For people who have a practical working knowledge of a belief in God, and the brotherhood of man, for those who have the great and often rare courage to face reality, Stevenson spoke with the voice of America, and even the voice of mankind."[81] But Stevenson's campaign was again ineffectual because it was disorganized and his supporters suffered from low morale regarding their candidate's chances. Stevenson gave more public speeches than Eisenhower, but the incumbent president was the darling of the mainstream media, and his advisors guided the production of highly effective commercials. His advisors had a firm grip on employing "personality"—as opposed to issue advertising—on TV, a strategy Stevenson rejected because he found the medium repugnant, and his awkward appearances on it affirmed his view.[82]

In August 1956, Brown was part of the Mutual team that covered the Democratic National Convention in Chicago. One listener indicated his impression in a letter to Mutual. "While all your special commentators were good ... our favorite was Cecil Brown, who is the nonpareil of all newscasters and almost without peer in the USA!" The anonymous writer went on to say that anyone could recap the day's headlines, but Brown, "thanks to his background, combined with his technical competence, high intelligence, courage and intellectual curiosity, add to his broadcasts that degree of originality and independence which is a *sina qua non* from anyone who is anything more than semi-literate!"[83] At the convention, Stevenson's platform called for the nations of the world to ban hydrogen bomb tests. Brown had been a consistent opponent of nuclear testing since the U.S. had used the weapon to end World War II, but Republicans attacked Stevenson, saying such a ban would diminish the nation's ability to defend itself. When the Suez and Hungary crises both occurred in October, the nation's voters decided it was no time to switch leaders. Thus, the Stevenson-ticket went down to defeat a second time.

Throughout the 1950s, the civil rights movement gained momentum, thanks to activist activities as well as at least in part to Brown's periodic commentaries. He believed Eisenhower needed to follow up on Truman's initiatives to end segregation in America, and he was disappointed when the president signaled that his approach was going to be more reactionary than proactive. Eisenhower's reticence did not stop Brown's determination to keep the issue in front of the national audience. In May 1954, a week after the *Brown v. Board of Education* decision, Brown sounded a clarion call. The court "banned racial segregation in public schools—and thereby speeded up a revolution that is going on in the hearts and minds of men.... The push for equality and democracy is on. And those who want to see steady progress [like the NAACP] aim to keep up the momentum."[84] His commentaries in support of civil rights continued throughout the mid–1950s and generated a large amount of feedback, including letters of appreciation from across the spectrum of those who had a stake in the movement. In April 1956, the chairman of the railroad dining car union, William Pollard, thanked Brown for his commentaries: "You are to be commended for the forth right [sic] position taken on important issues, particularly Civil Rights. Far too many commentators, columnists and other key dispensers of the news are silent on matters that should be laid naked before the public."[85] Dorothy Zeigler, a sociology professor at Ohio's Central State University, wrote, "Thank you for the service you are doing in pointing out how racial discrimination today is akin to treason. As a member of the Caucasian group I hang my head in shame."[86] A Dallas man wrote, "I have searched so hard for any one [sic] who would stand up and tell the truth as it fits both sides [of segregation], that when I heard your accounting of the news as you did. I want to suggest that much good would be accomplished all over the country if it could be repeatedly [sic] exactly as you told it. You offended no one by being fair. Yet you told everything on both sides." From Arkansas, David Rugg wrote Brown, "I and many others make it our business to lisson [sic] to you in order to understand what it is all about. I can assure you that you have many listeners that look to you for their knowledge even though you do not advocate the things they themselves desire."[87] And from High Point, North Carolina, a librarian wrote, "We are almost fanatic in our favorable impression toward the C. Brown Morning Broadcast—so fanatical—so fair-minded—so fearless—so educational—so full of that nameless something which stirs one into realization and action."[88]

He persisted with his commentaries in favor of civil rights as violence against blacks in the South became more vicious. In February 1956, the University of Alabama suspended Autherine Lucy—the first African American student to attempt to attend class there, for her own safety—because of violent protests opposing her presence on campus. The incident marked the most vicious segregationist mob activity in the U.S. since the *Brown v. Board of Education* ruling. Brown, in reacting, announced, "In the modern world, reason and intelligence may be valued as virtues. But it's quite evident that emotion and violence are more honored tonight at the University of Alabama."[89] Six months later, he summarized what he saw as the reality of racially motivated attacks in Clinton, Tennessee, and Mansfield, Texas. "The story is a rather familiar one—white individuals, frightened, and driven by emotion instead of reason, coagulate into a mob, bent on savagery." He said the people in those towns were proving only that they were irresponsible: "The people marched as mobs—marching backward in time, calling themselves segregationists. They are actually, anarchists—at war with the laws of the United States." A week later, he devoted almost all of his fifteen-minute program to analyzing the civil-rights' related editorials of southern newspaper editors. Brown appreciated that while the majority of the editors opposed integration, they also disapproved of mob violence. He said the editors recognized "that these mobs are made up of the mental riff-raff of the communities involved, the type of people who would fit so well into the uniform of one of Adolf Hitler's Nazi Storm Troopers.... Even though they wear a mask of respectability."[90]

In early September 1957, when schools attempted to desegregate in Little Rock and Nashville, riots broke out, with white crowds shouting, "Go home niggers." A crowd of 500 threw rocks and bottles at black children and destroyed black-owned property in Nashville. Police arrested dozens of white protestors, but the mobs succeeded in intimidating black students and their parents as they approached all-white schools. In Arkansas, Governor Orval Faubus called out the National Guard to prevent blacks from attending Central High School. Brown had this to say about the incidents: "White *mobsters* [emphasis mine] in the South in such places as Nashville and Little Rock are earning distinguished service awards for the cause of communism. The spectacle they offer the world ... is so valuable to communism ... that Soviet

Russia owes a deep debt of gratitude to [them]." He sympathized with the challenge Eisenhower faced in representing the U.S. to the rest of the world as a free country when the demonstrators were "stabbing him in the back with such spectacles." He wondered aloud what Eisenhower thought about the violence and what he planned to do, but he acknowledged that the president faced a situation that presented only difficult solutions. He speculated that Eisenhower's "attitude seems to be—there are enough people reacting with inflammatory emotion. He will show patience and perseverance—and await the actions of the courts, and uphold them while they handle this matter."[91]

Not surprisingly, Brown's stories generated negative feedback from the South—with many comments coming from MBS-affiliate station managers. The manager of the Kent Broadcasting System in Shreveport, Frank Ford, Jr., accused Brown of using only stories from the UPI newswire, which he said were pro-integration, instead of his own reporting. Ford charged, "You're not doing yourself justice by this and you're certainly not endearing yourself to your many listeners in the South. Do not allow yourself to become an unwilling accomplice of the NAACP. Though the word 'nigger lover' is seldom used or heard anymore, it's still thought of and is in many people's minds." He further advised Brown to only do stories that were of "real news value."[92] Brown replied that he had only used about 5 percent of the available stories from UPI during the past week, and that he employed independent sources to confirm the truth about southern occurrences. WMFR Station Manager Frank Lambeth, in High Point, wrote that Brown's pro-integrations comments were "against the South."[93] Ralph Goodwin, Jr., of WRUF in Gainesville, criticized Brown's use of his forum to encourage integration. Brown did not directly respond to Goodwin's integration charge, although it was true. Rather, he used the occasion to explain the value of his job as a commentator: "The goal of the analyst is to examine and evaluate the news with fairness, balance and understanding. Its worth is contingent on the background, experience, wisdom and integrity of the commentator." He contended that it was not possible to scrutinize the news without "the expression of opinion. How it is expressed ranges from the violent and small-minded to the calm, logical and tasteful. In many circumstances, I consider it a function of the analyst to distinguish between right and wrong, and to so state it." He continued that he thought news analysis had a beneficial effect on public opinion. Although he did not directly address segregation, Brown clearly was referring to it as a matter of right versus wrong. He said the job of commentary was to arouse the public's interest in domestic and international issues, so they might become personally involved in solving them. He concluded with: "In the light of problems today, compared to the 1930s and the greater complexity of news, the need for competent news analysis is probably ten times greater now than it was then.

However, the need is not synonymous with the gratification of the need."[94] His comments served as one of his clearest philosophical statements about the value of radio commentary.

Brown's comments also aroused the indignation of other southerners. A Stanton, Texas, listener penned, "While listening to a number of your unreasonable, unfounded, vituperative, vitriolic, vindictive, abusive tirades against southern people, I have been strongly inclined to write a letter to you and tell you just what I think of you and your kind."[95] A Texas minister wrote, "Why not tell the whole truth? Why don't you tell us what has happened to the Constitution under the Supreme Court decision and the civil rights' legislation? Or are you too blind to see what has happened? Is it no longer important that the rights of the states and local self-government be maintained?"[96] The negative comments did not dissuade Brown. In May 1957, he remarked: "There is no room for moderation. Regardless of the laws saying there should be no difference in the rights of Americans because of the color of their skin, there is not room for moderation either. Thus, in a sense, everybody who takes a basic position on this racial issue is an extremist."[97] If nasty responses constituted the worst reaction to Brown's pro-integration commentaries, he should have counted himself fortunate. Some liberal commentators said they received rat poison in the mail from listeners who took offense with their civil rights' viewpoints.[98] Davis said he received "fan mail" during the 1950s "with a good many gleeful predictions that I am going to be lynched."[99] Brown did not mention if he received such threats, but segregationist pressure on Brown's sponsors mounted. To its credit, at least one of those refused to succumb. State Farm maintained its sponsorship of Brown despite receiving threats from listeners that they intended to cancel their policies because the company sponsored Brown. State Farm VP, Thomas Merrill, responded to a particularly vicious attack. "I think you will agree it would be most un–American for any advertiser to use his financial pressure in an attempt to control the press…. Freedom of the press is important to all of us and this includes freedom from financial pressure by advertisers. Freedom of the press will continue to be important long after the current controversy is over."[100]

Although Brown spent a lot of time addressing racial turmoil at home, he also kept listeners informed about developments overseas. After combat wrapped up in Korea in 1954, so it was coming to a climax in another part of the world. It was an area with which Brown was particularly familiar, the Far East, and it was within a country that ten years later would come to be known as the next war that the U.S. could not win: Vietnam. Fighting had been ongoing there between the French and communist forces since 1946. In the spring of 1954, negotiations were underway between the two warring factions in Geneva, in an attempt to end the conflict. At the time, few Americans knew where Vietnam was, let alone that the U.S. was subsidizing 80 percent

10. Fighting for Unpopular Causes

of the French cost of fighting the war.[101] Brown foresaw the danger in a negotiated peace that left Vietnam partitioned, much like Korea. As had been the case in Korea, China and Russia were supporting communist forces in Vietnam. "The dangers in partition are obvious. If the Communists get a foothold in Indochina—a foothold accepted by other nations—then they can use that foothold as a springboard to take the rest of Indochina," Brown contended. In late April, French control of Vietnam hung in the balance as combat raged at Dien Bien Phu. Brown warned, "The far heavier duty that is now hovering over—not only the American Army—but every home in the United States—is, to fight Communists—not in headlines—but perhaps in a real, shooting war ... for our own security and survival." The Eisenhower Administration agreed that the communists had to be stopped, and the president considered sending troops to support the French. With or without American support, Brown did not hold out much hope for the French. Two months later, after the French defeat, and with partition in place, Brown put the situation in context: "We have just accepted a Munich in Asia—a Bataan—a Dunkirk.... This big communist success ... is not due to communist strength. It is mostly due to western division and shortsightedness."[102] A few years later, Brown's observations about the perils of U.S. involvement came to fruition.

The communist threat also redrew the political map in another Far Eastern nation after World War II. The U.S. had sent millions of dollars' in munitions and supplies to Chiang Kai-Shek's Nationalist Chinese. In opposition, the Russians supported Mao Tse-tung's Red Army. Despite a disadvantage in troop strength, the communists defeated the Nationalists, and forced Chiang and nearly 3,000,000 of his troops and civilian sympathizers to retreat to the island of Taiwan (Formosa). Brown's assessment of the debacle was that the Communists won because "we worked with as nice a gang of crooks, cutthroats, grafters, reactionaries, and enemies of the Chinese people as could be found." Nevertheless, in 1949, the Browns had made the first of several stops they would make in Taiwan to interview Chiang. The meeting also resulted in the creation of a personal friendship between Chiang and his wife and Martha and Cecil that continued until the expatriate leader died in 1975. The relationship prompted Cecil to voice encouragement for the Nationalists to regain control of mainland China on more than one occasion. One listener wrote Brown that he was "the only commentator I've heard who has mentioned what would become of China after we put Chiang back on the mainland, and defeated the Reds."[103] Throughout the 1950s, Brown opposed U.S. recognition of the Peking government, saying Taiwan would simply "disappear" if the U.S. quit supporting it. He argued that if the U.S. recognized the communist Chinese government that it would "compel other Asian nations to recognize the Maoist regime. This in turn would allow the Chinese to station military, economic, and political missions in those countries, thereby giving China a fifth column with which to overthrow neighboring governments." His perspective represented the classic "domino effect" view of communist aggression. "If we recognize Communist China, we are in effect kissing off Southeast Asia," Brown argued.[104]

Although he had criticized conservatives whom he considered "hysterical commentators," Brown was a staunch anti–Russian. Although some Americans continued to label Brown a communist, his commentaries and writings indicate a far different position. In September 1948, *See*, a New York City magazine, published Brown's article "How Close Are We to War with Russia?" It was unfortunate the article did not receive wider distribution because it served as a primer on the status of the relationship between Russia and the U.S. In the article, Brown posed and answered thirty-four questions concerning the possibility of war with Russia. He said the two nations were involved in a "game of chicken" regarding nuclear weapons. At that early point in the Cold War, Brown sought to educate readers about the nations' relationship. He said the Russians would attempt to achieve as many territorial gains as they could, without entering into armed conflict with the U.S. But to make no mistake that the Russians wanted all of Europe under their control. If the two became engaged in a war it would likely cost millions of lives, because, unlike the previous two world wars, combat would come to America. He said the U.S. was in actuality already at war with Russia—"a war for the souls of men," and that totalitarian and free nations were waging it around the world. He argued that the only way to stop the Russians was with a show of force. He encouraged readers to be "concerned" about the relationship, not just "curious." He concluded that a system of world government, in the form of the United Nations, was the preferred strategy to safeguard one nation from overstepping the sovereignty of others.[105]

If Russian leaders had tuned into Brown's broadcasts during the mid-1950s, they would not have been pleased with what they heard about their political affairs. A power struggle was underway with Communist Party activists Nikita Khrushchev and Nikolai Bulganin squaring off against Soviet Premier Georgy Malenkov. In February 1955, Bulganin became premier. Brown's assessment of the new leadership was that "Bulganin and Khrushchev are died-in-the-wool thugs, with a code of ethics made to measure for their business." Brown later said Khrushchev's claim that he knew the U.S. did not want war with Russia was contrary to the propaganda he was feeding his own people. After taking control of the Politburo, Bulganin and Khrushchev undertook a campaign to eradicate many of Stalin's policies, such as the forced labor economy, as well as his legacy, by removing monuments dedicated to him. Brown was unimpressed. While many hailed it as a new era in Russia, Brown announced, "In their campaign to de-sanctify Joseph Stalin and his twenty-five year reign of tyranny and murder, those gangsters are thereby condemning themselves."[106] His prediction was correct in that only two years later Khrushchev turned on Bulganin and forced him out of office, making himself First Secretary of the Communist Party, Russia's top political post.

In June 1957, Brown returned to Russia for the first time since his trip there as a youth, with Martha and twenty-two other Americans, to tour and gather facts for a series of stories. He said many of his American friends were aghast that the group would travel to a country that had become an adversary, but he was anxious to see what understanding civilians could achieve face-to-face: "We are, I think, doomed to years of tension between the U.S. and Russia. It will be interesting to note whether meeting non-political people can achieve a better understanding, and if they can, what effect that can have on governmental policies." During the twenty-four-day excursion, the group visited Copenhagen, Helsinki, Leningrad, Kiev, Moscow, Warsaw and Berlin. Brown recorded eighteen reports on life in Russia and Poland, giving Mutual listeners a perspective they could not receive elsewhere on U.S. airwaves. He told them that the appearance of the Russian people in Leningrad appalled Brown. He said the expressions on the faces of the people in the streets told him everything he needed to know about how Khrushchev's reforms were succeeding: "I have seen nothing but grim, tight and tired faces—as though the burden of existence took almost all the spark of gayety out of them."[107] Concerning Khrushchev, who had recently dismissed longtime protégé Vyacheslav Molotov, Brown said he figured "Khrushchev had put himself out on the edge of a springboard" with his revision of his nation's economic policies. If his initiatives failed, "the determined, ruthless and conniving Khrushchev will get the same treatment that he is now handing out to his ruthless, determined and conniving colleagues." In his final broadcast from Russia, Brown noted that most of the people were suffering without the essentials of life. But, said Brown, "it is no serious concern of the Soviet planners ... they don't care if no home in Russia has a lamp shade.... Soviet Russia is engaged in a war—an economic war ... to overtake the United States. That's the slogan everywhere—to equal and exceed the United States."[108]

One of the most important Mutual-affiliate relationships was with the Don Lee Broadcasting System on the West Coast. Lee Broadcasting owned high-powered stations in Los Angeles, Santa Barbara and San Diego, and held stock in MBS. In 1950, the Lee stations began airing Brown's programs after the Stebbins Advertising Agency convinced the group's management that he would provide a boost to their stations' listenership. Account executive Leon Wray said Brown may not have had the highest ratings, but "he's got something you can't measure with rate cards.... He has the sustained confidence of his listening audience. They believe in him—in his integrity; in his seasoned judgment; in his ability to sift the real from the phony." Because of these attributes, the agency claimed that Brown's advertising support had grown 53 percent in the previous three years.[109] In turn, a Lee Broadcasting sales pitch to advertisers proclaimed that Brown "has been called the most famous of all radio correspondents," and that his morning news show was reaching 229,000 homes on the West Coast.[110]

These were good years for Brown at Mutual. The network had allowed him to speak his mind, with limited sponsor or network interference. There were a number of reasons for that, including the fact that despite its growth Mutual did not wield the clout with advertisers or command respect with the mass audience that the major networks did. The fact that Mutual was willing to air divergent ideological views in an attempt to generate a large and diversified audience also played a role. However, television changed all that once it began entering the American home in the late 1940s. By 1957, the mass audience had abandoned radio and the heyday of the radio commentator was nearly over. Brown saw it coming, and he had been busy trying to make a transition to the new medium. He had proposed program ideas to television network executives and had floated the idea of presenting the same news-commentary type of program on television that he had been doing on radio.[111] But network executives were not yet ready to invest in news programming because they were uncertain what role news would play in television programming. Nevertheless, on March 25, 1957, Brown bid farewell to Mutual: "There is ... a wrench in leaving, for they have indeed been exciting and momentous years.... I feel rather proud of the devotion of my listeners to these, and other programs I've done on Mutual, the listeners who approve of what I say and those who do not, for both, I hope these broadcasts have been informative, stimulating or thought-provoking, or all three."[112] But he was not without prospects. Brown was leaving Mutual because one of the network's executives had decided to take a chance on utilizing his expertise as an experiment at its New York flagship station. Brown already had been on the air for six months at WABC TV when he left Mutual, providing news and commentary weeknights at 11 p.m. He believed television presented a seasoned analyst such as himself with an opportunity to continue presenting opinion, and he was the first to take advantage of it in New York City, the nation's most influential media market. As he would quickly discover, the new medium was not ready for his outspokenness. Yet, it provided a new opportunity for him to adjust the trajectory of his career.

♦♦ 11 ♦♦

Back to the Far East for a New Medium

Few radio commentators successfully made the transition to television. Kaltenborn, Davis, Lewis, and others who had talked Americans through World War II and the difficult years thereafter, saw their careers come to an unceremonious end. Winchell—along with Brown—were two who tried. The others did not even attempt the transition, and Winchell's foray was short lived. David Brinkley, who was a member of the new breed of broadcast journalists who began their careers in television, said most of the old radio guard "were afraid of it, and reluctant to try anything new."[1] The reasons for the demise of the radio commentator are multifaceted. Howe attempted to explain the end of the era that lasted barely twenty years. He said commentators owed their popularity to World War II, but by 1957, "the news itself had lost its wartime urgency and flowed less abundantly." He also speculated that with the higher production costs and increase in advertising rates, television executives could not risk the controversy in which commentators specialized.[2] Others observed that few of the radio commentators could make the transition because appearance and showmanship played a bigger role than they had in radio. Knoll argued that a contributing factor was that the new generation of television reporters lacked the journalism skills and knowledge of their radio predecessors. Specifically, he believed they were deficient in their ability to construct the thoroughly researched, convincingly argued thought pieces that characterized the radio veterans' work. Another reason was that commentary did not play well on television, which prioritized visual appeal, at the expense of thoughtful content. NBC's John Chancellor said, "You could deal with abstractions on radio in a way you couldn't on television." Hugh Downs—who began his career with NBC radio during World War II and successfully made the transition to television as a *Today* and game show host—confirmed that network executives believed there was a psychological difference between the way topics were presented on the two mediums.

"[NBC] believed that anything I would say on radio would be perceived by the listener as my personal opinion, but anything I'd say on television would be perceived by the viewer as company policy." Knoll lamented that television executives did not appreciate the value of "the gifted essayist whose function was to extract meaning and context from the day's news." As radio attempted to compete with television, it turned to newscasts that were fast-paced and featured short sound bites, instead of documentaries and commentaries that had characterized the glory days of radio news.[3]

Brown was typically confident—perhaps naively so—that he and his style of analysis could transition to television. In 1950, he pitched the idea of a half-hour television news show that would "report and interpret the news in an informal, comprehensive, authoritative and behind-the-scenes manner" to Robert Kintner, ABC president. Kintner was in the process of trying to make ABC more competitive with the other networks, but news was not a priority as a means of accomplishing it. Instead, he cut deals with Warner Brothers and Disney to provide entertainment fare. *Walt Disney's Disneyland* and Warner's *Cheyenne*—TV's first successful western series—put ABC on sound financial footing. The network's shining moment in the area of news during the 1950s was its live coverage of the Army-McCarthy hearings while NBC and CBS carried them only intermittently.

However, on July 2, 1956, ABC's owned and operated television station in New York City (WABC), began airing a fifteen-minute news and commentary program at 11 p.m. each weekday. Its first host was Brown, and, with a summer start date, it constituted a trial effort during a time of the year when audience ratings were at their lowest. The first ten minutes of the program were devoted to straight news, sports and weather, and the final five to commentary. It was the first attempt by a U.S. TV station to present commentary. At the time, ABC—much like Mutual a decade earlier—was the proverbial also-ran in television. The network was born in 1945 after a FCC anti-monopolistic ruling that NBC divest itself of one of its two radio networks. Sarnoff decided to give up the network's "Blue network" because its affiliates were in smaller markets and less productive financially than NBC-Red-Network affiliates. So in 1956 ABC was under-capitalized, and lacked the strong affiliate roster that CBS and NBC possessed. Therefore, the network was willing to experiment with news programming. All the networks were trying to discover how best to present news on television, so instead of trying Brown's commentary at the network, Kintner decided to give him a trial at WABC, thus constituting a "test case" in the nation's largest market.

Brown approached television with suspicion, but he knew he had to give it a try because the future of his career in broadcasting depended on trying to make the transition. Almost everyone at the networks believed television was going to replace radio as the audience's medium of choice. Brown had

11. Back to the Far East for a New Medium

no experience as a TV anchor; the situation was much like the fledgling days of radio news when he had broken in with CBS as an intrepid reporter in Italy. The night before he went on the first time, Brown told a newspaper reporter that he did not consider himself either an actor or a comedian, the two skills that he observed TV personalities displaying in those early days. On the eve of his first appearance, he expressed views about the medium that, in hindsight, indicated that his stay would not last long. He had recently viewed another New York's station's newscast in which film of an Atlantic City "bathing beauty contest" had been its lead story. Brown said, "I don't want to make the program too visual and become a prisoner of film. If it adds depth to the news, film is fine. But so much of it is used only to bring movement to the show. There seems to be too much emphasis on charm and personality." He insisted the networks would have to designate a place in their schedules for news analysis: "I can't believe that news on television is supposed to be purely entertainment. Somehow the medium will have to find a solution to the daily [radio] commentator." He recognized that his television scripts would have to be more conversational than the ones he had employed in radio: "I want people to feel that a fairly well-informed neighbor has dropped in to speak with them. People have many problems on their minds that are much closer to them on the surface. You have to make the news understandable to them.... And that doesn't mean making concessions by deluging them with trivia."[4] He was convinced that solid news content would attract and retain an audience.

Indeed, Brown displayed a conversational, even humorous approach in a story he presented in the first week of his WABC gig. There were three international heads-of-state at the time that he found particularly distasteful, because he believed they were undependable. They were Egyptian President Abdel Nasser, India's Jawaharlal Nehru and Yugoslavia's Prime Minister Josip Tito. In this particular story, Brown found a way to link the continually shifting political policies of the three together with the most popular American icon that year: Elvis Presley. "In international affairs there's not one Elvis the Pelvis—but three of them. Their names are Nasser of Egypt, Tito of Yugoslavia and Nehru of India. The more these three Elvis the pelvises gyrate the more they end up where they started from."[5] New York entertainment columnists gave Brown's program mixed reviews. It appears a reason for the disparity was that at this early stage of television news programming they also were unsure whether substance or style mattered more. The *New York Times'* Richard Shepard offered a backhanded compliment when he wrote that Brown's "major contribution on his three week-old telecast has been to add to the bare news bulletins an idea and some judgment as to their significance." But Shepard complained that the show did not make enough use of film or other visuals, and that Brown's on-air style was problematic. He said Brown expresses "a deadpan physical and vocal delivery ... in which a top national story and a baseball score are delivered with the same monotonous intonations. It's a rather uncomfortable show to watch because of this." Nonetheless, Shepard liked the commentary portion: "He makes amends with the latter portion ... which he devotes entirely to one story, spicing it with film and commentary. On the night watched ... he did a bang-up job of setting forth the issues with wry but pertinent observations. It's this latter portion in which Brown stands out." Often-acerbic television critic Jack Gould was able to look beyond Brown's performance deficiencies to appreciate the content, saying, his show "is a good one, too—swift-moving, complete and concerned only with the real hard news of the day, not inconsequential newsreel features. Interestingly enough, Mr. Brown also presents his own commentary on the news and is sensible enough to do the normal thing—read from the copy he wrote rather than look fishy-eyed into the teleprompter. He held interest, too."[6]

Unfortunately, Brown did not attract enough interest to satisfy ABC, especially after it was unable to secure a sponsor for the show. WABC management's solution was to replace Brown with John Cameron Swayze, and eliminate the analysis portion of the program after only eight months, on April 1, 1957. Swayze had previously anchored NBC's evening news program, but the network had replaced him with Chet Huntley and David Brinkley the previous year. Swayze conveyed a nearly manic style of presentation, set up by his introductory line "Let's go hopscotching the world for headlines." As a commercial pitchman for Timex ("takes a licking and keeps on ticking"), he was not a credible journalist. Thus, he failed to communicate the tenor of substantive journalism Brown had. The change made it clear that from the beginning television was about entertainment and making money, not about thoughtful journalism. Swayze possessed a more upbeat style than Brown, and he was more comfortable with the camera. The fact that industry personnel did not consider him a journalist, did not matter at this date in network television's development.

Afterward, it became clear that in the short time he was on the air, Brown attracted a devoted, if small, following. When loyal viewers learned that ABC was replacing him, several wrote the network. One viewer said Brown's was "the only real television news program on the air." Suzanne Weltman, an employee of the French Broadcasting Network in Manhattan, wrote, "It was the first daily television news program that tells us what the big events mean."[7] In responding to her, network vice president Robert Stone wrote, "We at ABC share your high opinion of Mr. Brown as a reporter and analyst, but regret that the network could no longer afford to carry his news program on an unsponsored basis." The network sold the time to Esso Standard Oil, whose managers had stipulated they wanted the more charismatic Swayze as host.

The termination of Brown seems to have been purely an issue of economics. In the *New York Post,* television critic Jay Tuck wrote of the change, "John Cameron Swayze has returned to television news, as always complete with carnation and a joy that we could get together. He replaced Cecil Brown.... Brown's sharp and incisive mind will be badly missed by many of us."[8]

As Brown had already severed his ties with Mutual, ABC decided to retain him for its radio network. Actually, the parting with Mutual had not altogether been Brown's idea. In October 1956, one of Brown's biggest sponsors, Kraft, which had previously stood with him, abandoned him over a controversy that began ten months earlier. The issue had to do with civil rights, Mississippi Senator James Eastland, and the *New York Times.* Although a Democrat, Eastland was chair of the Senate Internal Security Subcommittee, which was investigating the Communist Party in the U.S., and he was an ardent segregationist. He opposed implementation of the *Brown v. Board of Education* ruling in Mississippi. The *Times* took Eastland to task, and he retaliated by issuing subpoenas for *Times* reporters' notes. On January 5, 1956, a *Times* editorial said that long after Eastland, segregation and McCarthyism were dim memories, and "long after the last Congressional committee has learned that it cannot tamper successfully with a free press, the *New York Times* will be speaking for [those] who make it, and only for [those] who make it, and speaking, without fear or favor, the truth as it sees it." It was a cause to which Brown could lend his voice, and he did, commenting over Mutual that he wholeheartedly supported the *Times'* position. Newspaper editorials across the country likewise defended the *Times.* Nonetheless, a representative from Kraft's advertising agency told Brown it had received a large amount of protest mail that complained about him being "radically liberal." Brown reiterated that his commentaries did not adhere to any particular partisan or philosophical perspective. He said his search for and presentation of the truth could take him anywhere across the ideological spectrum. "The essential point as I see it is the conduct of the searcher after the truth, the principles which motivate that search and the capacity to find a tolerable amount of it. It is inescapable that any view excites some disagreement."[9]

But Kraft was unsatisfied with Brown's explanation. Its ad. agency representative Ray Fowler wrote Brown he was sorry to have to disassociate his client from his program, but "the criticism—both from within and outside the organization—has continued over such a long period of time that we had no recourse.... A great deal of feeling that your commenting has frequently struck many people as being slanted and expressive of your own personal feelings more than that of an objective view" led to the decision.[10] Despite the amount of listener support Brown received, the negative correspondence that Kraft received outweighed it. Brown's outspokenness on controversial public issues had alienated the conservative ownership that dominated corporate America. Kraft could no longer tolerate Brown's track record of controversial opinions because they threatened sales of their products. Corporate temerity outweighed association with journalistic integrity. Brown's foray into television probably also played a role in his years at Mutual ending. By 1957 Mutual was on tenuous financial ground. With the incredible growth of the television audience, advertisers were leaving radio, shifting their advertising to television. WOR and a number of other affiliates defected from Mutual, thus diminishing its audience in major markets. Ownership of the network changed hands several times, ending up in the hands of Hal Roach, Jr., but then the FCC launched an investigation into Roach's association with a totalitarian foreign government. The turmoil led to a turnover of its formerly talented management team. With the network's precarious financial status, it could not afford controversy that alienated listeners and advertisers. In 1959, MBS would file for Chapter 11 bankruptcy.[11] Fortunately, ABC offered an employment alternative for Brown: ABC Radio.

In one of his final Mutual broadcasts, Brown had devoted time to a sensitive recognition of the importance of America's immigrants. The impetus for the story was Eisenhower's executive order, the first of its type, to authorize the placement of nearly 1,000 international orphans into the custody of American military families. U.S. soldiers who had either fathered and/or were stationed on Cold War outposts overseas had informally adopted the children—and they wanted to make the arrangement permanent in the States. With congressional approval, the orphans were granted permanent U.S. residence status. Brown began by noting that the U.S. possessed a number of attributes, but its greatest strength was "the stranger in our midst—the immigrant." He said Americans tended to take immigrants for granted in the mid-1950s, but the foreign-born makeup of the American population was what he believed made the nation vividly different from totalitarian countries. "They are afraid of strangers; we are not." He said it was a basic American idea "that a dynamic nation is built on many viewpoints—many enthusiasms—many cultures and tongues.... Every time a stranger in our midst—the immigrant—ceases to be a stranger—our country takes on new strength and decency."[12] He spoke from personal experience.

Upon his move to ABC Radio, Brown began doing a fifteen-minute news and commentary program between 8 and 8:15 each morning, Monday through Saturday, replacing old-friend Martin Agronsky. Following the final night of his television broadcast, ABC's Stone told Brown that he appreciated how he had ended his TV show: "I want you to know how pleased I was with the dignified and effective way in which you handled the farewell to your viewers and also the plug for John Cameron Swayze. Very often this kind of thing is handled awkwardly and rather begrudgingly on the air by talent, and I want you to know I appreciate your handling of it."[13] Ironically, on April 26,

1957, the Overseas Press Club presented Brown and WABC with its award for "Best Interpretation of Foreign Affairs within the U.S." for his now-terminated nightly newscast. WABC managers had nominated the program because they believed it was the first daily commentary program in television that "showed an understanding of American foreign policy (in advance of official decisions), and that no other regular television news program and few other analysts in any media had subjected American foreign policy to as searching and critical an examination."[14] On May 1, after bestowing the award on Brown, the Press Club elected him its president for the following year.

At the time of his introduction as a commentator, the ABC news division was underfunded and understaffed. Its nightly network newscast, anchored by John Daly, ran a distant third in the ratings behind CBS and NBC.[15] On ABC Radio, the most popular news program was *Paul Harvey's News & Comment*. It was a tabloid-style, politically conservative newscast. Winchell and Davis had provided commentary at ABC in the early 1950s, but by the time Brown arrived they both had moved on.[16]

On the inaugural program of his ABC radio newscast, Brown told his audience that he and they both had the same objective, which was to understand what the news meant and how it affected them. He said it was his responsibility "to be fair and balanced ... and to seek to bring you all the facts I can gather to illuminate and explain an event." He did not categorize himself as right or left wing, "whatever those vague terms may mean.... Rather, I prefer to consider my broadcasts—sensible. That, of course, is an opinion. You will judge them as time goes on, for yourself."[17] A number of listeners soon made Brown's commentaries appointment listening. "It is a delight to listen to a man like this [Brown]; frank ... and plenty of courage. He hits hard and in the right place and in the right way," wrote C.F. Pearce from Hillsboro, Texas. He added that Brown "is fair.... I cannot tell to which political party he belongs, which as it [sic] should be with a news commentator—just the truth and let the chips fall where they may."[18]

On his daily newscast, Brown continued to be critical of the Eisenhower Administration. He complained about the president for seemingly reversing the Truman Administration's pro–Israel stand when he compelled the Israelis to evacuate the Sinai Peninsula following the Suez War. Especially galling to Brown was the administration's collaboration with the Soviet Union at the U.N. in condemning Israel, England and France in their fight with Egypt for control of the Suez Canal. The three nations had attacked Egypt because they all saw it as a threat in their Middle Eastern interests. The U.N. action strengthened Nassar's regime, allowed Egypt to threaten Israel's existence for decades into the future, and drove another stake into England's decline as a world power.[19]

To Brown, the president's actions showed that he favored Arab elements in the Middle East, as opposed to old U.S. allies and Israel. In July 1957, after the Egyptian takeover of the canal, Brown announced, "The Stock of Egyptian President Nasser is ace high tonight in the Arab world. In the western world, his name is bandit." Brown said Nasser's "grab of the Suez Canal ... can carry him, or his country, or both to disaster.... It is no wonder the British are calling him 'Hitler of the Nile.'" Brown labeled him "frantic, frenzied, [and] irresponsible." Brown's assessment was accurate, but he failed to acknowledge that the administration also took steps during Eisenhower's two terms to support Israel.[20] As additional communist aggression unfolded around the world, Brown was angered that U.S. foreign policy seemed immobilized. In 1954, the Soviets engineered the Warsaw Pact. Two years later, Russia stopped the Hungarian revolt and established a communist government in that country. That same year, Soviet troops crushed the Polish workers' strike. As Russia became more and more aggressive across Europe, Brown was convinced that the U.S. was not doing enough to stop it. He charged that the president and Dulles "were either woefully misinformed about American policies and needs or were desperately determined to avoid reality."[21]

On his November 7, 1956, newscast, one day after Eisenhower's reelection, Brown cautioned his audience, "If we have been in a state of hypnosis—that all is safe, secure and serene—that often-repeated assurance, unhappily, does not make us safe." He blamed the administration for not being more transparent with the steps it was taking to confront the problems around the globe. He ticked off issues such as fallout from nuclear testing, a Middle East policy that he said was "an imaginary one that we pretended to have for the past three years," threats from the communist world and a "ragged and frayed" free world alliance. In light of the European and Middle Eastern developments, Brown criticized the president for communicating a false sense of security to Americans. "President Eisenhower is fond of saying—never was the United States stronger—never was American prestige higher. That, of course, is a masquerade of our real position. No better evidence of this is available right now than the diplomatic disaster we are suffering over the Suez Canal." A year later, when the Soviets beat the U.S. into outer space by launching Sputnik I, Brown commented, "So many of our chickens are coming to roost. That isn't a very optimistic way to begin today's report. But I think it's a fair appraisal of what we have been hiding from for the past five years—and what burden and dangers we now face.... One cannot be sure that we are awake. For our sleep for these past five years has been rather sound. And when Sputnik falls out of the skies, we may hit the sack again."[22] Historians agree with Brown. "Sputnik was responsible for an ominous national cloud of fear and uncertainty, a dilemma Eisenhower brought upon himself by trying to maintain that a space race did not exist," according to Allen.[23] Brown stopped short of blaming the administration for not solving all the problems, but he added, "The need seems to be to take the problems out from under the rug—where they have been concealed—and building up to spontaneous combustion. Only when the problems are out in bright and airy sunlight do we have a chance, at least, to tackle and solve them." He concluded that the U.S. was in a "cult of personality—the personality being Mr. Eisenhower's."[24]

In a manner reminiscent of his verbal campaign against Germany during World War II, Brown seemed almost obsessed with Eisenhower's impassiveness. His haranguing of the administration raised the ire of a number of ABC affiliates and listeners. They believed Brown was neglecting to balance his criticism with recognition of the administration's positive steps in keeping the nation at peace and for perpetuating a growing economy. On May 15, 1957, KGW Program Director Jack Moyes, in Portland, Oregon, complained to network executives that his station was receiving a large amount of listener complaints about Brown. He said Brown seemed to have embarked on a "one-man, anti–Eisenhower crusade." Moyes said he was confident the letters were coming from listeners whom he described as "calm and intelligent—not the mass political type of call." He asserted that a number of those writing had been loyal Brown listeners when he was at Mutual. Moyes said KGW's management was Democratic, and they did not presume to tell commentators what to say, and they believed occasional criticism of the president was in order. Nevertheless, they felt that "Brown simply hasn't been doing a good reporting job from the standpoint of talking about other subjects aside from Eisenhower." Moyes said if Brown did not provide more variety in the subjects he discussed, they would seriously consider dropping his program from the KGW schedule. In November, Simon Goldman of the James Broadcasting Company in Jamestown, New York, also complained about Brown's Eisenhower criticism. This time, in a personal response to Goldman, Brown defended his approach. "I owe no responsibility to unreality or evasion of facts. That is not a service to the American people, although I am quite aware that many people, a great many, would prefer a myth to a fact." He said there were quite a few commentators who provided exactly that, but he was not one of them. He added, "I do not discharge my responsibility either by entertaining or alarming people. I do discharge it by being ... penetrating and perceptive." He argued that his record of accomplishment demonstrated that he was good at anticipating events, and he believed that if he did not warn the public of the issues Eisenhower was ignoring that a bigger calamity was in the offing: "Many people cannot and will not believe that a bomb can drop, until it hits the ground. I think a responsibility of a commentator is to know the story before the bomb hits, however irksome it may be to some people to hear the news before the bomb." But even if Brown disputed the grievances, ABC executives had to take the letters seriously because affiliates are the lifeblood of a network's existence.[25]

Brown's negative assessment of the Eisenhower presidency was not without some substance. While historians in recent years have been more charitable in reassessing the former general's eight years in office, political analysts during the 1950s and '60s agreed with Brown that Eisenhower's presidency was a disappointment. While the president succeeded in ending the Korean War, kept the U.S. out of a new war, and allowed most of the New Deal policies to remain intact, he failed to lead strongly in a number of domestic areas. Two of those, as Brown had noted, were civil rights and McCarthyism, issues that Brown believed needed timely attention. Coming from nearly three decades of proactive, Democratic governance, and given his "justice for all" philosophy, Brown found Eisenhower's reactionary approach a weak successor to Roosevelt's and Truman's strategies.[26] Of course, these matters were not a concern for the conservative Republican management that dominated network and station ownership. During the 1950s, economic prosperity fueled consumer spending and thus broadcasters' affluence via plentiful advertising sales. Television was developing, radio was transitioning from keeping the public informed to featuring escapist pop music, and management had little tolerance for men like Brown who wanted to distract from the good times by telling the public about issues that were bubbling underneath seemingly "happy days." Brown moderated his comments regarding the president after the criticism, and the affiliates remained with ABC. Regardless, Brown's days at the network were numbered.

Controversial issues aside, with Brown already skating on thin ice at ABC, he permanently fractured his relationship a few months later when he complained about how they were paying him. It is not clear what the original contractual arrangements were, but on May 24 Brown sent a memo to ABC Radio's Director of News and Public Affairs Francis Littlejohn to say that for five weeks he had been doing his Saturday morning news show without any compensation.[27] He felt his salary only covered his Monday through Friday newscasts. In addition, he noted that he was re-announcing his morning program three hours later for the network's West Coast affiliates, without additional compensation. Littlejohn wanted Brown to do the Saturday newscasts live, and Brown said he made several alternative suggestions for Saturday coverage, but Littlejohn had rejected all of them. Instead, the two reached a temporary agreement in which Littlejohn would pay Brown for the Saturday newscast while allowing him to record it Friday afternoon after Brown's final broadcast each week. Occasionally, Brown did the Saturday morning show live when major news broke over Friday night, but the disagreement damaged the men's relationship. The dispute festered, then reached a breaking point near midnight on January 31, 1958, when NASA successfully launched its first satellite, Explorer I, into orbit. The launch represented U.S. entrance into the space age and was the nation's reaction to the Soviet Union's launch of Sputnik three months earlier.

11. Back to the Far East for a New Medium

The problem was that Brown had recorded his Saturday newscast on Friday, so he did not do a live newscast Saturday morning. The other radio networks presented multiple updates on the historic launch—ABC had not only been scooped, it had failed to report the story at all. Littlejohn was irate that Brown had not broadcast live Saturday morning. He accused Brown of refusing to report to the studio after a producer called him at his apartment. Littlejohn said Brown had embarrassed the network because it had not provided affiliates with the breaking news that morning. Brown claimed that no one had called him, and Littlejohn subsequently agreed. Nevertheless, on February 10, he sent a registered letter to Brown's apartment in which he said ABC was terminating him as of March 29. Four days later, Brown's response stated, "It is interesting ... that with two exceptions ... not a single promise, assurance or hope given me before coming to ABC was fulfilled regarding my becoming a part of the news team and operation."[28] Only those intimately involved with the situation knew the real reason behind ABC's decision to fire Brown. Littlejohn had not fully integrated Brown into the news department. Brown's frank commentaries may have been offensive, or perhaps he felt ABC executives had thrust Brown upon him. Without question, Brown had not enjoyed the freedom to express the views as he had been accustomed to airing at Mutual. Regardless, Brown felt as if Littlejohn treated him like an outsider, and the news director found a reason to get rid of him.

The short-term employment and moving among jobs equaled a difficult time personally for Cecil and Martha; it strained their marriage. With each job change, there were weeks and months of insecurity concerning whether he would secure a position with another broadcast company. The uncertainty was difficult, and the absence of a paycheck caused belt-tightening. Brown told a reporter during this time that he insisted "on paying his grocery bills only with what money he earn[ed] from his work."[29] He knew many people in New York broadcasting whom he could call about positions, but he also had burned some bridges. He was an experienced, knowledgeable journalist, but his forthrightness and devotion to doing work his way alienated many. Martha said she at times doubted the value of what Cecil was doing. "I never had the confidence in the American public that they cared. They enjoyed his broadcasts, but I don't think they thought he was telling us what to think and what to do." Jonathan Brown had a different take on why his uncle eventually worked for and left three of the four major networks. "I think it's remarkable that he lasted in New York as long as he did. He was critical in a way that was often unexpected. He had his own views, and I think that's what made some people and some sponsors very uncomfortable."[30]

Then on June 1, 1958, Brown completed a full circuit of network employment when Kintner—who also had left ABC over a policy disagreement and had become NBC President—hired Brown again. Obviously, Kintner was familiar with Brown's abilities and believed he would be a quality addition to the NBC news team he was expanding.

The NBC position would take Brown out of New York, but return Cecil to the area of the world with which he was familiar: The Far East. It was part of the reason the position was offered, and definitely the reason why Brown accepted it. It carried with it both administrative and reporting duties for the first time in his career. He would be NBC's Far East Bureau Chief in Tokyo. In announcing that Brown would join the network, NBC's Vice President of News William McAndrew said he was delighted to add Brown to his staff. "[His] appointment emphasized the growing importance NBC News places on its world-wide operation." NBC already had James Robinson reporting from Tokyo, but McAndrew relocated him to Hong Kong as bureau chief there.[31]

This was during a period in the late-1950s when the television networks were building their foreign bureaus, seeking to garner respect with viewers for their news operations. NBC, in particular, under new president Kintner (who had left ABC after a disagreement over policy), was intent on elevating the network above CBS in both news show ratings and prestige. Kintner was directing more money to the news department to achieve the goal of making NBC the best television network news organization. He and McAndrew became a formidable team that achieved the network's goal of topping CBS during their tenure. One of Kintner's dictates to the news department was that NBC stay on a good story thirty minutes longer than CBS, "no matter what."[32] During the four years that Brown would work for the network, NBC expanded its news team to include nearly 700 correspondents and technicians. It stationed 338 correspondents in seventy countries around the globe, including England, France, Germany, multiple nations bordering the Mediterranean, Africa, the Soviet Union, Japan, Asia and Latin America. McAndrew said the regions represented "major squares on the Cold War checkerboard." For its foreign correspondents, NBC utilized its men as "regional reporters ... [each responsible] for a wide area and ... fully familiar with all the problems of the parts of the world that constitute his beat." He added that "each [correspondent is] an experienced observer, skilled and trained in the art of digging out the significant news and presenting it in a clear, cogent style that places every new development in the context of what has gone before and what has happened elsewhere." McAndrew said Brown and the other correspondents were chosen because each was "intimately acquainted beforehand with the politics, the social and economic problems and the mores which they are likely to encounter. They are also sensitive to the hopes and objectives of the peoples in these lands."[33]

McAndrew assigned Brown to travel throughout the Asian rim to keep the U.S. apprised of developments in that part of the world, and there were plenty of them taking place. In addition to Japan, he covered stories in Taiwan, Korea, South Vietnam, Thailand, Malaya, Burma, Laos, Cambodia and his old CBS posting, Singapore. In Tokyo, the Browns rented a house in the Shibuya section of the city. During the U.S. occupation of Japan between 1945 and 1952, most Americans had lived in that neighborhood. Therefore, it remained popular with American business and military personnel.

In September 1958, soon after beginning his new assignment, Brown, as the lone U.S. reporter in the region, reported the struggle between Communist and Nationalist China over the Quemoy Islands. The fight over the twelve islands in the Taiwan Strait—which separate mainland China from Taiwan by only ninety miles—dated to the Korean War when both claimed rightful possession of the islands. Hostilities between the two nations escalated in 1955 when Mao authorized bombing of the islands. Eisenhower resolved the crisis by sending a U.S. Naval group to the Straits on behalf of Taiwan, and Mao backed down. Three years later, though, Communist planes bombed the islands again, and Mao charged the U.S. with "deliberate war provocation" by flying warplanes over the Strait. Brown said "unimpeachable" U.S. spokespersons in Taiwan had informed him they had recommended that the Seventh Fleet accompany Taiwanese ships to Quemoy's beaches instead of stopping at the international boundary. Brown said Eisenhower would decide whether to send the fleet within twenty-four to forty-eight hours, putting U.S. ships within firing range of the Red Chinese mainland. The White House denied Brown's report, but the president did dispatch the fleet to Taiwan within days.[34]

In his first appearances on NBC television later that month, Brown participated in a special program "Far East: Clear Danger," a report on the Quemoy crisis. He appeared with Pauline Frederick, James Robinson, Brinkley, and moderator Frank McGee. After the program aired, reviewer Bob Foster said the show was a quality analysis that "might well make thinking Americans a little more thoughtful." He praised the insight of all the NBC reporters, but wrote that Brown and Robinson were overly pessimistic about the prospects of the U.S. successfully defending Taiwan against the communists[35] However, in October, Red China ceased hostile action against the islands. During the crisis, Brown spent six weeks in Taiwan. On one occasion, Martha marveled at her husband and Chiang's deep concentration in an interview. An earthquake rocked Taiwan and the aftershocks continued for several minutes during the interview, but neither man paid any attention and continued the interview. Soon thereafter, Brown appeared on the *Today* show and told host Dave Garroway, "You have a sense [in Taiwan] of sitting on a simmering volcano. That kind of perch raises blistering questions: Whether the American people consider the survival of Generalissimo Chiang Kai Shek and his ambition to return to the mainland as essential to American interests."[36]

In one of his first stories from Japan, Brown interviewed the twenty-six-year-old youngest daughter of Hideki Tojo, Japan's Prime Minister who had been in charge of that nation's military during World War II and had ordered the bombing of Pearl Harbor. Convicted of war crimes, an international tribunal had hanged him in 1948. Brown's interview of the young Kamei Tojo put a sympathetic, human face on what many Americans had previously believed to be an evil man and a universally immoral people. When Brown queried her about feelings of guilt regarding her father's actions, she innocently claimed to be naïve about what her father had perpetrated. "It is difficult for me to make an opinion about this ... so difficult for a student who has not studied enough." She said that when some Japanese girls heard her name, they made her feel uncomfortable by the way they looked at her. She insisted her greatest desire was to attend a U.S. university to study law.[37] Despite the bad feelings Americans still had regarding her father, the story did not cause Brown any trouble, but not so another one he conducted soon thereafter.

In early October, he conducted an extended interview with Japan's Prime Minister Nobusuke Kishi. During the interview, the prime minister told Brown, "The time has come for Japan to abrogate the no-war provision [Article 9] in the Japanese Constitution." He said world conditions had changed since the U.S. drew up the constitution at the end of the war. He went on to say that China's communist leadership was demanding that Japan recognize it as a condition of economic trade, but Kishi said he would not do so because of Red China's incursion into the Korean War.[38] When Brown's story aired on the Huntley-Brinkley Report, international newspapers picked it up, and the prime minister's statements sent shockwaves around the world.

Kishi's comment astounded many, with memories of Japan's attack on Pearl Harbor and subsequent prisoner-of-war abuses fresh in many people's minds. McAndrew wrote Brown, "Ever since the story of your interview broke out here, the telephones have not stopped ringing. We had inquiries from the following news organizations, requesting more details: UP, AP, Kyodo, NHK, JOKR TELEVISION, Time Life, NTV, Japan Cultural Broadcasting and Hokkaido Press." One of the news agencies questioned whether Brown's report had misinterpreted Kishi's remarks, and asked for recorded proof of the interview, but Brown had not recoded it. Despite the uproar that resulted, McAndrew was thrilled that Brown had scooped the other networks. When questioned by the Japanese press, Kishi denied he had made the statements, but Brown said the quotes were accurate. The Diet—Japanese equivalent of the U.S. Congress—investigated the incident. It called Kishi to testify and he claimed that Brown's story did not "accurately convey what he really meant." Brown said he was ready to testify as to the truth of his report, but the Diet did not ask him to appear.[39] Brown had been away from Japan when the story broke, but public demonstrations erupted in Tokyo when the story broke because most of the population disagreed with Kishi's statements. When the demonstrators learned that Brown was on his way back to Tokyo, they marched to the airport to protest his return. In a society where news was strictly controlled, they objected to him broadcasting such a provocative, internal-affairs story. When Martha learned of the planned reception, she got a message to the plane's pilot, who conveyed it to Brown. She told him: "Only say something innocuous when you get off the plane, which he did, although he resented" not being able to speak freely. The demonstration dissolved without incident.[40]

During Brown's years in Japan, NBC flew its bureau chiefs back to New York at the end of each year to review the year's events for a national broadcast. They also speculated about what might occur in their part of the world in the upcoming year. The shows were titled *Kaleidoscope: Projection*. For the first program, on December 28, 1958, Brown appeared with Irving R. Levine, Joseph C. Harsch, John Chancellor, and Brinkley. The others were bureau chiefs in Moscow, Paris, Vienna and Washington; McGee moderated. Brown summed up the situation in the Far East by saying, "Chiang Kai Shek, India's Nehru, Indonesia's Sukarno, Japan's Kishi, and ... Red China's Mao Tse Tung ... [were all] trying to walk a tightrope that's been swayed and whipped by the ferments of revolution in Asia. All these statesmen have to be acrobats to stay on their precarious perch."[41] Unfortunately, Brown became overzealous about the importance of events within his coverage area. He dominated nearly twenty-three minutes of the hour-long program, going on at length about Nationalist China's claims to the Quemoy Islands. "It was too long a defense," wrote AP observer Charles Mercer in a review afterward. Brown's control of the time ended up limiting Brinkley's report to only two minutes, from whom Mercer said, in his opinion, the audience needed to hear more. "The most dogmatically opinioned man [Brown] held the floor longest and some of the most trenchant comments were made by those nipping at the heels of the charging bull," added Mercer. Brown had difficulty containing himself in excitedly detailing what was occurring in the Far East.[42] If Brown alienated the other correspondents with his monopolizing of the discussion, they did not let their feelings toward him affect their professional relationship. During their assembly in New York, Brown suggested that it would be a good idea if they joined him on a tour of Pacific Rim nations, so they could improve their knowledge of the countries in that part of the world. They agreed, and the correspondents alternately hosted one another on tours of their areas of responsibility thereafter.[43]

While back in the States for his appearance on *Kaleidoscope*, Brown spoke to the National Press Club in Washington and told those in attendance how thrilled he was to be with NBC. He said that when McAndrew hired him he promised Brown he would regularly be working eighteen hours a day. In the few months he had been in Japan, however, he had "been working twenty-three and one-half hours, seven days a week," but he was not complaining. "That [kind of effort], I think, helps to make NBC the greatest news-gathering organization in the electronic age." He said NBC was trying its best to help the public comprehend the ever-changing status of a confusing and dangerous world. That reality required that he and his colleagues do their best to keep them informed and to try to explain the meaning of the news. "We all feel keenly, what I wished all Americans felt more zealous about— and that is the right to know. And with the right to know, there's also the duty to care," he concluded.[44]

In April 1960, Brown went to South Korea to cover the protests against eighty-four-year-old President Syngman Rhee. Rhee had served three terms in office, which the Korean Constitution stated was the maximum number, but during his third term Rhee pushed legislation through the National Assembly that allowed him to be reelected to a fourth term. Many Koreans, especially college-age students, were displeased that Rhee had robbed them of their ability to practice the democratic principle of choosing a new president. The protestors told Brown: "We are no better off here than the Communists in the North. In fact, it would be better for us to be in the North. There, education is free." Unfortunately, the demonstrations turned violent, as police tried to control them and 114 students were killed. Brown summarized, "It was a typical youth-led revolution, its leadership vague and its direction uncertain." He said the demonstration was emblematic of the turmoil he was witnessing in the Far East.[45] Brown produced several on-the-scene segments soon thereafter for a special hour-long NBC program that updated Americans on the status of South Korea, including status updates on U.S. military and economic involvement there.

Upon returning to Tokyo, Brown again found himself reporting on college-age students protesting political activities. Throughout the 1950s, opposition had been growing in Japan concerning the presence of U.S. military bases there. Many Japanese believed the bases presented an open invitation to Russia and Red China to attack their country. The opposition became more strident in 1957 after Kishi became controversial. Upon taking office, Kishi declared his intention to revise the security treaty with the U.S. The new treaty would renew the U.S. right to maintain bases in Japan, and obligated the two countries to assist one another in case of enemy attacks on Japanese territories. Because of Kishi's announcement, a coalition of diverse groups, including Socialists, university students, labor union representatives and intellectuals, mounted a campaign to stop ratification of the amended treaty. Demonstrators broke through the fence at the Sunakawa Military Base near Tokyo. While conducting a hearing to consider prosecution of the

11. Back to the Far East for a New Medium 207

demonstrators, a Tokyo District Court ruled that the portion of the security treaty that said the U.S. could station troops in Japan contradicted the constitution MacArthur had engineered at the end of World War II. The judges ruled that the constitution forbade the U.S. from placing military troops and weaponry in Japan. Brown did a series of interviews with Japanese citizens regarding the ruling. The majority of them told him they felt it was imperative that the U.S. military remain in Japan because the treaty prohibited their nation from having its own defense force, but they considered this a ridiculous treaty provision.[46]

Despite the protests and court opinion, in January 1959 Kishi flew to the U.S. where he and Eisenhower signed the revised treaty, but Kishi needed Diet approval. In May, police removed protestors from the Diet proceedings so the members could debate the changes to the treaty. Other youthful protestors marched and chanted outside, and fights broke out between those who supported or opposed Kishi's initiative. Police used Billy clubs to restrain the crowd, and one woman died during the melee. Although the Diet affirmed the treaty, Kishi's autocratic tactics further inflamed the protestors. Brown said, in reference to the new treaty, "Japan is a classic example of a country that commits itself to nothing while Americans pretend they have a deal."[47] He said the Diet may have approved the treaty, but that did not mean the Japanese people accepted it. In the midst of the dispute, Eisenhower planned a visit to Japan as a goodwill gesture regarding U.S. agreement to the treaty, but the demonstrators had other ideas. They planned mass protests during his visit. When White House Press Secretary James Haggerty arrived at the Tokyo Airport in the second week of June, a few days before Eisenhower's planned visit, mobs pelted his car with stones. In his story about the incident, Brown said the protestors were poised to kill, if necessary. They did not want Eisenhower on Japanese soil, and he cancelled his visit after learning of the hostile reception that was planned for him. Later, more than 120,000 protestors surrounded the Diet and chanted for Kishi's resignation. Seeing that he had lost any hope of effectively governing Japan, he resigned on June 23. Brown's assessment of the relationship between the countries was that the U.S. had failed to communicate its benevolence toward Japan. "For fifteen years the Japanese had been nodding their heads in agreement while Uncle Sam talked, but precious little had percolated and even less has coursed to their hearts."[48]

Throughout his years in Japan, Brown focused many of his stories on Japanese-U.S. relations. He said the problems that existed between the two countries were the result of the Allied military occupation. In one broadcast, he presented a hypothetical conversation with a Japanese individual to encapsulate the issue. "All our troubles come because you defeated us.... I suppose I should say that many of our good things come from you, too.... So if you are disappointed in what we have become or where we are going, it is because you forget so easily." He added that the typical Japanese man or woman would say McArthur had given Japan "a divorce from international responsibilities. We were delighted! [But] the irritations come between us because you want to marry us to international troubles." The final part of the individual's response referred to the Allies' ability to maintain military bases in Japan to engage in the Cold War. With Red China sending signals that it was increasing its expansionist activities in the Far East, fear grew in Japan that Mao intended to invade their country. In a story in which Brown metaphorically spoke to President-elect John Kennedy, he said the new president needed to mend fences, not just with Japan's government, but with the Japanese people. "The task is immensely difficult, since Japanese governments are tragically inept in communicating information to their own people and to the outside world, and the Japanese press is highly resistant to information contrary to her neutralist convictions."[49]

As the 1960s began, Brown and his NBC colleagues turned their attention to new threats to the U.S. in the Far East. In April 1960, during a furlough in the States, Brown spoke to the Detroit Economic Club about Mao: "Red China is the mushrooming terror of this new decade.... In our time, the hinge of our fate has moved steadily eastward from the Rhine to the Volga and now to the Yangtze. There it is now, and there I believe it will be in the decade of the Sixties." He told the audience that he believed Communist China, not Russia, posed the biggest threat to world peace. He said Red China was the nation least interested in peace. He told the Motor City audience that while the Soviets had decided there was a "virtue in a certain measure of decent behavior," Communist China felt otherwise. He said the Peking government intended to "suffocate every non-communist independent nation of Asia; to make subservient ... more than one and a half billion people in Asia, from Japan to Ceylon, from Pakistan to Indonesia." Red China's goals, he insisted, constituted "a fearful challenge to free world strength and decision." He added that the people of the other Asian nations were fighting, not for communism, but "to win the fruits of the twentieth century," including adequate nourishment and decent health. He predicted that Communist China would one day possess a nuclear bomb, and he called on the U.S. to extend economic, medical and education help to Far Eastern nations to bolster their economies. By doing so, he argued, "the stiffer their [Asian nations'] spines will become to resist Red China." He concluded that the more the U.S. supported Taiwan, the greater it would become "a magnet" in attracting dissatisfied émigrés from mainland China.[50]

The network reporters of that era could be placed in three categories regarding their attitudes about communism, according to McDonald: Sevareid, McGee, Smith, CBS's Alexander Kendrick and NBC's Wells Hangen were "middle-of-the-road thinkers who could criticize both sides in the Cold War but still remain conspicuously pro–American." CBS's Daniel Schorr and Robinson were more objective, but Hottelet and Brown were conspicuously anti-communist in their on-air work. That point became clear during the *Projection '60* end-of-the-year NBC program. During the course of the discussion, Robinson and some of his fellow panelists attempted to cultivate a conciliatory appreciation for the Communist Chinese point of view. Brown was having none of it. "I'm shocked by your remarks," he replied and accused Robinson of "putting the stamp of virtue on banditry and murder.... It seems to me you're applying upside-down logic about what Red China is trying to do: It's trying to destroy every non-communist country in Asia." NBC's Edwin Newman thereafter referred to his colleague's recurrent outbursts on the shows as "The Brown Buzzsaw."[51]

But Brown never held a grudge regarding differences of opinion with colleagues for long, and neither, apparently, did they. The following year he collaborated with nine other NBC correspondents, including Robinson, in writing portions of a unique book *Memo to JFK from NBC News* that Putnam published. Other contributors included Chancellor, Sander Vanocur, Newman, Harsch, Levine and Hangen. While the title indicated the intended audience, the book also sought to update the American public on the international challenges the new administration faced in the 1960s. Somewhat presumptuously, the network believed its correspondents could provide the new president with a more objective briefing on world situations than the State Department or diplomatic corps. McAndrew claimed in the introduction that the book "pulls together a comprehensive pattern of fact and analysis that helps to make sense of our tangled foreign relations in a crucial period of history." He said the contents included both "background and proposals [for action]," and that the correspondents' chapters were "frank and forthright. They note where U.S. policy or practice has been good and where it has gone astray. There has been no attempt to cover up or excuse diplomatic action."[52]

Among those threats were warnings that Red China had designs on annexing other nations in the Far East. In January 1959, Brown's segment, "Southeast Asia: Target for Communism," about the threat of Communist China to Vietnam, appeared as part of a special NBC report. "It is a truism in the animal world that dragons are bigger than bears. And the Chinese Communist dragon is hungrier than the Russian bear—it needs more food, more living space, wants more quick and deadly prestige." He said the Southeast Asian countries were the most vulnerable because the people in those nations were "untutored, untrained, often hungry, usually in ill health." Brown called on the U.S. to send not just aid but "farm missionaries, technical missionaries, doctors and nurses ... if you will, downright do-gooders" to save

Asia from communism. Soon after his report, he asked McAndrew for the opportunity to present increased coverage of events in Asia during the nightly *Huntley-Brinkley Report*, but McAndrew rejected the proposal.[53]

In February 1960, though, McAndrew approved an NBC special news program *Journey to Understanding*, which constituted an in-depth investigation of the status of Indochina. Brown was one of a number of correspondents who participated. He anticipated that Vietnam was going to become an ongoing story, and that the U.S. would be involved there more deeply as the '60s progressed. "American interests and the dynamics of world development will produce the thrust that pushes us westward toward Asia.... This will be an explosive decade in Asia ... a decade filled with conflict, political, military and economic.... Asia may be more vital to our future than Europe," Brown wrote in an unpublished document.[54] Eisenhower also feared that Southeast Asia was going to be trouble, and before leaving office he warned Kennedy that he needed to make the situation a priority during his presidency, and he advised him to intervene in Laos. But Kennedy did not feel Laos was sufficiently vital to U.S. interests to risk a war. Believing that the U.S. already had overcommitted in Southeast Asia, Kennedy put his faith in Laotian Prince Souvanna Phouma's neutralization strategy, a tactic in which Brown had little confidence.

The following summer, Brown wrote a script for a multi-hour documentary on Vietnam, titled *Land of the Dragon*, which included an in-depth look at the nation's history and socio-political makeup. But McAndrew did not see fit to produce it. The U.S. was not yet involved in combat in Vietnam, yet Brown saw the U.S. suffering losses already: "We're losing the war in Vietnam. Partly because we haven't understood the country and its vastly complex history." He said the Vietnamese, especially the Vietcong, had a "fierce desire for independence. [And] we are faced with a major catastrophe here." He concluded that the U.S. had advisors in Vietnam to help defend a presumably free country, "but in fact, we and the Vietnamese are still trying to nurse one into existence."[55] On the January *Projection '61* show, Brown said Kennedy would have to deal with the civil war in Laos and mainland China along with Middle East issues as soon as he entered office. At the time, most Americans did not even know where to locate Vietnam on a map.[56]

During one of his visits to Vietnam, Brown secured another exclusive when he interviewed South Vietnam's *de facto* First Lady, Madame Nhu (Tran Le Xuan). The American ambassador had not been able to gain access to her, but Brown did. Madame Nhu was the wife of Ngo Dinh Nhu, the brother of South Vietnamese President Ngo Dinh Diem. Because Diem was a bachelor, the South Vietnamese people considered the outspoken Madame Nhu the nation's First Lady. She told Brown, "When you no longer need us, when you have missiles that can fire from the United States to any warfront, then you will not need us, and you will desert us." The U.S. was just beginning to send troops to defend the South against North Vietnam at the time. Yet, in the interview, Madame Nhu demonstrated the cynicism that continued to characterize her opinion of American leadership, especially after her husband and President Diem were assassinated in a 1963 coup. She accused U.S. officials of orchestrating the assassinations.[57] Her prediction that South Vietnam could not depend on the U.S., was borne out in 1975 when the last American soldiers evacuated Saigon as the North Vietnamese overwhelmed the city. Kennedy's intentions regarding U.S. involvement in Vietnam remained unclear after his own assassination in November 1963. He escalated the number of U.S. advisors in Vietnam during his time in office, but Senate Majority Leader Mike Mansfield said that two months before his death Kennedy told him it was up to the South Vietnamese people to win or lose the war on their own.[58]

Along with Vietnam and Japan, there was a significant amount of news taking place around the Pacific Rim. Brown traveled up and down the expanse of the region securing interviews with various nations' leaders and accompanying dignitaries as they toured the region. He interviewed Indonesian President Sukarno, India's Nehru, Japanese Prime Minister Hayato Ikeda, Russian First Deputy Premier Anastas Ivanovich Mikoyan, and Diem. He was among the journalists who accompanied Khrushchev on his tour of Indochina, Eisenhower when he visited India, MacArthur when he returned to the Philippines in 1961, and Secretary of State Dean Rusk when he visited Japan. He also accompanied Attorney General Robert Kennedy and wife Ethel during their visit to Hong Kong and Japan, Bali, Bangkok, Singapore and Taiwan. Brown was impressed with the president's younger brother: "Bobby Kennedy attracted enormous and excited and admiring crowds—everywhere he went he searched out and shook every hand he could grab." Brown later said that Kennedy moved so fast that he could barely keep up with him.[59]

Brown being Brown, he campaigned relentlessly to get stories on the NBC airwaves. At one point, while back in the States, he told a speech audience that "a correspondent out in the field, in one respect, is like a general out in the field. He thinks his area is the most important in the world—most deserving of attention, most acutely in need of reformation. For me to feel that way about Asia requires no effort."[60] In one such endeavor, in July 1960, he met with NBC's Vice-President of Programming Julian Goodman, and proposed production of a ten-minute weekly film segment on the *Today* show, or a one-half hour, twice weekly, radio show in which Brown provided international analysis from Tokyo. Goodman had McAndrew respond. "On the question of more news from your beat, this is partly beyond our control. American media in general have been playing down the Far East simply because of more urgent developments elsewhere," wrote Goodman. But he assured Brown that "we will try to bring up Tokyo more frequently for radio spots," and he was true to his word.[61]

As part of Kintner's dedication to building news offerings at NBC, he introduced a new radio news program titled *Emphasis*. The approximately three-minute opinion or insight pieces, international in scope, were closer to creative essays than features. They were a precursor to today's NPR style of longer-form reports. Reporters were encouraged to discard the traps of standard radio journalistic form and to eschew the conventional. McAndrew later commented that NBC received a lot of positive listener comments regarding the segments, especially from younger and professional members of the audience. He said some of the "most touching" letters came from the blind or shut-ins, who said the segments served as their "window on the world."[62]

Brown contributed several segments to the program that exposed the U.S. audience to Japanese culture. They included reports on birth control, a nation dealing with its memories of war atrocities, the booming television culture and a better understanding of the difference between American and Japanese journalism. His pieces demonstrated an ability to help Americans understand—without making value judgments—Japanese life. The segments served as a departure for Brown, as did much of his reporting during his four-years with NBC. In the birth-control segment, Brown probably shocked the American audience when he noted that abortions in Japan were common (1,200,000 per year) and inexpensive ($8.00). Regarding World War II, Brown said the historical facts embarrassed the everyday Japanese person, and as a result, they were staunchly anti-military. He noted that one of the most popular television shows in Japan was titled *I Want to Be a Sea Shell* about a mild-mannered barber who was ashamed of the atrocities his commander had forced him to commit during the war. Consequently, many people in Japan employed the show's title in daily conversation as an idiom to represent their revulsion toward militarism.

Brown's story on how Japanese television differed from that in the U.S. depicted a society in which its members were attempting to adopt the U.S. culture. "It is frantic ... imitative, artistic, wooden, earnest and alert. Japanese television is a genuine mirror of a Japan torn between East and West, between traditional and modern." As an example of what he meant, he said, "Watch a Japanese girl strolling down the Ginza wearing a kimono, her hair in a ponytail and you can picture the mental tug of war."[63] In other stories, he observed that the majority of Japanese did not have refrigerators, televisions, washing machines or apartments ... [and] most Japanese women still wear kimonos. But the trend is obvious. "Traditions are in turmoil, so are the minds of the Japanese. The old ways are dying out. The Japanese are going American—and they wonder if they'll be happier for it."[64]

11. Back to the Far East for a New Medium   213

Brown's story about Japanese journalism had to strike Americans as particularly odd. The segment began with his description of an anomaly known in the culture as "face, or stomach, reading (*Haragei*)." Brown described it as a practice in which a person did not take at face value what another person said, but rather accepted communication that suited "his own desires." In Japanese journalism, this meant that what a person said in an interview his newspaper might report quite differently from the interviewee's actual comments. Brown provided an example in which a reporter included a long interview in a newspaper story with the alleged survivor of a plane crash. The problem was that there were no survivors. When an editor asked the reporter about the discrepancy, without a hint of embarrassment, the reporter replied, "If there had been a survivor of the air crash ... the survivor would have said what the story said he said."[65]

One of the last stories Brown reported from Tokyo featured a reflection on the impact of Marilyn Monroe's death on the Japanese. He noted many in Japan had met her when she and baseball icon-husband Joe DiMaggio honeymooned there in 1954. Brown said the Japanese "adored Monroe [because] ... she put humor and wit into her acting." He remarked that it might surprise many Americans that the Japanese remembered Monroe— not for her blond beauty—but for her modesty. When she and DiMaggio arrived in Tokyo, "she attracted an unprecedented crowd of screaming fans at the airport. But she won the hearts of Japanese by shifting the attention onto her husband whose big baseball days were over."[66]

During a February 1962 visit home, Brown appeared in Oakland on a panel of network correspondents at the World Affairs Council. Joining him from NBC were some other foreign correspondents, including Piers Anderton, who was based in West Berlin. In writing about the appearance, *Oakland Tribune* reporter Bill Fiset commented that each of the correspondents tried to outdo the others when it came to telling stories about their experiences. Concerning Brown's comments, Fiset wrote, "Hell hath no fury like a television correspondent at a luncheon. [Brown] declared that in Southeast Asia this is the year for the U.S. to take the offensive. 'We should impose in North Korea, North Vietnam and Red China the same subversion, hardship and sabotage that they impose on others.'" Fiset concluded that the correspondents' remarks were "pretty impressive, but then a network's overseas men have to get in their licks when they can. The idea is to say something to make people sit up."[67] It was one of the last public appearances Brown made as an NBC employee.

NBC had provided Brown with the opportunity to participate in the pioneering and innovative years of news department development. It was a period of expansion and acclaimed news coverage that is now only a memory at network news departments. Brown had provided U.S. viewers with insightful news from an area of the world where bureau no longer exists. The only time Americans now get a glimpse of the Far East is when a disaster occurs or U.S. interests are threatened. But, in 1962, at age fifty-five, health issues began to catch up with him. A Tokyo doctor told Brown in May that he needed hernia surgery again. The malady that had dogged him since 1930, was hindering his ability to fulfill the responsibilities of a big job that required long hours and extensive travel. He decided not to have the surgery in Japan, and asked for a new assignment in the States. McAndrew kindly allowed him to return to the U.S. for a new position.[68]

McAndrew provided Brown with the option of returning to New York or going to Los Angeles with NBC. When they had moved to Tokyo in 1958, the Browns had rented their penthouse to George Vila, the president of Uniroyal, and he was still living there. They could not bring themselves to ask Vila to vacate. It was a difficult decision, but the Browns opted for Los Angeles. In July, Goodman notified Brown that the network was assigning him to KCRA TV, to do nightly commentary. Brown was pleased that the new assignment would provide him with a greater opportunity to be on the air regularly and to do analysis again. What he could not have envisaged was that his assignment in California would turn out to be more rewarding than he could have imagined, and would take his career in a completely new, unexpected and innovative direction.

❖❖ 12 ❖❖

Return to the U.S. to Open More Eyes

Relocating to California became one of the best moves Brown could have made. His homecoming to the States constituted the last of four phases of his career: 1. as a foreign correspondent; 2. as a radio commentator; 3. as a network bureau chief; and, 4. as a reenergized television commentator. Jonathan Brown believed the final phase of Cecil's career "was probably his most harmonious" because California was a "more tolerant place to live and work than New York City." He believed his uncle found work on the West Coast "liberating."[1] Then again, Brown's nephew may have been referring to his uncle's second job in Los Angeles, not the first one. Even as he moved into the fifth decade of his career, he remained committed to confronting challenges and helping his audience make sense of their world.

After recovering from surgery, Brown began delivering commentaries every other night in October 1962, on KRCA TV in Los Angeles. A month after Brown started there, NBC relocated the station to Burbank and changed its call letters to KNBC. Brown alternated every other night with AP and NBC veteran Elmer Peterson in presenting commentaries. Anchor Jack Latham presented L.A. and California news from 6–6:05, Gordon Weir did the weather between 6:05–6:10, and Brown or Peterson occupied the 6:10–6:15 time slot. When they started their nightly commentary, KRCA promoted them as the station's own "Huntley-Brinkley duo." The two continued their segment when the program grew to one-half hour in September 1963 after NBC increased the *Huntley-Brinkley Report* to one-half hour and moved it to 6:30–7:00 time slot. The ratings for the Brown-Peterson segments were the highest on KNBC and regularly "neck and neck with those of the *Huntley-Brinkley Report*."[2]

On Brown's first night on L.A. television, he picked up where he left off in 1958 with advocacy for civil rights. The latest confrontation was playing out in Mississippi, where James Meredith was trying to become the first African

American to enroll at Oxford. Segregationist Governor Ross Barnett opposed Meredith's enrollment, and President Kennedy and his brother, Robert, were attempting to negotiate with Barnett. Brown brought his perspective on the crisis in the South to Los Angeles viewers: "In his twenty months in the White House, President Kennedy has seldom faced a simpler decision or a more powerful one.... What is to happen in Mississippi now, and next in Alabama and South Carolina, is dictated by what has already happened." Placing the situation in historical context, Brown said, "Kennedy has to go on demonstrating now, what President Lincoln though he had defined 100 years ago ... that the authority of the United States is superior to the sovereignty of the state of Mississippi."[3]

The same day Brown delivered his commentary the president announced he was doing exactly what Brown hoped he would. Negotiations between the Kennedy brothers and Barnett had broken off, so the president ordered U.S. Marshals and National Guardsmen to accompany Meredith to campus to ensure his safety. During the ensuing conflict, that resulted in the deaths of two men, Meredith enrolled. In June 1963, the president had to take similar action to facilitate enrollment of two African Americans at the University of Alabama. Governor George Wallace had vowed that blacks would never attend the flagship university in his state. That night, in a national television address, Kennedy told the nation that civil rights was a "moral," not just a legal issue. He said he was introducing a civil rights act to Congress that outlawed discrimination based on race, color, religion, sex, or national origin. Although he would not live to see the bill become law, it did so in July 1964.

Then, only two weeks after Brown began his tenure at KRCA, the Cuban Missile Crisis erupted. The clash brought the U.S. and Russia to the brink of nuclear war. After the failed CIA-led Bay of Pigs invasion, Premier Fidel Castro convinced Khrushchev to send nuclear missiles to Cuba to deter further U.S. harassment. U.S. reconnaissance planes confirmed that Russia had delivered missiles, and Kennedy authorized a naval blockade to stop additional deliveries. Brown observed that "Khrushchev and Castro are playing a cat and mouse game with President Kennedy. The question is who will get tired first."[4] Eventually, negotiations between Russia and the U.S. led to an agreement in which Khrushchev pledged to remove the Cuban missiles in exchange for the U.S. retrieving its missiles from Turkey. Kennedy called off the Navy's blockade, and the Cold War's tensest crisis passed.

During the following months, Brown was a hit with Los Angeles viewers. The ratings documented that, as did viewers. Representative of the feedback was a letter from a North Hollywood viewer. "It is reassuring to hear commentary such as yours. Reassuring ... means that in existence there is still a voice that is forthright enough to present a point of view not edited and watered down to accommodate 'the big brainwash,' which we are subjected to by the wire services and the staff news reporters."⁵ On many evenings, Brown analyzed international events. He addressed developments in Russia, China, and Vietnam and other locations around the globe about which he believed the southern California audience should be knowledgeable. Given his background, KNBC believed it was fortunate to have an in-house expert on international affairs, and Brown was pleased to utilize his international expertise. But this was not the subject matter he had hoped for when he accepted the position at the most-watched station in Southern California. He yearned for the days at Mutual when he had had the freedom to comment on true public-interest issues. Greater Los Angeles and California witnessed a number of controversial issues during the early 1960s, but station management did not allow Brown to tackle those issues. KNBC management was unwilling to allow him to discuss topics that might alienate viewers or advertisers.

Among the topics on which he did not provide commentaries were the termination of Los Angeles streetcar service after ninety years, and merger of the *Los Angeles Examiner* with the afternoon *Herald Express* to form the *Herald-Examiner*. The merger—caused in part by KNBC's popularity—signaled the demise of two-a-day newspaper coverage in the nation's second largest metropolis. Other local issues on which Brown did not comment included the Baldwin Hills dam disaster, construction of the controversial Humboldt Bay nuclear power plant south of Eureka, migrant farmworker protest over working conditions, and damning of the Trinity River to supply California with a network of reservoirs, at the expense of Chinook salmon population. While KNBC reported the events as news, management forbid Brown from providing critical commentary about them. Instead, he was limited to national and international issues. When addressing those stories, he did his best to relate them to the lives of Los Angelenos. But as time passed, he became frustrated that he was not permitted to comment on controversial local or state activities. Instead, he relied on the wire services for leads from which he could develop relevant perspectives

The events of Friday, November 22, 1963, served as an example of how he was able to do that. On that day, Lee Harvey Oswald assassinated President Kennedy in Dallas. Brown had not met the president, but he was familiar with his brother, Robert. But Brown, like most journalists, was enamored with John Kennedy. Brown was in Japan during much of Kennedy's first two years in office, but the president provided a breath of fresh political hope for Brown, and like Roosevelt and Truman, Kennedy cooperated with journalists. Brown was most impressed with Kennedy's handling of the civil rights' confrontations in the South. He appreciated that Kennedy's time in office was too short to facilitate his agenda and to fix all the issues he faced. Kennedy presented Brown with the kind of optimism and transparency that he valued in the presidency. The president had related to young Americans and had rallied them to break through the complacency the 1950s had institutionalized. Kennedy's style and proposals reminded Brown of the idealism and outreach to the disadvantaged that had characterized the Roosevelt and Truman Administrations. The president's faith in public intelligence, reasoned discussion and human nature likewise resonated with Brown. Two days after the assassination, Brown offered a commentary in which he focused more on what the assassination said about America than on the act itself. He said there were two entities in the American body politic. One of those was a character filled with "generosity, and tremendous decency, and democracy and equality." On another hand, there existed in the U.S. people "venom and poison and tyranny and hatred and contempt for the rights of other human beings." Brown argued that those irreconcilable differences were what killed Kennedy, "The venom [that is] coursing through the bloodstream of American life, may be getting too powerful to stem—that it threatens to suffocate, or overwhelm the decencies in the American body politic." He said the racial violence in U.S. cities had to end and people needed to learn to see each other as equals because "hatred" was what had really killed the president. "He, for his historic and unequaled stand on civil rights, may be known in history as the Great Emancipator ... [but] the American people could really honor President Kennedy by emancipating themselves from bigotry," Brown concluded[6]

In April 1964, Brown interviewed Dwight Eisenhower in Palm Springs about the upcoming Republican presidential race. The former president expressed frank views concerning the campaign, and Brown's story about the interview appeared on the *Huntley-Brinkley Report*. Eisenhower had told Brown the GOP was in need of a candidate with two qualities: the ability "to project sincerity ... and he must have fire in his belly." Eisenhower did not think either of the two candidates at the time, Barry Goldwater or Nelson Rockefeller, had been able "to capture the imagination of the public." He refused to name his favorite candidate, other than to say the best-qualified man for the job was his brother, Milton, who was president of Johns Hopkins University. But, Milton was sixty-five, and Eisenhower said "the presidency is something I wouldn't wish on him."[7] Brown was stunned that the airing of his story was causing consternation among national Republicans. After the story aired, one of Eisenhower's advisers told Brown the former president was angry because he had assumed Brown understand that his candid comments were meant to be off the record. Brown called Eisenhower to say he had misunderstood the interview's conditions, but by the time Brown reached him, his anger had subsided, and Brown's supposed *faux pas*, from which Eisenhower was attempting to distance himself, was forgiven.

After eighteen months at KNBC, Brown commenced discussions with a number of sources regarding employment elsewhere. One of those was

Elmer Lower, president of ABC News. He responded that he was most impressed with Brown's work, and he wanted to hire him at KABC Radio, but his budget would not allow him to do so. In early 1964, San Francisco's KNBR FM broadcast Brown's show, *The World as I See It*, on a trial basis, but the station could not secure a sponsor and terminated it. On Cecil's behalf, Eugene Brown contacted Justus Lawrence—a New York PR specialist—to explore opportunities. Lawrence told Eugene that Cecil was in a difficult position because of the convoluted career path. He said his moves between commentary and foreign correspondence left him without "a sound strategy and long-term program." Lawrence said Cecil, whom he considered, "one of the best writers I have ever known," could write a book about his experiences in Italy or possibly even return to a foreign correspondence posting there. Nonetheless, he was uncertain if Brown's health would allow him to again undertake the rigors of foreign correspondence. (In fact, a Los Angeles cardiologist began treating Cecil for a heart condition in 1964.) Lawrence also doubted that Brown could rely on someone such as Kintner again: "Bob is, first of all, a realist, not a sentimentalist."[8] In addition, KNBC soon thereafter announced plans to eliminate commentary from the evening newscast. The reason was that Brinkley had begun doing commentary on the *Huntley-Brinkley Report*. Consequently, there was no reason to continue the Brown-Peterson segment at KNBC. Management wanted to reassign Brown and Peterson to reporter positions. Peterson was amenable to the new arrangement, but Brown was not.

Brown was at a crossroads in his career, but in the summer of 1964 a new opportunity presented itself. The position would not pay a great deal—it is unclear but more than likely it paid even less than he was making at KNBC—and the future of the enterprise was questionable. But it presented Brown with the prospect once again to do original commentary on a wide range of local and international issues for a new type of station whose management promised that they would not constrain him. At the end of July, Brown left KNBC to begin a new job as director of news and public affairs at KCET TV in Los Angeles. Channel 28 was the first noncommercial, educational television (now PBS) station to sign on the air in L. A. KCET's founding president, James Loper, and program director Jim Case, were preparing to put the station on the air, and they invited Brown to join them as a member of the station's management team. The station signed on September 28, 1964, operating in the former studios of KNXT TV on North Vine in Hollywood. Initially, KCET was only on the air Monday through Friday during the afternoon and evening.

Brown's position carried with it a broad range of responsibilities. Most importantly, he had free rein to do commentaries on topics of his choosing. Operating on a bare bone's budget, with limited staff, Brown would serve as his own researcher, producer, and show host. In making the announcement of Brown's appointment, Loper said Brown's program, titled *Comment*, "Will treat the news, not as an isolated moment in time, but as a part of a whole that forms a pattern for our daily lives." He added that although *Comment* would consider current events, it would use them only as a starting point to "provide the viewer with an opportunity to evaluate the present and perhaps anticipate the future by a better understanding of the past."[9]

Brown's first night on the air was November 9, 1964. He looked into the camera at 8:30 p.m. and asked the audience, "Are news commentators really necessary?" After a pause, he answered his own question by saying they were because there were "stirring events ... happening all around us ... most of them are highly controversial and, of course, they are mighty confusing." He said he would analyze the events and that he would do his best "to eradicate some of the confusion," instead of adding to it. He referenced the plain background in front of which he was sitting at a desk. It was a simple set that looked like a study, with books and magazines on the desk and landscape pictures on the wall behind. He said the set designers made it to look inviting, which is what he wanted to encourage the viewers to feel in joining him each night. The program, he said, would not do spot news—the L.A. commercial stations did that, and did it well. Rather, he assumed that by 8:30 it was a good time to sit back and relax, "and to add up the score—to try to bring some order out of the disorder of the day's avalanche of news." Brown would voice opinions about the day's controversial events because if he did not, "this program would be pointless, aimless, and senseless. But I trust you will find it to be balanced opinion. I hope that in the 35 years I've spent covering happenings in this country ... and in most countries of the world, I've gathered ... some wisdom to wrap around my opinions. Of course, one person's opinion is another person's stupidity—but then, that's what makes democracy so refreshing."[10]

He then presented his first commentary, concerning the nation's economy. Case and Loper considered themselves privileged to have such a respected journalist on the air as they launched the new station. Brown likewise considered himself fortunate to be back doing what he really loved. To add to the allure of the situation, was the fact that the time frames during which he would present commentaries ran ten minutes in length (a full half hour on Friday), and there were no sponsors who would interrupt or attempt to edit his content. Save for the lack of resources, it was an ideal situation, one rife with opportunity. A month after starting, he wrote a colleague, "I haven't worked this hard in 15 years, or enjoyed it more."[11] In addition to his nightly program, he began producing documentary and interview programs. During the coming months, he created and hosted programs with titles such as *Meet Your Public Servant*, and *Citizens in Action* in which he examined a broad range of topics. Among them were Los Angeles water fluoridation, birth control, the challenges of free trial versus free press, the Vietnam War, the California migrant workers' plight, the perils of the increasingly popular recreational drug LSD, as well as smoking and voter registration.[12] A few months after he began at KCET, *Los Angeles Times*' reporter Hal Humphrey interviewed Brown. He noted in the article that while Brown's audience was not nearly as large as the ones he previously had addressed at the commercial networks, he "feels useful again…. [And his] "twenty-five years of experience are not being wasted."[13] Records are incomplete, but Brown's commentaries may have been the first on educational TV in the U.S., if not among the first and few available.

Added to the new station's challenge in attracting an audience was the fact that KCET was the first Los Angeles station utilizing the UHF area of the electromagnetic spectrum. L.A.'s commercial stations were broadcasting in the VHF area of the band. In addition to the fact that UHF waves do not travel as great a distance as VHS waves do, many viewers' sets were not equipped with UHF tuners in the 1960s. In 1964, only about 60 percent of the more than 1,000,000 homes in greater Los Angeles possessed sets equipped with both types of tuners.[14] Yet, with its location in the second largest media market, KCET quickly became the second most watched educational station in the nation.[15] And within only a few weeks of going on the air, *Comment* became KCET's most watched program.

There were approximately 115 educational television stations on the air in the U.S. in the mid–1960s. At the time Brown began at KCET, the National Education Television (NET) quasi-network was coordinating programming for the stations. Unlike the commercial networks, NET could not afford to distribute programming electronically, so it had to be circulated among affiliates via the postal service. Besides its financial limitations, NET was under fire because it was airing documentaries that dealt with topics such as racism and poverty. Just as such programming had aroused indignation when Brown had been at Mutual, Southern-NET-affiliates voiced opposition to airing similar programs in the 1960s. That form of investigative journalism was not appearing regularly on the commercial networks, so audiences across the U.S. became upset when a supposedly benign education television service began airing uncompromising looks at controversial issues. Charges of liberal bias quickly became a common accusation.[16]

A 1966 study found that public affairs programs, which it defined as "the consideration of problems rather than events" had become a "bold program fixture" via NET by 1966. One of the significant changes in ETV programming that the study discovered had occurred during the past two years was the evolving "tone of public affairs programming…. What made Public Affairs so distinctive was that, at least on a national level and sometimes locally, it addressed itself to some topics that were infrequently, if ever, discussed on [national commercial] television," such as black history, and, similar to the "bottom up" program distribution arrangement that MBS had pioneered, NET disseminated local station productions to its affiliates.[17]

KCET, under Brown's direction, quickly became one of the stations contributing such programming for network distribution. Within his first few months at KCET, Brown and Wesley Willoughby, a veteran San Francisco journalist, teamed up to produce a documentary titled "The Radical Right in California: Extremism, Communism." Willoughby wrote much of the script as a counterpoint to the ultraconservative right movement in the U.S. that the book *None Dare Call It Treason* had helped perpetuate, by anti-communist John Stormer. The book's allegations helped propagate a revitalization of anti-communist accusations and unlawful actions across the nation, including in Southern California.

Brown served as the studio host for the program, which interspersed pre-recorded segments from a reporter, testimonials from harassed Southern California citizens, and a Santa Barbara publisher whose newspaper had editorialized against the movement. In addition, historian Allen Nevins explained Americans' constitutional rights. The set on which Brown appeared, was meager, reflecting both the low-budget quality of the production as well as the seriousness of the topic. While speaking, Brown walked among hanging posters that displayed the faces of extremist figures. The program outlined the activities of extremists such as John Birch Society founder Robert Welch, anti-communist radio preacher Carl McIntire, militant Minutemen founder Robert DePugh, and Liberty Amendment author Willis Stone. The program outlined the tactics and dangers of rightwing extremism. Brown began with: "It is hard to believe that so many Americans, living in the midst of prosperity, are willing to believe they are living in the midst of a grand conspiracy, dragging us to impending ruin." He provided a history of rightwing fanaticism, dating to the 1850s, and noted that the various extreme-right organizations had raised $25,000,000 in recent years. This far exceeded the U.S. Communist Party's $1,000,000 raised during the peak of popularity in the 1930s. Brown said there presently were more than 3,000 Radical Right groups in the U.S.

He called the members of the organizations "outright bigots," but explained that "all extreme right-wingers are not bigots, but almost all professional bigots are right wingers." He said they were targeting Jews, Negroes, Roman Catholics and Communists for persecution. Brown said there had been eight violent attacks in the previous two-and-one-half-years in Southern California where right-wingers had sought to disrupt peaceful activities or intimidate law-abiding citizens. A Presbyterian minister said he had received threatening phone calls and his house had been bombed. A librarian said

Birch members had attempted to burn what they considered offensive books at her library. Brown said the vast majority of Southern Californians were not extremists, but the extremists were gaining influence because they were working in concert with one another. "The radical right may not be an imminent threat to our survival as a free, democratic society. [But] with their resources and dedicated followers, the radical right will touch most Americans sooner or later." He said that if viewers were courageous in standing up to the extremists that they could be defeated.[18]

Brown closed the program by citing John Milton's *Areopagitica* statement concerning the principle of a representative society's right to freedom of expression.[19] NET distributed the program nationwide, and the national press critically acclaimed it as revelatory and courageous. Overall, the format and intellectual approach of the program resembled an episode of *Bill Moyers' Journal*, a respected issues and commentary program that would appear from 1971 to 2010 on PBS.

The following June, as more civil rights' incidents occurred in major U.S. cities, Brown related the extremist movement to the situation: "The more possible that civil rights becomes, the more the extremists take over the opposition to civil rights." This comment came two months after the winter and spring of marches, in which police assaulted and jailed hundreds of African-Americans. Throughout the period, Brown did a number of programs in which he criticized what he termed "suspect southern justice." In one of the June *Comment* shows, he speculated that the activities would soon be reaching a climax. "That 200-year-old-game that some Americans enjoyed so much was to shoot Negroes, to beat them, to abuse them, or to kill them. And to do all that securely confident that they … would not be punished or even restrained." He said the game was coming to an end because they themselves were in danger of being beaten, bombed or murdered." He called it a "sensational development in the dark and unresolved story" of U.S. race relations.[20] A partial resolution to the struggle moved ahead in August that year when President Johnson signed the Civil Rights Act that prohibited racial discrimination in the voting booth.

After moving to KCET, Brown again became an in-demand speaker in greater Los Angeles, with his topics typically concerning international affairs or journalism. In 1966, he spoke at Claremont McKenna College, where he displayed a passion for educational television and the advantages and disadvantages that exemplified it in comparison to commercial broadcasting's news programming. At the time, few people understood those differences. Brown explained that the commercial networks devoted "fortunes" to news coverage, but that their monetary investment made them "prisoners of economics." He argued that the gap between what they were reporting and what they could be reporting was "enormous." They are, he argued, "prisoners of timidity. By comparison, we [educational television] are puny ... we are severely handicapped by a shortage of professional people." Yet, "In the field of news and public affairs ... educational television has a niche to fill.... We certainly can ... break some of the chains [of public ignorance]. The fact is ... we already have broken some of the chains."

He said KCET managers wanted them to watch their programs, of course, but they were not concerned if they did not get maximum viewership for every program. Smaller audiences, he clarified, were not as much of a concern for channel 28 because it did not have to please sponsors, and he called that "a whole wide-world of difference" for KCET. He promoted *Comment*, explaining how he prepared analysis. He said he relied on his years of experience to inform his commentaries, which he attempted to present in a manner that allowed the audience to understand "the way things seem to be and where we seem to be going." His job was to "analyze, assess, estimate, evaluate, distill, interpret and offer explanations of the day's event." He argued that the public was "hungry for news commentary on television," and that commercial television was failing to satisfy that hunger. Commercial television was not doing its job, in his opinion, because it was failing "to trace the pattern of events so that they show the pattern of history. I'm convinced that the networks will eventually summon the courage and develop the will to do this." He called the way the networks and stations were using television "disorderly." Thus, the sky was the limit for those who wanted to produce programming that explored the issues facing the nation.[21]

In a similar speech a few months later, at Chico State College, he acknowledged that he had made mistakes during his career, "In forty years of journalism I have contributed my share of preconceived notions, and I certainly have compounded the public's bewilderment, and unhappily, every other journalist can make that same statement." The years of combat with managers and sponsors had mellowed Brown. His commentaries at KCET reflected the thoughts of a man who was wiser, after having been through the network news wars, but he still was not ready to cease agitating his audience's sensibilities with assertive opinions and exposure of controversial subjects. During the next few years, in addition to his busy KCET schedule, and appearances before college audiences, he addressed professional and civic groups, and lectured at the UCLA Institute of Lifelong Learning.[22]

The mid-to-late 1960s saw the rise in America of the so-called counterculture, and California universities were at the epicenter of the movement. More young people than ever were attending college, and they were politically aware and liberally minded. While many were solely interested in getting an education and launching a career, an increasingly visible group considered U.S. cultural values outdated and narcissistic. They found a Caucasian-dominated culture that was fixated on the perks of secure employment, consumer goods, a suburban home and escapist television to be vapid philosophically and culturally. The inability of the nation to deal with civil rights' issues in a peaceful manner and questions concerning involvement in the Vietnam War also bothered students. Rebellious music lyrics, uninhibited sex, and recreational drug use became the norm for thousands of students. Brown tried to contextualize the activities and their meaning.

He produced a special program titled "Revolt on the Campus." It dealt with the demonstrations at the University of California at Berkeley. Cal-Berkeley had made national headlines in October 1964 when police arrested the campus chairperson of the Congress of Racial Equality, Jack Weinberg, for violating university rules regarding activism. Campus administrators summoned police to break up the protests and they arrested Weinberg, but before the patrol car in which he was held could leave campus students blocked the street. The protests continued the next day, with nearly 7,000 mostly students present and giving speeches that called for free speech on campus. Following the demonstrations, administrators and student groups met and reached an agreement that allowed the students to speak freely about public issues. Two months later, however, students occupied Sproul Hall in response to the administration's decision to expel Weinberg and other members of the Free Speech Movement for staging anti–Vietnam protests. Fifteen-hundred students crowded into Sproul and stated their intention to occupy it for two-to three-days, but the police forcibly removed them, arresting nearly 800.

The free speech protests resonated with Brown.[23] He believed that once an independent observer set aside the students' inappropriate strategies for change and their questionable morals, they were on a wavelength not unlike his own. For him, and them, the Kennedy idealism for a more progressive America was going unrealized. Like Kennedy, Brown embraced Randolph Bourne's "beloved community" thinking, which identified that "realizing the national destiny required struggle and even violence."[24] Before the end of the decade, the men who championed the causes of nonviolent civil rights, and uplifting the disenfranchised (King, Jr., John and Robert Kennedy all would be assassinated). Yet, many Americans refused to acknowledge the deep-seated issues in America or acted to rectify them. It was a disquieting time for men like Brown, who recognized that few others in journalism were being of much help in making sense of or recommending action to rectify the causes behind the extemporaneous events that were playing out on television each evening.

Brown produced a number of additional programs regarding student protests, making an effort to balance the views of those who supported or opposed the campus activities. But in late 1965, he made it clear with which side of the controversy he agreed. On his Thanksgiving Day broadcast, Brown told viewers that instead of criticizing the student protestors, they should be acknowledged for doing something that was necessary and valuable. "There is an extraordinary ferment among the young people of America. They are using words and they are taking actions that question America's behavior and purpose," he began. He appreciated that the students were calling for a new interpretation of terms such as "right wing," "liberal," "conservative" and "radical." He thought something special was playing out: "When young people question standards, values and clichés—then the whole nation is cooking with gas, or it's being cooked." He reasoned that it was important that the students were forcing Americans to "reexamine our nation's conduct and to reassess its purpose." He said other nations had been observing how the U.S. was addressing foreign and domestic challenges, and they were being critical of America. He was referring to the Vietnam War and the civil rights' struggle. Consequently, he concluded, the students were showing all Americans that reassessment was exactly what needed to be taking place.[25]

In later programs, he continued his efforts to enlighten the audience on the value and context of campus protests. In March 1966, Brown composed a commentary in which he attempted to put the activities in international context: "The notion that students are boiling with rage and eager to show it is fantastically wrong," he said. He cited a survey the Educational Testing Service had conducted of 850 colleges and universities across the nation. It found that students protested about food service and dormitory rules more than they did U.S. Vietnam policy. Students in other countries, he explained, did not only demonstrate but attempted to force leaders to resign, citing recent occurrences in Japan, India, Indonesia and South Korea. What stood out to him was not necessarily the focus of the demonstrations, but "how vital they are in the political affairs of other countries. How important their attitudes are. And how much care and attention have to be paid to the students' hopes, determinations and intentions. It's well to remember—today's students will be running tomorrow's show."[26]

In May, Brown presented another perspective on student protests. He said the rebellion that the nightly commercial newscasts were covering was no doubt making older adults "nervous and annoyed." Yet he believed that the challenges to the established way of doing things and rebellion against authority "may yet prove to be one of the healthiest signs of progress. Changes are often denounced at the time they occur—not as progress—but as steps backward. Then, a few years pass, and [things have improved]. Something better could be the result of all this present-day turmoil, and upside-down values."[27] A month later, he introduced his commentary by citing Weinberg's mantra—that the protestors had adopted—"Don't trust anyone over thirty." Brown said the remark was naive, but then he said it was no wonder the students were criticizing their elders: they had messed up the world, in Brown's view. "Consider the kind of world, the scale of standards, the range of ethics, business, social and personal, that older people are giving to the oncoming youth." He said older Americans' questionable standards and ethics had guaranteed that a "great burden was being dumped" on America. He argued that it was a wonder the students were not causing more trouble. "It could be that it's the adults who need a searching examination far more than the current crop of young people."[28]

Brown's commentaries indicate he was fully back in his contrarian element. Instead of presenting the perspective that many commercial newscasts were giving, that the students were spoiled, acting inappropriately and causing social unrest, Brown saw their activities as necessary and a response to an America that had become dangerously satisfied with its values. By this time, Brown was nearly sixty years old. Yet, unlike many Americans of that era, he was encouraged, instead of threatened, by the willingness of the young to challenge political policies and social practices. Consequently, Brown's unconventional views elicited mixed responses. That did not surprise him; indeed, it pleased him. One writer, who apparently had watched Brown since he had appeared at KRCA, told him "We believe you are one of the most-sound public affairs' analysts on the American scene today." Another long-term viewer, said he thought Brown's presentation ability had improved and that since moving to KCET, he had "acquired new confidence and the courage of your convictions." A third addressed the value of *Comment*: "To me the most important 10 minutes on non-commercial TV." A female viewer said she and her husband never missed Brown: "[We] enjoy your studious, factual, highly intelligent reporting.... We are only sorry that only ten minutes is allotted to you, since we feel the news these days especially, requires much more time for you to do 'in-depth' reporting." Another woman said she had been listening to Brown since World War II, and she knew of "no one who can cover current happenings with such clear objectiveness as you." Other viewers wrote that they found Brown's commentaries "refreshingly different," and "You always leave the listener with food for thought and reflection.... Most commentators ... are so boringly conformist that we know beforehand what they are going to say.... You generally have a little surprise for the viewer." Another praised Brown's interviewing skill: "You [are] successful in allowing or prompting guests to expose their real feelings on the subject discussed."[29]

Among those who were displeased with Brown's strategies, one woman wrote that she found it inappropriate for educational television to present commentary. "We thought that this station was going to be a cultural agent for the entire community.... [Perhaps] we should look elsewhere for cultural and refining agencies." Another voiced mixed reactions: "We have found you provocative as well as occasionally irritating." Others were upset with Brown's defense of the Berkeley protestors. Emily Zabriskie wrote Program Director Case, "After having heard your commentator, Cecil Brown, make disparaging remarks about Governor [Ronald] Reagan on several occasions, we wonder if he is related to ex-Governor [Jerry] Brown because he seems to have a phobia when it comes to Governor Reagan."[30] In another, a man complained about a documentary on the right of protestor speech Brown had produced. Case's replay was representative of a number of responses he or Loper wrote that supported Brown's right to speak as he saw fit. Case said he understood a program of comment and news analysis could be controversial and might upset some people. Nevertheless, "We also know that it causes a great number of people to think seriously about serious world problems; to inquire, to study, and to make judgments as individual citizens based on their own experience." Case added that anyone was welcome to utilize KCET's airwaves to rebut Brown's remarks. Regardless, "since the broadening of all human experience is the ultimate objective of educational television, we feel that a program of news commentary is a vital part of a vigorous educational television station."[31] There is no record any viewer accepted Case's offer, or that he or Loper revised any of Brown's commentaries.

As had been the custom throughout his career, Brown took time to write responses to viewers who disagreed with him. To a woman who criticized a Vietnam commentary as biased, he replied that he had re-read the script to which she alluded, and found it a balanced treatment.

He explained that during his nearly forty years as a journalist he had written thousands of newspaper stories, dozens of magazine articles, and thousands of radio and television broadcasts. Thus, he believed he knew how to write one properly. He concluded by saying he attempted to construct commentaries that provided a full picture of situations without resorting to partiality. "The broadcast to which you object is … a textbook example of explaining the forces at work on a critical situation, laying them out for an audience to examine so that people would have a better understanding of those forces, without my approving or disapproving."[32]

On the other hand, given Brown's views regarding campus unrest, one of his viewer's comments was particularly surprisingly. Glenn Dumke became the chancellor of the California University System beginning in 1962. He opposed student protests and banned faculty strikes—two strategies Brown supported. Brown interviewed Dumke on several occasions, they became friends, and Dumke later helped Brown with his next career move. He later wrote of Brown: "As an historian interested in bringing some perspective and reason to our understanding of world affairs, I found Cecil's view of the world to be that to which all of us should aspire—balanced, reasoned, never afraid of the truth, and always with human compassion."[33]

In January 1966, Ronald Reagan became California's governor. Thus began the tenure of a politician, the identity of which Brown believed had been fabricated. He said Reagan's PR "handlers" had successfully created the former actor's political persona: "Reagan is being handcrafted and carefully packaged.... His words are measured, weighed and tested ... his appearances are calculated, rehearsed and nothing is left to spontaneity." Once in office, Brown found Reagan's policies similarly fabricated from questionable material. It soon became clear, too, that Reagan was uncomfortable with the press; when he had to go "off-script," during a press conference he quickly ran into trouble formulating ad-lib responses. Brown offered on-the-air advice to Reagan to improve his interactions with journalists. He said he needed to be more honest with the public, and Brown counseled that when Reagan was unable to answer a question he should simply respond: "I will look into that and get back to you, instead of stumbling during press conferences."[34]

During Reagan's tenure as governor, Brown's unfavorable analyses contradicted popular opinion. He pointed out how Reagan's decisions failed to help California's needy and disenfranchised. One of those groups was Mexican-American. In 1966, Brown spoke at a UCLA Conference that addressed the Hispanic plight: "There's ferment among Mexican-Americans to get off the bottom of the economic totem pole—to better define their identity and to win higher respect for it." On *Comment*, he saluted Cesar Chavez for organizing migrant workers. In September 1965, Mexican American and Filipino farmworkers struck California's grape growers over wages. Reagan was unsympathetic, supporting the vineyard owners' dubious labor practices. He fought the efforts of the workers to win union contracts, vetoing the Agricultural Labor Relations Act, a bill that would have granted farmworkers collective bargaining rights. The strike lasted five years and many consumers refused to buy California grapes until vineyard owners agreed to bargain with the newly formed United Farmworkers Union. (The Labor Relations Act was enacted after Reagan left office).[35] Brown was pleased with Reagan's intent to balance the state budget, but he criticized his means for doing it, including reductions in education funding. Regarding a number of the governor's other policies, Brown balanced his opinion, saying Reagan had made mistakes, but he had surprised others with some progressive policies. On balance, however, Brown made it clear—through programs he produced about California's poor and minorities—that he believed the governor's policies failed to address their needs.[36]

In a February 1967 *Comment*, Brown turned his attention to the *Los Angeles Times*, taking its editors to task concerning their Reagan coverage. He said the newspaper had done an incomplete job of reporting the controversy between Reagan and the California Higher Education System. In running for governor, Reagan had made two promises: "To get the welfare bums back to work," and "to clean up the mess at Berkeley." The second one is what Reagan devoted much of his first term in office to addressing. He was critical of the Berkeley administration and faculty as well as the state university system for failing to punish what Reagan called the "spoiled" students, whom he said were taking advantage of their taxpayer-supported education. Three weeks after taking office, Reagan fired nationally respected Cal-Berkeley President Clark Kerr. He also threatened to reduce the university's budget unless the administration restored order at the campus. In 1964, FBI Director J. Edgar Hoover had pressured Kerr to deal more vigorously with the Free Speech Movement, which he considered a communist front, but Kerr had refused. Hoover found a willing ally in Reagan who had told Hoover that if he won the governorship he would deal harshly with the students and Kerr. (This agreement did not become public knowledge until 2002 when the *San Francisco Chronicle* uncovered the details.) Brown was unaware of such a plan, but he said Reagan and the Board of Regents had handled the Kerr firing badly and that the action would not end student protests—and he was correct. Reagan's contentious relationship with Cal-Berkeley continued throughout his years in office. On May 15, 1969, he had to call out the National Guard to quell a 3,000-strong-student protest at Berkeley. During the melee, about two-dozen students were hospitalized with injuries, and police arrested nearly 1,000.[37]

Throughout Brown's tenure at KCET, Johnson continued to escalate America's involvement in Vietnam. In 1965, it had become clear that the South Vietnamese were unable to repel the increased number of Viet Cong and North Vietnamese infiltrating the South. Adding to the strength of the invading forces was the fact that Red China and the Soviet Union were aiding and abetting the efforts by increasing their support of North Vietnam. In an effort to bolster South Vietnam's defenses, U.S. combat units had begun operations in the South. In March 1965, the White House ordered a controversial increase in bombing missions over North Vietnam. Although the number of protests against the war were growing on U.S. campuses, Congress and the majority of Americans continued to support prosecution of the war. So did Brown, but he began raising questions about the wisdom of escalating the war. He asked his audience what price they thought the U.S. and they individually were prepared to pay to save South Vietnam. Brown asserted that the expenditures the U.S. was outlaying were proving insufficient to secure victory. He said both U.S. leaders and the American people were merely "pretending" that they were curtailing the Communists in Southeast Asia. He argued that the price had to go up if the U.S. expected to save South Vietnam. "President Johnson has been remarkably, and ominously, uninformative about the worsening crisis.... One result could be that the president has ill-prepared the American people for the dreadful decisions that now must be made."[38]

Johnson's Great Society efforts pleased Brown because they enacted much of Kennedy's New Frontier program. But the Vietnam conundrum and civil rights' confrontations dominated the president's efforts and sabotaged his hopes of fully implementing his domestic initiatives.[39] Brown told an audience at the University of Southern California during this period that the president was suffering from a "crisis of communication." Johnson, said Brown, "is often not believed when he tells the truth because his listeners fail to take into account what he says by both word and deed." He noted that the previous year Johnson had said the U.S. would do "everything necessary to win the war in Vietnam." But war hawks, Brown said, felt "betrayed because he isn't doing literally 'everything.'" Yet, taken along with Johnson's other statements and orders, it was clear the president intended to "make the U.S. the policeman of the world." Americans did not fully comprehend the president's mixed messages, Brown noted. In the same speech, Brown said Reagan suffered from a similar "crisis of communication," and consequently Californians were complaining that the governor had lied to them. Brown, however, defended him on this count, saying if anyone took the time to re-read the newspaper accounts of what Regan had said he would do if elected, then "nobody can say he is deceiving the voters. He is giving the people what he said he would give them."[40]

Up until early 1965, Brown had favored taking whatever steps necessary to halt the spread of communism across Asia. But by the following year he began presenting *Comments* in which he sought to balance the positive and negative effects resulting from U.S. involvement there. "Our stand in Vietnam has produced all kinds of favorable results.... The revolt in Indonesia, the overthrow of Sukarno and the release of Indonesia from its tie-up with Red China would not have occurred had it not been for our stand in Vietnam. We are convincing the Communists in Asia that they cannot subvert their neighboring countries and take them over—That is what we are proving in Vietnam."[41] But, conversely, he was unconvinced that the conflict was worth the cost. Viewers witnessed a commentator who on multiple evenings was voicing a view that the war—as the U.S. was conducting it—was unwinnable.

Consequently, Brown began exploring Johnson's Vietnam quandary as a confusing situation that more broadly characterized contradictory U.S. international policy. He said he had spoken with a Beverly Hills' woman whose son was in the Navy. His ship had sailed for Japan recently and she was concerned his next stop would be Vietnam. She had voted for Johnson, thinking he was doing a "wonderful job ... being firm and aggressive" with the Communists, but now that her son might have to fight she was disappointed in him, and said the U.S. had no business being in Vietnam. Brown did not criticize the woman, saying instead, "There's nothing reprehensible or even unpatriotic about the mother's attitude. In fact, it's no more than normal and natural for a mother to react that way. It's natural for her to resent and to resent bitterly and even politically the circumstances that combines with a president to take her son away from a comfortable home and plop him down where there's shooting going on."[42] In October 1966, with the American body count escalating, Brown looked into the camera and soberly said, "Vietnam is a nasty, miserable war, but there never was a war that wasn't nasty and miserable. Americans have a tendency to say 'Let's get things over with.' But there will be other Vietnams, other Berlin crises, other Dominican Republic uprisings. We can only put them in their proper framework and deal with them."[43] Although he did not call directly to discontinue the escalation of American involvement in Vietnam at that point, the evidence Brown provided, and continued to provide, indicated that he had serious reservations about prosecution of the war. Jonathan Brown—who was an anti-war activist at Yale—remembers having heated discussions with Cecil about the Vietnam War. Because of his belief that Communism had to be checked, Cecil was conflicted about the proper course of action, but his misgivings about Johnson's policies alienated some viewers: "Goodness me—where did you get the script you read on tonight's news [concerning Vietnam]? What hogwash—and you knew it," wrote Ester Langlois in December 1966.[44] Once again, Brown was ahead of other journalists by more than a year in questioning the evidence in favor of American prosecution of the war. Not until February 1968 did Walter Cronkite voice his now-famous commentary in which he said the war was headed for a stalemate. Contrary to myth, and like Brown, Cronkite did not call for American withdrawal from Vietnam, only for a negotiated peace.[45] Overall, Brown supported prosecution of the war, and esteemed U.S. soldiers, but just as he had more than twenty years before with the British in Singapore, he questioned the political and military motivation and strategies of America's leaders.

In the fall of 1968, Brown was on the road again. He and Martha traveled to their favorite part of the world, visiting eight nations in the Far East, with stops in Japan, Thailand, Hong Kong, Taiwan, South Vietnam, Singapore and Indonesia. In Indonesia, he met with Foreign Minister Adam Malik, and on Taiwan he again interviewed old friend Chiang. Brown learned that Chiang remained "cockily certain" that his forces would soon retake control of the Chinese mainland. The interview took place at Chiang's palace at Yangmingshan, outside of Taipei. It had been nineteen years since the communists had forced Chiang and the 2,000,000 Chinese loyal to him from mainland China. In the years since, Chiang had talked often of returning to power in Peking, but at the time Brown interviewed him the likelihood that it could happen seemed more plausible than it had previously. Mao was directing the Cultural Revolution in Red China, which was resulting in turmoil and death. Millions were starving to death or Mao's troops were executing them because they opposed the revolution. Chiang's agents on the mainland were reporting chaos. Indeed, his agents were perpetrating some of the trouble by organizing and arming Chinese rebels, sabotaging factories and delaying rail transportation. Many

12. Return to the U.S. to Open More Eyes

in Red China remained loyal to Chiang, and he believed that if his forces invaded, they would join with his Nationalist forces to defeat Mao. During his exile on Taiwan, Chiang had never given up hope that he would eventually return to mainland China, but he did not tell Brown of any specific plans. The *Los Angeles Times* published Brown's findings in two articles, which constituted one of the most comprehensive reports on the status of the situation between the two Chinas at the time.

While many of Chiang's exiled brethren joined him in dreaming of a return to the mainland, Brown doubted the U.S. would facilitate or permit it to happen. He said U.S. policy had "chained" Chiang to Taiwan, what with a U.S. military umbrella helping protect Taiwan against a Red Chinese invasion. In addition, Brown doubted that the 11,500,000 native-born Taiwanese had any interest in supporting Chiang's plans. Nevertheless, Chiang had a strategy in mind to attack Red China with air and naval forces. But, following Brown's

In July 1941, Brown sits on an ammunition crate typing a story while in the West African desert with British troops. At the time, the temperature was over 120 degrees, and the Tommies were exchanging artillery rounds with German batteries across Halfaya Pass. The stark, unforgiving brutality of the desert stunned Brown and he lost weight when he contracted "gyppy-tummy." *Life* magazine published his article about the experience in "The Desert Is Hell" (courtesy Wisconsin Historical Society).

visit, the White House informed Chiang that he was to abandon the idea, and that if he did not American planes and warships would deploy to stop Chiang. Johnson wanted to avoid any reason for Red China to escalate its involvement in Vietnam into a war with the U.S. Two years later, the U.S. Ambassador to the U.N., Charles Woodruff Yost, joined the majority in the vote that affirmed Red China's right to assume that nation's seat at that international body. The development permanently ended any hope Chiang had of returning to power in his homeland. Brown found the native Taiwanese not completely happy that the Nationalist Chinese regime constituted foreign rule over their country, but in Brown's words, "Freedom is an ambiguous term in Asia.... [Because] personal economic improvement" is more important than sovereignty.[46]

That fact was the most impressive reality Brown witnessed during his visit to Taiwan, which enjoyed the second highest standard of living in Asia. After pumping $14,000,000,000 into the Taiwanese economy since Chiang became its president, U.S. aid to the nation had ended in 1965. After the influx of U.S. dollars stopped, private U.S. investments had been boosting Taiwan's economy by locating manufacturing plants there. During Brown's travels around the island, he witnessed the results of $80,000,000 in investments from companies such as Singer, Gulf Oil, Procter and Gamble and Philco. The Chiang Administration was making U.S. locations in Taiwan attractive by offering inexpensive land, income and tax incentives. Each week, up to one-thousand U.S. military personnel, on leave from Vietnam, also contributed to the economy by spending furlough money freely. Brown concluded that although Chiang never stopped dreaming of returning to power on the mainland, few of his Taiwanese neighbors had any intention of doing anything that jeopardized the economic boom they were enjoying.[47] Chiang died in 1975.

In addition to his analysis of international and domestic political and social affairs, Brown devoted numerous programs to examining the state of broadcast journalism. Of course it was a topic with which he had been intimately acquainted for many years. Dating to its beginnings, the commercial networks have done an inadequate job of publicly analyzing their own activities. But Brown had the freedom to do that: "The men who made television possible—[Guglielmo] Marconi, [Thomas] Edison, [Allen] DuMont—must be turning over in their graves if they knew what commercial television is offering this season." He noted that the networks aimed their cameras at much that was going on in American society "except, naturally, themselves." National television critics, Brown commented, were appalled at what NBC, CBS and ABC were offering in their 1965 primetime lineup of shows. Among the programs was escapist fare such as *My Favorite Martian, Petticoat Junction, My Mother the Car, Green Acres* and *The Munsters*. There was only one investigative news show among the three networks, *CBS Reports*, on the air. Brown said former Curtis Publishing Company executive Edward Bok had made a comment in a previous decade that was applicable to the network situation in the 1960s. "Come down to the level which the public sets, and it will leave you the moment you do," Bok had said, then added, "Perhaps someday, possibly but not probably, the commercial television networks will discover that the public always wants something a little better than it asks for."[48]

During an interview with Brown, *Los Angeles Times*' reporter Hal Humphrey asked him his views on the state of network news. Brown was concerned about the absence of commentary on the commercial networks of the type he had voiced throughout his career. He asserted that "news on radio and TV today almost puts you to sleep. At least we used to be able to arouse indignation from listeners, but now the general public either misses what's significant, or it is beyond their comprehension as delivered by most newscasters." He said high-financial stakes were mainly to blame. In the mid–1960s, only four commentators remained on the commercial networks: Lewis at MBS, Harvey and Edward P. Morgan on ABC radio and Sevareid on CBS television. "I recognize the difficulties inherent in commenting on the news, but the public is ill-served by the lack of it," Brown argued, and augmented his thought with, "It calls for someone to evaluate it…. There is a risk involved in freeing the airwaves for commentary—if it isn't responsible and safeguarded against demagoguery."[49]

In February 1966, in an incident that accentuated Brown's concern with the network's lack of dedication to keeping the public informed, Fred Friendly resigned his post as CBS News President. Friendly quit when CBS Vice President John Schnieder decided the network would not interrupt a rerun of *The Lucy Show* to broadcast live coverage of the Senate hearings that were investigating American involvement in Vietnam. Friendly resigned, making himself a martyr for the cause of quality network news. The developments did not escape Brown's attention. He said Friendly had resigned in the hope it would make network executive reconsider television's responsibility to the public, but said Brown, "It didn't do that at all. Fred Friendly said several months ago that broadcasting had a curious quirk that causes it to cast out the men most dedicated to advancing the media." Although he did not name names, Brown had to be thinking of himself, and Murrow, and other respected journalists he had known through the years that CBS had jettisoned. "Friendly hardly realized that he would be the next to be driven from the broadcasting jungle. The real issue was put in a nutshell in the title of an article in the *New York Times Magazine* last January 23rd. The title of the article was 'TV shows are not supposed to be good—they are supposed to make money,'" Brown noted.[50]

In March 1967, when Friendly was in L.A., Brown interviewed him about his book *Due to Circumstances Beyond Our Control*. Friendly borrowed the title from a broadcast axiom that the networks employed to indicate that a technical problem was preventing them from delivering a program. However, Friendly utilized it to indicate that journalists could not deliver important news *because of circumstances* that the networks controlled. He outlined how behind the scenes at the networks there was a continual struggle between executives and the news divisions to get quality news coverage on the air. In the volume, which constituted the first critical history of television news, Friendly expressed thoughts that were similar to Brown's concerning the state of network news. Friendly warned that a future in which coverage of important news was subservient to Nielsen ratings and profits would put the nation at peril. At the height of the Vietnam War—before the truth concerning government manipulation of the war situation was made public—Friendly's book served as a public indictment of network news practices. Viewer letters confirmed that they felt it was an important program.

In May of that year, Brown wrote an article for a Pasadena newspaper in which he described "the courage gap in television news." He said the gap to which he referred existed between the daring journalists who were covering the Vietnam War and the "button-down-collar broadcast executives high in the steel and stone towers in New York." He said there was a vast "chasm" that existed between reporters and the network executives who lacked "economic courage. [And] falling deeper and faster into the chasm is the long-denied and more-confused public." He called the situation reprehensible because the networks possessed the resources to provide the public with the news coverage it needed and deserved. Brown called NBC's executives disingenuous in their recent claims that it was somehow admirable not to permit their reporters to air opinion. He was referring to NBC's McAndrew, who had said he did not permit his journalists to comment because doing so breached the boundaries of objective journalism. That's a "disclaimer that is supposed to allow Huntley and Brinkley to make wry remarks and gentle asides to titillate the public into imagining it is getting the salt and pepper of opinion in its supposedly 'objective' and 'straight news,'" observed Brown.[51]

He called on the networks to utilize what he termed the "daily historian" (commentator), to help the public understand where current events fit into history and how international developments were changing the direction of the world. He said the public did not understand the war in Vietnam nor even what was causing unrest within their own neighborhoods. One of these was the first major racial uprising in Los Angeles since World War II. The Watts Riots that occurred in August 1965 cost thirty-four lives and $40,000,000 in damages. Although the national media blamed police racism and unemployment, Brown said the Watts incident provided Los Angeles with an opportunity to focus on the need to improve medical services in the

African American area of the city, which was one of the primary—but rarely mentioned—reasons for the riots.[52] He stated: "Because television news has a fantastic fear of depth ... [journalists] may lose all capacity for opinion, even about the weather." He concluded that if television did not recommit itself to courageous reporting and in-depth analysis, it would miss what he termed "the most important story of all—the destiny of the human race."[53]

In 1968, CBS launched *60 Minutes*. Brown was pleased to see CBS put a news magazine on the air because he considered it "about the only [network news] program that was doing a meaningful job of informing" the American people. Nevertheless, he was concerned that it was "carrying advocacy a little far." What he meant was that the program did not provide a broad enough perspective on the topics it investigated to help the audience understand their context. Only educational television, Brown explained, had the latitude to do that.[54]

Brown continued his campaign to bring commentary back to broadcasting during a 1969 speech at California State Polytechnic University in Pomona. He charged that the short-form visually driven presentation of television news was inadequate. "When you consider that 64 percent of the public gets its information from the 'box' ... the TV industry owes the public a presentation that provides the most accurate impression of what has occurred." He referenced cameras focusing on the violence at the Chicago Democratic Convention demonstrations the previous August, without journalists providing contextual information. "Without interpretation," he said, "[it] leaves only an incomplete, distorted and confused impression." He said an ardent viewer could turn the next day to a syndicated column, such as "Today and Tomorrow," by Walter Lippman. The viewer would receive a fuller appraisal of the confusing situation there, but most Americans did not take time to do that. "TV defaulted its responsibility to the newspapers" in that case, he said.[55]

In addition to his opinions regarding the media, Brown remained one of the best-informed American journalists on events in the Far East. While the majority of reporters focused on developments in Vietnam, he continued to view the war as a struggle that represented a larger conflict that was playing out in that area of the world. In July 1968, he had proposed writing a book for Doubleday titled *The '70s Belong to Asia*, and the editors were interested in publishing it, but Brown failed to produce a completed manuscript. It was the last of a number of writing projects that he never completed. In spite of the fact that he wrote millions of words for broadcast and print outlets during his career, he never completed another book after *Suez to Singapore*. The reason is not clear; he wrote segments of an autobiography, but he never pulled it all together into a complete book.

Nevertheless, throughout his years in L. A. Brown remained a voluminous letter writer. Whenever he saw an accolade in the news regarding one of his acquaintances, he wrote the person a letter of congratulations and included a copy of the clipping. If he heard that one of them was traveling to California, he invited them to dinner or in the case of public figures, such as Benett Cerf or William Benton, encouraged them to sit for an interview on one of his programs. In June 1964, old colleague Kaltenborn died. Brown had not forgotten that Hans was the one commentator who stood with him and his right to speak his mind in 1943 during his rift with CBS. In a letter to Kaltenborn's widow, Olga, Brown told her that her husband had made a "monumental contribution to public communication" by being the best and most influential early news analysts on radio. Hans had accomplished that, he said, by "bridg[ing] the gap for the first time between printed means of reporting the news and the verbal methods that came with electronic journalism." He added that broadcasting owed a debt of gratitude to Kalternborn for making commentary essential. It was Hans, Brown added, that "established and maintained the need, the integrity, and the endurance of the commentator."[56]

Jonathan was right that his uncle's relocation to California paid off for him as several journalism organizations recognized the quality and legitimacy of Brown's work. In 1965, the AP selected him for the Best News Commentator Program in California for his broadcasts concerning the Pay ("cable") TV controversy. The National Association of Theater Owners had mounted a successful campaign to prohibit any form of subscription television in the state. The campaign influenced voters to approve Proposition 15, which banned pay television. In a series of programs, Brown documented how the theater owners had employed manipulated statistics and slanted testimonials to convince the public to support the referendum. A federal court later ruled the referendum as unconstitutional.

In 1966, former smoker Brown won the AP Commentator Award again for programs he did about the perils of smoking. Following issuance of the 1964 Surgeon General's Report on the dangers of smoking, he presented several programs that expressed his opinion on the subject. "When it comes to choosing between dying of cancer and smoking a cigarette, the American people are making their fateful and fatal choice. That has now become the postscript, the sequel, the net result of the great cigarette scare of 1964. Americans are smoking more cigarettes than ever." He also criticized tobacco company advertising that targeted young people. In 1966, he joined with FCC Chairman William Henry in criticizing broadcasters for continuing to accept cigarette advertising two years after the Surgeon General's report.[57] Brown interviewed healthcare professionals and illustrated the deadly effects of smoking.

The most esteemed recognition Brown received came in the form of the national Alfred I. DuPont Award. In April 1965, DuPont Committee presented

Brown with its award for Outstanding Work by an Individual in the Field of News, Commentary and Public Affairs. In recognizing him, the committee said, "Brown provides thoughtful, forthright opinion.... His stimulating and informative analyses are in the finest tradition of public affairs broadcasting, and add a vigorous and effective voice to public discussion and understanding."[58] In the late '60s, the Hollywood Chamber of Commerce recognized Brown—along with Murrow—by implanting stars on the Hollywood Walk of Fame with their names on them (none of the other Murrow Boys received that distinction).

Along about this time, a reporter asked Brown if his forty years of experience commenting on U.S. affairs had not made him "a cynical man." "No," Brown responded, "Rather, I consider U.S. foreign policy since 1945 to be the most generous, decent and honorable pursued by any nation in the whole history of mankind."[59] The comment reflected a patriotic side to Brown's personality that perhaps some of his critics had missed. It seemed the antithesis of his commentaries over the years in which he had accentuated how a number of leaders had fallen short of his expectations. Brown had repeatedly put forth a vision for America that it become a nation that would serve as a model of morality and benevolence for the rest of the world. Only exceptional leadership, he believed, would help it attain that goal.

In 1969, Brown left KCET and launched into a different career, one he had been considering for several years, and one that Dumke had encouraged him to pursue. He did not cite a reason for leaving broadcasting. It may have been that with his increasing age, he was tired of the production, research, writing and hosting load he was shouldering at KCET. His health also may have played a role. With PBS' founding (and congressional funding) still a year away, local non-commercial TV stations continued to operate with meager budgets and a lack of operational staff. Regardless, Brown was not ready to retire. Rather, he was ready to pass along the knowledge he had gained over four decades to the generation of students that would take his place.

Epilogue

In 1969, Cecil Brown finally earned his bachelor's degree by completing nine hours of coursework at UCLA, which allowed him to complete the Ohio State degree he had left unfinished for forty years. Although he lacked the normally required graduate degree, his years of media experience and undergraduate degree made it possible for him to lecture at the college level in California. He accepted a position to teach at California State Polytechnic University in Pomona. In switching careers, he said it did not constitute as great a change as some might have thought. "I came to realize that teaching was what I was doing all those years. Working to give audiences the information and encouragement they needed to act coherently as good citizens so they could experience fully the world in their own time and make an impact on it."[1] Teaching at Cal-Poly required a forty-mile commute from Brown's apartment on Wilshire Boulevard in L.A., but the new opportunity energized him. Cal. Poly hired him to teach courses in communications, but later reassigned him to the Social Sciences Department where he taught courses in American Civilization. Cal. Poly administrators were pleased to hire a man they termed "in a class by himself—an expert on international affairs, a journalist with few peers, a keen observer of human foibles, a man of insight, wit and humor.... He speaks authoritatively on the issues of our time."[2] When a department chair introduced him to the other faculty in a beginning-of-the-schoolyear meeting, Professor David Levering leaned over and whispered to a colleague, "My God, I thought he was in Hong Kong."[3]

In addition to teaching, Brown produced and directed more than fifty public affairs video programs in collaboration with other Pomona faculty during the next few years. Known as *The Cal-Poly Forum*, the programs took the form of panel discussions or interviews. Part of the responsibility included teaching his colleagues how to write and perform appropriately on television. He devoted the time to it because he thought, "People in the community ought to have access to information about matters of concern to them; we need to reach people with all that we have to offer."[4] The guests included not just faculty, but notable individuals such as diplomats, visiting scholars, authors, artists and working journalists from greater Los Angeles. The university showed the programs on local cable television, and some of them were subsequently screened in classes throughout the University of California system. In the classroom, Brown encountered students who could not afford the newspaper or magazine subscriptions he required as part of their homework, and the debate team needed financial support to travel to meets. Brown loaned them the money for the subscriptions, and talked some philanthropic Southern California friends into financially supporting the debate team and funding scholarships.

Meanwhile, he remained in demand as a speaker in greater Los Angeles. He continued to address international issues, recognizing that for many in his audiences his job was to familiarize them to what was going on in the world and why it should matter to them. In a 1973 letter to a friend, Brown commented, "Since no one really knows what U.S. foreign policy is I am able to speak without fear of contradiction. What our policy, foreign or domestic will be, after Watergate, not even a professor would dare to predict."[5] Coincidentally, the Watergate scandal presented Brown with another opportunity to comment on the performance of the press. Speaking before a Society of Professional Journalists' (SPJ) meeting in Riverside, Brown criticized the job the U.S. press had done in its reporting about Watergate. He told the journalists he disagreed with those who were saying coverage of Watergate had spotlighted "the vigor and vitality of the press." He charged that journalists had been reticent and absent in their coverage. The reality, he said, was that the Nixon Administration's contempt for the First Amendment had exposed the press in a way that should "make us all shiver in our boots." On the other hand, the situation also showed that a great many Americans no longer believed in a free press. He concluded, "Too many people who uphold freedom of the press are weak on responsibility ... and too many people who scorn freedom of the press are hypocrites who think that they—and they are not alone—are privy to and guardians of the whole truth."[6]

Students enjoyed his classes, which they said were demanding but in which they learned to see the world in a different way. He commented to a friend who asked about what he thought of teaching: "Too many young minds are frozen in concrete; too many young people are fitting in a little too readily. The stakes are too high for that."[7] He attracted many students to his classes because they were impressed that when he talked about seminal developments in twentieth-century history, he had experienced many of them firsthand. A colleague who sat in on one of his classes said, "His professional career as a journalist was predicated on the belief in people's right to know; his career as a teacher has as its parallel the belief that people have a responsibility to know."[8] One student commented that Brown "brought the entire world into perspective for [her]. I felt at times that the various 'hot spots' were burning right on campus." Another wrote Brown that "I have nothing but the highest regard for your one-man crusade for awareness of what is going on in the world." Brown told journalism students that he had spent his life fighting censorship, and he encouraged them to have the courage to do the same. He urged them: to be "fighters rather than automatons. Too much is at stake to be namby-pamby in communications.... Make the fight but be prepared to accept the consequences."[9]

In a letter to a friend, Brown wrote that his "years of teaching have been the happiest and most serene of my life. We are dealing with people who are making decisions about the future, and I think we can inspire them to be better people, citizens who believe that they have the ability to change things."[10] Brown spent eleven years at Pomona. He retired in 1980, but not before he was named Outstanding Teacher in the California University System. One of his nominators had written of Brown, "He epitomizes everything we believe a man of international renown should be. His quiet dignity and his self-effacing manner are admired by those who know him. He stands as a model for those of us teaching at the university."[11]

For the next seven years, he remained active in civic activities and speaking about the state of American journalism and world affairs. But in October 1987, Brown suffered a ruptured aorta, and died within a couple of hours at the UCLA Medical Center. His brother Eugene died of prostate cancer three years later. A month before his death, Brown had responded to a letter from a student who had written him for advice regarding a journalism career. He counseled the student: "Whatever else you seek, first must be dedication to honesty and integrity in what you do.... You ought to be able to face yourself in the mirror and be proud over what you see. Your integrity must match your contribution to society."[12] It was the code by which Cecil Brown had lived. In November 1987, the Cal. Poly community held a memorial service on campus for Brown. A number of former faculty colleagues eulogized him. Representative of them were comments by Professor Donald Pfluger:

> If Cecil Brown were thirty years old today he would be living in Beirut, or possibly in Tehran on a forged Canadian passport. One way or another he would be getting the news out to the world, the kind of objective news the world needs to evaluate situations and make rational decisions. Long before Pearl Harbor this giant among journalists knew where the action was, where the decisions were being made, and from where the alarms needed to be sounded. He had a feel for the past, was totally in touch with the present, and saw more clearly than most what the future held for mankind.[13]

For some historians, Cecil Brown has not represented a journalist worthy of consideration. There are probably a number of reasons for this. Perhaps it was because he worked for so many different media outlets during his career that he failed to establish a high-profile identity. Maybe it was because he spent so many years with the Mutual Broadcasting System, which trailed the other networks in market penetration. Possibly it was because he alienated a number of influential individuals—both within broadcasting and government—with his pugnacious reporting and sometimes combative personality. Or perhaps it was because he was willing to do the work to discover the truth and was unafraid to share his findings, even if they were unpopular. Regardless, he is one of those people who practiced his craft in a way that communicated virtue in an unambiguous mode that is uncommon in the media today. Those who listened to him appreciated his candor. His career is worthy of recounting for what it represents in the development of broadcast journalism and in serving as a testing ground in defining broadcast press freedom.

Brown spent forty-three years as a journalist. It was quite an adventure for a first-generation Jewish-American who fell in love with the idea of keeping the public informed as well as challenging them to think. He believed that by doing so he could make America and the world a better place. That may seem like a grandiose claim, but he shared it with other members of the Murrow team. Howard K. Smith, for example, said he viewed his career as aiming for "nothing less than improving the world."[14] Like all human beings, Brown was flawed. His rapid rise to fame resulted in an inflated ego—making him excessively self-assured and strong-willed—and probably hurt his opportunities. Yet, when not behind the microphone, he was known for kindness and benevolence. His sense of self-importance moderated over time, but he clung to an aggressiveness that distinguished him as a hard-working reporter and fearless commentator. Although an exact comparison is impossible, among network commentators he traveled around the world more than most of them so he could personally witness international activities and interview foreign personages. The power he wielded with the typewriter and microphone was dynamic in his hands. His personal files indicate that he often pushed too hard, and asked for too much from his colleagues and superiors. But during the heyday of broadcast commentary, he distinguished himself as an independent, progressive spokesman for social vigilance and accountability.

Although he did not employ the term to describe himself, Brown was a libertarian. He believed in absolute freedom of the press, unrestrained by government, managerial or advertiser censorship. From his perspective, anyone who got in the way of telling the complete story was impeding truth. He believed that information was knowledge and knowledge was power. There is no evidence that he formally studied libertarian theory, but other journalists most certainly informally tutored him during his neophyte years. His painful observation of nonexistent press freedom overseas also informed his respect for the principle. Moreover, Brown grew up in a different era, which made his upbringing distinct from the current generation of journalists. David Brooks identified the difference when he observed: "People in earlier times inherited a vast moral vocabulary and set of moral tools, developed over centuries and handed down from generation to generation. This was a practical inheritance, like learning how to speak a certain language."[15] Although the FCC's Mayflower and Fairness Doctrines, and the Hutchins Commission's recommendations regarding broadcasting's freedom to address issues were all issued during the 1940s, Brown never mentioned them either on the air on in correspondence as informing his practices. Yet he clearly was motivated by a public-service vision for how the First Amendment could grow broadcast journalism into a provocative news medium.

Just as Brown has been overlooked, so has the influence radio commentary had on the nation from the 1930s-1950s. Its period of popularity lasted less than two decades, but it is "not an exaggeration," wrote John Hohenberg, that during their halcyon days radio commentators had "more influence than any other factor in molding the opinions of adult Americans." What the commentators thought represented "in a very large measure what the great American public [thought]."[16] Newspaper and magazine columnists quoted them, and listeners identified with their voices in an intimate way that they could not with columnists. In the years soon after World War II, there were dozens of commentators on the air. They spanned the philosophical spectrum, especially at Mutual, where the financial and political stakes were not as high as at NBC or CBS. And, like Brown, Mutual has not received the credit it deserves for surpassing the larger networks in the breadth of opinion its stable of commentators provided. Early radio journalists believed that to hide their opinions constituted a disingenuousness to the knowledge they possessed and their listeners' right to hear it. Today, only on rare occasions do Americans hear the kind of dispassionate, analytical analysis men like Brown provided. "Never has he or she [the commentator] been more needed in a world where truth is more difficult to find and in which the loudest instead of the most reasoned voices dominate the airwaves," notes Steve Knoll.[17] Instead, Americans are led to believe they are getting truthful commentary from men such as Rush Limbaugh, Bill O'Reilly and Sean Hannity who appeal primarily to conservative, white men and disparage anyone who dares question their viewpoints. Even in the decades after Brown left network radio, CBS's seemingly principled attempt to disseminate commentary on television fell short, ironically enough, in the person of Eric Sevareid. Paley allowed the former Murrow Boy to offer his perspective on the news only because Sevareid accepted the chairman's conditions for editorial neutering. Former colleague David Schoenbrun said of Sevareid's commentaries on the *CBS Evening News* from 1964 to 1977: "[Sevareid] has a great felicity of phrase, but he doesn't really say anything."[18]

Brown was a skeptic. For him, the glass of official explanation always seemed half-full. Like all great reporters, he never stopped "questioning, challenging, probing," in the words of H.G. Wells.[19] It was an approach that sometimes got him into trouble, but also allowed him to deliver thought-provoking commentary. Much like the term he created to describe Robert Taft, he was an "againster." Brown's commitment to doggedly striving to accurately represent reality can be traced to his genealogy. Uniquely, and most certainly, the gratefulness Brown inherited from his immigrant parents for receiving the privilege of a life of freedom in America informed his work. He was acutely aware of the persecution of minority groups, including members of his own ethnicity. His upbringing made him impatient with people who did not appreciate the preciousness of freedom. This energized his intolerance with those who dishonored the common person's trust. He was a patriot who cared deeply about the ability of America to achieve the Founding Fathers' vision for exceptionalism.

Brown esteemed the sanctity of the truth, as opposed to practicing political correctness or accepting the relativism that characterizes much of current journalistic practices. Murrow concurred with that sentiment. In the 1950s, he estranged himself from Bill Paley for criticizing the broadcast networks for hiding the truth from their audiences: "The American public is more reasonable, restrained and more mature than most of our industry's program planners believe."[20] Brown believed if a news organization had sufficient faith in a journalist's abilities to put him or her on the air, then it should trust that person's judgment enough to allow him or her to speak unreservedly. Both men embraced Os Guinness' definition that "if truth is truth, it strikes a chord in hearts everywhere that are yearning for deeper freedom.... Human beings are truth-seekers by nature, and truth persuades by the force of its own reality."[21]

Did that label, Crusader for Truth, which Isaac Stone accorded Brown in 1943, actually result in Brown attaining the truth? Yes, and no. Few present-day journalists believe securing truth is possible because they have accepted the tenets of positivism (rationally justifiable assertions can be scientifically verified or are capable of logical or mathematical proof), or relativism (truth exists only in relation to culture, society, or historical context). Oddly, although they universally agree that they are obligated to disclosing the truth, they disagree over what constitutes it. They argue that for knowledge to be objective it must be value-free. They promote "objectivity" as a more realistic goal, but they confess that being an objective journalist is not really attainable. Yet, they believe it is the closest they can get to truth. Unfortunately, journalists' reliance on objectivity as their defining goal has resulted in confusion and fallacious information for the audience. As Juan Ramon Munoz-Torres points out: "That knowledge is subjective does not necessarily imply its being 'arbitrary,' or 'whimsical,' [or] 'unwarranted.'" Positivism, he argues, "Wrongly equates objectivity with truth and subjectivity with lack of it, thus establishing a false dilemma between subject and object ... [which] does not stem from experience and cannot be verified through it."[22]

Brown and the other members of the Murrow team thought striving for objectivity insufficiently served the audience. They believed that humankinds' relationship with the real world was at stake in their ability to help listeners grasp a true appraisal of reality. This required a "sorting-out process" that stripped information of "misinformation, disinformation, or self-promoting information."[23] Jeffrey Abramson argues that "a commitment to truth provides journalism with its ethical center of gravity." Achieving it is demanding because so many institutions have a "vested interest ... in public ignorance ... for the truth in so many of these areas of public debate, we are dependent on a press that understands itself to be an adversary of power everywhere, private as well as public."[24] Brown considered himself an adversarial or an "advocacy journalist." That is, research and ethical standards motivated him to sort through the clutter, arrive at a transparent understanding of reality, and advocate social or political change that would benefit the Greater Good. U.S. journalists who have defined their *modus operandi* in this manner have historically paid a high price for the approach. There is a similarity between Brown's recalcitrant career and that of Chris Hedges, a commentator for the website *Truthdig*. The *New York Times* fired the Pulitzer Prize winner in 2005 for his criticism of U.S. prosecution of the Iraq War. "Journalists [he insists] ... have to take sides.... The idea that something is objective and impartial is just a lie ... really great journalists care fundamentally about truth, and truth and news are not the same thing." Those who pursue the truth at any cost, Hedges insists "are management headaches because they care about truth at the expense of their own careers."[25]

By its very nature, commentary was subjective and often controversial. But commentary—supported by research and reflective analysis—which distinguished Brown's technique—was superior to the superficial, melodramatically presented opinions of many commentators. With each story, he searched for deeper implications. He looked to keep his audience abreast of how activities or policies were historically, culturally or politically significant. He was not always right, but more often than not impartial evidence, devotion to human rights and the reliance on independent evidence validated his positions. He was repeatedly ahead of public opinion or official policy in identifying issues and calling for change, the need for which was subsequently borne out by developments. In a medium that has been notoriously inept or uncaring in responding to audience feedback, his extensive correspondence with members of the audience demonstrated a concern for helping them think through issues and arrive at knowledgeable solutions. The correspondence was also a signifier of the give-and-take process neces sary for uncovering truth. Brown grasped the fact that achieving truth required an ongoing conversation that eventually lead to revelation. The letter writing demonstrated that he did not take his listeners for granted. When they registered confusion over his comments or disputed his conclusions, he took time to clarify his views.

Latter-day network journalist Jeff Greenfield has written that "the legend of Edward R. Murrow and his colleagues ... has cast its shadow for more than half a century, and for good reason. The performance of all broadcast journalists is measured against what the CBS team accomplished during World War II and as individuals thereafter.... [They were] "remarkably gifted, remarkably courageous, [and] remarkably ambitious."[26] Brown's career epitomized those characteristics, but the Boys' dreams for what broadcast news could become were unceremoniously dashed. Their vision for beneficent public service, which allowed them to build an enterprise during World War II that came closest to realizing its First Amendment potential, could not coexist with the broadcast industry's economic values. Brown's run-in with CBS was only the first in a series of contentious incidents regarding freedom of the airwaves that played out over the following decades. Executives dashed the journalists' vision of being allowed to candidly scrutinize public issues and recommend corrective actions. The members of the most esteemed broadcast news team, who believed they deserved editorial liberty, found themselves stymied. Thus, several of them became disenchanted with the profession. Smith, Murrow and Friendly all followed Brown out the CBS newsroom door in the 1950s and '60s. The post–World War II correspondents' ambition for a bolder journalism thrived only for a short time. The vision of the Commission on Freedom of the Press for broadcast journalism to become vibrantly responsible and incisively investigative was left unrealized.

Interestingly, however, Brown succeeded in espousing the Murrow Boys' ideals throughout his career, albeit often on experimental and less conspicuous stages. He did not become as well-known as his boss, or some of the other Boys, but the length and diversity of his career allowed him to have an impact on the development of broadcast news. His professional trajectory distinctly coalesced with that of the evolving broadcast journalism profession. Mutual allowed him to speak largely unfettered, ABC had him introduce commentary to commercial television, NBC utilized him to develops its impressive international TV news team, and his venture into noncommercial TV helped pave the way later for other experienced journalists to migrate to the venue (PBS) as an alternative to the editorially constrained news departments. Commercial network veterans such as Robert MacNeil, Daniel Schorr and Bill Moyers all followed Brown's lead. They sought a platform where— although similarly less visible—they could explore controversial issues in an atmosphere free of restraint.

As he had been in the South China Sea in 1942—Brown was a survivor. His career was marked by conflict and controversy, but he kept finding new venues where he could speak. Late in his career, he commented, "It would have been easier to give in, but that would have made me a traitor to my craft, a betrayer of public trust."[27] Brown viewed journalism as a strategy for fulfilling the traditional Jewish democratic republicanism goals of social justice (*Tzedakah*), caring and compassion (*Chesed*) and repair of the world (*Tikkun Olam*). As an immigrant son, broadcast journalism had been his way to repay the debt his family believed they owed America for taking them in. The cost had been high, but Cecil Brown believed it had been his responsibility to tell the world the unvarnished truth.

Chapter Notes

Chapter 1

1. Jurgen Sielemann, "Eastern European Jewish Emigration via the Port of Hamburg: 1890-1914," http://kehilalinks.jewishgen.org/suchostaw/TheTailorShop/Eastern_European_Jewish_Emigration_Article.html (accessed August 31, 2013).
2. John Van Der Kiste, *The Romanovs: 1818-1959* (Stroud: Sutton, 2003), 94; and Sally Bedell Smith, *In All His Glory: The Life of William Paley, the Legendary Tycoon and His Brilliant Circle* (New York: Simon & Schuster, 1990), 27.
3. Casey Horton, *We Came to America: The Jews* (New York: Crabtree Publishers, 2000), 2-5.
4. "Russian Jewish Immigration to the United States in the Late Nineteenth Century," http://www2.needham.k12.ma.us/nhs/cur/kane98/kane_p6_immig/russian/eklbab.html (accessed August 31, 2013).
5. U.S. Bureau of Census, "1910 U.S. Census," http://search.ancestry.com/search/db.aspx?dbid=7884&s_kwcid=+1910++census&oxid=21892&o_lid=21892&o_sch=Search (accessed October 19, 2013).
6. Martha Brown, phone interview by author, August 23, 2013.
7. Rabbi Jonathan Spira-Savett, "7 Hebrew Words and Phrases Every Activist Should Know," *The Jewish Federation of North America*, last modified 2013, http://www.jewishfederations.org/page.aspx?id=14231 (accessed November 15, 2014).
8. Jonathan Brown, phone interview by author, November 4, 2013.
9. *The Jewish Americans: Migration: The Diaspora in America*, directed by David Grubin (2013; Washington, D.C.: JTN Productions and WETA TV), DVD.
10. John Higham, *Strangers in the Land: Patterns of American Nativism, 1860-1925* (New Brunswick: Rutgers University Press, 2002), 284; and Howard M. Sachar, *A History of Jews in America* (New York: Alfred A. Knopf, 1992), 311.
11. Marvin Perry and Frederick Schweitzer, *Anti-Semitism: Myth and Hate from Antiquity to the Present* (New York: Palgrave Macmillan, 2005), 168-169.
12. Martha Brown, phone interview by author, March 7, 2014.
13. "Teacher of Brown Resigns in Massillon," *Youngstown Vindicator*, July 7, 1942.
14. "Obituary: Cecil Brown, Broadcaster for Networks," *Pittsburgh Post-Gazette*, October 29, 1987.
15. *The Echoes*, Warren Senior High School Yearbook (Warren, OH, June 1925), 91.
16. *Ibid.*, 51, 100.
17. Cecil Brown, letter to Harry W. August, Pittsburgh, PA, January 14, 1941, box 27, folder 23, Brown Papers.
18. *Ibid.*, letter to Martha (Kohn) Brown, January 21, 1931, box 26, folder 15, Brown Papers.
19. *Ibid.*, "Canoeing Down the Ohio: Warren Boys Off to Start of Planned 400 Mile Trip," *Warren [OH] Tribune-Chronicle*, August 13, 1926.
20. *Ibid.*, "All's Well That Ends Well, River Traveler's Quote," *Warren Tribune-Chronicle*, September 1, 1926.
21. *Ibid.*, "Boys Run into Storm and Lose Their Pup Tent," *Warren Tribune-Chronicle*, August 20, 1926.
22. *Ibid.*, "All's Well That Ends Well."
23. *Ibid.*, "Scorching Sun Hard on Warren Adventurers," *Warren Tribune-Chronicle*, August 14, 1926.
24. *Ibid.*, "Canoe Boys See Odd River Sights," *Warren Tribune-Chronicle*, August 7, 1926.
25. *Ibid.*, "Warren Lads Sail as 'Stowaways' on Rio Cruise," *Youngstown Vindicator*, October 31, 1928.

26. *Ibid.*
27. *Ibid.*
28. Eugene Brown, "Dancing Is for Her," *The Oneonta Star*, August 6, 1964.
29. "Naval Officer Tells of Cecil Brown's First Sea Trip," *Galveston News*, December 5, 1943.
30. "Around Town," *Youngstown Vindicator*, May 17, 1943.
31. Cecil Brown, diary, undated, box 11, folder 8, Brown Papers.
32. "Hillel Players Have Triumph," *[Columbus] Ohio Jewish Chronicle*, May 3, 1929, 3.
33. Fay Wray, *On the Other Hand: A Life Story* (New York: St. Martin's Press, 1989), 219.
34. Cecil Brown, quoted in Esther Hamilton, "Browm Thinks Bridge Is Game for Stupid," *Youngstown Telegram*, July 9, 1931.
35. Harry August, "From Pittsburgh to War Reporting," *Pittsburgh Press*, May 7, 1941.
36. Cecil Brown, letter to Martha (Kohn) Brown, January 21, 1931, box 26, folder 15, Brown Papers.
37. *Ibid.*, "The *Vindicator* Adventure Boys, Cecil and Eugene Brown, of Warren, Are Off for New Thrills in the Forbidden Russia," *Youngstown Vindicator*, January 12, 1930.
38. *Ibid.*, "Fights, Illusions and More Briny Thrills," *Youngstown Vindicator*, January 19, 1930.
39. *Ibid.*, "Into the Hellespont, On to Grim Russia," *Youngstown Vindicator*, February 2, 1930.
40. *Ibid.*, news script, Mutual Broadcast Service (hereafter MBS), April 16, 1952, box 11, folder 8, Brown Papers.
41. *Ibid.*, "Fear Dominates Russian Citizens Today," *Youngstown Vindicator*, March 3, 1930.
42. *Ibid.*, "We Look at Daring Experiment," *Youngstown Vindicator*, February 9, 1930.
43. *Ibid.*
44. *Ibid.*, "A Youngstown Yankee in the Soviet's Fort," *Youngstown Vindicator*, February 16, 1930.
45. *Ibid.*, "Fear Dominates Russian Citizens Today," *Youngstown Vindicator*, March 2, 1930.
46. *Ibid.*, "A Land of Peasant Kings and Bread Lines," *Youngstown Vindicator*, March 9, 1930.
47. *Ibid.*, "Warren Boys Reach Russia," *Youngstown Vindicator*, November 2, 1929.
48. *Ibid.*, "Good-by Russia! You Deserve a Better Fate," *Youngstown Vindicator*, March 16, 1930.
49. *Ibid.*, "Speaking of Climate—We'll Take Morocco" *Youngstown Vindicator*, March 23, 1930.
50. *Ibid.*, "Our Last Port of Call—Gay, Gaudy Morocco," *Youngstown Vindicator*, March 30, 1930.
51. *Ibid.*
52. *Ibid.*
53. Francisco Balderrama and Raymond Rodriguez, *Decade of Betrayal: Mexican Repatriation in the 1930s*, interview by Terry Gross, *Fresh Air*, National Public Radio, September 10, 2015, transcript, http://www.npr.org/2015/09/10/439114563/americas-forgotten-history-of-mexican-american-repatriation (accessed January 29, 2016).

Chapter 2

1. Cecil Brown, diary, February 10, 1943, box 28, folder 2, Brown Papers.
2. *Ibid.*, March 12, 1933.
3. Mark Bernstein and Alex Lubertozzi, *World War II on the Air: Edward R. Murrow and the Broadcasts That Riveted a Nation* (Naperville, IL: Sourcebooks, 2003), 111.
4. Cecil Brown, letter to Harry W. August, Pittsburgh, PA, January 14, 1941, box 27, folder 23, Brown Papers.
5. Brown, diary, undated, 1949, box 28, folder 19, Brown Papers.
6. Kevin Osborne, "Cover Story: The Light Dims," *Cincinnati City Beat*, February 21, 2007.
7. *Ibid.*, "Brooklyn Bulldog," *Pittsburgh Press*, January 19, 1935.
8. *Ibid.*, "CCC Invades Somerset County," *Pittsburgh Press*, May 11, 1936.
9. Cecil Brown, "Pittsburgh Hosts Hobo Convention," *Pittsburgh Press*, April 21, 1935.
10. William A. White, "It's a Wonder Cecil Brown Lived to Write His Remarkable Story," *The Pittsburgh Press*, November 1, 1942.
11. *Ibid.*, letter to August.
12. *Ibid.*
13. *Reporting America at War: Episode 1: The Romance of War*, directed by Steven Ives (2003; Washington, D.C.: Insignia Films and WETA TV, Public Broadcasting Service), DVD.
14. David H. Hosley, *As Good as Any: Foreign Correspondence on American Radio, 1930–1940* (Westport, CT: Greenwood Press, 1984), 99.
15. John McNamara, *Extra! U.S. War Correspondents in Action* (Boston: Houghton Mifflin, 1945), 134.
16. *Ibid.*, 135.
17. *Ibid.*, 136.
18. *Ibid.*, 135–136.
19. Cecil Brown, "A Nut Between Crackers," *Ken*, May 5, 1938, box 25, folder 6, Brown Papers.
20. *Ibid.*, "Tomorrow the World Is Ours," *Ken*, June 16, 1938, box 25, folder 6, Brown Papers.

21. *Ibid.*, "Mussolini's Always Right," *Ken*, June 2, 1938, box 25, folder 6, Brown Papers.
22. Brown, letter to August.
23. Cecil Brown, International News Service, May 3, 1938, box 27, folder 28, Brown Papers.
24. *Ibid.*, letter to August.
25. McNamara, 136–137.
26. Cloud and Olson, 126.
27. Erik Barnouw, *The Golden Web: A History of Broadcasting in the United States, Vol. II—1933–1953* (New York: Oxford University Press, 1968), 165.
28. Robert S. Benjamin, *The Inside Story: By Members of the Overseas Press Club of America* (New York: Prentice Hall, 1940), 78.
29. Cecil Brown, diary, May 2, 1940, box 32, folder 1, Brown Papers.
30. *Ibid.*, December 8, 1940, box 27, folder 46, Brown Papers.
31. Martha Brown, interview by Adelaide Hawley, on "Woman's Page of the Air," CBS Radio, October 22, 1942, box 28, folder 7, Brown Papers.
32. *Ibid.*, phone interview with author, August 16, 2013.
33. Cecil Brown, diary, January 22, 1940, box 27, folder 45, Brown Papers.
34. Cloud and Olson, 2.
35. Hosley, xi.
36. Douglas, 178.
37. *Ibid.*
38. Editors, *American Heroes: Edward R. Murrow* (Hackensack: Salem Press, 2008), 638.
39. Robert J. Landry, "Edward R. Murrow," *Scribner's Magazine*, December 1938, 9.
40. Cloud and Olson, 1–2.
41. Smith, *In All His Glory*, 175.
42. Douglas, 190.
43. *Ibid.*, 389.
44. Mark Bernstein, "Edward R. Murrow: Inventing Broadcast Journalism," *American History* 40, no. 2 (2005): 46.
45. Barnouw, 150.
46. Dan Rather, interview by Larry King, *Larry King Live*, Cable News Network, June 12, 2003, http://transcripts.cnn.com/transcripts/0306/12/lkl.00.html (accessed October 19, 2014).
47. Cloud and Olson, 126.
48. Stuart Hyde and Dina A. Ibrahim, *Television and Radio Announcing*, 12th ed. (New York: Pearson, 2013), 48.
49. Frank Colby, "Take My Word," *Ogden [Utah]Standard-Examiner*, July 4, 1946.
50. Paul White, *News on the Air* (New York: Harcourt, Brace, 1947), 157.
51. Brown, letter to August.

Chapter 3

1. Cecil Brown, letter to Harry W. August, Pittsburgh, PA, January 14, 1941, box 27, folder 23, Brown Papers.
2. *Ibid.*, "America's Fifth Column in Europe," *Liberty*, June 27, 1942.
3. Susan Douglas, *Listening In: Radio and the American Imagination* (Minneapolis: University of Minnesota Press, 1999), 178.
4. Mark Bernstein and Alex Lubertozzi, *World War II on the Air: Edward R. Murrow and the Broadcasts that Riveted a Nation* (Naperville, IL: Sourcebooks, 2003), 103.
5. Cecil Brown, diary, May 4, 1940, box 32, folder 2, Brown Papers.
6. Martha Brown, "Inside Italy," *Collier's*, April 26, 1941, 13–15.
7. Bernstein and Lubertozzi, 27.
8. Brown, "America's Fifth Column in Europe," *Liberty*, parts I and II, June 27, 1942, 28.
9. Brown, diary, July 17, 1940, box 27, folder 10, Brown Papers.
10. Martha Brown, "Life in Nazified Italy," *Woman's Home Companion*, August 1941, 20.
11. Editors worldwide utilized the color blue in the days before computer editing to show required revisions in written copy. Blue was utilized because it would not show in some lithographic or photographic reproduction processes
12. John Maxwell Hamilton, *Journalism's Roving Eye: A History of American Foreign Reporting* (Baton Rouge: Louisiana State University Press, 2009), 277.
13. Robert W. Desmond, *Tides of War: World News Reporting 1931–1945* (Iowa City: University of Iowa Press, 1984), 150–151.
14. Cecil Brown, original manuscript, *Suez to Singapore*, box 30, folder 1, Cecil Brown Papers and (New York: Random House, 1942), 103.
15. *Ibid.*, diary, June 12, 1940, box 27, folder 45, Brown Papers.
16. *Ibid.*, "America's Fifth Column in Europe," 24.
17. John McNamara. *Extra! U.S. War Correspondents in Action* (Boston: Houghton Mifflin, 1945), 138.
18. Cecil Brown, letter to Telesio Interlandi, July 11, 1940, box 26, folder 16, Brown Papers.
19. *Ibid.*, letter to Guido Rocco, July 27, 1940, box 26, folder 16, Brown Papers.
20. *Ibid.*, "America's Fifth Column in Europe," 24; and McNamara, 138.
21. *Ibid.*
22. Harry W. August, "From Pittsburgh to War Reporting," *Pittsburgh Press*, May 7, 1941, 4.
23. "Correspondent's Wife," *Radio Mirror*, March 1942, Brown Papers.

24. Brown, diary, April 1, 1941, box 32, folder 1, Brown Papers.
25. Columbia Broadcasting System, *World News Roundup*, broadcast transcript, May 1, 1941, box 1, folder 7, Brown Papers.
26. "A War Reporter Talks About His Job," *PM*, April 6, 1942, 12.
27. Brown, *Suez to Singapore*, 2.
28. Cecil Brown, "Keeping Posted," *Saturday Evening Post*, August 23, 1941, 4.
29. Michael Chinigo, Radiogram to CBS, April 25, 1941, microfilm 2107, vol. II, Brown Papers.
30. "A War Reporter Talks About His Job."
31. Cecil Brown, "The Germans Are Coming," *Saturday Evening Post*, August 23, 1941, 59–61.
32. "A War Reporter Talks About His Job."
33. Ibid., letter to Martha Brown, October 2, 1941, box 28, folder 7, Brown Papers.
34. Ibid., letter to Alfred Haworth Jones, March 30, 1973, box 27, folder 5, Brown Papers.
35. Ibid., "The Germans Are Coming," 62.
36. Ibid.
37. Ibid., diary, April 29, 1941, box 27, folder 46, Brown Papers.
38. Columbia Broadcasting System, *World News Roundup*, May 1, 1941, audio recording #1314A/1, Brown Papers.
39. Sam Brewer, "Writer Tells of Thwarting Death as Spy in Belgrade," and "Four Americans Reach Budapest by Auto," *Chicago Times*, April 25 and 26, 1941; reprinted in *A Nation's Fight for Survival: The 1941 Revolution and War in Yugoslavia as Reported by the American Press* (London: Royal Yugoslav Embassy, 1944), 154, 228.
40. Brewer, *A Nation's Fight for Survival*, 228.
41. Columbia Broadcasting System, *World News Roundup*, broadcast transcript, May 1, 1941, box 1, folder 7, Brown Papers.
42. Cecil Brown, diary, May 4, 1941, box 27, folder 46, Brown Papers.
43. Paul White, cable to Cecil Brown, May 5, 1941, box 26, folder 20, Brown Papers.
44. Cecil Brown, *Suez to Singapore*, 9.
45. Ibid.
46. Cecil Brown, "The Germans Are Coming," *Saturday Evening Post*, August 23, 1941, 59–61.
47. Ibid., diary, May 7, 1941, box 26, folder 20, Brown Papers.
48. Ibid., diary, May 14, 1941, box 27, folder 46, Brown Papers.
49. Cecil Brown, diary, June 15, 1941, box 27, folder 47, Brown Papers
50. Brown, *Suez to Singapore*, 27.
51. Ibid., letter to Paul White, May 28, 1941, box 27, folder 38, Brown Papers.
52. Ibid.
53. *Ibid.*, July 7, 1941.
54. *Ibid.*, June 15, 1941.
55. *Ibid.*, June 14, 1941.
56. *Ibid.*, June 11, 1941.
57. Brown, diary, June 19, 1941, box 28, folder 1, Brown Papers.
58. *Ibid.*, June 22, 1941.
59. *Ibid.*, June 27, 1941.

Chapter 4

1. Cecil Brown, diary, July 5, 1941, box 27, folder 46, Brown Papers.
2. Ibid., "Life's Reports: The Desert Is Hell," *Life*, December 8, 1941, 18.
3. Ibid., diary, July 7, 1941, box 28, folder 1, Brown Papers.
4. Ibid., *Suez to Singapore*, 92.
5. Ibid., "A War Reporter Talks About His Job," *PM*, April 6, 1942, 12.
6. Ibid., *Suez to Singapore*, 104.
7. Ibid., diary, May 18, 1941, box 27, folder 46, Brown Papers.
8. Ibid., *Suez to Singapore*, 118.
9. Cecil Brown, diary, July 26, 1941, box 28, folder 1, Brown Papers.
10. "Cecil Brown, Famous Correspondent, Visits Williamsburg Restoration," *The Flat Hat*, April 28, 1942.
11. Karl Hack and Kevin Blackburn, *Did Singapore Have to Fall? Churchill and the Impregnable Fortress* (New York: Routledge Curzon, 2004), 26.
12. Cecil Brown, diary, August 1–3, 1941, box 32, folder 2, Brown Papers.
13. Russell Braddon, *The Naked Island* (Leicester: Charnwood Edition, 1982), 28.
14. Cecil Brown, *Suez to Singapore*, 373.
15. Peter Thompson, *The Battle for Singapore: The True Story of the Greatest Catastrophe of World War Two* (London: Portrait Books, 2005), 3.
16. Barbara Leitch Lepoer, ed., *World War II, 1941–45: A Country Study: Singapore* (Washington, D.C.: National Archives, Federal Research Division, 1991), para. 3, http://lcweb2.loc.gov/cgi-bin/query/r?frd/cstdy:@field(DOCID+sg0025 (accessed March 22, 2014); and Brown, book review of *Singapore is Silent*, BR3.
17. Hack and Blackburn, 20.
18. Ibid.
19. Cecil Brown, diary, August 3, 1941, box 32, folder 2, Brown Papers.
20. Ibid., August 5, 1941.
21. "Radio War Reporting," *Time*, December 22, 1941, 52.
22. Cecil Brown, diary, August, 8, 1941, box 32, folder 3, Brown Papers.

23. *Ibid.*, August 6, 7, 1941.
24. Cecil Brown, diary, August 13, 1941, box 32, folder 3, Brown Papers.
25. *Ibid.*, *Suez to Singapore*, 151.
26. James W. Gould, *The U.S. and Malaysia* (Boston: Harvard University Press, 1969), 73.
27. *Ibid.*, diary, October 3, 1941, box 28, folder 1, Brown Papers.
28. *Ibid.*, *Suez to Singapore*, 179.
29. Weller and Weller, 197.
30. *Ibid.*, 1, 170, 195.
31. Eric Davis, Malayan Broadcast Corporation, August 31, 1941, letter to Brown, and Brown reply, September 2, 1941, box 26, folder 16, Brown Papers.
32. Cecil Brown, letter to Paul White, September 7, 1941, box 27, folder 38, Brown Papers.
33. Editorial, *Singapore [Malaya] Strait-Times*, September 11, 1941, box 26, folder 16, Brown Papers.
34. Cecil Brown, diary, September 16, 19, 1941, box 32, folder 2, Brown Papers.
35. *Ibid.*, September 16, 1941.
36. Lepoer, para. 3.
37. Cecil Brown, diary, September 22–23, 1941, box 32, folder 2, Brown Papers.
38. Paul White, cable to Brown, September 26, 1941, box 26, folder 38, Brown Papers.
39. Cecil Brown, cable to Paul White, October 18, 1941, box 26, folder 38, Brown Papers.
40. O.P. Gallagher, letters to Major Fisher, November 4, 5, 1941, box 26, folder 38, Brown Papers.
41. Peter Thompson, *The Battle for Singapore: The True Story of the Greatest Catastrophe of World War Two* (London: Portrait Books, 2005), 2.
42. Cecil Brown, diary, September 30, 1941, box 32, folder 3, Brown Papers.
43. Louis Allen, *Singapore, 1941–1942* (New York: Routledge, 2013), 213.
44. Cecil Brown, diary, October 3, 1941, box 32, folder 3, Brown Papers.
45. Jacqui Murray, *Watching the Sun Rise: Australian Reporting of Japan, 1931 to the Fall of Singapore* (New York: Lexington Books, 2004), 228.
46. Cecil Brown, letter to Martha Brown, October 20, 1941, box 26, folder 21, Brown Papers.
47. *Ibid.*, *Suez to Singapore*, 238.
48. *Ibid.*, diary, October 12, 1941, box 32, folder 3, Brown Papers.
49. Cecil Brown, diary, September 28, 1941, box 32, folder 3, Brown Papers.
50. *Ibid.*, August 11, 1941.
51. Cecil Brown, *Suez to Singapore*, 235.
52. Cecil Brown, diary, November 6, 1941, box 32, folder 3, Brown Papers.
53. *Ibid.*
54. *Ibid.*, November 19, 1941.
55. Hack and Blackburn, 17.
56. Cecil Brown, diary, December 8, 1941, box 32, folder 4, Brown Papers.

Chapter 5

1. "Planes vs. Ships," *Newsweek*, December 22, 1941, 20.
2. Bernard Ash, *Someone Blundered: The Story of the "Repulse" and the "Prince of Wales"* (New York: Doubleday & Company, 1961), 12, 238.
3. Peter Thompson, *The Battle for Singapore: The True Story of the Greatest Catastrophe of World War Two* (London: Portrait Books, 2005), 106.
4. Ash, 213.
5. *Ibid.*
6. Swinson, 6; and John Toland, *But Not in Shame: The Six Months After Pearl Harbor* (New York: Random House, 1961), 77–82 and 89–98.
7. Cecil Brown, diary, December 8, 1941, box 32, folder 3, Brown Papers.
8. Matthews, *Sailors' Tales*, 73–74.
9. Thompson, 144–145.
10. *Ibid.*, 148.
11. Alan Matthews, "The Sinking of the *Prince of Wales* and *HMS Repulse*: Final Departure," para. 1, www.forcez-survivors.org.uk/sinking2.html (accessed December 18, 2013).
12. Brown, diary, December 8, 1941, box 28, folder 1, Brown Papers.
13. *Ibid.*, December 9, 1941.
14. Matthews, *Sailors' Tales*, 1.
15. Brown, *Suez to Singapore*, 307.
16. Matthews, "The Sinking of the *Prince of Wales* and *HMS Repulse*: A Series of Personal Accounts: Eyewitness Accounts from The Crew," para. 5.
17. "A War Reporter Talks About His Job," *PM*, April 6, 1942, 12. (*PM*—or *Picture Magazine*—was a liberal newspaper that Marshall Field III founded in 1940. Its editors said, "It was dedicated to making sure the little guy wasn't pushed around." It published stories by Ernest Hemingway, Erskine Caldwell and Don Hollenbeck, among others, accepted no advertising, and went out of business in 1948 because of accusations that it was pro-communist, although it had published anti-communist articles.)
18. Brown, *Suez to Singapore*, 318.
19. Matthews, *Sailors' Tales*, 92.
20. *Ibid.*, 97.
21. Arch Whitehouse, *The Years of the War Birds* (Garden City, NY: Doubleday & Company, 1960), 172.

22. Middlebrook and Mahoney, 197.
23. Matthews, *Sailors' Tales*, 103–104.
24. Brown, "Cable: Sinkings of the *Repulse* and *Prince of Wales*: A Blow-by-Blow Account," *Newsweek*, December 22, 1941, 18.
25. Ash, 269.
26. Matthews, "The Sinking of the *Prince of Wales* and *HMS Repulse*: Summary of Battle," para. 3.
27. Ash, 266–267.
28. Middlebrook and Mahoney, 193.
29. *Ibid.*, 212.
30. Whitehouse, 173.
31. "Indestructible," *Broadcasting: The Weekly Newsmagazine of Radio*, December 29, 1941, 26
32. George Weller and Anthony Weller, *Weller's War: A Legendary Foreign Correspondent's Sage of World War II on Five Continents* (New York: Three Rivers Press, 2009), 1.

Chapter 6

1. Louis L. Snyder and Richard B. Morris, *A Treasury of Great Reporting: Literature under Pressure* (New York: Simon & Schuster, 1962), 595.
2. Cecil Brown, *Suez to Singapore*, 342.
3. Martin Middlebrook and Patrick Mahoney, *Battleship: The Sinking of the Prince of Wales and the Repulse* (New York: Charles Scribner's Sons, 1979), 196.
4. Arch Whitehouse, *The Years of the War Birds* (Garden City, NY: Doubleday & Company, 1960), 171.
5. Piers Brendon, *The Decline and Fall of the British Empire, 1781–1997* (New York: Alfred A. Knopf, 2008), 426; and Peter Thompson, *The Battle for Singapore: The True Story of the Greatest Catastrophe of World War Two* (London: Portrait Books, 2005), 151.
6. Alan Matthews, "The Sinking of the *Prince of Wales* and *HMS Repulse*, Summary of Battle," para. 1, www.forcez-survivors.org.uk/sinking2.html (accessed December 18, 2013).
7. Bennett Cerf, interview by Robin Hawkins, September 20, 1968, "Interviews with Notable New Yorkers," Columbia University Libraries, Oral History Research Office, http://www.columbia.edu/cu/lweb/digital/collections/nny/cerfb/introduction.html (accessed June 16, 2014).
8. Bennett Cerf, *At Random: The Reminiscences of Bennett Cerf* (New York: Random House, 1977), 162
9. William J. Dunn, *Pacific Microphone* (College Station: Texas A&M Press, 1988), 48.
10. Louis L. Snyder and Richard B. Morris, *Literature Under Pressure: From the Sixteenth Century to Our Own Time* (New York: Simon & Schuster, 1962), 595.
11. Cecil Brown, diary, December 16, 1942, box 32, folder 4, Brown Papers.
12. *Ibid.*, *Suez to Singapore*, 361.
13. *Ibid.*
14. "A War Reporter Talks About His Job," *PM*, April 6, 1942, 12.
15. *Ibid.*
16. Katharine Sansom, *Sir George Sansom and Japan: A Memoir* (Tallahassee: Diplomatic, 1972), 127.
17. Cecil Brown, *Suez to Singapore*, 399; and Brown, diary, January 8, 1942, box 32, folder 4; both Brown Papers.
18. *Ibid.*
19. *Ibid.*, diary, January 10, 1942, box 32, folder 4, Brown Papers.
20. *Ibid.*, *Suez to Singapore*, 400.
21. "CBS Appeals Brown Suspension," *New York Herald Tribune*, January 13, 1942.
22. Paul White, cable to Cecil Brown, January 14, 1942, box 26, folder 20, Brown Papers.
23. Cecil Brown, "Morale in Malaya." *Time*, January 19, 1942, 20.
24. O'Dowd, Gallagher, "American Journalist Banned," *[London] Daily Express*, January 15, 1942.
25. Giles Playfair, *Singapore Goes Off the Air* (New York: E.P. Dutton, 1943), 117.
26. Cecil Brown, "Malay Jungle War," *Life*, January 12, 1942, 32–38.
27. Cecil Brown, *Suez to Singapore*, 434–435.
28. *Ibid.*, diary, January 21, 1942, box 32, folder 4, Brown Papers.
29. *Ibid.*, January 22, 1942.
30. *Ibid.*, January 23, 1942.
31. Cecil Brown, letter to Martha Brown, January 31, 1942, box 26, folder 22, Brown Papers.
32. *Ibid.*, diary January 24, 1942.
33. "A War Reporter Talks About His Job," *PM*, April 6, 1942.
34. Cecil Brown, diary, February 3, 1942.
35. *Ibid.*, February 5, 1942.
36. *Ibid.*, "War Pilot's Story," *Life*, May 11, 1942, 35–36.
37. *Ibid.*, diary, February 10, 1942.
38. *Ibid.*, *Suez to Singapore*, 495.
39. Headlines cited in story about the impact of Brown's broadcasts in *[Perth] Daily News*, February 14, 1942.
40. *Ibid.*
41. Paul White to Cecil Brown and Brown to White, cables, February 13 and February 15, 1942, box 26, folder 21, Brown Papers.
42. Cecil Brown, radio script, CBS, February 15, 1942, box 1, folder 5, Brown Papers.
43. *Ibid.*, "How Cecil Got the Story," and

"Take 'er Down," *Collier's*, May 16, 1942, 12–13, 57–59.
44. Knightley, 269.
45. Gunther, 327. Collingwood's broadcast quoted in Mark Bernstein and Alex Lubertozzi, *World War II on the Air: Edward R. Murrow and the Broadcasts That Riveted a Nation* (Naperville, IL: Sourcebooks, 2003), 132.
46. *Ibid.*, diary, February 17, 1942, box 32, folder 4, Brown Papers.
47. Legendary American foreign correspondents Floyd Gibbons and Webb Miller formed the Overseas Press Club in New York in 1939. By the time of Brown's recognition, it counted among its members the majority of U.S. journalism's most notable foreign correspondents.
48. Cecil Brown, acceptance speech to the Overseas Press Club, box 25, folder 19, Brown Papers.
49. *Ibid.*, *Suez to Singapore*, 515.
50. *Ibid.*, diary, February 27, 1942, box 32, folder 4, Brown Papers.
51. *Ibid.*, "Australians," *Life*, June 8, 1942, 82–91.
52. "Australians Termed Lazy, But Superb Fighting Men," *The [Brisbane] Sunday Mail*, June 7, 1942, 3.
53. Brown, Diary, March 6–29, 1942, box 28, folder 3, Brown Papers.
54. Brown, *Suez to Singapore*, 532.

Chapter 7

1. Cecil Brown, diary, March 29, 1942, box 28, folder 3, Brown Papers.
2. "Radio Reporting Tougher, Says Brown," *Broadcasting*, April 6, 1942, 14.
3. Adelaide Hawley, "Interview with Martha Brown," *Women's Page of the Air*, October 22, 1942, CBS radio transcript, box 27, folder 18, Brown Papers.
4. Timothy M. Gay, *Assignment to Hell: The War Against Nazi Germany with Correspondents Walter Cronkite, Andy Rooney, A. J. Liebling, Homer Bigart, and Hal Boyle* (New York: Penguin Group, 2012), 247.
5. John Maxwell Hamilton, *Journalism's Roving Eye: A History of Foreign Reporting* (Baton Rouge: Louisiana State University Press, 2009), 2.
6. Samuel L. Hynes, *Reporting World War II: American Journalism, 1938–1946* (Washington, D.C.: Library of Congress, 1995), x.
7. Susan J. Douglas, *Listening In: Radio and the American Imagination* (Minneapolis: University of Minnesota Press, 1999), 194.
8. "Radio's Spring Honors List," *New York Times*, April 12, 1942.
9. Douglas, 191.
10. *Ibid.*, 189–194.
11. "Radio Reporting Tougher," 14.
12. "A War Reporter Talks About His Job," *PM*, April 4, 1942, 12.
13. "Radio Reporting Tougher," 14.
14. Isaac Stone, "Review of *Suez to Singapore*," *Washington Post*, October 25, 1942.
15. Martha Brown, interview by author, March 7, 2014.
16. "Cecil Brown to Speak Here," *[Columbus] Ohio Jewish Chronicle*, May 22, 1942.
17. "Cecil Brown to Lecture Tonight at Local School," *Spartanburg [SC] Herald-Tribune*, April 23, 1942.
18. "War Correspondent Speaks," *The Flat Hat*, April 29, 1942.
19. "A War Reporter Talks About His Job," 12.
20. "Time at Hand for Supreme Effort," *[Mansfield, OH] News-Journal*, April 4, 1942.
21. Martha Brown, interview by author, August 16, 2013.
22. "State Irked by Apathy Charges of Cecil Brown," *[Warsaw, IN] Daily Times*, May 27, 1942.
23. "Ace Correspondent's Fine Letter," *The Charleville [Brisbane] Times*, Aug. 14, 1942.
24. Bennett Cerf, *At Random: The Reminiscences of Bennett Cerf* (New York: Random House, 1977), 162.
25. Bennett Cerf, "Books That Shook the World," *Saturday Evening Post*, April 3, 1943, 19, 84.
26. Martha Brown, Hawley interview.
27. Bennett Cerf, letters to Cecil Brown, May 22, 25 and June 22, 1942, box 26, folder 16 and box 30, folder 1, Brown Papers.
28. N.R. Howard, letter to Saxe Commins, and Commins' response to Howard, September 10, 11, 1942, box 30, folder 1, Brown Papers.
29. Cecil Brown, diary, October 13, 1942, box 28, folder 2, Brown Papers.
30. Leonard Lyons, "Broadway Medley," *[San Mateo] Times and Daily News Leader*, March 19, 1943.
31. Bennett Cerf, interview by Robin Hawkins, "Interviews with Notable New Yorkers," Columbia University Libraries, Oral History Research Office, New York, September 20, 1968, http://www.columbia.edu/cu/lweb/digital/collections/nny/cerfb/introduction.html (accessed June 16, 2014).
32. Frank W. Adams, "Cecil Brown Narrates the History Which He Saw Made," *New York Times*, October 25, 1942.
33. "Candid Correspondent," *Newsweek*, October 26, 1942, 77–78.
34. "*Suez to Singapore* Review," *Boston Globe*, October 28, 1942.
35. William Shinnick, "Cecil Brown's

Clashes with Censors," *Chicago Sunday Tribune*, November 8, 1942.
36. Keith Hutchinson, "Brown Among the Brass Hats," *Nation*, November 7, 1942, 482–483.
37. Robert G. Woolbert, "*Suez to Singapore* Review," *Foreign Affairs*, April 1943.
38. Lewis Gannett, "Review of *Suez to Singapore*," *New York Herald Tribune*, October 22, 1942.
39. Murray Harris, "Reporter-at-Large," *Saturday Review of Literature*, November 14, 1942, 9–10.
40. Stanley Cloud and Lynne Olson, *The Murrow Boys: Pioneers on the Front Lines of Broadcast Journalism* (New York: Houghton Mifflin, 1996), 153.
41. Cecil Brown, letters to reviewers, undated, box 26, folder 11, Brown Papers.
42. Harry Hansen, "Writers Divided on Question of Building Up More Hatred," *Chicago Tribune*, November 8, 1942.
43. Bennett Cerf, Donald Klopfer, and Robert D. Loomis, "Cerf letters to Klopfer, June 23, September 26 and October 6, 1942," *Dear Donald, Dear Bennett: The Wartime Correspondence of Bennett Cerf and Donald Klopfer* (New York: Random House, 2002).
44. Cecil Brown, "How Japan Wages War," *Life*, May 11, 1942, 98–108; and Cecil Brown, speech text, July 24, 1943, Portland, OR, box 1, folder 19, Brown Papers.
45. "Cecil Brown of CBS Wins Award for 'Best Reporting of the News,'" *Christian Science Monitor*, April 11, 1942.
46. "Awarding Stories That Matter: Personal Award: Cecil Brown for Outstanding Reporting of the News, Winner 1941: CBS Radio," Peabody Awards, Grady College, University of Georgia, http://matt.jhousemedia3.com/peabody/award-profile/personal-award-cecil-brown-for-outstanding-reporting-of-the-news (accessed September 3, 2014).
47. Craig D. Tenney, "The 1943 Debate on Opinionated Broadcast News," *Journalism History* 7, no. 1 (1980): 13
48. Paul White, letter to Cecil Brown, June 3, 1942, box 27, folder 38, Brown Papers.
49. Cecil Brown, CBS news script, September 22, 1942, box 1, folder 7, Brown Papers.
50. Ibid., CBS news scripts, box 1, folder 7, September 22, 29, November 4, December 25, 1942, Brown Papers.
51. Gay, 77.
52. David Nichols and Studs Terkel, *Ernie's War: The Best of Ernie Pyle's World War II Dispatches* (New York: Random House, 1986), 64–65.
53. Cecil Brown, CBS news script, January 15, 1943, box 1, folder 13, Brown Papers.

54. Cecil Brown, *Suez to Singapore* (New York: Random House, 1942), ix; and Weller and Weller.
55. Cecil Brown, CBS news scripts, January 15, February 4, March 25, 1943, box 1, folder 9, Brown Papers.
56. "Cecil Brown Given Degree by College," *The San Antonio [TX] Light*, May 3, 1943.
57. Cecil Brown, letter to Alfred Haworth Jones, March 30, 1937, box 27, folder 5, Brown papers.
58. According to Fang, "Commentary on the air built a following after the networks decided to identify the news broadcast by the name of the news reader. Adding a name to a disembodied but distinctive voice created a personality. Within a few years, program titles tacked on the names told listeners the kind of news and expertise they were getting. [William] Wile gave us 'The Political Situation,' George R. Holmes tipped in with 'The Washington News,' [and] Edwin C. Hill offered 'The Human Side of the News.'" Irving E. Fang, *Those Radio Commentators* (Ames: Iowa State University Press, 1977), 5.
59. Ibid., 3.
60. In comparison, CBS paid Murrow $125,000 per year when he returned to New York after the war. Exact figures are unavailable, but because of Brown's noteworthy position on the CBS schedule, his salary was likely higher than the other members of the Murrow team when they resumed Stateside broadcasting. It was not, however, the highest commentator salary in U.S. radio, according to broadcast sources. Again, although exact figures are unavailable, that privilege belonged to Raymond Gram Swing, who was doing commentary for the Mutual Radio Network.
61. Editors, *American Heroes, Vol. I: "Edward R. Murrow"* (Hackensack: Salem Press, 2008), 344.
62. Gay, 65.
63. Mitchell Charnley, *News by Radio* (New York: Macmillan, 1948), 304, 315.
64. Ibid., 320.
65. Fang, 2.
66. William Frayer, "Some Comments on Commentators," *Quarterly Review of the Michigan Alumnus: A Journal of University Perspectives* 51, no. 4 (1944): 8.
67. Louise Benjamin, "Radio Comes of Age, 1900–1945," in *The Media in America: A History*, 9th ed., Wm. David Sloan, ed. (Northport, AL: Vision Press, 2014), 379.
68. Stone, "Review."
69. Cecil Brown, diary, November 2, 1942, box 28, folder 2, Brown Papers.
70. James Kates, "Kicking Nixon: Howard K. Smith and the Commentator's Imperative,"

ArNet, http://www.americansc.org.uk/Online/Nixon.html (accessed January 18, 2013).
71. *Ibid.*
72. Eric Sevareid, *Not So Wild a Dream* (New York: Alfred A. Knopf, 1946), 111, 132.
73. Cloud and Olson, 22.
74. Brown, interview by Craig D. Tenney, "The 1943 Debate on Opinionated Broadcast News," 13.
75. Joe Cohen, "Cecil Brown," *Billboard*, July 4, 1942, 10.
76. CBS, Press Release, June 20, 1942, box 27, folder 38, Brown Papers.
77. Cloud and Olson, 167.
78. "Radio's Best," *New York World-Telegram*, January 22, 1943.
79. Dorothy Rockwell, "Radio Censors Itself," *Nation*, August 26, 1939, 217.
80. Robert S. Benjamin, ed., *The Inside Story: By Members of the Overseas Press Club of America* (New York: Prentice Hall, 1940), 85.
81. Smith, *In All His Glory*, 191; and Cesar Searchinger, "Radio, Censorship and Neutrality," *Foreign Affairs*, January 1940, 344.
82. *Variety*, January 21, 1942, 25; and "War Code Brings Program Changes," *Broadcasting*, January 19, 1942, 10.
83. Benjamin, 84.
84. Smith, *In All His Glory*, 191.
85. James J. Martin, *Revisionist Viewpoints: Essays in a Dissident Historical Tradition* (Colorado Springs: Ralph Myles, 1971), 152.
86. Fang, 7–8.
87. Halberstam, *The Powers That Be*, 34; and Paley, quoted in *Broadcasting*, December 15, 1937, and cited in Barnouw, 135.
88. Smith, *In All His Glory*, 190.
89. *Ibid.*, 190–192.
90. Cited in Fang, 6.
91. MacDonald, *Television and the Red Menace*, 6.
92. "Radio Gets Ready," *Broadcasting*, July 3, 1950, 15.
93. Charnley, 301.
94. International Press Institute, *The Flow of News: A Study of Knowledge of International Affairs* (New York: Arno Press, 1972), 49–71.
95. Robert S. Benjamin, *The Inside Story*, 82; and Benjamin, *Eye Witness: By Members of the Overseas Press Club* (New York: Alliance Book Company, 1940), 301.
96. Fang, 3, 7–8.
97. Ned Midgley, *The Advertising and Business Side of Radio* (New York: Prentice Hall, 1948), 190–200.
98. Charnley, 304, 308.
99. Benjamin, *Eye Witness*, 301.
100. Gay, 247.
101. Gerald Nachman, *Raised on Radio* (Berkeley: University of California Press, 2000), 401.
102. Charnley, 321.
103. Brown, CBS radio script, April 2, 1943, box 1, folder 10, Brown Papers.
104. *Ibid.*, May 28, 1943.

Chapter 8

1. Malcolm Cowley, *New Republic*, 450; cited in James J. Martin, *Revisionist Viewpoints: Essays in a Dissident Historical Tradition* (Colorado Springs: Ralph Myles, 1971), 148.
2. Mark Bernstein and Alex Lubertozzi, *World War II on the Air: Edward R. Murrow and the Broadcasts That Riveted a Nation* (Naperville, IL: Sourcebooks, 2003), 223.
3. Cecil Brown, CBS news script, April 22, 1943, box 1, folder 13, Brown Papers.
4. *Ibid.*, CBS news script, May 7, 1943, box 1, folder 13, Brown Papers.
5. Bernstein and Lubertozzi, 132.
6. "Edward R. Murrow: Inventing Broadcast Journalism." Historynet, http://www.historynet.com/edward-r-murrow-inventing-broadcast-journalism.htm (accessed October 22, 2015).
7. Ed Bliss, Jr., *Now the News: The Story of Broadcast Journalism* (New York: Columbia University Press, 1991), 142.
8. Erik Barnouw, *The Golden Web*, 151.
9. Elsa Maxwell, "Party Line," *Pittsburgh Post-Gazette*, November 25, 1943.
10. Martin, 54.
11. Cecil Brown, "Do You Know Why You're Fighting," *Colliers*, December 11, 1943, 14–15 and 52–53; and Cecil Brown, "Report on America," *[Zanesville, OH] Times Recorder*, August 14, 1943.
12. "CBS Man Sees 7- to 10-Year Job Before Japs Whipped," *Louisville Times*, July 24, 1943.
13. Eleanor Roosevelt, "My Day," March 30, 1943, www.gwu.edu/~erpapers/myday (accessed October 19, 2013).
14. Brown, *Suez to Singapore*, ix.
15. "Brown and White," *Time*, October 4, 1943, 72.
16. Charles A Siepman, *Radio's Second Chance* (Boston: Little, Brown, 1946), 91; and Bosley Crowther, "Review of *Mission to Moscow*," *New York Times*, April 30, 1943.
17. Robert Trout, interview by Craig D. Tenney, December 1977, cited in Tenney, "The 1943 Debate on Opinionated Broadcast News," 13.
18. Brown, CBS news script, August 25, 1943, box 1, folder 15, Brown Papers.
19. Kenneth D. Nichols, *The Road to Trinity* (New York: William Morrow, 1987), 17; and

"Churchill, Roosevelt Hold War Conference in Quebec City," Canadian Broadcasting Corporation, digital archives, http://www.cbc.ca/archives/categories/society/celebrations/quebec-city-400-years-of-history/war-conference-at-quebec.html#tabs-2 (accessed December 18, 2014).
  20. Edward R. Murrow, quoted in R. Franklin Smith, *Edward R. Murrow: The War Years* (Kalamazoo: New Issues Press, 1978), 63.
  21. Paul White, CBS Office Communication, August 27, 1943, box 26, folder 23, Brown Papers. It was not known until years later what Roosevelt and Churchill had agreed upon during the Quebec conference because much of it was top secret and the two statesmen had agreed not to discuss the details with the press. See "Joint Statement by Prime Minister Churchill and President Roosevelt," August 24, 1943, http://avalon.law.yale.edu/20th_century/decade06.asp (accessed March 11, 2013).
  22. Paul White, letter to Brown, August 27, 1943.
  23. Brown, letter to Craig Tenney, September 14, 1978, cited in "The 1943 Debate on Opinionated Broadcast News," 13.
  24. Brown, letter to Bill Paley, September 2, 1943; and Paley, response to Brown, September 7, 1943; box 26, folder 23, Brown Papers.
  25. Halberstam, *The Powers That Be*, 145.
  26. Richard W. Steele, "The Great Debate: Roosevelt, the Media, and the Coming of the War, 1940–1941," *Journal of American History* 71, no. 1 (1984): 88–92; and Steven Casey, *Cautious Crusade* (New York: Oxford University Press, 2001), xix, 217.
  27. Gay, *Assignment to Hell*, 48.
  28. Robert W. Desmond, *Tides of War: World News Reporting 1931–1945* (Iowa City: University of Iowa Press, 1984), 461–462.
  29. Kendrick, 263.
  30. *Institute for Education by Radio, Education on the Air Yearbook* (Columbus, OH: Institute for Education by Radio Annual, 1942), 71.
  31. "Kaltenborn Dissents," *New York Times*, September 15, 1943.
  32. Eric Barnouw, *The Golden Web: A History of Broadcasting in the United States, Vol. II—1933 to 1953* (New York: Oxford University Press, 1968), 135.
  33. White, letter to H.V. Kaltenborn, September 15, 1943, box 27, folder 38, Brown Papers.
  34. "CBS News Policy Explained by White," *Broadcasting*, September 27, 1943, 10.
  35. "FDR and the Four Freedoms Speech," Franklin Delano Roosevelt Presidential Library and Museum, http://www.fdrlibrary.marist.edu/fourfreedoms (accessed May 12, 2015).
  36. H.V. Kaltenborn, *Fifty Fabulous Years* (New York: Putnam, 1950), 301.
  37. Shirer, quoted in *PM*, September 30, 1943; cited in Sperber, 226.
  38. Shirer, letter to Murrow, September 21, 1943, Edward R. and Janet Murrow Papers, # MS 0576 (LD 7082.18 Murrow), Archives and Special Collections, Mount Holyoke College, MA.
  39. Halberstam, 33.
  40. Murrow, letter to Shirer, October 15, 1943; and Janet Murrow, letter to family, October 29, 1943; both quoted in Sperber, *Murrow: His Life and Times*, 226–227.
  41. Halberstam, 39.
  42. "Why Neither CBS News Broadcasters nor CBS Sponsors 'OPINIONATE' the News," *New York Times* and *Washington Post*, September 20, 1943.
  43. White, *News on the Air* (New York: Harcourt, Brace, 1947), 205.
  44. "Debate of CBS News Policy," *Billboard*, September 25, 1943, 13.
  45. Walter Winchell, "On Broadway," *New York Daily Mirror*, September 17; and Winchell's September 21 article in the *Mirror* quoted in "Brown Quits CBS in Censor Protest," *Broadcasting*, September 27, 1943, 10.
  46. "White-Brown CBS Dither on 'Hooks' in the News Seen as Personalized Tug-O'-War," *Billboard*, October 2, 1943, 12; and "Opinionated News and the Easy Chair of Martyrdom," *Billboard*, October 2, 1943, 8.
  47. John K. Hutchens, "The Columbia Network Tells Its Analysts to Keep Their Opinions to Themselves," *New York Times*, September 26, 1943.
  48. "Analysts Analyze CBS Policy," *Billboard*, October 9, 1943, 8.
  49. "Breach of Promise," *Newark [NJ] Star-Ledger*, September 25, 1943.
  50. "Brown and White," *Time*, October 4, 1943, 72.
  51. Dorothy Thompson, "Is Thinking Dangerous," *The Hartford [CT] Times*, September 27, 1943.
  52. "What Kind of Radio Newspaper?" *St. Louis Post-Dispatch*, September 24, 1943.
  53. Kendrick, 265–266.
  54. "Fly Defends Analysts' Right to Opinions," *Broadcasting*, October 11, 1943, 11.
  55. Arthur Robb, "Shop Talk at Thirty," *Editor & Publisher*, September 24, 1943, 96.
  56. White, 207.
  57. Siepman, 85–86.
  58. Cecil Brown, letters to Paul White and

William Paley, September 22, 1943, box 26, folder 7, Brown Papers.

59. "Brown-Trouble in a Romance," *Variety*, September 29, 1943, 30.

60. Edwards, Trout and Holles' comments from 1977 and 1978 interviews by Tenney, in "The 1943 Debate on Opinionated Broadcast News," 14.

61. Maxwell.

62. "Army Talk, Orientation Fact Sheet #64, FASCISM!" Unites States War Department, March 24, 1945, http://fascism-archive.org/books/atofs-fascism.html (accessed June 10, 2015).

63. Kendrick, 266.

64. Maxwell.

65. Brown, "What's Going to Happen to Our Women Workers?" *Good Housekeeping*, December 1943, 42, 78–83.

66. Brown, speech notes, microfilm reel 2107, reel P11–920, Vol. III, February 6, 1944, Brown Papers.

67. Elsa Maxwell, "Party-Line: Gag-Buster-Brown," *Pittsburgh Post-Gazette*, November 25, 1943.

68. Paul White, "Letters," *Newsweek*, April 12, 1954, 6.

69. William Sommers, "White Caps on San Diego's Air Waves," *Nation*, October 10, 1953, 281.

70. David L. Levering, "Remarks, Cecil Brown Memorial Service," Cal Poly Pomona, November 7, 1987.

71. Brown, letter to Craig D. Tenney, September 14, 1978, box 26, folder 38, Brown Papers.

72. Brown, notes from outline for unpublished autobiography, box 11, folder 8, Brown Papers.

Chapter 9

1. Edward Bliss, *Now the News* (New York: Columbia University Press, 1991), 34–36, 60–61, 97–98; Robert J. Brown, *Manipulating the Ether: The Power of Broadcast Radio in Thirties America* (Jefferson, NC: McFarland, 1998), 180; and Dan Nimmo and Chevelle Newsome, *Political Commentators in the United States in the 20th Century: A Bio-Critical Sourcebook* (Westport, CT: Greenwood Press, 1997), 173.

2. J. Fred MacDonald, *Television and the Red Menace: The Video Road to Vietnam* (New York: Praeger, 1985), 3.

3. Edgar Kobak, "Statement Presented on Behalf of MBS 'Broadcasting and the Bill of Rights,'" cited in R. Franklin Smith, "Cecil Brown: A Case Study in Broadcast Commentary" (Ph.D. diss., University of Wisconsin, 1961), 301.

4. Walt Taliaferro, "News Commentator Lauds Independence in Broadcasts," *Los Angeles Daily News*, January 19, 1949.

5. Irving Fang, *Those Radio Commentators!* (Ames: Iowa State University Press, 1977), 9.

6. "Book Reviews," *New York Times*, January 23, 1944.

7. Martha Brown, phone interview by author, March 14, 2014.

8. Mutual Broadcasting System, advertisement, February 1944, box 28, folder 37, Brown Papers.

9. Richard W. Steele, "American Popular Opinion and the War against Germany: The Issue of Negotiated Peace, 1942," *The Journal of American History* 65, no. 3 (1978): 716–719; and John Byrne Cooke, *Reporting the War: Freedom of the Press from the American Revolution to the War on Terrorism* (New York: Palgrave Macmillan, 2007), 113.

10. Office of War Information, Martin Agronsky, Raymond Gram Swing, Cecil Brown, "What American Commentators Say: Daily Review of the Comments and Opinions of Leading News Analysts," audio recording, Washington, D.C., Library of Congress, LC # 2003645979, RGA 0582 PN0 07, OWI RWD 3274 B3, file: Q389E, disk: 1114082, 1945.

11. Stephen Roth, *Anti-Semitism Worldwide* (Lincoln: University of Nebraska Press, 2002), 14; Frederic C. Jaher, *The Jews and the Nation: Revolution, Emancipation, State Formation, and the Liberal Paradigm in America and France* (Princeton: Princeton University Press, 2002), 230; and Marc Dollinger, *Quest for Inclusion* (Princeton: Princeton University Press, 2000), 66.

12. Martha Brown, phone interview by author, March 7, 2014.

13. Martha Brown, phone interview by author, August 16, 2013.

14. Robert L. Benson, *The Venona Story* (Fort George G. Meade, MD: National Security Agency Center for Cryptologic History, 2001), 1–34.

15. Federal Bureau of Investigation, "FBI Monograph-Soviet Defectors, A Study of Past Defectors from Official Soviet Establishments Outside the USSR," January 1955, http://archive.org/stream/foia_FBI_MONOGRAPH-Soviet_Defectors/FBI_MONOGRAPH-Soviet_Defectors_djvu.txt (accessed May 14, 2015); Boris Volodarsky, *Stalin's Agent: The Life and Death of Alexander Orlov* (New York: Oxford University Press, 2015), 515; and Martha Brown, phone interview by author, August 16, 2013.

16. Martha Brown, phone interview by author, August 16, 2013.

17. John Moore, Jr., email to author, April 24, 2013.

18. Jonathan Brown, phone interview by author, November 4, 2013. Following graduation from Yale, Jonathan spent three years in Chad with the Peace Corps. He completed a masters' degree from the Annenberg School of Communication at the University of Pennsylvania, and another masters from the Harvard Business School. He then worked for the World Bank for thirty-five years. As an activist at Yale, he was executive director of the Americans for Reappraisal of Far Eastern Policy, and worked with Martin Luther King, Jr., in the South for a couple of years. During his high and college summer vacations, his father, Eugene, employed him at the newspapers he managed in New York and Connecticut.

19. Ibid.
20. Editors, *American Heroes: Edward R. Murrow* (Hackensack: Salem Press, 2008), 700.
21. Smith, *In All His Glory*, 298.
22. Martha Brown, phone interview by author, August 16, 2013.
23. Cecil Brown, MBS news script, March 3, 1944, box 1, folder 14, Brown Papers.
24. Ibid., "A Noteworthy Broadcast," *[Columbus] Ohio Jewish Chronicle*, January 12, 1945.
25. Ibid., CBS news scripts, February 10 and May 8, 1943, box 1, folder 16, Brown Papers.
26. Ibid., CBS news scripts, February 10, 1943, May 8, 1943 and August 4, 1944, box 1, folders 17 and 18, Brown Papers.
27. Neal Ivey, letter to Brown, September 18, 1944, box 26, folder 22, Brown Papers.
28. Benjamin, "The Media and National Crises, 1917–1945," 351.
29. Steven Casey, *Cautious Crusade* (New York: Oxford University Press, 2001), xix, 217.
30. Office of War Information, Martin Agronsky, Raymond Gram Swing, Cecil Brown, "What American Commentators Say: Daily Review of the Comments and Opinions of Leading News Analysts," audio recording, Washington, D.C., Library of Congress, LC # 2003645894, RGA 0572 PNO 07, OWI RWD, file: N7560J, Disk: 81780, 1945.
31. Casey, *Cautious Crusade*, xix, 213.
32. Cecil Brown, MBS news script, April 9, 1945, box 1, folder 16, Brown Papers.
33. Ibid., MBS news scripts, April 13, 1945, box 1, folder 16, Brown Papers.
34. Ibid., MBS news script, September 3, 1945, box 2, folder 4, Brown Papers.
35. Ibid., MBS news script, October 2, 1946, box 3, folder 9, Brown Papers.
36. Fang, *Those Radio Commentators*, 12.
37. Paul F. Lazarsfeld and Harry Field, *The People Look at Radio: Report on a Survey Conducted by The National Opinion Research Center* (Chapel Hill: University of North Carolina Press, 1946), vii, 42–45, 76–78.

38. Fang, *Those Radio Commentators*, 4.
39. Ibid.
40. James J. Martin, *Revisionist Viewpoints: Essays in a Dissident Historical Tradition* (Colorado Springs: Ralph Myles, 1971), 141.
41. Harry S. Truman, "The President's Special Conference with the Association of Radio News Analysts," May 13, 1947, Washington, D.C., in *Public Papers of the Presidents of the United States: Harry S. Truman, 1945–1953*, http://trumanlibrary.org/publicpapers/viewpapers.php?pid=2155 (accessed June 4, 2015).
42. Harry S. Truman, *Memoires: Vol. I: Years of Trial and Hope* (Garden City, NY: Doubleday & Company, 1956), 32–35, 74–79.
43. Paul F. Lazarsfeld, Patricia L. Kendall and Clyde Hart, *Radio Listening in American: The People Look at Radio—Again* (New York: Prentice Hall, 1948), 53–56.
44. "More for Your Money with Mutual Shows," *Billboard*, March 30, 1946.
45. Cameron C. Stineman, letter to KPAB AM, Laredo, TX; cited in Bertram J. Hauser, "Newscasts Still Do the Sponsor's Job," *Broadcasting*, May 12, 1947, 50.
46. J. Fred McDonald, *Don't Touch That Dial! Radio Programming in American Life, 1920–1960* (Chicago: Nelson-Hall, 1980), 298; and C.E. Hooper, Inc., *Uniform Network Competition, Comprehensive Hooperatings* (New York: C.E. Hooper, Inc., 1946), 10–35.
47. Fang, *Those Radio Commentators*, 6.
48. Bertram J. Hauser, "Newscasts Still Do the Sponsor's Job," *Broadcasting*, May 12, 1947, 50.
49. MacDonald, *Don't Touch That Dial*, 292.
50. Gay, *Assignment to Hell*, xiii, 447.
51. MacDonald, *Don't Touch That Dial*, 310.
52. Bruce J. Evensen, *Truman, Zionists and the Press: Framing a Palestine Policy at the Coming of the Cold War* (Ph.D. diss., University of Wisconsin, 1989), 385.
53. Martha Brown, phone interview by author, March 7, 2014.
54. Fang, *Those Radio Commentators*, 11.
55. Gary Gerstle, "The Crucial Decade: The 1940s and Beyond," *The Journal of American History* 92, no. 4 (2006): 1292–1299.
56. Elizabeth Fones-Wolf, *Selling Free Enterprise: The Business Assault on Labor and Liberalism, 1945–1960* (Urbana: University of Illinois Press, 1994), 5–57; and John Blum, William McFeely, Edmund Morgan, Arthur Schlesinger, Jr., Kenneth Stampp and C. Vann Woodward, *The National Experience: A History of the United States*, 6th ed. (New York: Harcourt Brace Jovanovich, 1985), 772.
57. Graham J. White, *F.D.R. and the Press* (Chicago: University of Chicago Press, 1979), 70.

58. J. Fred MacDonald, *Television and the Red Menace*, 153.
59. Quincy Howe, "Policing the Commentator: A News Analysis," *Atlantic Monthly*, November 5, 1943, 47–49.
60. Alfred E. Kahn, *Treason in Congress: The Record of the House Un-American Activities Committee* (New York: Progressive Citizens of America, 1948), www.trussel.com/hf/treason.htm (accessed September 13, 2013).
61. "Un-Amer. Comm. Gets Work As Representative Hook Plans to Force Anti-Bill to Floor," *Billboard*, November 3, 1945, 10.
62. John Cogley, *Report on Blacklisting: II: Radio-Television* (New York: The Fund for the Republic, Inc., 1956), 71.
63. Kahn, *Treason in Congress*.
64. A.M. Sperber, *Murrow: His Life and Times* (New York: Freundlich Books, 1986), 275.
65. "Punishment for Commentators," *The Charlotte [NC] News*, November 9, 1945; and "House Hears of Threat to Free Speech," *Stars and Stripes*, October 27, 1945.
66. Cecil Brown, MBS news script, February 12, 1943, box 1, folder 16, Brown Papers.
67. "Why Columbia Waives the Rule," *Variety*, December 27, 1950, 19.
68. Bryce Oliver, "Thought Control—American Style," *New Republic*, January 13, 1947, 12–13; Juan Gonzalez and Joseph Torres, *News for All the People: The Epic Story of Race and the American Media* (Brooklyn: Verso, 2011); and Smith, *In All His Glory*, 300.
69. "Fadeout of Liberal Gabbers," *Variety*, December 25, 1946, 29–30.
70. Alexander Kendrick, *Prime Time: The Life of Edward R. Murrow* (New York: Little, Brown, 1969), 297.
71. Cecil Brown, MBS news scripts, March 5 and October 28, 1947, box 12, folders 1 and 14, Brown Papers.
72. Ibid., MBS news script, October 8, 1947, box 4, folder 16, Brown Papers.
73. William Benton, letter to Brown, February 24, 1947, box 3, folder 14, Brown Papers.
74. Kendrick, *Prime Time*, 266.
75. Cecil Brown, MBS news scripts, October 26 and October. 28, 1947, box 4, folder 17, Brown Papers.
76. Ernest Pascal, letter to Cecil Brown, December 15, 1948, box 26, folder 17, Brown Papers.
77. Erik Barnouw, *The Golden Web*, 266; and Richard Goldstein, "Howard K. Smith, Broadcast Newsman, Dies at 87," *International New York Times*, February 18, 2002, http://www.nytimes.com/2002/02/18/obituaries/18CND-SMITH.html (accessed July 15, 2014).
78. Suzanne Clark, *Cold Warriors: Manliness on Trial in the Rhetoric of the West* (Carbondale: Southern Illinois University Press, 2000), 110–111.
79. David G. Mitchell, letter to MBS, New York, January 7, 1949; box 26, folder 16, Brown Papers.
80. Cecil Brown, reply letter to Mitchell, January 10, 1949; and Mitchell reply letter to Brown, January 14, 1949; box 26, folder 16, Brown Papers.
81. Mrs. Marguerite B. Pratt, letter to MBS, New York, August 25, 1949, box 26, folder 16, Brown Papers.
82. Cecil Brown, letter to Marguerite B. Pratt, September 9, 1949, box 26, folder 16, Brown Papers.
83. Mrs. Lawrence Sheehy, letter to MBS, February 22, 1950, box 26, folder 17, Brown Papers.
84. Cecil Brown MBS news script, March 28, 1950, box 7, folder 15, Brown Papers.
85. A.D. McNeil, of W. Colston Leigh, Inc. (agent), Pacific Coast Office, San Francisco, letter to Cecil Brown, October 6, 1950; Cecil Brown, reply letter to McNeil, October 9, 1950; George H. Armacost, President, Redlands University, reply letter to Brown, October 11, 1950, box 26, folder 17, Brown Papers.
86. Cecil Brown, MBS news script, March 15, 1949, box 7, folder 9, Brown Papers.
87. Victor Van Der Linde, letter to Mrs. Engs, Oakland, CA, May 12, 1950, box 26, folder 17, Brown Papers.
88. Van Der Linder, letter to Cecil Brown, MBS, New York, April 13, 1950, box 26, folder 17, Brown Papers.
89. Cecil Brown, letter to Mrs. Agnes Engs, Oakland, CA, April 12, 1950, box 26, folder 17, Brown Papers.
90. David R. Davies, "The Media in Transition, 1945–1974," *The Media in America: A History*, 470–471.
91. Gerald Weales, "The Voice of Elmer Davis," *The Virginia Quarterly Review* 71, no. 3 (1995): 503–509.
92. Cecil Brown, MBS news script, February 22, 1954, box 12, folder 15, Brown Papers.
93. Ibid., "A Designing Beauty," *New Outlook*, August 1954.
94. Ibid., MBS news script, December 8, 1954, box 13, folder 18, Brown Papers.
95. Bill Watters, letter to Cecil Brown, April 26, 1950, box 26, folder 17, Brown Papers.
96. Cecil Brown, letter to Frank R. Warren, Sepulveda, CA, May 15, 1950, box 26, folder 17, Brown Papers.
97. Ibid., MBS news script, May 3, 1957, box 18 folder 1, Brown Papers.
98. Robert Spiers, *The Inside Story: By*

Members of the Overseas Press Club of America (New York: Prentice Hall, 1940), 86.
99. Sam Goldwyn, letter to Brown, March 20, 1950, box 26, folder 17, Brown Papers.
100. Anonymous letter to Brown, October 19, 1950; and letter from O.W. Chandler, Hannibal, MO, to Brown, box 26, folder 17, Brown Papers.
101. Cecil Brown, letter to Pratt.
102. *Ibid.*, letter to Seniel Ostrow, Sealy Mattress Company, March 9, 1948, box 26, folder 17, Brown Papers.
103. George Wright, "The Umbrellas of Liberalism: The Impact of Ideology on Post-World War II U.S.," http://www.csuchico.edu/~gwright/index.htm (accessed December 2, 2015).
104. Cecil Brown, letter to Ray Fowler, January 21, 1956, box 26, folder 22, Brown Papers.
105. Jonathan Brown, phone interview by author, November 4, 2013.

Chapter 10

1. William A. Frayer, "Some Comments on Commentators," *Quarterly Review of the Michigan Alumnus: A Journal of University Perspective* 51, no. 4 (October 18, 1944), 8–18, Wilfred B. Shaw, ed., University of Michigan.
2. "It's News to Mutual," *New Republic*, January 3, 1955, 10. The article considered the other Mutual commentators to be "untrained spokesmen" of differing pressure groups.
3. Arthur Nadel, Filmation Co., letter to Martha Brown, November 5, 1987, and Donald Pluger, "Remarks at Cecil Brown Memorial Service," Cal Poly Pomona, November 7, 1987, box 27, folder 43, Brown Papers.
4. "Cecil Brown Warns Against Efforts to Divide Allies," *The Lewiston [ME] Daily Sun*, October 6, 1944.
5. Jean Gaines, "No Staccato for Brown," *Radio-Television Life* (n.d.), microfilm P11–920, Vol. 3, Brown Papers.
6. Cecil Brown, letter to Ray Fowler of Needham, Louis and Brorby, Inc. Advertising, January 16, 1956, box 26, folder 19, Brown Papers.
7. Portions of this rhetorical analysis are derived from R. Franklin Smith, "Cecil Brown: A Case Study in Broadcast Commentary" (Ph.D. diss., University of Wisconsin, 1961).
8. Kernis quoted in Jonathan Kern, *Sound Reporting: The NPR Guide to Audio Journalism and Production* (Chicago: University of Chicago Press, 2008), 288.
9. Melvin L. DeFleur and Margaret H. DeFleur, *Mass Communication Theories: Explaining Origins, Processes and Effects* (New York: Routledge, 2010), 110.
10. Walter Lippman, *Public Opinion* (New York: Harcourt, Brace, 1922), 215; and Gerald Nachman, *Raised on Radio* (Berkeley: University of California Press, 2000), 406.
11. Office of War Information, Cecil Brown, "What American Commentators Say: Daily Review of the Comments and Opinions of Leading News Analysts," audio recording, Washington, D.C., Library of Congress, LC # 2003645979, RGS 0582 PNO 07, OWI RWD 3274 B3, file: Q389E, disk 1114082, July 10, 1945.
12. Office of War Information, Cecil Brown, "What American Commentators Say: Daily Review of the Comments and Opinions of Leading News Analysts," audio recording, Washington, D.C., Library of Congress, LC # 2003645894 RGS 0580 PNO 06, OWI RWD 3272 B2, file T10E, disk: 4093, August 7, 1945.
13. Cecil Brown, MBS news script, cited in Kathy R. Forde and Matthew W. Ross, "Radio and the Civic Courage in the Communications Circuit of John Hersey's *Hiroshima*," *Literary Journalism Studies* 3, no. 2 (2011): 41.
14. *Ibid.*, MBS news script, June 23, 1948, box 5, folder 6, Brown Papers.
15. *Ibid.*, "How Close Are We to War with Russia," *See*, September 1948, 30.
16. Cecil Brown, MBS news script, June 10 and July 24, 1946, box 2, folder 21, and box 3, folder 1, Brown Papers.
17. *Ibid.*, MBS news script, March 5, 1947, box 12, folder 1, Brown Papers.
18. For a thorough examination of the Truman Administration's struggle concerning support of Israel, see David McCullough, *Truman* (New York: Simon & Schuster, 1992), 600–620.
19. Cecil Brown, MBS news script, September 1, 1947, box 13, folder 4, Brown Papers.
20. *Ibid.*, MBS news script, May 25, 1948, box 5, folder 5, Brown Papers.
21. *Ibid.*, MBS news scripts, September 29, 1947, March 22, 30, and May 25, 1948, boxes 14 and 16, folder 1, Brown Papers.
22. *Ibid.*, MSB news script, March 19, 1948, box 16, folder 1, Brown Papers; and Bruce J. Evensen, *Truman, Zionists and the Press: Framing a Palestine Policy at the Coming of the Cold War* (Ph.D. diss., University of Wisconsin, 1989).
23. Reverend Thomas Kirkman, Jr., letter to Brown, August 17, 1950, box 26, folder 23, Brown Papers.
24. Cecil Brown, MBS news script, WNYC Media Archives, New York, script # 68838.1 LT236 R208, February 13, 1950.
25. "Cecil Brown Will Speak at Giant Rally," *[Pittsburgh]American Jewish Outlook*, January 16, 1951.

26. "Cecil Brown, News Analyst, Appears Here," *[Westport, CT] Herald News*, April 8, 1951.
27. Cecil Brown, MBS news script, October 29, 1951, box 8, folder 16, Brown Papers.
28. "Noted Author to Speak for Jewish Appeal," *Massena [NY] Observer*, April 30, 1951, 21.
29. "UFJ Women's Pledge of $40,000 Is 25% Increase," *[Columbus] Ohio Jewish Chronicle*, May 25, 1951.
30. "Cecil Brown Here Sunday," *[San Diego] Southwestern Jewish Press*, March 6, 1953; and San Diego United Jewish Fund, "What Can I Do?" March 1953, box 25, folder 21, Brown Papers.
31. "Brown Asserts U.S. at War with Russia," *Ellensburg [WA] Daily Record*, October 11, 1950.
32. Will-Matthis Dunn, letter to Brown, MBS, November 1, 1950, box 26, folder 17, Brown Papers.
33. "Cecil Brown to Speak Thursday," *[State College, PA] Daily Collegian*, May 1, 1951.
34. "U.S. Journalists Die in Air Crash," *[Perth] West Australian*, July 13, 1949; and Eugene Brown, "About Town," *Oneonta [NY] Star*, July 18, 1949.
35. WNYC, Cecil Brown, interview by anonymous reporter, audio recording, courtesy of NYC Municipal Archive, WNYC Collection, catalog # 68839, LT236, 1949.
36. Brown, MBS news script, May 14, 1951, box 8, folder 11, Brown Papers.
37. "The Tape Recorder Is Revolutionizing Radio Programming," *Sponsor*, October 1, 1951, 37–38; and MBS press release, May 25, 1951, box 28, folder 37, Brown Papers.
38. Eugene Brown, "His All-Wool Humble Jacket," *Oneonta [NY] Star*, December 4, 1971.
39. "Army of 6 Million for China Invasion Claimed by Chiang," *Stars and Stripes*, November 19, 1951.
40. Cecil Brown, "World Report 1952 Memo to State Farm Insurance," February 1952, box 28, folder 37, Brown Papers; and Eugene Brown, "U.S. Must Prepare for More Rigorous Living, Cecil Brown Says on Visit to Oneonta," *Oneonta Star*, December 26, 1950.
41. Mutual Broadcasting System, "A Biography from the Press Information Department," April 13, 1954, courtesy of CBS Archives, New York City.
42. ABC Radio, "Biography: Cecil Brown and the News," May 13, 1957, courtesy CBS Archives, New York City.
43. Brown, MBS news script, April 10, 1951, box 8, folder 11, Brown Papers.
44. Brown, MBS news scripts, April 12 & 13, 1951, box 8, folder 11, Brown Papers.
45. Edward Bliss, Jr., *Now the News: The Story of Broadcast Journalism* (New York: Columbia University Press, 1991), 263.
46. Mrs. R.J. Trumpfer, Berkley, CA; Evelyn Bing, Las Vegas, NV; Mrs. Walter Power, Albany, NY; and anonymous letters to Brown, box 26, folder 19, Brown Papers.
47. Dorothy Titland, San Francisco; Helen Eberhard, Artesia, CA; and Mrs. Walter D. Powell, Albany, NY; letters to Brown, April 12, 1951; box 26, folder 17, Brown Papers.
48. "Cecil Brown to Speak Thursday," 1.
49. Eugene Brown, "U.S. Must Prepare for More Rigorous Living."
50. Cecil Brown, MBS news script, Nov. 23, 1952, box 10, folder 9, Brown Papers.
51. Eugene Brown, "U.S. Must Prepare for More Rigorous Living."
52. *Ibid.*
53. Cecil Brown, MBS news script, July 27, 1953, box 11, folder 17, Brown Papers.
54. McCullough, 587.
55. Barbara Dianne Savage, *Broadcasting Freedom: Radio, War, and the Politics of Race 1938–1948* (Chapel Hill: University of North Carolina Press, 1999), 121, 199, 325 and 345; and Michele Hilmes and Jason Loviglio, *Radio Reader: Essays in the Cultural History of Radio* (New York: Routledge, 2001), 219.
56. Fang, *Those Radio Commentators*, 331.
57. Cecil Brown, MBS news scripts, January 14, 1949, July 26, 1950, and February 2, 1954; box 6, folder 14; box 8, folder 1; and box 12, folder 20, Brown Papers; and Cecil Brown, "Can Asia Be Saved from Communist China's Aggression?" Speech delivered before the Economic Club of Detroit, January 4, 1960, *Vital Speeches*, April 1, 1960, 365.
58. Garland Powell, letter to Brown, MBS, July 20, 1949; and Brown response, July 22, 1949; box 26, folder 17, Brown Papers.
59. J. Fred MacDonald, *Television and the Red Menace: The Video Road to Vietnam* (New York: Prager, 1985), 21–22.
60. John K. Galbraith, *The Affluent Society: The Economics of the Age of Opulence-A Literate and Expert Revision of the Basic Ideas* (New York: Houghton Mifflin, 1958), 112–115.
61. Art Preis, "Myth of 'People's Capitalism,'" *International Socialist Review* 23, 1 (Winter 1962): 3–9.
62. Eugene Brown, "U.S. Must Prepare for More Rigorous Living."
63. Cecil Brown, MBS news script, August 11, 1944, box 1, folder 19, Brown Papers.
64. *Ibid.*, MBS news script, April 9, 1951, box 26, folder 19, Brown Papers.
65. *Ibid.*, MBS news script, February 14, 1952, box 9, folder 1, Brown Papers.
66. Mrs. W. MacFarlane, South Pasadena,

CA, letter to Brown, April 19, 1951, box 26, folder 19, Brown Papers.

67. Cecil Brown, MBS news script, July 31, 1953, box 11, folder 11, Brown Papers.

68. *Ibid.*, MBS news script, June 6, 1952, box 9, folder 15, Brown Papers.

69. *Ibid.*, MBS news script, Dec. 6, 1953, box 12, folder 4, Brown Papers.

70. *Ibid.*, MBS news script, December 7, 1953, box 12, folder 3, Brown Papers.

71. Craig Allen, *Eisenhower and The Mass Media: Peace, Prosperity, & Prime-Time TV* (Chapel Hill: University of North Carolina Press, 1993), 190; and David Brooks, *The Road to Character* (New York: Random House, 2016), 67.

72. Cecil Brown, MBS news scripts, March 10 and June 6, 1954, box 12, folders 16 and 20, Brown Papers.

73. Allen, 51.

74. *Ibid.*, 50.

75. Cecil Brown, MBS news script, March 10, 1954, box 12, folder 16, Brown Papers.

76. Arthur M. Schlesinger, *A Thousand Days: John F. Kennedy in the White House* (New York: Houghton Mifflin, 1965), 239.

77. John Bartlow Martin, *Adlai Stevenson and the World* (Garden City, NY: Doubleday & Company, 1977), 94

78. Cited in John M. Blum, William S. McFeely, Edmund S. Morgan, Arthur M. Schlesinger, Jr., Kenneth Stampp, C. Vann Woodward, *The National Experience: A History of the United States*, 6th ed. (New York: Harcourt Brace Jovanovich, 1985), 785.

79. Cecil Brown, MBS news scripts, October 5, 1952 and November 6, 1952, box 11, folders 20 & 22, Brown Papers.

80. *Ibid.*, MBS news script, June 6, 1954, box 12, folder 20, Brown Papers.

81. *Ibid.*, MBS news script, May 27, 1955, box 14, folder 16, Brown Papers.

82. Allen, 95.

83. Anonymous letter to MBS, August 1956, box 26, folder 19, Brown Papers.

84. Cecil Brown, MBS news script, May 24, 1954, box 12, folder 14, Brown Papers.

85. William E. Pollard, letter to Cecil Brown, MBS, April 27, 1956, box 26, folder 19, Brown Papers.

86. Dorothy Zeiger, Wilberforce, OH, letter to Brown, September 11, 1957, box 26, folder 22, Brown Papers.

87. David. R. Rugg, Hot Springs, AK, letter to Brown, October 16, 1957, box 26, folder 22, Brown Papers.

88. Ms. H.R. Broadhurst, letter to Brown, December 7, 1957, box 26, folder 22, Brown Papers.

89. Cecil Brown, MBS news script, February 7, 1956, box 16, folder 1, Brown Papers.

90. *Ibid.*, MBS news scripts, September 4 and 10, 1956, box 17, folders 3, 4, Brown Papers.

91. *Ibid.*, MBS news script, September 11, 1957, box 18, folder 7, Brown Papers.

92. Frank Ford, Jr., letter to Brown, MBS, February 3, 1956, box 26, folder 19, Brown Papers.

93. Frank Lambeth, WMFR, High Point, NC, letter to Brown, October 1957, box 26, folder 19, Brown Papers.

94. Cecil Brown, letter to Ralph E. Goodwin, Jr., Gainesville, FL, Feb. 25, 1956, box 26, folder 19, Brown Papers.

95. W.A. Kaderli, Stanton, TX, letter to Brown, September 12, 1957, box 26, folder 22, Brown Papers.

96. The Reverend C.E Kleber, St. Paul Lutheran Church, Lamesa, TX, letter to Brown, September 25, 1957, box 26, folder 22, Brown Papers.

97. Cecil Brown, MBS news script, May 4, 1957, box 18, folder 1, Brown Papers.

98. Steve Knoll, "Demise of the Radio Commentator: An Irreparable Loss to Radio Journalism," *Journal of Radio Studies* 6, no. 2 (1999): 359.

99. Gerald Weales, "The Voice of Elmer Davis," *The Virginia Quarterly Review* 71, no. 3 (1995): 504.

100. Thomas C. Merrill, letter to anonymous listener, January 1956, box 26, folder 19, Brown Papers.

101. Blum, et al., 802.

102. Cecil Brown, MBS news scripts, April 25 and 27, and June 7, 1954; box 12, folders and 17 & 21, Brown Papers.

103. *Ibid.*, MBS news script, April 25, 1949, box 7, folder 14; and anonymous letter to Brown, May 1951, box 26, folder 21, Brown Papers.

104. MacDonald, 97.

105. Cecil Brown, "How Close Are We to War with Russia?" 30–33.

106. *Ibid.*, MBS news scripts, May 18, 1955, and March 19, 1956; box 14, folder 22, and box 16, folder 2, Brown Papers.

107. *Ibid.*, MBS news script, June 8, 1957, box 18, folder 3, Brown Papers.

108. *Ibid.*, MBS news scripts, June 10 and 14, 1957, box 18, folder 3, Brown Papers.

109. Hal Stebbins, Inc. Advertising, letter to Mr. Leon Wray, Mutual Don Lee Broadcasting System, March 22, 1950; microfilm # P11–920, Vol. 3, Brown Papers.

110. Don Lee Radio Network, advertising flyer, 1954, box 8, folder 146, Brown Papers.

111. Cecil Brown, letter to Robert Kintner, box 30, folder 12, Brown Papers.

112. Cecil Brown, MBS news script, March 25, 1957, box 17, folder 19, Brown Papers.

Chapter 11

1. David Brinkley, cited in Gerald Nachman, *Raised on Radio* (Berkeley: University of California Press, 2000), 402.
2. Quincy Howe, "The Rise and Fall of the Radio Commentator," *Saturday Review*, October 26, 1957, 15; and Steve Knoll, "Demise of the Radio Commentator: An Irreparable Loss to Broadcast Journalism," *Journal of Radio and Audio Media* 6, no. 2 (1999): 365–367.
3. *Ibid.*, 356.
4. Richard Shepard, "Just News, No Antics," *New York Times*, July 22, 1956.
5. Cecil Brown, WABC news script, July 11, 1956, box 16, folder 15, Brown Papers.
6. "Review: Cecil Brown and the News on WABC TV," *New York Times*, July 11, 1956; and Jack Gould, "Television Review: Cecil Brown Presents Weekday News Show," *New York Times*, July 11, 1956.
7. Letters to ABC Television Network, March 15, 1956, box 20, folder 17, Brown Papers.
8. Jay Nelson Tuck, "On the Air," *New York Post*, April 2, 1957.
9. Brown, reply letter to Ray Fowler, Needham, Louis and Brorby, Inc. Advertising, January 18, 1956, box 26, folder 19, Brown Papers.
10. Ray Fowler, letter to Brown, October 16, 1956, box 26, folder 21, Brown Papers.
11. Ronald Garay, *Gordon McLendon: The Maverick of Radio* (Westport, CT: Greenwood Press, 1992), 64; and Jim Cox, *American Radio Networks: A History* (Jefferson, NC: McFarland, 2009), 83.
12. Cecil Brown, MBS news script, May 27, 1956, box 19, folder 22, Brown Papers.
13. Robert L. Stone, letter to Brown, April 4, 1957, box 26, folder 24, Brown Papers.
14. ABC, unsigned letter to Annual Awards Committee, Overseas Press Club, March 15, 1957, box 20, folder 7, Brown Papers.
15. Members of the Murrow team would no doubt have adamantly opposed a broadcast journalist who also worked as a game show host. They would have considered it contrary to the standards of ethical journalism in that it violated the wall of separation they believed needed to exist between objective news reporting and entertainment programming.
16. Cox, 96–97.
17. Brown WABC news script, April 1, 1957, box 17, folder 19, Brown Papers.
18. C.F. Pearce, Hillsboro, TX, letter to WABC, September 6, 1957, box 26, folder 22, Brown Papers.
19. Michael Mayer, *The Eisenhower Years* (New York: Infobase Publishing, 2010), 44; and George C. Peden, "Suez and Britain's Decline as a World Power," *Historical Journal* 55, no. 4 (2012): 1073–1096.
20. Cecil Brown, MBS news script, July 27, 1957, Brown Papers, box 18, folder 6, WHS. For more information on the Eisenhower Administration's relations with Israel, see Isaac Alteras, *Eisenhower and Israel: U.S.–Israeli Relations, 1953–1960* (Gainesville: University Press of Florida, 1993).
21. Cecil Brown, book review of John Robinson Beal's *Brinkmanship*, in *Saturday Review*, April 27, 1957, 19–20.
22. *Ibid.*, MBS news scripts, September 24, 1956 and October 19, 1957, box 17, folder 2; and box 18, folder 10, Brown Papers.
23. Craig Allen, *Eisenhower and The Mass Media: Peace, Prosperity, & Prime-Time Television* (Chapel Hill: University of North Carolina Press, 1993), 152.
24. Cecil Brown, MBS news script, November 7, 1956, box 20, folder 5, Brown Papers.
25. *Ibid.*, letter to Simon Goodman, James Broadcasting Co., Jamestown, NY, November 18, 1957, Brown Papers, box 26, folder 22, WHS; and Pat O'Reilly, letter to Thomas Velotta, "ABC Interdepartmental Correspondence," May 15, 1957, box 26, folder 19, Brown Papers.
26. David Frum, *How We Got Here: The '70s* (New York: Basic Books, 2000), 27; and Blum, McFeely, Morgan, Schlesinger, Jr., Stampp, Woodward, *The National Experience*, 809.
27. In January 1961, Littlejohn resigned from ABC, a little more than a month after the network's vice president in charge of news, John Daly, resigned over ABC television network programmers' decision to air episodes of *Bugs Bunny* and *The Rifleman* instead of coverage of the Nixon-Kennedy presidential race. Littlejohn had worked at ABC since 1945 and had been the radio network's news director since 1954. ABC replaced Daly with former Eisenhower press secretary James Haggerty.
28. Cecil Brown, letter to Francis Littlejohn, ABC Radio Network, February 14, 1961, box 27, folder 18, Brown Papers.
29. Shepard, "Just News, No Antics."
30. Jonathan Brown, phone interview by author, November 4, 2013.
31. "Cecil Brown, Noted Commentator-Author, Will Join NBC News and Cover Far East Area," NBC press release, May 5, 1958, courtesy of CBS Archives, New York.
32. Edward Bliss, Jr., *Now the News: The Story of Broadcast Journalism* (New York: Columbia University Press, 1991), 308.
33. NBC News, *Memo to JFK: From NBC News* (New York: G.P. Putnam and Sons, 1961), 9, 21.
34. "U.S. Warned on Plane Violation," *Oakland [CA] Tribune*, September 10, 1958.

35. Bob Foster, "Bob Foster on Television: Review of Fast East: Clear Danger," *San Mateo Times*, September 20, 1958.
36. Cecil Brown, NBC *Today* show script, October 16, 1958, box 28, folder 40, Brown Papers.
37. *Ibid.*, transcript of filmed interview with Kameii Tojo on NBC's *Outlook*, September 7, 1958, box 20, folder 8, Brown Papers.
38. "Biography: Cecil Brown NBC News' Tokyo Correspondent," NBC press release, November 18, 1958, courtesy of CBS Archives, New York.
39. Cecil Brown, NBC news script, October 9, 1958, box 28, folder 28, Brown Papers.
40. Martha Brown, phone interview by author, August 16, 2013.
41. Cecil Brown, "Kaleidoscope: Projection '59," NBC transcript, December 28, 1958, box 28, folder 40, Brown Papers.
42. Charles Mercer, "NBC Correspondents Get Together for Bull Session," *Ocala fl Star-Banner*, October 20, 1958.
43. At the time Brown initiated the program, Walter Coombs was the Director of the World Affairs Council. Coombs became Brown's department chair in 1970, in the Department of Social Sciences at Cal-Poly, when Brown began teaching there in 1970. Coombs recalled the 1959 beginning of the tour arrangement in a letter to Ruth Harmer, English Department, Cal Poly Pomona, January 29, 1980.
44. Cecil Brown, speech notes, October 20, 1958, box 25, folder 22, Brown Papers.
45. *Ibid.*, NBC news script, April 27, 1960, box 20, folder 9, Brown Papers.
46. Stuart Addy and Dieter Flectk, *The Handbook of the Law of Visiting Forces* (New York: Oxford University Press, 2001), 404; and Cecil Brown, NBC filmed report, April 5, 1959, NBC News Archives, NY, ID # 00C9065.
47. Cecil Brown NBC news film, June 16, 1960, NBC News Archives, NY, ID # S600616.
48. "Global Nonviolent Global Database: Japanese Protest Security Treaty with U.S. and Unseat Prime Minister, 1959–1960," at http://nvdatabase.swarthmore.edu/content/japanese-protest-security-treaty-us-and-unseat-prime-minister-1959-1960 (accessed September 22, 2015); and NBC News, *Memo to JFK from NBC News*, 204.
49. NBC News, *Memo to JFK from NBC News*, 195, 235.
50. Cecil Brown, "Can Asia Be Saved from Communist China's Aggression?" (speech to The Economic Club, Detroit, MI, January 4, 1960), *Vital Speeches* 26, no. 12 (1960): 362–365.
51. J. Fred MacDonald, *Television and the Red Menace: The Video Road to Vietnam* (New York: Praeger, 1985), 94–96.
52. NBC News, *Memo to JFK from NBC News*, 9, 24.
53. Cecil Brown, special NBC Report script, January 4, 1959; and Brown, letter to William R. McAndrew, VP, NBC News, January 12, 1959, box 20, folder 9, and box 26, folder 24, Brown Papers.
54. *Ibid.*, unpublished book notes, 1958, box 26, folder 1, Brown Papers.
55. *Ibid.*, unpublished script, "Vietnam: Land of the Dragon" documentary, 1960, box 26, folder 14, Brown Papers.
56. MacDonald, *Television and the Red Menace*, 169–171.
57. *Ibid.*, NBC news script; 1960, box 11, folder 8, Brown Papers; and Howard Jones, *Death of a Generation: How the Assassinations of Diem and JFK Prolonged the Vietnam War* (New York: Oxford University Press, 2003), 433.
58. Blum, et al., 817.
59. Cecil Brown, *Comment* script, KCET, June 1966, box 22, folder 19, Brown Papers.
60. *Ibid.* (speech, National Press Club, Washington, DC, January 8, 1958), box 25, folder 22, Brown Papers.
61. William McAndrew, letter to Brown, April 13, 1960, box 26, folder 24, Brown Papers.
62. Arthur W. Hepner, ed., *The Best of Emphasis: Opinions and Insights by the World-Wide NBC News Staff* (Westminster, MD: The Newman Press, 1962), v–xi.
63. Cecil Brown, NBC news script, November 5, 1959, box 28, folder 40, Brown Papers.
64. *Ibid.*, NBC news script, November 9, 1959, box 28, folder 40, Brown Papers.
65. *Ibid.*
66. *Ibid.*, NBC Radio News script, August 6, 1962, box 20, folder 10, Brown Papers.
67. Bill Fiset, "About Television: An Era of Unlimited Possibilities," *Oakland [CA] Tribune*, January 19, 1962.
68. Martha Brown, phone interview by author, August 16, 2013.

Chapter 12

1. Jonathan Brown, phone interview by author, November 4, 2013.
2. NBC, interoffice memo re: Brown-Peterson *Comment* show ratings, April 1, 1963, box 28, folder 34; and KNBC Press Release, October 1, 1962, box 28, folder 34, Brown Papers.
3. Cecil Brown, *Comment* script, KRCA TV, October 1, 1962, box 20, folder 11, Brown Papers.
4. Brown, *Comment* script, KNBC TV, No-

vember 19, 1963, box 28, folder 34, Brown Papers.

5. Carl Brandt, letter to Brown, KNBC TV, cited by Brown in biographical sketch when he applied for the KCET position, August 21, 1964; box 28, folder 20, Brown Papers.

6. Cecil Brown, script, KNBC TV, November 24, 1963, box 20, folder 5, Brown Papers.

7. "As Ike Sees the Candidates Now," *U.S. News & World Report*, April 20, 1964, 14.

8. Justus B. Lawrence, International Fact Finding Institute, to Eugene Brown, March 9, 1964, box 28, folder 7, Brown Papers. Lawrence was capable of making this assessment because during World War II he served as PR chief, with the rank of colonel, under Supreme Allied Commander Dwight Eisenhower. Lawrence started his career in Los Angeles as a journalist, then was advertising and publicity director for movie producer Samuel Goldwyn from 1933 to 1939, and PR director of the Motion Picture Film Producers Association from 1939 to 1942. Lawrence was originally from Akron, but it is unclear if Eugene knew him in Ohio or when both lived near New York City.

9. "Cecil Brown Joins Staff of KCET as Director of News and Public Affairs," *Camera 28, KCET TV Program Guide*, November 1964, 5, 20; James Loper Papers, box 15, file 4, Special Collections, University of Maryland Libraries, Hornbake Library, College Park, MD.

10. Cecil Brown, *Comment* script, KCET TV, November 11, 1964, box 21, folder 9, Brown Papers.

11. *Ibid.*, letter to Larry G. Newman, December 31, 1964, box 26, folder 26, Brown Papers.

12. *Ibid.*, *Comment* script, KCET TV, April 26, 1966, box 22, folder 17, Brown Papers.

13. Hal Humphrey, "There's Bad News Tonight," *Los Angeles Times*, April 8, 1965.

14. "Population History of Los Angeles from 1890–1990," http://physics.bu.edu/~redner/projects/population/cities/la.html (accessed November 6, 2015).

15. James Loper Papers, Special Collections, series 1:7, box 15, file 4, University of Maryland Libraries, Hornbake Library, College Park, MD; and Jeannine Stein,"R.S.V.P.: Black-Tie Gala Helps KCET Celebrate 25 Years on the Air," *Los Angeles Times*, June 16, 1989.

16. "National Educational Television (NET) History," http://www.museum.tv/eotv/national educ.htm (accessed August 3, 2015); and University of Maryland Libraries, http://web.archive.org/web/20120822192909/http://www.lib.umd.edu/ NPBA/subinfo/net.html (accessed July 20, 2015).

17. Mass Communication Research Center, Brandies University, Waltham, MA, and the National Center for School and College Television, Bloomington, IN, "One Week of Educational Television," no. 4, April 17–23, 1966.

18. Radical Right in California; Extremism, Communism, [1964], Los Angeles, CA, moving images series, motion pictures subseries, MP # 59, Edmund S. Muskie Papers, Edmund S. Muskie Archives and Special Collections Library, Bates College, Lewiston, Maine.

19. John Milton, *The Areopagitica and of Education: With Autobiographical Passages from Other Prose Works*, 1644 (Wheeling, IL: Harlan Davidson, Inc., 1987), 1–49.

20. Cecil Brown, *Comment* script, KCET TV, June 7, 1965, box 22, folder 1, Brown Papers.

21. *Ibid.* (speech, Claremont-McKenna College, Claremont, CA, November 14, 1966), box 25, folder 27, Brown Papers.

22. *Ibid.*, letter to Ercole Graziadei, Rome, Italy, July 1973, box 27, folder 5, Brown Papers.

23. *Berkeley in the Sixties*, directed by Mark Kitchell (1990: Alexandria, VA: POV Theatrical Films, Public Broadcasting Service, 2002), DVD; "Free Speech Movement Chronology," *California Monthly*, http://bancroft.berkeley.edu/FSM/chron.html (accessed July 17, 2015); and Kathleen E. Gales. "A Campus Revolution," *British Journal of Sociology* 17, no. 1 (1966): 1–19.

24. Christopher Rasmussen, "Kennedy's Amerika: The Transcendent Turn in American Propaganda, 1961–1963," *Journalism History* 42, no. 3 (2016): 139.

25. Cecil Brown, *Comment* scripts, KCET TV, November 25, 1965, box 22, folders 8 and 11, Brown Papers.

26. *Ibid.*, *Comment* script, KCET TV, April 5, 1966, box 24, folder 11, Brown Papers.

27. *Ibid.*, *Comment* script, KCET TV, May 30, 1966, box 24, folder 11, Brown Papers.

28. *Ibid.*, *Comment* script, KCET TV, June 28, 1966, box 24, folder 20, Brown Papers.

29. David Bentz, letter to Brown, January 27, 1967; Hiram Gallagher, M.D., letter to Brown, July 7, 1967, Morris Korot, letter to Brown, March 27, 1967, and Irma Dobriner, letter to Brown, March 27, 1967; KCET TV, box 27, folder 4, Brown Papers;

30. J.S. Galindo, letter to Brown, Whittier, CA, unknown date; George Kuyper, letter to Brown, January 18, 1967; Ester Langlois, letter to to Brown, December 22, 1966; Emily Zabriskie, letter to KCET TV Manager, March 25, 1967; box 27, folder 4, Brown Papers.

31. James W. Case, response letter to F.R. Joos, May 12, 1965, box 26, folder 27, Brown Papers.

32. Cecil Brown, response letter to Ester

Langlois, December 22, 1966, box 26, folder 19, Brown Papers.

33. Frank E. Reynolds, letter to Brown, January 17, 1967; Alvin Karbru, letter to Brown, January 3, 1967, box 27, folder 1; and Glenn Dumke, comment at the Brown Memorial Service, November 5, 1987, Cal Poly Pomona, box 27, folder 43, Brown Papers.

34. Cecil Brown, *Comment* scripts, KCET TV, January 3, 1966, and February 20, 1967; box 22, folder 11, Brown Papers.

35. Lisa Morehouse, "Grapes of Wrath: The Forgotten Filipinos Who Led a Farmworker Revolution," *Weekend Edition*, National Public Radio, September 19, 2015.

36. Cecil Brown, *Comment* scripts, KCET TV, May 11, 1966 and February 20, 1967, box 22, folder 18; and box 23, folder 18, Brown Papers.

37. Jeffrey Kahn, "Ronald Reagan Launched Political Career Using the Berkeley Campus as a Target,? *UCBerkeleyNews*, June 8, 2004, http://www.berkeley.edu/news/media/releases/2004/06/08 _reagan.shtml (accessed July 23, 2015).

38. Cecil Brown, *Comment* script, KCET TV, February 9, 1965, box 21, folder 17, Brown Papers.

39. Blum, et al., 840.

40. Stan Metzler, "Faculty Told LBJ Suffers from Crisis of Communication," *[University of Southern California] Daily Trojan*, February 9, 1967.

41. "Pacific Tide Seen Running for U.S. as Result of Firm Stand in Vietnam," *Long Beach [CA] Independent*, October 6, 1966.

42. Cecil Brown, *Comment* script, KCET TV, June 2, 1965, box 22, folder 1, Brown Papers.

43. "Pacific Tide Seen Running for U.S. as Result of Firm Stand in Vietnam."

44. Ester Langlois, letter to Brown, December 22, 1966; KCET TV, box 27, folder 4, Brown Papers.

45. John Marciano, "Walter Cronkite Opposed the Vietnam War Because It Was Unwinnable," *LA Progressive*, June 21, 2016, https://www.laprogressive.com/walter-cronkite-vietnam (accessed December 23, 2016).

46. *Ibid.*, "View from Taiwan: Chiang Sees Communists Crumbling," *Los Angeles Times*, September 3, 1968; and Heyamigoes, "Chiang Kai-Shek Had One Last Shot in 1968," *All Empires History Forum*, August 31, 2012, http://www.allempires.com/forum/forum_posts.asp?TID=32335 (accessed July 23, 2015).

47. Cecil Brown, "View from Taiwan: No. 2 Economic Miracle of Asia," *Los Angeles Times*, September 5, 1968, II: 5; and "Chiang Kai-Shek Had One Last Shot in 1968."

48. *Ibid., Comment* script, KCET TV, November 24, 1965, box 22, folder 8, Brown Papers.

49. Humphrey, "There's Bad News Tonight."

50. Cecil Brown, *Comment* script, KCET TV, February 28, 1966, box 22, folder 14, Brown Papers.

51. *Ibid.*, "A Courage Gap in Television News," *Pasadena [CA], Independent Star-News TV Week*, May 29, 1966.

52. *Ibid., Comment* script, KCET TV, May 17, 1966, box 22, folder 18, Brown Papers.

53. Kenneth Harwood, "Why Not?" *Pasadena [CA] Independent Star-News TV Week*, May 29, 1966.

54. Cecil Brown, cited in *Leader, School and Community*, Cal Poly Pomona newsletter, n.d., box 27, folder 22, Brown Papers.

55. "TV Must Analyze, Evaluate, Cal-Poly Pomona Lecturer Cecil Brown Says," *Montclair [CA] Tribune*, February 5, 1969.

56. Cecil Brown, letter to Olga Kaltenborn, June 25, 1965, box 26, folder 27, Brown Papers.

57. *Ibid., Comment* script, KCET TV, March 29, 1966, box 22, folder 18, Brown Papers; and Jane Lang McGrew, *History of Tobacco Regulation*, The National Commission on Marihuana and Drug Abuse, Schaffer Library of Drug Policy, http://www.druglibrary.org/Schaffer/LIBRARY/studies/nc/nc2b.htm (accessed July 23, 2015).

58. Alfred I. DuPont Awards Committee (presentation to Cecil Brown, Washington, DC, April 19, 1965); box 26, folder 28, Brown Papers.

59. Stan Metzler, "Faculty Told LBJ Suffers from Crisis of Communication," *[University of Southern California] Daily Trojan*, February 9, 1967.

Epilogue

1. Cecil Brown, quoted in Professor Ruth Harmer, Cal-Poly, letter to Dr. Nicholas Hardemann, Academic Senate, California State University and Colleges, Long Beach, CA, February 12, 1980; box 27, folder 21, Brown Papers.

2. "1970 Annual Review of Cecil Brown," n.d., Cal Poly Pomona, box 27, folder 5, Brown Papers.

3. Professor David L. Levering, comment at Cecil Brown Memorial Service, October 1987, Cal Poly Pomona.

4. Cecil Brown, Harmer letter.

5. *Ibid.*, letter to Ercole Graziadei.

6. Cecil Brown (speech, Society of Professional Journalists' meeting, Riverside, CA, May 1, 1974), box 25, folder 32, Brown Papers.

7. Harmer letter.
8. *Ibid.*
9. *Ibid.*
10. Cecil Brown, narrative to Teacher of the Year nominating committee, California Polytechnic State University, Pomona, 1974, box 27, folder 21, Brown Papers.
11. Professor Barbara Lingenfelter, Teacher Preparation Center, Cal Poly, Pomona, January 2, 1980; cited in Harmer nomination packet. Levering made his comment at Brown's Cal Poly Pomona memorial service, November 5, 1987.
12. Cecil Brown, letter to Martin Treese, Jr., Las Vegas, October 1, 1987, box 27, folder 17, Brown Papers.
13. Donald Pfluger, "Remarks at Cecil Brown Memorial Service," Cal Poly Pomona, November 7, 1987.
14. Scott Donaldson, "Media in Decline," *Sewanee Review* 104, no. 4 (1996): 674.
15. David Brooks, *Character* (New York: Random House, 2016), 56.
16. John Hohenberg, *Foreign Correspondent: The Great Reporters and Their Times* (New York: Columbia University Press, 1964), vii.
17. Steve Knoll, "Demise of the Radio Commentator: An Irreparable Loss to Broadcast Journalism," *Journal of Radio Studies* 6, no. 2 (1999): 356.
18. David Schoenbrun, "The Best of Barry Gray," WMCA Radio, New York, December 23, 1972; quoted in Knoll, "Demise of the Radio Commentator," 366.
19. The attributes are attributed to H.G. Wells. Cited in Louis L. Snyder and Richard B. Morris, *A Treasury of Great Reporting: Literature under Pressure* (New York: Simon & Schuster, 1962), xxv–xxiv.
20. Edward R. Murrow, "Wires and Lights in a Box" (speech, Radio Television News Directors Association Convention, Chicago, October 15, 1958), http://www.rtdna.org/content/edward_r_murrow_s_1958_wires_lights_in_a_box_speech (accessed December 17, 2015).
21. Os Guinness, "The Meaning of Truth," in *Belief: Readings on the Reason for Faith*, ed. Francis S. Collins (New York: Harper One, 2010), 69.
22. Juan Ramon Munoz-Torres, "Truth and Objectivity in Journalism: Anatomy of an Endless Misunderstanding," *Journalism Studies* 13, no. 4 (2012): 566, 576–580.
23. Bill Kovach and Tim Rosenstiel, "Principle One: Journalism's First Obligation is to Tell the Truth," *NiemanReport Special Issue 2001*, June 15, 2001, http://niemanreports.org/articles/journalisms-first-obligation-is-to-tell-the-truth/ (accessed February 4, 2017).
24. Jeffrey B. Abramson, "Four Criticisms of the Press," *Democracy and the Mass Media*, Judith Lichtenberg, ed. (Cambridge: Cambridge University Press, 1990), 264–265.
25. Chris Hedges, interviewed by Bill Moyers, "The Price for Truth in Journalism (Israel Gaza)," *Bill Moyers & Company*, November 12, 2012, https://www.youtube.com/watch?v=h9gFbrEmejw (accessed February 1, 2017).
26. Jeff Greenfield, "Before the Network Fall, review of *The Murrow Boys: Pioneers on the Front Lines of Broadcast Journalism*, by Stanley Cloud and Lynne Olson," *Time*, May 20, 1996, 73.
27. William Frayer, "Some Comments on Commentators," *Quarterly Review of the Michigan Alumnus: A Journal of University Perspectives* 51, no. 4 (1944): 8–18.

Bibliography

Manuscript and Archival Sources

Brown, Cecil. Correspondence, news scripts, diaries, photographs, audio recordings. Wisconsin Historical Society, Madison, WS.

Columbia Broadcasting System. Press releases and news scripts. CBS Network Archives, New York.

Loper, James. Papers. Library of American Broadcasting, Special Collections and University Archives. University of Maryland, College Park, MD.

Multiple Speakers, November 7, 1987, Cecil Brown Memorial Service, California State University, Pomona.

Murrow, Edward R. Papers. Digital Collections and Archives, Tufts University, Medford, MA.

Murrow, Edward R., and Janet Murrow. Papers. Archives and Special Collections, Mount Holyoke College, MA.

Muskie, Edmund S. Documentary. Edmund S. Muskie Archives and Special Collections Library, Bates College, Lewiston, ME. Collections, Mount Holyoke College, MA.

National Broadcasting Company. Press releases. NBC Network Archives, New York.

Recorded Sound Research Center. Audio recordings. Motion Picture, Broadcasting and Recorded Sound Division, Library of Congress. Washington, D.C.

WNYC. Audio recordings. WNYC radio archives, New York.

Internet Postings, Interviews and Recordings

"Army Talk, Orientation Fact Sheet #64, FASCISM!" Unites States War Department. Last modified March 24, 1945. Accessed June 10, 2015. http://fascism-archive.org/books/atofs-fascism.html.

"The BBC Story: The BBC at War—Censorship and Propaganda." Accessed August 15, 2013. http://www.bbc.co.uk/historyofthebbc/resources/bbcatwar/censor_prop.shtml.

Berkeley in the Sixties. Directed by Mark Kitchell. 1990. Alexandria, VA: POV Theatrical Films, Public Broadcasting Service, 2002. DVD.

Brown, Martha. Interview by Adelaide Hawley. "Woman's Page of the Air." CBS Radio, October 22, 1942.

———. Phone interviews by author. Digital recordings. August 16 and 23, 2013, and March 7 and 14, 2014.

———. Transcript of interview by John Moore. Westwood, CA, April 19, 2013.

Cerf, Bennett. Interview by Robin Hawkins. *Interviews with Notable New Yorkers*. Columbia University Libraries, Oral History Research Office, New York, September 20, 1968. Accessed June 16, 2014. http://www.columbia.edu/cu/lweb/digital/collections/nny/cerfb/introduction.html.

"Churchill, Roosevelt Hold War Conference in Quebec City." Canadian Broadcasting Corporation, Digital Archives. Accessed December 18, 2014. http://www.cbc.ca/archives/categories/society/celebrations/quebec-city-400-years-of-history/war-conference-at-quebec.html#tabs-2.

Federal Bureau of Investigation. "FBI Monograph-Soviet Defectors, a Study of Past Defectors from Official Soviet Establishments Outside the USSR." January 1955. Accessed May 14, 2015. http://archive.org/stream/foia_FBI_MONOGRAPH-Soviet_Defectors/FBI_MONOGRAPH-Soviet_Defectors_djvu.txt.

"Global Nonviolent Global Database: Japanese Protest Security Treaty with U.S. and Unseat Prime Minister, 1959–1960." Accessed November 15, 2014. http://nvdatabase.swarthmore.edu/content/japanese-protest-security-treaty-us-and-unseat-prime-minister-1959-1960.

Hedges, Chris. Interview by Bill Moyers. "The Price for Truth in Journalism (Israel Gaza)." *Bill Moyers & Company*, Public Broadcasting Service, November 12, 2012. Accessed February 1, 2017. https://www.youtube.com/watch?v=h9gFbrEmejw.

The Jewish Americans: Migration: The Diaspora in America. Directed by David Grubin. 2013. Washington, D.C.: JTN Productions and WETA TV. DVD.

Johannessen, Kenneth I. "Mutual Broadcasting System: Ed Kobak Gets a Network." Last modified 2009. Accessed September 28, 2015. http://misterk60.com/Kobak.html.

"Joint Statement by Prime Minister Churchill and President Roosevelt." August 24, 1943. Accessed March 11, 2013. http://avalon.law.yale.edu/20th_century/decade06.asp.

Kates, James. "Kicking Nixon: Howard K. Smith and the Commentator's Imperative." *ARNet*. Accessed January 18, 2013. http://www.americansc.org.uk/Online/Nixon.html.

KCET TV, and National Education Television. "Radical Right in California: Extremism, Communism." Producers: Cecil Brown and Wesley Willoughby. Edmund S. Muskie Papers, Edmund S. Muskie Archives and Special Collections Library, Bates College, ID: MC105.15.

Kovach, Bill, and Tim Rosenstiel. "Principle One: Journalism's First Obligation Is to Tell the Truth." Nieman Report Special Issue, June 15, 2001. Assessed February 1, 2017. http://niemanreports.org/articles/journalisms-first-obligation-is-to-tell-the-truth/.

Marciano, John. "Walter Cronkite Opposed the Vietnam War Because It Was Unwinnable." *LA Progressive*, June 21, 2016. Accessed December 23, 2016. https://www.laprogressive.com/walter-cronkite-vietnam.

Matthews, Alan. "The Sinking of the *Prince of Wales* and *HMS Repulse: A Series of Personal Accounts Compiled from Crewmembers*." Accessed March 3, 2014. http://microworks.net/pacific/personal/pow_repulse.htm.

McGrew, Jane L. "History of Tobacco Regulation." The National Commission on Marihuana and Drug Abuse. Schaffer Library of Drug Policy. Accessed July 23, 2015. http://www.druglibrary.org/Schaffer/LIBRARY/studies/nc/nc2b.htm.

Moore, John, Jr. Email to author, April 24, 2013.

Morehouse, Lisa. "Grapes of Wrath: The Forgotten Filipinos Who Led a Farmworker Revolution." *Weekend Edition*, National Public Radio, September 19, 2015. Accessed January 24, 2016.

Murrow, Edward R. "Wires and Lights in a Box." Speech to the Radio Television News Directors Association Convention, Chicago, October 15, 1958. Accessed December 17, 2015. http://www.rtdna.org/content/edward_r_murrow_s_1958_wires_lights_in_a_box_speech.

The National Educational Television Center. Accessed July 20, 2015. http://www.museum.tv/eotv/nationaleduc.htm.

National Public Radio Staff. Interview with Anthony Doerr, author of *All the Light We Cannot See*. May 25, 2014. Accessed May 26, 2014. http://www.npr.org/2014/05/25/314566791/world-war-ii-in-a-new-light-empathy-found-in-surprising-places.

Pew Research Center. "What Americans Know: 1989–2007." Accessed August 12, 2015. http://www.people-press.org/2007/04/15/public-knowledge-of-current-affairs-little-changed-by-news-and-information-revolutions/April 15, 2007.

"Population History of Los Angeles from 1890–1990." Accessed November 6, 2015. http://physics.bu.edu/~redner/projects/population/cities/la.html.

"Radio News Broadcasting and CBS in the Twenties and Thirties." The Edward R. Murrow Papers, Tufts University. Accessed May 3, 2014. https://wikis.uit.tufts.edu/confluence/display/MurrowCollection/Home.

Reporting America at War: Episode 1: The Romance of War. Directed by Steven Ives Washington, D.C.: Insignia Films and WETA TV, 2003, Public Broadcasting Service, DVD.

Roosevelt, Franklin Delano. "FDR and the Four Freedoms Speech." January 6, 1941. Franklin Delano Roosevelt Presidential Library and Museum. Accessed May 12, 2015. http://www.fdrlibrary.marist.edu/fourfreedoms.

Sielemann, Jurgen. "Eastern European Jewish Emigration via the Port of Hamburg: 1890–1914." Accessed August 31, 2013. http://

kehilalinks.jewishgen.org/suchostaw/The TailorShop/Eastern_European_Jewish_ Emigration_Article.html.

Smitha, Frank E. "Roosevelt and Approaching War: The Economy, Politics and Questions of War, 1937–38." *Macrohistory and World Timeline.* Accessed March 19, 2014. http://www.fsmitha.com/h2/ch22.htm.

Soldiers Without Swords: The Black Press. Director Stanley Nelson, Jr., 1999. A Half Nelson Production, Chicago: WTTW TV, Public Broadcasting Service. DVD.

Spira-Savett, Rabbi Jonathan. "7 Hebrew Words and Phrases Every Activist Should Know." *The Jewish Federation of North America.* Last modified 2013. Accessed November 15, 2014. http://www.jewishfederations.org/page.aspx?id=14231.

Truman, Harry S. "The President's Special Conference with the Association of Radio News Analysts." May 13, 1947. *Public Papers of the Presidents of the United States: Harry S. Truman, 1945–1953.* Washington, D.C. Assessed June 4, 2015. http://trumanlibrary.org/publicpapers/viewpapers.php?pid=2155.

U.S. Bureau of the Census. *1910 U.S. Census.* Accessed October 19, 2013. http://search.ancestry.com/search/db.aspx?dbid=7884&s_kwcid=+1910++census&o xid=21892&o_lid=21892&o_sch=Search.

"What American Commentators Say: Daily Review of the Comments and Opinions of Leading News Analysts." Audio recording. Martin Agronsky, Raymond Gram Swing and Cecil Brown. Washington, D.C.: Office of War Information, 1945. Library of Congress, Washington, D.C. LC # 2003645894, RGA 0572 PNO 07, OWI RWD, file: N7560J; LC # 2003645979, RGA 0582, OWI RWD 3274 B3 RGA 0572 PNO 07, OWI RWD, file: N7560J, disk: 81780; LC # 2003645979, RGS 0582 PNO 07, OWI RWD 3274 B3, file: Q389E, disk 1114082; LC # 2003645894 RGS 0580 PNO 06, OWI RWD 3272 B2, file T10E, disk: 4093.

Wright, George. "The Umbrellas of Liberalism: The Impact of Ideology on Post-World War II U.S." Accessed December 2, 2015. http://www.csuchico.edu/~gwright/index.htm.

Books

Abramson, Jeffrey B. "Four Criticisms of the Press," in *Democracy and the Mass Media*, Judith Lichtenberg, ed. Cambridge: Cambridge University Press, 1990.

Addy, Stuart, and Dieter Flectk. *The Handbook of the Law of Visiting Forces.* New York: Oxford University Press, 2001.

Allen, Craig. *Eisenhower and The Mass Media: Peace, Prosperity, & Prime-Time TV.* Chapel Hill: University of North Carolina Press, 1993.

Alteras, Isaac. *Eisenhower and Israel: U.S.-Israeli Relations, 1953–1960.* Gainesville: University Press of Florida, 1993.

Alwood, Edward. *Dark Days in the Newsroom.* Philadelphia: Temple University Press, 2007.

American Press. *A Nation's Fight for Survival: The 1941 Revolution and War in Yugoslavia as Reported by the American Press.* London: Royal Yugoslav Embassy, 1944.

Ash, Bernard. *Someone Had Blundered: The Story of the "Repulse" and the "Prince of Wales."* New York: Doubleday & Company, 1961.

Balderrama, Francisco, and Raymond Rodriguez. *Decade of Betrayal: Mexican Repatriation in the 1930s.* Albuquerque: University of New Mexico Press, 2006.

Barnouw, Erik. *The Golden Web: A History of Broadcasting in the United States, Vol. II—1933 to 1953.* New York: Oxford University Press, 1968.

Benjamin, Robert S. *Eye Witness: By Members of the Overseas Press Club of America.* New York: Alliance Book Corporation, 1940.

Benjamin, Robert S. *The Inside Story: By Members of the Overseas Press Club of America.* New York: Prentice Hall, 1940.

Benson, Robert L. *The Venona Story.* Fort George G. Meade, MD: National Security Agency Center for Cryptologic History, 2001.

Bernstein, Mark, and Alex Lubertozzi. *World War II on the Air: Edward R. Murrow and the Broadcasts That Riveted a Nation.* Naperville, IL: Sourcebooks, 2003.

Bliss, Edward, Jr. *Now the News.* New York: Columbia University Press, 1991.

Blum, John, William McFeely, Edmund Morgan, Arthur Schlesinger, Jr., Kenneth Stampp, and C. Vann Woodward. *The National Experience: A History of the United States*, 6th ed. New York: Harcourt Brace Jovanovich, 1985.

Bowen, Croswell. *Back from Tobruk.* New York: Potomac Books, 2013.

Braddon, Russell. *The Naked Island.* Leicester: Charnwood Edition, 1982.

Brendon, Piers. *The Decline and Fall of the British Empire, 1781–1997.* New York: Alfred A. Knopf, 2008.

Bibliography

Brooks, David. *The Road to Character*. New York: Random House, 2016.

Brown, Cecil. *Suez to Singapore*. Box 30, folder 1, Cecil Brown Papers, Wisconsin Historical Society; and New York: Random House, 1942.

Brown, Robert J. *Manipulating the Ether: The Power of Broadcast Radio in Thirties America*. Jefferson, NC: McFarland, 1998.

Carleton, Don, and Walter Cronkite. *Conversations with Cronkite*. Austin: Center for American History, 2010.

Casey, Steven. *Cautious Crusade*. New York: Oxford University Press, 2001.

C.E. Hooper, Inc. *Uniform Network Competition: Comprehensive Hooperatings*. New York: C.E. Hooper, Inc., 1946.

Ceplair, Larry, and Steven Englund. *The Inquisition in Hollywood: Politics in the Film Community, 1930–1960*. Urbana: University of Illinois Press, 2003.

Cerf, Bennett. *At Random: The Reminiscences of Bennett Cerf*. New York: Random House, 1977.

Cerf, Bennett, Donald Klopfer, and Robert D. Loomis. *Dear Donald, Dear Bennett: The Wartime Correspondence of Bennett Cerf and Donald Klopfer*. New York: Random House, 2002.

Charnley, Mitchell. *News by Radio*. New York: Macmillan, 1948.

Clark, Suzanne. *Cold Warriors: Manliness on Trial in the Rhetoric of the West*. Carbondale: Southern Illinois University Press, 2000

Cloud, Stanley, and Lynne Olson. *The Murrow Boys: Pioneers on the Front Lines of Broadcast Journalism*. New York: Houghton Mifflin, 1997.

Cogley, John. *Report on Blacklisting: II: Radio-Television*. New York: The Fund for the Republic, Inc., 1956.

Commission on Freedom of the Press. *A Free and Responsible Press; a General Report on Mass Communication: Newspapers, Radio, Motion Pictures, Magazines, and Books Free and Responsible Press*. Chicago: University of Chicago Press, 1947.

Cooke, John B. *Reporting the War: Freedom of the Press from the American Revolution to the War on Terrorism*. New York: Palgrave Macmillan, 2007.

Cox, Jim. *American Radio Networks: A History*. Jefferson, NC: McFarland, 2009.

DeFleur, Melvin L., and Margaret H. DeFleur. *Mass Communication Theories: Explaining Origins, Processes and Effects*. New York: Routledge, 2010.

Desmond, Robert W., and Harold J. Laski. *The Press and World Affairs*. New York: D. Appleton-Century, 1937.

_____. *Tides of War: World News Reporting 1931–1945*. Iowa City: University of Iowa Press, 1984.

Diner, Hasia. *The Jews of the United States. 1654 to 2000*. Berkeley: University of California Press, 2006.

Dixon, Norman. *On the Psychology of Military Incompetence*. London: Pimlico, 1994.

Dollinger, Marc. *Quest for Inclusion*. Princeton: Princeton University Press, 2000.

Douglas, Susan. *Listening in: Radio and the American Imagination*. Minneapolis: University of Minnesota Press, 1999.

Dunn, William. *Pacific Microphone*. College Station: Texas A&M Press, 1988.

The Echoes. Warren, OH: Warren High School Yearbook, 1925.

Editors. *American Heroes: Edward R. Murrow*. Hackensack: Salem Press.

Fang, Irving E. *Those Radio Commentators*. Ames: Iowa State University Press, 1977.

Fones-Wolf, Elizabeth. *Selling Free Enterprise: The Business Assault on Labor and Liberalism, 1945–1960*. Urbana: University of Illinois Press, 1994.

Frum, David. *How We Got Here: The '70s*. New York: Basic Books, 2000, 27.

Galbraith, John K. *The Affluent Society: The Economics of the Age of Opulence-A Literate and Expert Revision of the Basic Ideas*. New York: Houghton Mifflin, 1958.

Garay, Ronald, and Gordon McLendon. *The Maverick of Radio*. Westport, CT: Greenwood Press, 1992.

Gay, Timothy M. *Assignment to Hell: The War Against Nazi Germany with Correspondents Walter Cronkite, Andy Rooney, A. J. Liebling, Homer Bigart, and Hal Boyle*. New York: Penguin Group, 2012.

Gonzales, Juan, and Joseph Torres. *News for All the People: The Epic Story of Race and the American Media*. New York: Verso Books, 2011.

Gould, James W. *The U.S. and Malaysia*. Boston: Harvard University Press, 1969.

Guinness, Os. "Differences Make a Difference" and "The Meaning of Truth," in *Belief: Reading on the Reason for Faith*, edited by Francis Collins. New York: Harper One, 2010.

Gunther, John. *Inside Asia: 1942 War Edition*. New York: Harper & Brothers, 1942.

Hack, Karl, and Kevin Blackburn. *Did Singapore Have to Fall? Churchill and the Impregnable Fortress*. New York: Routledge Curzon, 2004.

Halberstam, David. *The Powers That Be*. New York: Alfred A. Knopf, 1979.

Hallin, Daniel C., and Robert Giles. "Presses and Democracies," in *Institutions of American Democracy: The Press*, edited by Geneva Overholser and Kathleen Hall Jamieson. New York: Oxford University Press, 2005.

Hamilton, John M. *Journalism's Roving Eye: A History of American Foreign Reporting*. Baton Rouge: Louisiana State University Press, 2009.

Harbutt, Fraser, J. *The Cold War Era*. New York: Wiley-Blackwell, 2002.

Hepner, Arthur W., ed. *The Best of Emphasis: Opinions and Insights by the World-Wide NBC News Staff*. Westminster, MD: The Newman Press, 1962.

Higham, John. *Strangers in the Land: Patterns of American Nativism, 1860–1925*. New Brunswick: Rutgers University Press, 2002.

Hilmes, Michele, and Jason Loviglio. *Radio Reader: Essays in the Cultural History of Radio*. New York: Routledge, 2001.

Hohenberg, John. *Foreign Correspondence: The Great Reporters and Their Times*. New York: Columbia University Press, 1964.

Horton, Casey. *We Came to America: The Jews*. New York: Crabtree Publishers, 2000.

Hosley, David H. *As Good as Any: Foreign Correspondence on American Radio, 1930–1940*. Westport, CT: Greenwood Press, 1984.

Hyde, Stuart, and Dina A. Ibrahim. *Television and Radio Announcing*, 12th ed. New York: Pearson, 2013.

Hynes, Samuel, L. *Reporting World War II: American Journalism, 1938–1946*. Washington, D.C.: Library of Congress, 1995.

Institute for Education by Radio. *Education on the Air Yearbook*. Columbus: Ohio State University, 1942.

International Press Institute. *The Flow of News: A Study of Knowledge of International Affairs*. New York: Arno Press, 1972.

Jefferson, Thomas. *Writings: Autobiography/Notes on the State of Virginia/Public & Private Papers/Addresses/Letters*, edited by Merrill D. Peterson. Washington, D.C.: Library of America, 1984.

Johanningmeier, Erwin J. *Equality of Educational Opportunity and Knowledgeable Human Capital*. Scottsdale: Information Age, 2009.

Jones, Howard. *Death of a Generation: How the Assassinations of Diem and JFK Prolonged the Vietnam War*. New York: Oxford University Press, 2003.

Kahn, Alfred E. *Treason in Congress: The Record of the House Un-American Activities Committee*. New York: Progressive Citizens of America, 1948.

Kallen, Stuart A. *The War at Home*. San Diego: Lucent Books, 2000.

Kaltenborn, Hans V. *Fifty Fabulous Years*. New York: Putnam, 1950.

Kendrick, Alexander. *Prime Time: The Life of Edward R. Murrow*. New York: Little, Brown, 1969.

King, Charles A. *Ottaway Newspapers: The First 50 Years*. Campbell Hall, NY: Ottaway Newspapers, Inc., 1986.

Klehr, Harvey. *The Heyday of American Communism: The Depression Decade*. New York: Basic Books, 1984.

Knightley, Phillip. *The First Casualty: From the Crimea to Vietnam: The War Correspondent as Hero, Propagandist, and Myth Maker*. New York: Harcourt Brace Jovanovich, 1975.

Lazarsfeld, Paul F., and Harry Field. *The People Look at Radio: Report on a Survey Conducted by The National Opinion Research Center*. Chapel Hill: University of North Carolina Press, 1946.

Lazarsfeld, Paul F., Patricia L. Kendall, and Clyde Hart. *Radio Listening in American: The People Look at Radio—Again*. New York: Prentice Hall, 1948.

Lippman, Walter. *Public Opinion*. New York: Harcourt, Brace, 1922.

Lepoer, Barbara Leitch, ed. *World War II, 1941–45: A Country Study: Singapore*. Washington, D.C.: National Archives, Federal Research Division, para. 3, 1991. Accessed March 22, 2014. http://lcweb2.loc.gov/cgibin/query/r?frd/cstdy:@field(DOCID+sg0025).

Martin, John, B. *Adlai Stevenson and the World*. Garden City, NY: Doubleday, 1977.

Mass Communication Research Center, Brandeis University, Waltham, MA, and the National Center for School and College Television, Bloomington, IN. *One Week of Educational Television, April 17–23, 1966*. Waltham, MA, Brandeis University, 1966.

Matthews, Alan. *Sailors' Tales*. Llangollen, Wales: Small Print, 1997.

———. "The Sinking of the *Prince of Wales* and *HMS Repulse*," accessed December 18, 2013, www.forcez-survivors.org.uk/sinking2.html.

Matthews, Joseph. *Reporting the War*. Westport, CT: Greenwood Press, 1957.

Macdonald, J. Fred. *Don't Touch That Dial: Radio Programming in American Life, 1920–1960*. Chicago: Nelson-Hall, 1980.

_____. *Television and the Red Menace: The Video Road to Vietnam*. New York: Praeger, 1985.

Martin, James J. *Revisionist Viewpoints: Essays in a Dissident Historical Tradition*. Colorado Springs: Ralph Myles, 1971.

McCullough, David. *Truman*. New York: Simon & Schuster, 1992.

McNamara, John. *Extra! U.S. War Correspondents in Action*. Boston: Houghton Mifflin, 1945.

Middlebrook, Martin, and Patrick Mahoney. *Battleship: The Sinking of the Prince of Wales and the Repulse*. New York: Charles Scribner & Sons, 1979.

Midgley, Ned. *The Advertising and Business Side of Radio*. New York: Prentice Hall, 1948.

Miller, Donald L. *D-Days in the Pacific*. New York: Simon & Schuster, 2008.

Milton, John. *Areopagitica and of Education: With Autobiographical Passages from Other Prose Works*. 1644. Reprint, Wheeling, IL: Harlan Davidson, Inc., 1987.

Moore, Michaela H. *Know Your Enemy: The American Debate on Nazism, 1933–1945*. Cambridge: Cambridge University Press, 2010.

Mayer, Michael. *The Eisenhower Years*. New York: Infobase, 2010.

Morrison, Ian. *The War Against Japan*. London: Faber and Faber, 1943.

Murray, Jacqui. *Watching the Sun Rise: Australian Reporting of Japan, 1931 to the Fall of Singapore*. New York: Lexington Books, 2004.

Nachman, Gerald. *Raised on Radio*. Berkeley: University of California Press, 2000.

NBC News. *Memo to JFK: From NBC News*. New York: G.P. Putnam and Sons, 1961.

Nichols, David, and Studs Terkel. *Ernie's War: The Best of Ernie Pyle's World War II Dispatches*. New York: Random House, 1986.

Nichols, Kenneth, D. *The Road to Trinity*. New York: Morrow, 1987.

Nimmo, Dan, and Chevelle Newsome. *Political Commentators in the United States in the 20th Century: A Bio-Critical Sourcebook*. Westport, CT: Greenwood Press, 1997.

Perry, Marvin, and Frederick Schweitzer. *Anti-Semitism: Myth and Hate from Antiquity to the Present*. New York: Palgrave Macmillan, 2005.

Roth, Stephen. *Anti-Semitism Worldwide*. Lincoln: University of Nebraska Press. 2002.

Sachar, Howard M. *A History of Jews in America*. New York: Alfred A. Knopf, 1992.

Sansom, Katharine. *Sir George Sansom and Japan: A Memoir*. Tallahassee: Diplomatic PR Research, 1972.

Savage, Barbara D. *Broadcasting Freedom: Radio, War, and the Politics of Race 1938–1948*. Chapel Hill: University of North Carolina Press, 1999.

Schlesinger, Arthur M., Jr. *A Thousand Days: John F. Kennedy in the White House*. New York: Houghton Mifflin, 1965.

Schroth, Raymond A. *The American Journey of Eric Sevareid*. South Royalton, VT: Steerforth Press, 1995.

Sevareid, Eric. *Not So Wild a Dream*. New York: Alfred A. Knopf, 1946.

Siepmann, Charles A. *Radio's Second Chance*. Boston: Little, Brown, 1946.

Sloan, Wm. David, ed. *The Media in America: A History*, 9th ed. Northport, AL: Vision Press, 2014.

Smith, R. Franklin. *Edward R. Murrow: The War Years*. Kalamazoo: New Issues Press, 1978.

Smith, Sally B. *In All His Glory: The Life of William Paley, the Legendary Tycoon and His Brilliant Circle*. New York: Simon & Schuster, 1990.

Snyder, Louis L., and Richard B. Morris. *A Treasury of Great Reporting: Literature Under Pressure: From the Sixteenth Century to Our Own Time*. New York: Simon & Schuster, 1962.

Sperber, Ann M. *Murrow: His Life and Times*. New York: Freundlich Books, 1986.

Swinson, Arthur. *Defeat in Malaya: The Fall of Singapore*. New York: Ballantine Books, 1970.

Thompson, Peter. *The Battle for Singapore: The True Story of the Greatest Catastrophe of World War Two*. London: Portrait Books, 2005.

Toland, John. *But Not in Shame: The Six Months after Pearl Harbor*. New York: Random House, 1961.

Toro, Amy L. "Fairness Doctrine (Historical Development and Update)." Vol. 3 of *Encyclopedia of the American Constitution*, 2d ed., edited by Leonard W. Levy and Kenneth L. Karst. Detroit: Macmillan Reference, 2000.

Truman, Harry S. *Memoires: Vol. II: Years of Trial and Hope*. Garden City, NY: Doubleday & Company, 1956.

Van Der Kiste, John. *The Romanovs: 1818–1959*. Sutton: Stroud, 2003.

Vatter, Harold G. *The U.S. Economy in World War II*. New York: Columbia University Press, 1985.

Volodarsky, Boris. *Stalin's Agent: The Life and Death of Alexander Orlov.* New York: Oxford University Press, 2015.
Warren, Donald. *Radio Priest: Charles Coughlin, the Father of Hate Radio.* New York: Free Press, 1996.
Weller, George, and Anthony Weller. *Weller's War: A Legendary Foreign Correspondent's Sage of World War II on Five Continents.* New York: Three Rivers Press, 2009.
White, Graham J. *F.D.R. and the Press.* Chicago: University of Chicago Press, 1979.
White, Llewellyn. *The American Radio: A Report on the Broadcasting Industry in the United States from the Commission on Freedom of the Press.* Chicago: University of Chicago Press, 1948.
White, Paul. *News on the Air.* New York: Harcourt, Brace, 1947.
Whitehouse, Arch. *The Years of the War Birds.* Garden City, NY: Doubleday & Company, 1960.
Wilkie, Wendell. *One World.* Melbourne: Cassell, 1943.
Wray, Fay. *On the Other Hand: A Life Story.* New York: St. Martin's Press, 1989.

Newspaper Articles

"Ace Correspondent's Fine Letter." *Charleville [Brisbane] Times,* August 14, 1942.
Adams, Frank W. "Cecil Brown Narrates the History Which He Saw Made." *New York Times,* October 25, 1942.
August, Harry. "From Pittsburgh to War Reporting." *Pittsburgh Press,* May 7, 1941.
"Australians Termed Lazy, But Superb Fighting Men." *[Brisbane] Sunday Mail,* June 7, 1942.
Baldwin, Hanson W. "Defeat at Singapore." *New York Times,* February 12, 1942, p. 4.
"Book Reviews." *New York Times,* January 23, 1944.
"Breach of Promise." *[Newark, NJ] Star-Ledger,* September 25, 1943.
"Brown Asserts U.S. at War with Russia." *Ellensburg [WA] Daily Record,* October 11, 1950.
Brown, Cecil. "All's Well That Ends Well, River Traveler's Quote." *Warren [OH] Tribune-Chronicle,* September 1, 1926.
——. "Boys Run into Storm and Lose Their Pup Tent." *Warren Tribune-Chronicle,* August 20, 1926.
——. "Brooklyn Bulldog." *Pittsburgh Press,* January 19, 1935.
——. "Canoe Boys See Odd River Sights." *Warren Tribune-Chronicle,* August 7, 1926.
——. "Canoeing Down the Ohio: Warren Boys Off to Start of Planned 600 Mile Trip." *Warren Tribune-Chronicle,* August 13, 1926.
——. "CCC Invades Somerset County." *Pittsburgh Press,* May 11, 1936.
——. "A Courage Gap in Television News." *Pasadena [CA] Independent Star-News TV Week,* May 29, 1966.
——. "A Designing Beauty." *New Outlook,* August 1954.
——. "Do You Know Why You're Fighting." *Colliers,* December 11, 1943.
——. "Fear Dominates Russian Citizens Today." *Youngstown Vindicator,* March 2, 1930.
——. "Fights, Illusions and More Briny Thrills." *Youngstown Vindicator,* January 19, 1930.
——. "Good-by Russia! You Deserve a Better Fate." *Youngstown Vindicator,* March 16, 1930.
——. "Into the Hellespont, On to Grim Russia." *Youngstown Vindicator,* February 2, 1930.
——. "A Land of Peasant Kings and Bread Lines." *Youngstown Vindicator,* March 9, 1930.
——. "Mother of Dead Butler Boy Forgives Accused Killers." *Pittsburgh Press,* January 4, 1935.
——. "A Noteworthy Broadcast." *[Columbus] Ohio Jewish Chronicle,* January 12, 1945.
——. "Our Last Port of Call—Gay, Gaudy Morocco." *Youngstown Vindicator,* March 30, 1930.
——. "Pittsburgh Hosts Hobo Convention." *Pittsburgh Press,* April 21, 1935.
——. "Report on America." *[Zanesville, OH] Times Recorder,* August 14, 1943.
——. "Scorching Sun Hard on Warren Adventurers." *Warren Tribune-Chronicle,* August 14, 1926.
——. "Speaking of Climate—We'll Take Morocco." *Youngstown Vindicator,* March 23, 1930.
——. "The *Vindicator* Adventure Boys, Cecil and Eugene Brown, of Warren, Are Off For New Thrills in the Forbidden Russia." *Youngstown Vindicator,* January 12, 1930.
——. "Warren Boys Reach Russia." *Youngstown Vindicator,* November 2, 1929.
——. "Warren Lads Sail as 'Stowaways' on Rio Cruise." *Youngstown Vindicator,* October 31, 1928.
——. "We Look at Daring Experiment." *Youngstown Vindicator,* February 9, 1930.

_____. "View from Taiwan: Chiang Sees Communists Crumbling." *Los Angeles Times*, September 3, 1968.

_____. "View from Taiwan: No. 2 Economic Miracle of Asia." *Los Angeles Times*, September 5, 1968.

_____. "A Youngstown Yankee in the Soviet's Fort." *Youngstown Vindicator*, February 16, 1930.

"Brown Classified 4F." *Ohio Jewish Chronicle*, May 22, 1942.

Brown, Eugene. "About Town." *Oneonta [NY] Star*, July 18, 1949.

_____. "Dancing is for Her." *Oneonta Star*, August 6, 1964.

_____. "His All-Wool Humble Jacket." *Oneonta Star*, December 4, 1971.

_____. "U.S. Must Prepare for More Rigorous Living, Cecil Brown Says on Visit to Oneonta." *Oneonta Star*, December 26, 1950.

"CBS Appeals Brown Suspension." *New York Herald Tribune*, January 13, 1942.

"CBS Man Sees 7 to 10-Year Job Before Japs Whipped." *Louisville Times*, July 24, 1943.

"Cecil Brown, Famous Correspondent, Visits Williamsburg Restoration." *[College of William and Mary] Flat Hat*, April 28, 1942.

"Cecil Brown Given Degree by College." *San Antonio Light*, May 3, 1943.

"Cecil Brown Here Sunday." *Southwestern Jewish Press*, March 6, 1953.

"Cecil Brown, News Analyst, Appears Here." *[Westport, CT] Herald News*, April 8, 1951.

"Cecil Brown of CBS Wins Award for 'Best Reporting of the News.'" *Christian Science Monitor*, April 11, 1942.

"Cecil Brown to Lecture Tonight at Local School." *Spartanburg [SC] Herald-Tribune*, April 23, 1942.

"Cecil Brown to Speak Here." *Ohio Jewish Chronicle*, May 22, 1942.

"Cecil Brown to Speak Thursday." *[State College, PA} Daily Collegian*, May 1, 1951.

"Cecil Brown Warns Against Efforts to Divide Allies." *Lewiston [ME] Daily Sun*, Oct. 6, 1944.

"Cecil Brown Will Speak at Giant Rally." *[Pittsburgh, PA] American Jewish Outlook*, January 16, 1951.

Cerf, Bennett. "Try and Stop Me." *Marin [County, CA] Independent Journal*, January 14, 1952.

Chamberlain, John. "Review of *Suez to Singapore*, by Cecil Brown." *New York Times*, October 22, 1942.

Colby, Frank. "Take My Word." *Ogden [UT] Standard-Examiner*, July 4, 1946.

Crowther, Bosley. "Review of *Mission to Moscow*." *New York Times*, April 30, 1943.

Deming, Walt. "Behind the Mike." *Oneonta Star*, November 18, 1949.

"Editorial." *Singapore [Malaya] Strait-Times*, September 11, 1941.

Fiset, Bill. "About Television: An Era of Unlimited Possibilities." *Oakland [CA] Tribune*, January 19, 1962.

Foster, Bob. "Bob Foster on Television: Review of NBC's "Fast East: Clear Danger." *San Mateo Times*, September 20, 1958.

Gallagher, O'Dowd. "American Journalist Banned." *[London] Daily Express*, January 15, 1942.

Gannett, Lewis. "Review of *Suez to Singapore*, by Cecil Brown." *New York Herald Tribune*, October 22, 1942.

Goldstein, Richard. "Howard K. Smith, Broadcast Newsman, Dies at 87." *International New York Times*, February 18, 2002.

Gould, Jack. "Television Review: Cecil Brown Presents Weekday News Show." *New York Times*, July 11, 1956.

Hansen, Harry. "Writers Divided on Question of Building Up More Hatred." *Chicago Tribune*, November 8, 1942.

Harwood, Kenneth. "Why Not?" *Pasadena [CA] Independent Star-News TV Week*. May 29, 1966.

"Hillel Players Have Triumph." *[Columbus] Ohio Jewish Chronicle*, May 3, 1929.

"House Hears of Threat to Free Speech." *Stars and Stripes*, October 27, 1945.

Humphrey, Hal. "There's Bad News Tonight." *Los Angeles Times*, April 8, 1965.

Hutchens, John K. "The Columbia Network Tells Its Analysts to Keep Their Opinions to Themselves." *New York Times*, September 26, 1943.

Kahn, Jeffrey. "Ronald Reagan Launched Political Career Using the Berkeley Campus as a Target." *UCBerkeleyNews*, June 8, 2004.

Lyons, Leonard. "Broadway Medley." *[San Mateo] Times and Daily News Leader*. March 19, 1943.

_____. "The Lyon's Den." *Pittsburgh Post-Gazette*, April 21, 1944.

_____. "Screenwriter Demands More Service Than Ex-Empress." *St. Petersburg Times*, November 28, 1948.

"Kaltenborn Dissents." *New York Times*, September 15, 1943.

Maxwell, Elsa. "Party-Line: Gag-Buster-Brown." *Pittsburgh Post-Gazette*, November 25, 1943.

McDaniel, C. Yates. "Last Foreign Correspondent to Leave Sees Defenders Fighting in a

Hell Without the Protection of Aircraft." *New York Times,* February 12, 1942.
Mercer, Charles. "NBC Correspondents Get Together for Bull Session." *Ocala Star-Banner,* October 20, 1958.
Metzler, Stan. "Faculty Told LBJ Suffers from Crisis of Communication." *[University of Southern California] Daily Trojan,* February 9, 1967.
"Naval Officer Tells of Cecil Brown's First Sea Trip." *Galveston News,* December 5, 1943.
"1944 Army Statistics." *Yank,* September 17, 1944.
"Noted Author to Speak for Jewish Appeal." *Massena [NY] Observer,* April 30, 1951.
"Obituary: Cecil Brown, Broadcaster for Networks." *Pittsburgh Post-Gazette,* October 29, 1987.
Osborne, Kevin. "Cover Story: The Light Dims." *Cincinnati City Beat,* February 21, 2007.
"Pacific Tide Seen Running for U.S. as Result of Firm Stand in Vietnam." *Long Beach Independent,* October 6, 1966.
"Punishment for Commentators." *Charlotte [NC] News,* November 9, 1945.
"Radio's Spring Honors List. *New York Times,* April 12, 1942.
"Review: Cecil Brown and the News on WABC TV." *New York Times,* July 11, 1956.
"Review of *Suez to Singapore,* by Cecil Brown." *Boston Globe,* October 28, 1942.
Roosevelt, Eleanor. "My Day." March 30, 1943. Accessed October 19, 2013. www.gwu.edu/~erpapers/myday.
"Scouts Bike to Erie." *[Beaver, PA] Daily Times,* August 25, 1922.
Shepard, Richard. "Just News, No Antics." *New York Times,* July 22, 1956.
Shinnick, William. "Cecil Brown's Clashes with Censors." *Chicago Sunday Tribune,* November 8, 1942.
"State Irked by Apathy Charges of Cecil Brown." *[Warsaw, IN] Daily Times,* May 27, 1942.
Stein, Jeannine. "R.S.V.P.: Black-Tie Gala Helps KCET Celebrate 25 Years on the Air." *Los Angeles Times,* June 16, 1989.
Stone, Isaac. "Review of *Suez to Singapore,* by Cecil Brown." *Washington Post,* October 25, 1942.
Taliaferro, Walt. "News Commentator Lauds Independence in Broadcasts." *Los Angeles Daily News,* January 19, 1949.
"Teacher of Brown Resigns in Massillon." *Youngstown Vindicator,* July 7, 1942.
Thompson, Dorothy. "Is Thinking Dangerous?" *Hartford [CT] Times,* September 27, 1943.
"Time at Hand for Supreme Effort." *[Mansfield, OH] News-Journal,* April 4, 1942.
"Tragic Singapore Fiasco." *New York Journal-American,* "Australia Takes up Critic of Britain." *New York Post,* and "Bungling Lost Singapore." *PM.* Reprinted in *[Perth] Daily News,* February 14, 1942.
Tuck, Jay N. "On the Air." *New York Post,* April 2, 1957.
"TV Must Analyze, Evaluate, Cal-Poly Pomona Lecturer Cecil Brown Says." *Montclair [CA] Tribune,* February 5, 1969.
"UFJ Women's Pledge of $40,000 is 25 % Increase." *Ohio Jewish Chronicle,* May 25, 1951.
"U.S. Journalists Die in Air Crash." *[Perth] West Australian,* July 13, 1949.
"U.S. Warned on Plane Violation." *Oakland Tribune,* September 10, 1958.
"War Correspondent Speaks." *Flat Hat,* April 29, 1942.
"What Kind of Radio Newspaper?" *St. Louis Post-Dispatch,* September 24, 1943.
White, William A. "It's a Wonder Cecil Brown Lived to Write His Remarkable Story." *Pittsburgh Press,* November 1, 1942.
"Why neither CBS News Broadcasters nor CBS Sponsors 'OPINIONATE' the News." *New York Times,* September 20, 1943.
Winchell, Walter. "On Broadway." *New York Daily Mirror,* September 10, 17, 21, 1943.

Magazine Articles

"Analysts Analyze CBS Policy." *Billboard,* October 9, 1943.
"Army of 6 Million for China Invasion Claimed by Chiang." *Stars and Stripes,* November 19, 1951.
"As Ike Sees the Candidates Now." *U.S. News & World Report,* April 20, 1964.
Brown, Cecil. "America's Fifth Column in Europe," parts I & II." *Liberty,* June 27, 1942.
_____. "Australians." *Life,* June 8, 1942.
_____. "Cable: Sinkings of the *Repulse* and *Prince of Wales*: A Blow-by-Blow Account." *Newsweek,* December 22, 1941.
_____. "Can Asia Be Saved from Communist China's Aggression?" Speech, Economic Club, Detroit, MI, January 4, 1960, *Vital Speeches* 26, no. 12 (1960): 361–365.
_____. "The Germans are Coming." *Saturday Evening Post,* August 23, 1941.
_____. "How Cecil Got the Story" and "Take 'er Down." *Collier's,* May 16, 1942.

———. "How Close Are We to War with Russia?" *See*, September 1948.
———. "How Japan Wages War." *Life*, May 11, 1942.
———. "Keeping Posted." *Saturday Evening Post*. August 23, 1941.
———. "Life's Reports: The Desert Is Hell." *Life*, December 8, 1941.
———. "Malay Jungle War." *Life*, January 12, 1942.
———. "Morale in Malaya." *Time*, January 19, 1942.
———. "Mussolini's Always Right." *Ken*, June 2, 1938.
———. "A Nut Between Crackers." *Ken*, May 5, 1938.
———. Review of *Free Men Are Fighting*, by Oliver Gramling. *Saturday Evening Review*, December 5, 1942.
———. "Tomorrow the World Is Ours." *Ken*, June 16, 1938.
———. "War Pilot's Story." *Life*, May 11, 1942.
———. "What's Going to Happen to Our Women Workers?" *Good Housekeeping*, December 1943, 42, 78–83.
"Brown and White." *Time*, October 4, 1943.
"Brown Quits CBS in Censor Protest." *Broadcasting*, September 27, 1943.
"Brown-Trouble in a Romance." *Variety*, September 29, 1943.
"Candid Correspondent." *Newsweek*, October 26, 1942.
"Cecil Brown Joins Staff of KCET as Director of News and Public Affairs." *Camera 28, KCET TV Program Guide*, November 1964.
"CBS News Policy Explained by White." *Broadcasting*, September 27, 1943.
Cerf, Bennett. "Books that Shook the World." *Saturday Evening Post*, April 3, 1943.
Cohen, Joe. "Cecil Brown." *Billboard*, July 4, 1942.
"Correspondent's Wife." *Radio Mirror*, March 1942.
"Debate of CBS News Policy." *Billboard*, September 25, 1943.
"Fadeout of Liberal Gabbers." *Variety*, December 25, 1946.
"Fly Defends Analysts' Right to Opinions." *Broadcasting*, October 11, 1943.
"Free Speech Movement Chronology." *California Monthly*, July 17, 2015.
Gaines, Jean. "No Staccato for Brown." *Radio-Television Life*, n.d.
Greenfield, Jeff. "Before the Network Fall," review of *The Murrow Boys: Pioneers on the Front Lines of Broadcast Journalism*, by Stanley Cloud and Lynne Olson. *Time*, May 20, 1996.

Harris, Murray. "Reporter-at-Large." *Saturday Review of Literature*, November 14, 1942.
Hauser, Bertram J. "Newscasts Still Do the Sponsor's Job." *Broadcasting*, May 12, 1947.
"Home Front." *Time*, December 22, 1941.
Howe, Quincy. "Policing the Commentator: A News Analysis." *Atlantic Monthly*, November 5, 1943.
———. "The Rise and Fall of the Radio Commentator." *Saturday Review*, October 26, 1957.
Hutchinson, Keith. "Brown Among the Brass Hats." *Nation*, November 7, 1942.
"Indestructible." *Broadcasting: The Weekly Newsmagazine of Radio*, December 29, 1941.
"It's News to Mutual." *New Republic*, January 3, 1955.
Landry, Robert J. "Edward R. Murrow." *Scribner's Magazine*, December 1938.
Marsh, Melissa A. "Fido Goes to War." *America in WW II: The War: The Home Front, The People*, April 2015.
Menchen, Henry L. "A Sorry Lot." *Time*, January 14, 1946.
"More for Your Money with Mutual Shows." *Billboard*, March 30, 1946.
Oliver, Bryce. "Thought Control—American Style." *New Republic*, January 13, 1947.
"Opinionated News and the Easy Chair of Martyrdom." *Billboard*, October 2, 1943.
"Planes vs. Ships." *Newsweek*, December 22, 1941.
"Radio Gets Ready." *Broadcasting*, July 3, 1950.
"Radio Reporting Tougher, Says Brown." *Broadcasting*, April 6, 1942.
"Radio War Reporting." *Time*, December 22, 1941.
Robb, Arthur. "Shop Talk at Thirty." *Editor & Publisher*, September 24, 1943.
Rockwell, Dorothy. "Radio Censors Itself." *Nation*, August 26, 1939.
Searchinger, Cesar. "Radio, Censorship and Neutrality." *Foreign Affairs*, January 1940.
Sommers, William. "White Caps on San Diego's Air Waves," *Nation*, October 10, 1953.
"The Tape Recorder Is Revolutionizing Radio Programming." *Sponsor*, October 1, 1951.
"Three Americans." *Time*, September 20, 1943.
"Un-Amer. Comm. Gets Work as Representative Hook Plans to Force Anti-Bill to Floor." *Billboard*, November 3, 1945.
"War Code Brings Program Changes." *Broadcasting*, January 19, 1942.

"War Commentators' Wives refuse to be 'Forgotten Women.'" *Movie-Radio Guide*, February 11–25, 1942.

"A War Reporter Talks About His Job." *PM*, April 6, 1942.

"White-Brown CBS Dither on 'Hooks' in the News Seen as Personalized Tug-O'-War." *Billboard*, October 2, 1943.

White, Paul. "Letters." *Newsweek*, April 12, 1954.

"Why Columbia Waives the Rule." *Variety*, December 27, 1950.

Woolbert, Robert G. Review of *Suez to Singapore*, by Cecil Brown. *Foreign Affairs*, April 1943.

Scholarly Journal Articles, and Dissertations

Bernstein, Mark. "Edward R. Murrow: Inventing Broadcast Journalism." *American History* 40, no. 2 (2005): 40–46.

Brown, Ralph S., Jr. "Book Review: The Commission on Freedom of the Press, A Free and Responsible Press: A General Report on Mass Communications, Newspapers, Radio, Motion Pictures, Magazines and Books," *Yale Law School Legal Scholarship Repository* 22, no. 1 (1948): 892.

Clark, David G. "H.V. Kaltenborn and His Sponsors: Controversial Broadcasting and the Sponsor's Role," *Journal of Broadcasting* 12, no. 4 (1968): 309–321.

Donaldson, Scott. "Media in Decline." *Sewanee Review* 104, no. 4 (1996): 673–687.

Evensen, Bruce J. "Truman, Zionists and the Press: Framing a Palestine Policy at the Coming of the Cold War," Ph.D. diss., University of Wisconsin, 1989.

Forde, Kathy R., and Matthew W. Ross. "Radio and the Civic Courage in the Communications Circuit of John Hersey's 'Hiroshima.'" *Literary Journalism Studies* 3, no. 2 (2011): 31–53.

Frayer, William A. "Some Comments on Commentators." *Quarterly Review of the Michigan Alumnus: A Journal of University Perspectives* 51, no. 4 (1944): 8–18.

Gales, Kathleen E. "A Campus Revolution." *British Journal of Sociology*, 17 (1966): 1–19.

Gerstle, Gary. "The Crucial Decade: The 1940s and Beyond." *Journal of American History* 92, no. 4 (2006): 1292–1299.

Hammersmith, Jack L. "The U.S. Office of War Information (OWI) and the Polish Question, 1943–1945." *The Polish Review* 19, no. 1 (1974): 67–76.

Johnson, Matthew D. "Propaganda and Sovereignty in Wartime China: Morale Operations and Psychological Warfare Under the Office of War Information." *Modern Asian Studies* 45, no. 2 (2011), 303–344.

Knoll, Steve. "Demise of the Radio Commentator: An Irreparable Loss to Radio Journalism." *Journal of Radio Studies* 6, no. 2 (1999): 356–370.

Mullally, Donald P. "The Fairness Doctrine: Benefits and Costs." *Public Opinion Quarterly* 33, no. 4 (1969–1970): 523–536.

Munoz-Torres, Juan Ramon. "Truth and Objectivity in Journalism: Anatomy of an Endless Misunderstanding." *Journalism Studies* 13, no. 4 (2012): 566–582.

Peden, George C. "Suez and Britain's Decline as a World Power." *The Historical Journal* 55, no. 4 (2012): 1073–1096.

Schickleral, Eric, and Devin Caugheyal. "Public Opinion, Organized Labor, and the Limits of New Deal Liberalism, 1936–1945." *Studies in American Political Development* 25, no. 2 (2011): 162–189.

Smith, R. Franklin. "Cecil Brown: A Case Study in Broadcast Commentary." Ph.D. Diss., University of Wisconsin, 1961.

Smith, Robert R. "The Origins of Radio Network News Commentary." *Journal of Broadcasting* 9, no. 2 (1965): 113–122.

Steele, Richard W. "American Popular Opinion and the War against Germany: The Issue of Negotiated Peace, 1942." *Journal of American History* 65, no. 3 (1978): 704–723.

Steele, Richard W. "The Great Debate: Roosevelt, the Media, and the Coming of the War, 1940–1941." *Journal of American History* 71, no. 1 (1984): 69–92.

Tenney, Craig D. "The 1943 Debate on Opinionated Broadcast News." *Journalism History* 7, no. 1 (1980): 11–15.

Torre, Richard M. "Finest Hour, Part I: Did Singapore Have to Fall? Hope Is Not a Strategy." *Journal of Winston Churchill* 138 (Spring 2008): 35–41.

Weales, Gerald. "The Voice of Elmer Davis: Review of *but We Were Born Free.*" *Virginia Quarterly Review* 71, no. 3 (1995): 503–510.

Weinberg, Sydney. "What to Tell America: The Writers' Quarrel in the Office of War Information." *Journal of American History* 55, no. 1 (1968): 73–89.

Index

Abrahams, Horace "Tubby" 70, 79
Adams, Frank 106
advocacy journalism 116, 121, 149, 215, 237, 246
Agricultural Labor Relations Act 229
Agronsky, Martin 43, 86–90, 196
alarm & despondency (A & D) 48, 52
Alexander II 5
Alexander III 5
Alfred I. DuPont Award 238
Alger, Horatio 32
Allies 56, 64, 84, 86, 89–90, 95–96, 105, 107, 109–110, 116, 123, 143, 152–153
American Broadcasting Company (ABC) 149, 157–158, 190–202, 219, 234–235, 247
American Business Consultants 154–155
American Farmer 22
Ampex tape recorder 170
Angly, Edward 44
Ankara, Turkey 42–43, 87
anti-semitism 7–8, 139
Aquitania 38
Areopagitica 223
Army-McCarthy Hearings 158, 192
Associated Press (AP) 25
Association of Radio News Analysts (ARNA) 126–129, 145–146
The Atlantic Monthly 149
Auchinleck, Claude 47
August, Harry 22, 32
Australia 43, 48, 53, 59, 91–98, 104–108
Austria 23–24, 159, 170
Avery, D.W. 76–77
Axis 26, *29*, 35, 38–40, 45, 52, 110, 122–125, 134, 143

Balter, Sam 138
Barnett, Ross 216
Baruch, Andre 22
Belgrade, Yugoslavia (Serbia) 39–42

Ben-Gurion, David 168
Benton, William 153, 238
Bigart, Homer 118
Biggers, Earl Derr 8–10
Bill Moyers' Journal 223
Billboard 113, 129–130, 147
Black Sea 15–16
blue pencil 36, 57, 65, 68, 97
Bok, Edward 235
Bonney, E.G. 94, 97
Bourne, Randolph 225
Boyer, Richard 94
Brewer, Sam 41–42
Brinkley, David 20, 129, 194, 203–205, 210, 215–219, 236
The [Brisbane, AU] *Sunday Mail* 98
British Empire 53–54, 83, 96; *see also* England; United Kingdom
Broadcasting 114, 148
Brooke-Popham, Robert 59–60, 68
Browm, Jenni (Broida) (mother) 6–7
Browm, Maurice Irvin (father) 6–7, 12, 17
Browm, Selma (sister) 6, 8–9, 13
Brown (Browm), Cecil 29, *46*, *81*, *141*, *233*; ABC termination 200–201; as Able-Bodied Seaman to Russia 10–12; accused of being a Communist 150–156, 188; advocating for Israel 165–170, 198; announcing characteristics 31–32, 34–35, 162, 227; audience ratings 147–148, 163, 189–190, 215, 221; CBS resignation 122–136; civil rights' advocacy 160, 163, 175–176, 181, 183–186, 195, 200, 215–218, 223–226; college teaching 237–242; complaints about his extreme German condemnation 142–145; criticism of American military censorship 110–111; criticism of British military censorship 44, 55–65, 71, 88–89, 97, 102–108, 110; criticism of Dwight Eisenhower 177–

178, 196–200; criticism of network TV news 223–224, 234–237; criticism of Ronald Reagan 228–231; criticism of Singapore defenses 39, 55, 59, 63, 67, 84, 89–91; as crusader for truth 3, 102, 138, 245; death of 242; as European freelancer 22–24; globetrotting 8–9, 16, 99, 169–172, 243; identification as liberal 150, 160–161, 163, 177, 195, 221, 246; Jewish heritage 1, 60, 13, 28, 119, 139, 160, 167–168, 176, 243, 248; as KCET commentator 219–239; as KCRA (KNBC) commentator 214–219; lifestyle 141–142, 170; listener responses 155–159, 169, 173, 177, 182–183, 185–186, 199, 216–217, 227–228; 236, 242; as Murrow Boy 1, 20, 100–101, 109, 118–120, 135, 152, 160, 239, 244, 247; with Mutual 137–196; as NBC Far East bureau chief 201–214; Ohio River adventure 9–10; as *Pittsburgh Press* reporter 21–22; reporting from Egypt 43–53; reporting from Italy 24–39; stowaway to South America 10–13; support of Adlai Stevenson 181–183; support of John Kennedy 210, 216–218, 225; support of student protests 225–230; surviving the Balkans 39–43; as WABC TV commentator 190–197; writing, reviews of *Suez to Singapore* 104–107, 122, 237; Brown (Browm), Eugene (brother) 6–7, 9–18, 23–24, 219, 242
Brown, Jerry 228
Brown, Jonathan (nephew) 7, 140, 161, 201, 215, 232, 238
Brown, Martha (Kohn) (wife) 3, 8, 26–**29**, 35–38, **46**–48, 63, 77, 80, 84, 100–112, 133, 138–142, 149, 167–170, 187–189, 201–205, 232
Brown v. Board of Education 183–184, 195
Budapest, Hungary 41–42
Buenos Aires, Argentina 12
Bukhage, H.R. 130
Burdette, Winston 30, 42

California State Polytechnic University, Pomona 237, 240, 242
Carley float 78–79
Carlyle, Thomas 1
Case, Jim 219–220, 227–228
Castro, Fidel 216
CBS *World News Roundup* 24, 32, 42, 45, 52, 55, 92, 101
censorship 34, 36, 44, 55–65, 71, 88–89, 97, 102–120, 130–131, 135–137, 178, 242–243
Central Washington College 169

Cerf, Bennett 84, 104–107, 134, 138–139, 238
Chancellor, John 191, 205, 209
Chapple, Wreford G. 93–96
The Charleville [AU] *Times* 104
Chavez, Cesar 229
Chesed 248
Chicago Daily News 24, 44, 46, 52, 57
Chicago Tribune 41, 106, 138
Chico State College 224
Christman, Elwyn 93–94
Churchill, Winston 58–59, 67, 83–84, 123, 164
Citizens in Action 220
civil rights 150, 160–163, 175–176, 180–186, 195, 200, 215–218, 223–230
Claremont McKenna College 223
Close, Upton 130, 137
Colby, Frank 31
Cold War 157, 166–169, 179, 188, 196, 202, 208–209, 216
Collingwood, Charles 30, 101
Columbia Broadcasting System (CBS) 1, 22–34, 37–39, 42–44, 48–50, 57–69, 82–85, 88–94, 99–102, 108–115, 120–158,164, 180, 192–197, 202–203, 208–209, 234–238, 244, 247
Columbus, OH 28, 30, 168
Comment 220–221, 223, 227, 229, 231
Commins, Saxe 105
Commission on Freedom of the Press 244, 247
communism 123, 135, 147, 150–160, 164, 166–171, 174–177, 180, 184–189, 195, 198, 203–204, 208–210, 222, 230–232
Communist China *see* Red China
Congress of Racial Equality 225
Coughlin, Father Charles 7
Counterattack 154
Cronkite, Walter 31, 232
Czechoslovakia 23–24, 170

Daily Worker 152
Daly, John 197
Darwin, AU 94–96
Davis, Elmer 2, 31, 108, 111, 113, 115, 118, 120, 146, 157–158, 186, 191, 197
Davis, Eric 55–58
De Lacy, Hugh 151
Democratic Party 110, 150, 157–160, 180–182, 195, 199–200, 237
Denny, Hal 52
DePugh, Robert 222
Dick, Elsie 170
Dill, John 54
Disney, Walt 192

Dolcin Corporation 157
Don Lee Broadcasting System 189
Donough, Cuthbert 83
Downs, Kenneth 23–24
Downs, William 30
Due to Circumstances Beyond Our Control 236
Duff Cooper, Alfred 58–62
Dumke, Glenn 228, 239
DuMont, Allen 234
Dunn, William 65, 85–88

Early, Stephen 114
Eastland, James 195
Edison, Thomas 234
Edwards, Douglas 112, 132
Edwards, Maurice 71
Egypt 28, 43–45, 50–51, 56, 61, 98, 193, 197–198
Eisenhower, Dwight 161, 177–187, 196–200, 203, 207, 210–211, 218
Eisenhower, Milton 218
Electra 67, 79–81, 83
Emperor Hirohito 171
Emphasis 212
England 15, 22–24, 50, 67, 84, 98, 105–107, 159, 170–172, 197; *see also* British Empire; United Kingdom
Exford 14–16
Exodus 166
Express 67, 82–83

Fair Deal 160
Fairholl, Thomas 68
Fairness Doctrine (FCC) 135, 244
fascism 37–38, 121–123, 126, 133–134
Fearon, O.K. 85–88
Federal Bureau of Investigation (FBI) 154, 230
Federal Communications Commission (FCC) 114, 131, 134–135, 149, 154, 192, 196, 238, 244
Field, Leonard 88–89
Fielding, Sean 51
fifth column 88, 95, 188
First Amendment 2, 126, 236, 241, 244, 247
Fly, Lawrence 114, 131
Flynn, John T. 153
Force Z 67–73, 80
Ford, Henry 7
Foreign Affairs magazine 106
Formosa *see* Nationalist China
Fortier, Louis 39–42
Founding Fathers 134, 172, 245
Four Freedoms 127, 144, 163

France 10, 23–24, 35, 38, 72, 96, 113, 143, 166, 170–172, 197, 202
freedom of speech 97, 115, 126–127, 129–131, 151, 153, 157, 225, 228–230
Friendly, Fred 30, 235–236, 247
Fuigi, Johnny 63

Gailmor, William 151
Gallagher, O'Dowd 59, 68–85, 90
Gannett, Lewis 106
Garroway, Dave 203
George Foster Peabody Award 108
Germany 15, 23–27, 35, 37–53, 59, 64, 67, 101, 109–111, 115, 118–120, 123, 126, 133, 143–145, 152, 159, 164, 169–174, 199, 202, 233
Gervasi, Frank 24, 84
Goebbels, Joseph 36, 124
Goldwyn, Samuel 159
Good Housekeeping 133
Goodman, Julian 211, 214
Goodman, Walter 162
Gould, Jack 194
Graney, Morris 78–79, 86
Great Depression 8, 17–18, 21, 104
Greece 45, 72, 158, 166, 171
Guadalcanal Diary 104
Gunther, John 96
gyppy tummy 50, 233

Haggerty, James 180, 207
Haifa, Palestine (Israel) 43, 48, 166
Halfaya Pass, Egypt 51–52, 233
Hangen, Wells 208–209
Haragei 213
Harris, Murray 106–107
Harvey, Paul 197, 235
Hauptmann, Bruno 21–22
Hauser, Bertram 148
Hawley, Adelaide 100
Hearst, William Randolph 138
Hedges, Chris 246
Hemingway, Ernest 24
Henry, Bill 123
Henry, William 238
hernia 16, 102, 140, 214
"Hiroshima" 165
Hiroshima, Japan 165
Hiss, Alger 157
Hitler, Adolf 24–27, 35, 184, 198
Holles, Everett 112
Hollywood Ten 154
Hollywood Walk of Fame 239
Hooper ratings 145–148
Hoover, J. Edgar 230
Hottelet, Richard C. 20, 30, 101, 113, 209

284 INDEX

House Un-American Activities Committee (HUAC) 151–155, 177
Howe, Quincy 130, 149–150, 191
Hull, Cordell 112
Huntley, Chet 194, 204, 210, 215, 218–219, 236
Hutchens, John 130
Hutchins Commission on Freedom of the Press 244, 247

I Want to Be a Sea Shell 212
Ikeda, Hayato 211
Imes, George Lake 176
India 43, 53–55, 84, 170–171, 193, 205, 211, 226
Interlandi, Telesio 37–38
International News Service (INS) 23–27, 101
Iron Curtain 153, 169
Israel 165–171, 197–198
Italian Ministry of Popular Culture 35–38
Italy 23–30, 32, 34–40, 43, 47, 51–52, 59, 60–62, 77, 101–102, 139–140, 170, 193, 219

J. Walter Thompson Agency 132
Jacob, Hans 151
Java, Indonesia 55, 90–92, 97–98
Jerusalem, Israel (Palestine) 43, 48, 165–168
Jewish 3, 5–9, 13, 28, 102, 119, 139, 160, 165–169, 176–177, 222, 243, 248
John Birch Society 222–223
Johns Manville 112
Johnson, Lyndon 160, 223; and Great Society 230–231, 234
Johnson Wax Company 163
Journey to Understanding 210
Judd, Winnie Ruth 19

KABC AM 219
Kai-Shek, Chiang **26**, 171, 187, 203–205, 208, 211, 232–234
Kalang Airport, Singapore 53, 91
Kaleidoscope: Projection 205, 209–210
Kaltenborn, Hans (H.V.) 2, 31, 126–127, 146, 159, 191, 238
KCET TV 219–224, 227–230, 239
KCRA TV (KNBC) 214–215, 217–219
Ken (magazine) 24
Kendrick, Alexander 209
Kennedy, John 208–211, 216–218, 225; and New Frontier 230
Kennedy, Robert 211, 216, 225
Keppel Harbor, Singapore 54, 65, 70, 82
Kerr, Clark 230

Kesten, Paul 132
Khrushchev, Nikita 188–189, 211, 216
King George II 45, 54, 65
Kingdom, Frank 152
Kintner, Robert 192, 201–202, 212, 219
Kirk, Alexander 38, 43–50
Kishi, Nobusuke 204–207
Klauber, Edward 115
Klopfer, Donald 104, 107
KNBR FM 219
Knickerbocher, H.R. 170
Knightley, Phillip 96
KNXT TV 219
Kohn, Adele (mother-in-law) 28
Kohn, Jerome (father-in-law) 28
Korea 169, 171–172, 203, 206, 213, 226
Korean War 172, 174–175, 186–187, 200, 204
Kraft Foods 160, 163, 195–196
Kuralt, Charles 31

Land of the Dragon 210
USS *Langley* 94
Latham, Jack 215
Lawrence, Justus 219
Layton, Geoffrey 59–61
Lazarfeld, Paul 145–147
Leach, John 67–69, 72, 80
Leech, Edward 21
Lenin, Vladimir 16
Leningrad (Saint Petersburg), Russia 189
LeSueur, Larry 30
Lett, Jack 11–14
Levine, Irving R. 205, 209
Lewis, Fulton, Jr. 2, 137
liberalism 2, 6, 24, 115, 126, 137–139, 143–163, 177–181, 186, 195, 221, 224, 226, 246; *see also* Brown, Cecil; Murrow Boys
Libya 28, 36, 51, 98
Liebling, A.J. 118, 126, 148
Life (magazine) 26, 52, 57, 87, 91, 94, 98, 107, 146, 204, 233
Lindbergh, Charles 21
Lindsay, Howard 84, 139
Lippman, Walter 164, 237
Littlejohn, Francis 200–201
Loesser, Frank 139
London Daily Express 59, 90
London Daily Sketch 64
Long Beach, CA 20, 158
Long Island Star 23
Look (magazine) 146
Loper, James 219–220, 228
Los Angeles, CA 19, 123, 141, 159, 175, 189, 214–223, 229, 233, 236, 241
Los Angeles Herald-Examiner 217

Index 285

Los Angeles Times 123, 221, 229, 233, 233, 235
Lower, Elmer 219
Luzon 93–94
Lyle, Jack 64
Lyon, C.A. 86

MacArthur, Douglas 172–174, 178, 207, 211
MacLeish, Archibald 120
MacNeil, Robert 247
Madame Nhu (Tran Le Xuan) 210–211
Malaya 53–59, 62–90, 98, 101, 107, 203
Malaya Broadcasting Corporation 55, 58, 88, 90
Malaya Tribune 54
Mankewitz, Joseph 177
Mansfield, Mike 211
March, Frederick 3, 139
Marconi, Guglielmo 234
Markel, Lester 149
marketplace of ideas 2, 134
Marshall Plan 147, 174, 178
Matthews, Ted 77–78
Maxwell, Elsa 134
Mayflower Doctrine 244; *see also* Federal Communications Commission
McAndrew, William 202–205, 209–214, 236
McCarthy, Joseph 135, 150, 156–159, 163, 180–181, 192, 193, 200
McCormick, Robert 138
McGee, Frank 203, 205, 208
McIntire, Carl 222
McLeod, Frank 80
Meet Your Public Servant 220
Memo to JFK from NBC News 209
Meredith, James 215–216
Mexican-Americans 18–19, 175, 229
Mikoyan, Anastas Ivanovich 211
Milton, John 223
Mission to Moscow 122, 152
Moley, Raymond 116
Monroe, Marilyn 213
Moore, Leon (Helfand) 139–140
Moore, Sonia (Helfand) 139–140
Moormacstar 98–100
Morgan, Edward P. 235
Moscow, Russia 49–50, 122, 140, 152, 155, 168, 189, 205
Mosely, Leonard 63–64
Mosely, Sydney 130
Motion Picture Daily 113
Mowrer, Edgar 24, **46**, 52
Moyers, Bill 223, 247
Mundt, Karl 154
Murrow, Edward R. 1–3, 20–32, 35, 39–40, 45, 100–101, 107–123, 128–137, 140–142, 148–149, 152, 158–160, 164, 235, 239, 243–247; conflicts with CBS 128, 135, 245–247; difference in lifestyle 141–142; relationship with Brown 22–33, 108, 122, 140–142, 239
Murrow, Janet 128
Murrow Boys 1, 20, 30–32, 100–101, 109, 118–120, 135, 152, 160, 239, 247; as celebrities and courageous 100–101; competition among 112–113; as idealists 1, 119, 135, 243; as liberal journalists 148, 160
Mussolini, Benito 24–26, 35–38, 46, 52
Mutual Broadcasting System (MBS) 115, 130, 133, 137–139, 142–143, 147–150, 155–157, 162–163, 170–172, 176–177, 180–182, 189–192, 195–196, 199–201, 217, 221, 243–244, 247; differences from other networks 137–138; as a pioneer in civil rights broadcasting 176; range of commentators 137, 149

NASA 200
Nasser, Abdel 193, 198
The Nation 106, 135
National Association of Broadcasters (NAB) 108, 114, 126, 138, 145
National Association of Theater Owners 238
National Broadcasting Company (NBC) 43, 57–60, 86, 90, 115–116, 129–130, 137, 152, 157, 191–194, 197, 201–219, 234–236, 244, 247
National Educational Television (NET) 221–223
National Opinion Research Center 145; *see also* Lazarfeld, Paul
National Public Radio (NPR) 164, 212
Nationalist China 171, 187, 203–205, 208, 211, 232–234; *see also* Kai-Shek, Chiang
Negev Desert 168
Nevins, Allen 222
The New Deal 121, 137–138, 149–150, 160, 178, 200
The New Republic 119, 152, 162
New York American 22
New York Daily Mirror 129
New York Herald-Tribune 44
New York Journal 22
New York Post 95, 107, 195
New York Times 52, 101, 106–107, 129–130, 138, 149, 195, 235, 246
New York Times Magazine 235
New York World-Telegram 113
The New Yorker 148, 165

286　Index

Newark [NJ] *Star Ledger* 130
Newman, Edwin 209
Newsweek 84, 106, 116, 135, 146
Nixon, Richard 182, 241
None Dare Call It Treason 222
nuclear warfare 165, 170, 181–183, 188

Oakland Tribune 214
Office of Censorship 105, 114–115
Office of War Information (OWI) 111, 120, 123, 145
Ohio Jewish Chronicle 13, 102
Ohio State University 10–13, 28, 145, 240
Oliver, Bryce 152
Oregon State University 155
Oswald, Lee Harvey 217
Ottoway Newspapers Inc. 17
Overseas Press Club 97, 107, 114, 197

Palestine 43–45, 165–167
Paley, William 59–61, 84, 115–118, 121–125, 132, 135, 148, 154, 180, 244–245; intolerance with commentary (or news analysis) 115, 118, 121–122, 125, 135, 148–149, 240–245
Parr, Jack 139
Pascal, Ernest 154
Pearl Harbor, HI 8, 66, 81, 84, 116, 179, 204, 242
Pearson, Drew 157
Percival, A.E. 62
Peterson, Elmer 215, 219
Philadelphia Inquirer 107
Phillies Cigars 138, 143
Phillips, Joseph 84
Phillips, Thomas 68–72, 79–80
Phoenix, AZ 18–19
Phouma, Souvanna 210
Pittsburgh Press 21–22
Playfair, Giles 90
PM (newspaper) 132
Pope Pius XI 25–27
Potsdam Conference 164–165
Pound, Dudley 84
Pox, Dixon Ryan 111
Prescott [AZ] *Journal-Miner* 20–21
press freedom 1, 44, 99, 118, 129, 148, 186, 243
HMS *Prince of Wales* 67–75, 80–84, 106–108
Public Broadcasting Service (PBS) 239, 247
Pulford, C.W. 69
Pulitzer, Joseph 2, 80, 108, 119, 246
Pulliam, Eugene 103–104
Purnell, William 93
Pyle, Ernie 110

Quemoy Islands 203–205

Radical Right 222
The Radical Right in California: Extremism, Communism 222–223
radio commentary 1–3, 111–118, 126–131, 137–139, 145–150, 159, 164, 185–186, 244
Radio Mirror 38
Raffles Hotel 54–56, 61, 65, 68–69, 83, 86, 89
Random House 84, 104–107, 138
Rankin, John 151
Reagan, Ronald 228–231
The Real News of the Day 163
Red Channels 155
Red China 175, 203–209, 213, 230–234
Red Scare 7, 157, 182
Redlands University 156
Report on America 138
Republican Party 110, 150, 160, 165, 178, 181–183, 200, 218, 248
HMS *Repulse* 67–84, 101, 106–108
Revolt on the Campus 225
Rhee, Syngman 206
Rio de Janeiro, BR 12
Riskin, Robert 13
Roach, Hal, Jr. 196
Robb, Arthur 131
Robinson, James 202–203, 209
Roosevelt, Eleanor 122, 130
Roosevelt, Franklin D. 7, 21, 67, 71, 90, 111–116, 121–127, 137–138, 142–144, 147, 150, 159, 178–180, 200, 217–218
Roosevelt, James (Jimmy) 45
Rusk, Dean 211
Russia 5–7, 14–16, 24, 48–52, 58, 67, 90, 109, 118, 123, 135, 139–140, 147, 152–153, 157–158, 165–170, 173–174, 185–189, 198, 206–211, 216–217

St. John, Robert 155
St. Louis Post-Dispatch 131
San Francisco Chronicle 230
Sansom, George 88–90
Sarajevo (Bosnia and Herzegovina) 39–40
Sarnoff, David 116, 148, 192
Saturday Evening Post 42, 57
Saturday Review of Literature 106
Schneider, John 235
Schorr, Daniel 209, 247
Scott, Robert 57–58
Scripps-Howard Newspapers 21
Sealy Mattress Company 160
See (magazine) 188
See It Now 135, 158
Seldes, George 24

Index

Sergio, Lisa 152
Services Public Relations Organization (SPRO) 55, 83, 88
Sevareid, Eric 1, 27, 30, 107, 113, 123, 131, 140, 146, 208, 235, 244
The '70s Belong to Asia 237
Sharett, Moshe 167
Sheehan, Vincent 105
Shepard, Richard 193-194
Shirer, William L. 1, 23-24, 27, 30, 107, 112, 127-130, 135, 155
Siepmann, Charles 131
Sigma Delta Chi 65
Singapore 50-72, 76, 79-96, 100-101, 104-110, 122, 126, 131, 145, 203, 211, 232, 237
Singapore Free Press 54, 64, 91
Singapore Herald 63
60 Minutes 237
Smith, Howard K. 1, 30, 155, 208, 243, 247
Smoot, Dan 153
Socialism 15, 153
Sommers, William 135
South America 11-13
South China Sea 69, 81, 84, 248
Soviet Union 15, 135, 140, 152-153, 168, 172, 179, 184, 188-189, 197-202, 208, 230
Sputnik I 198-200
Stalin, Joseph 15 67, 109, 123, 153, 164, 173, 188
Stanton, Frank 145
State Farm Insurance Company 163, 171, 186
Steel, Johannes 151
Sternberger, Estelle 152
Stettinius, Edward R. 165
Stevenson, Adlai 181-183
Stevenson, Robert Lewis 10, 12
Stickney, Dorothy 84, 139
Stone, Isaac 102, 245
Stone, Robert 194-196
Stone, Willis 222
Stormer, John 222
Suez Canal 43, 197
Suez to Singapore 105-107, 122, 237
Sukarno 205, 211, 231
Surgeon General's Report (on smoking) 238
Swayze, John Cameron 194-196
Swing, Raymond Gram 137, 151
Sydney [AU] *Telegraph* 68

Taft, Robert 178-179, 245
Taishoff, Sol 114
Taiwan *see* Nationalist China
television commentary 190-193, 197, 214, 220, 235-236

Tennant, William 70-72, 75-76, 80
Thailand 56-57, 64, 85, 203, 232
Thirty Seconds over Tokyo 104
This Is London: Witnesses to War 107
Thomas, J. Parnell 155
Thomas, Shenton 56, 61-62
Thompson, Dorothy 130
Tikkun olam 6, 247
Time (magazine) 57, 90, 122, 130, 146, 204
Times Square 13
Tod, Ronald 45-47, 53
Today Show 203, 211
Tojo, Hideki 204
Tojo, Kamei 204
Trout, Robert 30, 123, 132
Truman, Harry 146-147, 150, 160, 164-167, 172-180, 183, 197, 200, 217-218
The Truman Doctrine 166, 174
truth 2-3, 36, 85, 90, 95, 101-102, 108-112, 120, 129, 132-134, 138, 147-148, 157-159, 161, 173, 183-186, 195-197, 204, 228, 231, 236, 241-248
Tse-tung, Mao 157, 187, 203-205, 208, 232-233
Tsurumi, Ken 55, 63
Tunisia 28, 120
Turkey 39, 42, 50, 53, 166, 171, 216
typhoid 46, 63, 102
Tzedakah 6, 248

Union College 111
United Farmworkers Union 229
United Kingdom 55, 67, 105; *see also* British Empire; England
United Nations 96, 103-105, 109, 158, 164-168, 179, 188, 197, 234
United Press International (UP and UPI) 19, 185
University of Alabama 184, 216
University of California at Los Angeles (UCLA) 224, 229, 240, 242
University of California, Berkeley 225-230
University of Washington 155
University of Wisconsin 146

Vandercook, John 129
Van Der Linde, Victor 157
Vanocur, Sander 209
Variety 145, 152
Vietnam 186-187, 203, 209-213, 217, 221, 225-237
Vila, George 214
Voice of America (VOA) 139, 153

WABC TV 190-194, 197
Wallace, George 216

Walton, Sidney 152
War Bonds 103–104, 120–124, 134, 163
Warner Brothers 123, 192
Warren, OH 6–10, 17
Warren [OH] *Tribune-Chronicle* 10
Washington Post 102, 129
Watergate Scandal 241
Watts Riots 236–237
Wefing, Henry 132
Weinberg, Jack 225–226
Weir, Gordon 215
Welch, Robert 222
Weller, George 57–58, 80, 91, 110
Wells, H.G. 245
Western Reserve University 9–10
Western World 10
WGN AM 138
What American Commentators Say 139
Wheeling, W.VA 9, 157–158
Wheless, Hewitt 94
White, Paul 1, 27–32, 35, 40–45, 48–53, 56–65, 69, 82–85, 88–92, 95–97, 100, 108–118, 221–135
Wilkes, John 93
Willoughby, Wesley 222
Winchell, Walter 2, 31, 129, 148, 191, 197
Wood, Edward (Lord of Halifax) 105
Wood, John 151
WOR AM 138, 170, 196
The World as I See It 219
Wray, Fay 13
WRUF AM 177, 185
Wynn, Bert 71

Yale University 232
Yamamoto, Isoroku 70
Yami Yogurt Company 155
Yost, Charles Woodruff 234
Young, John 57–60
Youngstown [OH] *Vindicator* 14–16
Youngstown State University 13

www.ingramcontent.com/pod-product-compliance
Ingram Content Group UK Ltd.
Pitfield, Milton Keynes, MK11 3LW, UK
UKHW040610160426
5217IPUK00034B/345